Party politics and local government

Published in our
centenary year
≈ **2004** ≈
MANCHESTER
UNIVERSITY
PRESS

Party politics
and local government

Colin Copus

Manchester University Press
Manchester and New York

distributed exclusively in the USA by Palgrave

The right of Colin Copus to be identified as the author of this work has been asserted by him in accordance with the Copyright, Designs and Patents Act 1988.

Published by Manchester University Press
Oxford Road, Manchester M13 9NR, UK
and Room 400, 175 Fifth Avenue, New York, NY 10010, USA
www.manchesteruniversitypress.co.uk

Distributed exclusively in the USA by
Palgrave, 175 Fifth Avenue, New York, NY 10010, USA

Distributed exclusively in Canada by
UBC Press, University of British Columbia, 2029 West Mall,
Vancouver, BC, Canada V6T 1Z2

British Library Cataloguing-in-Publication Data
A catalogue record for this book is available from the British Library

Library of Congress Cataloguing-in-Publication Data applied for

ISBN 0 7190 6634 4 *hardback*
0 7190 6635 2 *paperback*

First published 2004

13 12 11 10 09 08 07 06 05 04   10 9 8 7 6 5 4 3 2 1

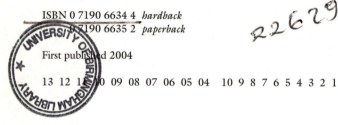

Typeset by Servis Filmsetting Ltd, Manchester
Printed in Great Britain
by CPI, Bath

Contents

Figures and tables

Figures

Tables

Preface and acknowledgements

The lack of widespread public interest in local government and the consistently disappointing turnout at local elections belies the intensity, excitement and passion with which local politics is conducted. The notion of local government as a dry, dusty bit player in the administration of centrally determined policies regarding service provision, masks the real and powerful dynamics of political life as it is conducted in what can only be described as 467 separate polities across Britain. That local government has always been synonymous with service delivery, coupled with the national political focus on the quality of public services, further detracts from the notion of local government as a set of politically representative institutions. Place all this in the context of a unitary state with a sovereign Parliament and many can be forgiven for thinking that the only politics that matter are the politics of the centre.

The intention behind this book is to explore the conduct of party politics at the local level and to highlight the passion, intensity, zeal and, yes, even excitement that the world of local party politics can generate, at least for those involved in it. But, the book's purpose is to expose local party politics as a closed and cosseted world. A world that exists in a hothouse, isolated from the outside environment by impenetrable structures, its own special language, its own peculiar customs and practices; fearful of strangers, suspicious of change and certain in its belief that only it understands the complexity and urgency of the world it inhabits. 'Party' claims local politics as its territory, which is to be defended from those outside the walls of the 'party', as well as against those from another party.

Political parties are a key element of the workings of a liberal representative democracy and draw their strength from the very nature of representative democracy, designed as it is, to avoid large-scale public participation in political decision making. Thus, parties themselves, and the way they conduct local politics, are at the heart of much of the disconnection between citizen and council, of which the Blair government complains. Yet, local democracy and local politics are not just what parties and elected representatives do, and, as a consequence, are not defined by the actions of parties and politicians alone. In this exploration of political parties at the local level, the focus is on the interpretations of, and approaches towards local democracy held by those involved in party politics, an approach that unsurprisingly places the party above all else in the local sphere.

Understanding the nature of local party political activity becomes all the more important as a result of the Local Government Act 2000. The ushering in of powerful political executives headed either by an indirectly elected council leader or a directly elected mayor has introduced a new set of powerful political institutions and dynamics to British councils. These 'executive arrangements' are already being recognised by parties and by party groups, as presenting them with an entirely new way of governing the locality. But, in so doing, also challenges many of the old assumptions and approaches to key party concerns, such as public unity, cohesion and loyalty.

The book will explore the role, organisation, impact and development of party politics in local government and more specifically, that discrete (and indeed, discreet) and distinct organisation of councillors: the political party group. For the party group has a longstanding and quite distinct role to play in the development of local government. Indeed, local government looks, feels and works the way it does because of coherent, organised and united *blocs* of councillors acting as a party group.

Many citizens and observers of local government often confuse political parties with the party group and not only fail to draw the distinction between them, but are not clear about the respective roles of party and group. Moreover, the specific role played in local political decision making by the party group, is under-researched and consequently not fully understood; the group is responsible for much of the opaque nature of local politics and council business. The book will bring this closed, private and secretive organisation into the open and examine what party groups (and parties) do to the processes of political decision making and local representation. Indeed, the private meetings of the ruling party group have long been elevated above full council as the place where council decisions are really taken and it is the group (and party), not the electorate that the councillor represents in the public settings of the council and beyond.

The book is the culmination of many years of research into party politics at the local level, through a number of formal research projects that employed standard research techniques. It also rests on my own on-going work with councillors and political parties through INLOGOV at the University of Birmingham. In writing the book I have also reflected on my own party political activity and a process that I have called simply: 'hanging around with councillors', much like a party political groupie. You notice very quickly when talking to councillors three interesting features of the life they lead: first; they can always tell you how many votes they received when first elected to the council, and the size of their initial majority; and, secondly, they can tell you how much their majority has gone up or down at each successive election. The third interesting factor is very similar to the experience you have when asking a young child how old they are: six and three quarters they will reply. When asking a councillor how long he or she has been a member of the party, they will reply in similar terms: 28 and three quarter years! Like the six-year-old and his or her contemporaries, those 'three quarters' can give you an edge over the fellow party member who has served a mere 28 years.

In January 2003 I celebrated, if that is the right word, 26 years party membership – more than some, less than others. As I write that period is now 26 and a half years. That period has informed the writing of this book more than I can explain here. Whilst some of what follows may sound cynical, bitter and twisted, that is what 26 and a half years in the same party can do for you I'm afraid. But, I'm still there and have no intention of going anywhere else. There is also much affection in this book too; I joined my party while still at school and have made many friends over the years. Like everyone involved in a political party, as long as the number of your friends outweighs the number of your deadly enemies (from your own party or course, no one hates the other side as much as they hate someone from their own side) then that's OK.

I have had the honour of representing the electorate on three councils: a London Borough, a county council and a district council; interesting, challenging and stimulating times they were too and lived, as they were, against the backdrop of party membership, these experiences become all the more intense. When I was elected to my first council, a long-standing member of some considerable years said to me: 'When you stop enjoying it, that's the time to quit, I should have gone 20 years ago you know!' That explains party and council membership – it gets in the blood and it is difficult to give up. Still I must say that my status as a former councillor was voluntarily obtained; I decided not to offer the electorate my services again, rather than the electorate deciding to dispense with them. All former councillors will know that is a very important thing to be able to say.

When running seminars for councillors through INLOGOV I often begin by saying: 'I'm not going to tell you which party I'm a member of and if you can guess by the end of the seminar then I have not been professional or balanced in my presentation.' But, party politics does not rest on the need for professionalism and balance! I do not declare my party allegiance here, but look carefully in the book; the clues are there if you spot them. There is for all involved in party politics a language that goes with your own party, a way of expressing yourself, a reference to cosy party institutions and familiar shared experiences, all of which helps to seal the party from the outside world.

Finally, there are two vital acknowledgements I must make. First, to all those hundreds of councillors and party activists I have met politically and professionally over the years and who have contributed wittingly and willingly, or otherwise, to this book – keep up the good work. Secondly, but most importantly of all, to Julia, Emma and Harriet, my long-suffering wife and two daughters, who, for reasons best known to themselves, have put up with my party political activity, council membership and with the writing of this book. Without their love and support I could not have started, let alone finished this project.

1

Party politics: an unwelcome partisan presence or a democratic necessity?

To the citizen with only the most passing of interest in what his or her council does, one thing will be abundantly clear: local government in Britain is party-based government. The local councillor, in the overwhelming majority of cases, will have stood for election on the basis of his or her party label. Indeed, Wilson and Game show that over five-sixths of all councils have what they refer to as a 'fully developed party system'.[1] Yet, despite the extent of party politicisation, the electorate have an ambivalent attitude towards the extent of party involvement in, and control of, local government.[2] In addition, distaste of party political intrusion into council affairs has been blamed for deterring many well-qualified potential candidates from seeking local office, even for subjugating the needs of the community to the needs of the party.[3] Alternatively, Jones highlights the importance political parties play locally in representing 'distinct sets of supporters, whose interests they promote'.[4] He displays how political parties merge the local and national political battle fought between the parties thus:

> The division over local politics was the same as that over national politics; the same parties competed, the same people argued, and the same people fought both municipal and Parliamentary elections . . . There was no meaningful antithesis between the parties' activities in local and national politics; the two skirmishes were part of one battle fought by the same armies.[5]

Little has changed in the way parties perceive and conduct the business of politics from when Jones was writing. Whether parties are seen as a bastion of democracy and the mechanism by which the electorate's policy preferences are transformed into a governing agenda, or parties are held as an unnecessary and anti-democratic partisan presence in local affairs, one thing is certain: today there is massive party political engagement with council and local political affairs. Parties touch every facet of political life and are involved, to one degree or another, in guiding and influencing the shape, nature and direction of our local communities. It is vital therefore that we understand what parties do at the local level, why and how they do it and the impact they have on local political decision-making and the local dimension of political representation.

Understanding party at the local level

Political parties at the local level fall between a number of stalls when it comes to constructing an analysis of their role and place within the political system. Much of the literature on political parties tends to ignore the local dimension almost completely.[6] Whilst, the general literature on local government, and more broadly local governance, recognises the existence of parties and party groups and indeed the power they wield locally, considerations of party are drowned out by consideration of managerial, financial, legal, structural and operational matters.

Much of our understanding of party at the local level comes from a considerable body of work focusing on the politics of local government in the form of case studies of the political and socio-economic development of a particular local authority.[7] Yet, there is a need to place party locally into a broader framework. One that borrows from the analysis of those political scientists concerned with party as a national and Parliamentary organisation, as well as from those considering party from a single authority perspective. To fully understand the impact and power of party locally, it is necessary to distinguish between the party outside the council and the party group of councillors operating on the council under a shared party label. The organisational and institutional separation and the role and power of these respective bodies makes a separate understanding of them a necessity. To treat party locally anything like as seriously as it requires, which is as a separate focus for study, with its own theoretical framework and models, a number of broader concerns must be addressed. Namely, how does party in the localities relate to democratic theory and to various models and concepts of representation and, further, can there be a separate theory of party and democracy at the local level?[8]

It is impossible to adequately consider party politics without first locating it within notions of democracy and representation. Parties are, after all, a principal feature of liberal democracy and the body through which the views, preferences and needs of the citizenry are articulated in representative institutions and beyond. But, as will be shown, party and more specifically the party group, is less about *re-presenting* citizens' views in the council and more about filtering out the views, preferences and needs of citizens which do not accord with its own political frame of reference, beliefs and assessment of the common good. What party represents is the party itself. What exists at the local level is less a democracy and more a *partyocracy* – rule for and by the party on behalf of the party.

The book does not approach the consideration of party from a dry institutional set of arrangements, rather it explores the dynamics, processes, power structures and struggles, personalities, issues, policies and approaches to politics and representation of those involved in local party politics. Moreover, it seeks to explain how the councillor, as part of the local political *elite*, makes sense of his or her role and interprets the day-to-day experiences of local democracy and representation. Further, it seeks to explore exactly what councillors mean when they refer to democracy and representation and what it is they (and their fellow party members) seek to 'represent'. It also examines the resilience of political processes and the approaches taken by councillors to notions of representation and local government faced, as the local arena is, with a constant barrage of government-inspired legislation and regulation to alter its shape, size, nature, boundaries and role and, potentially, its very existence. Councillors, and the parties of which they are members, are a vital part of the local political *elite*, yet they are also one amongst many players in the often-confused, complex and competing world of local politics and must engage with other groups and organisations in seeking power and influence. As such, political parties locally straddle the divide between *elite* and pluralistic theories, yet parties have a role beyond decision-making where power manifests itself.[9] They are crucial to the way political representation operates and the way in which the citizen and the party experience it.

Finally, the book introduces the notion of the local *party person*, that is the party member (whether holding an elected office or not) that places notions of party and party loyalty and cohesion at the centre of his or her political and social world. The party person is the individual that is totally immersed in the party, and views all of his or her activity, political or otherwise, through the prism of the party. Externally, the duty of the party person is to protect the party from criticism or challenge from any source and to present to the outside world the image of a united, cohesive and disciplined organisation, certain in its views of the world and of the rightness of its cause on any and all issues. Within the party, the party person is central to its organisation, structure and activities; the party person takes on positions within the party and membership of a wide array of internal party sub-units; they are central to all activity, political and social, that the party undertakes. Key to understanding the importance of the party person to the conduct of local politics is an appreciation of how he or she has built a life that fits around and into the party of which he or she is a member. The party is a vital element of all facets of the party person's existence. As a consequence, loyalty to the party is total and, whilst it may be strained to breaking point by personal and political rivalries inside the party, loyalty will not be broken except in the most extraordinary political and social circumstances. The party person in any political party is central to the conduct of local political activity and central to any attempts to change the structure, processes and dynamics of that activity. Much of the government's agenda for modernising local political decision-making rests on how the party person in all parties responds to that agenda.

Local government modernisation and the party: a new fiddle and an old tune

Local government today is very different from when much of our current understanding of political parties and the role they play locally was formulated. The Blair government's modernisation agenda for local government set out to modernise, revitalise and renew local government and to re-engage citizens with the councils that represent and serve them. Whilst the modernising agenda is clearly displayed in a number of government publications, *Local Democracy and Community Leadership*,[10] *Modern Local Government: In Touch with the People*,[11] *Local Leadership: Local Choice*,[12] and the white paper, '*Strong Local Leadership: Quality Public Services*',[13] the question remains: will this modernisation agenda reach as far as the practices and process of the political parties that control local government and that are such a prominent force within local democracy? Political modernisation touches party politics in two ways: first, a healthy dose of public participation is to be introduced into the system, both by legislative requirement and, second, by exhortation to greater citizen involvement. Indeed, a modern council is one where: 'public participation in debate and decision-making is valued, with strategies in place to inform and engage local opinion'.[14]

Enhanced public participation in local government, however, fundamentally challenges the deeply held notions that party people have about political parties and the place they have within local politics.

Moreover, greater public involvement in local political decision-making intensifies an already existing tension between increasingly assertive local communities and political party groups claiming a mandate for their every decision, based on references to the process of representative democracy and the local election.[15] But, as Stoker has pointed out 'the public is looking for politicians to reach beyond the boundaries of party politics'.[16]

Secondly, the Local Government Act 2000 introduced into British council chambers a political executive: either an indirectly elected leader or a directly elected mayor, both with their associated cabinets. It is here that the term modernisation becomes somewhat of a misnomer. As far back as 1967 the Maud Committee was recommending the creation of a small management board consisting of five to nine members, which would set the principle objectives for the authority and control its work, acting in all but name as a form of executive.[17] It was the Conservative government in 1991 that began to float the idea of directly elected mayors; something the Blair government has made a reality.[18] But, what is on offer from the political modernisation ushered in by the 2000 Act is less a New Labour vision of local government and more an old civil service one. Either way, it is no surprise that when central government starts to delve into the machinations of council political decision-making, it comes up with a solution that reflects the way government and party centrally conduct their activities.

The one change introduced by the 2000 Act that stands out as having no direct central equivalent – the directly elected mayor – has met with overwhelming hostility from councillors, councils and most of the local government establishment. The results of local referenda held so far on the introduction of such a new political office has indicated two things: first, the reactionary nature of much of the local government political establishment when faced with a change that destabilises exiting political relationships, structures, dynamics and power. Secondly, that the idea of directly elected mayors itself has singularly failed to ignite a spark of real interest amongst local citizens in local politics; the 30 referenda outside of London so far have delivered only 11 'yes' results. As we shall see later, the parties have had mixed fortunes when it comes to mayoral election campaigns.

The vast majority of councils have played it safe when it comes to political modernisation and introduced the option contained within the 2000 Act of an indirectly elected leader: an office open to the patronage and choice of the majority party group – or some arrangement between parties where no clear majority exists. Yet, despite the indirectly elected leader and cabinet representing minimal change in the outward appearance of council political decision-making, there is the potential for these new arrangements to usher in a new set of political dynamics. Executive leaders, mayors and cabinets, could potentially disturb some rather cosy and comfortable political worlds and open up a challenge to the notion of party in the locality as we currently understand it. Alternatively, parties and party groups can capture and colonise these new arrangements, diluting their potential for a new type of local politics and ensuring that locality remains the territory of the party. The likely result of attempts to modernise local politics, and the response of parties to it, is a central theme of this book.

A change that emphasises local sub-ordination

As a result of the Blair government's Local Government Act 2000, councils are now structured on a form of separation of powers that mirrors the national political and constitutional arrangements: a powerful central executive, or cabinet, headed by an indirectly (or directly elected) politician, held to account by an assembly (council) with a potentially powerful scrutiny role. Each council now also has a form of judiciary, that is, a *standards committee* that must monitor the ethical standards and practices of the council and ensure a healthy ethical environment exists within it. Councils have come to look more and more like Britain's national political institutions, but party locally and particularly council party groups are not necessarily set to change the way they do business and conduct council affairs. That local government must now look like central government makes the role of party locally even stronger than before.

The very terms local party, local politics and local democracy emphasise the subordination of powerful elements of the political processes and culture to an overarching, or overbearing, national political framework. Even the term 'sub-national politics or government' tends to relegate local politics to a sub-division of some broader and more important political system.[19] The terms 'territorial government' and 'territorial politics' come closest to highlighting both the distinct nature of local politics and local government.[20] Yet, Bulpitt's use of the terms 'high' and 'low' politics to separate national policy concerns, which are the domain of the central state, from concerns over service delivery by local government, rather than emphasising local political representation and leadership, powerfully implies that local politics is a subservient world to the high politics of the centre.[21] Whilst such terminology again relegates local politics in importance, it does emphasise the distinct and discrete nature of the local from the central, which is at the heart of Bulpitt's dual polity model. The term 'territorial politics' binds together the three elements of the local, politics, democracy and government, and displays their separateness from and connection with each other and the centre. It is a term which also conveys the largely exclusory way in which parties and party groups view and conduct local political decision-making.

The debate is not merely one of semantics, but of alighting on a term that enables local democracy, politics and government to be recognised as distinct and separate features of the political landscape. Moreover, reference to territorial politics emphasises that politics is about much more than what political parties and local councils do. Political parties have little or no loyalty to recognisable local communities as such. Rather, they are concerned with capturing control of a council – a specific local government unit – the boundaries of which are more likely to be drawn for administrative convenience and to meet technocratic and managerial needs, rather than reflect communities of place. Parties will transfer their interest and loyalty to any set of artificially drawn boundaries that represent any new local government units that may be formed, as it is power and the control of those units, more than community representation, that interest political parties.

The focus political parties have on capturing control of, or securing representation in any council chamber, results in the loosening of the bond between the councillor and the community and a strengthening of the ties between the councillor and his or her political party, for it is the party that can guarantee or withhold election to the council. Parties conduct their business and the business of local politics in broadly similar ways, wherever they are located. They will organise, structure themselves and operate within a framework that all party people recognise as constituting a 'political party' proper. As a consequence of this, parties have led to the nationalisation of local politics, that is, a squeezing out from the local political arena of diversity of practice and form and a substitution of local difference with local conformity in political processes. What local variation remains between parties of the same political affiliation and different parties is surprisingly minimal; parties have a homogenising affect on local politics. Thus, it is outside the walls of the party that we must look, to community and single-issue groups, if we wish to observe expressions of the rich, deep and diverse local political environment.

What follows in the book, however, is not intended to be a hatchet job on local party politics. Rather it is an exploration of the long-standing interconnection between local government, local democracy and local politics and the political party – more specifically, the political party group of councillors. It will be a sceptical, rather than cynical journey through local party politics to highlight the negative and positive impact party has within the locality, however the boundaries of that locality may be drawn. In addition, the book will draw together a number of different theoretical and conceptual threads to provide a framework through which to analyse and understand the conduct of local politics by the political party and the role it plays and power it wields locally.

Finally, an underlying theme of this book is the relationship between political party and notions of civic virtue, pride and splendour. Not by way of romanticising some mythical golden age of party-free local government, more to question how party can contribute to a new civic life within our communities that is apart from the dry administration of council services – as important as they may be. Can and does party provide local communities with powerful political leaders in tune with the needs of their communities? Or, does it provide us with elected managers who are immersed in and overwhelmed by the minutiae of service administration and thus distracted from the need to stimulate a vibrant and healthy local democracy?

The book is about what party does both to and within local politics, that is politics conducted within and aimed at the locality – not politics conducted locally but aimed at some national result. On that note, perhaps the springboard into the rest of the book should be Ostrogorski's solution to what was perceived as, the problem of political parties: 'Down with the party and up with the league.'[22] In other words, formal, structured and permanent organisations such as political parties have a damaging effect on democracy and representation and should be replaced by single-issue or multi-objective temporary bodies that seek to deal with a particular political problem and then remove themselves from the political arena. The political party acting as an uniformed and disciplined *bloc* of members with a broad political purpose would be replaced by loose-knit organisations seeking coalitions and alliances around particular issues. We shall see in what follows whether in today's local government that solution is appropriate, desirable and achievable.

Structure of the book

The main theme of the book is how those involved in party politics interpret politics, democracy and representation and how they equate representation with governing locally and more importantly with governing through and by the political party. The focus of the book is deliberately on the three main UK-wide political parties, as it is they that have responsibility for shaping and dominating the local political landscape. Indeed, it is the organisation, structure, activities and approach of the three main parties that has resulted in the homogenisation of the conduct of local politics. Smaller parties such as the Greens, the British National Party and the small array of local organisations that have secured election to council chambers, are far from having anything like a significant impact on the dominant practices of local politics shaped by the three main parties. Moreover, the Scottish National Party and Plaid Cymru are well-established elements of their own nations four party systems and conduct local politics and the politics of the council chamber in broadly similar ways to the three UK-wide parties. Thus, the Conservative and Labour parties and the Liberal Democrats face little challenge when it comes to the conduct of local politics, cast, as it is, in their own images. As a consequence the three main parties are the main, though not exclusive focus of the book.

The book is structured in the following way. The next chapter explores the relationship between notions of representation and the role of the political party within a local representative system. It considers the tension between the role of party locally and the growing assertiveness of local communities when it comes to decision-making around local issues; it considers how local communities are driven more by local issues and events than by concerns with political affiliation and party. Chapter 3 looks at how the main national political parties organise and structure themselves in the localities for the conduct of political activity. It explores the similarities and distinctions in organisation and approach to local politics taken by the main parties. It looks at how parties concentrate on very specific political activities, such as the local election, and how they interpret what for them constitutes political activity and legitimate politics.

Chapter 4 focuses on the organisation, role and power of that very specific unit of local party structure: the political party group of councillors. It explores the reasons for and affects of party group cohesion and public unity when it comes to the conduct of council affairs and local politics more widely. The chapter presents the party group as a *leviathan* that directs and controls all facets of council political activity and the way in which councillors approach the business of local representation. Chapter 5 continues the exploration of the party group, but focuses on the relationship between party groups and the national political party. It looks at the differences and similarities between the way in which the three main parties attempt to bring form and order to the organisation and activities of their local party groups. Chapter 6 presents the findings of research into five different local authorities, where the dynamics of the interactions within and between party groups were explored. The chapter illuminates the way in which the group becomes the centre of the councillor's political world and replaces loyalty to the electorate with loyalty to the group. It also displays very clearly the homogenising effect of political party on local politics and the uniformity with which political decision-making and political leadership manifest themselves locally. Chapter 7 examines how the *party person's* loyalty to the party and the councillor's loyalty to his or her party and party group on the council can generate a *crisis of representation* when the views of the party clash with the views of the electorate around specific local issues and concerns. It explores how councillors manage the tension between loyalty to the party and the representation of local interest.

Chapter 8 considers the changes to local government political decision-making introduced by the Local Government Act 2000. It explores how the creation of a council executive, specifically the indirectly elected leader and cabinet option within the Act, poses a challenge to notions of party group supremacy within council chambers. It looks at how councils have introduced this type of executive and the relationship between leaders, cabinet members and the party groups of which they are members. Chapter 9 looks at how political party groups have responded to the new office of directly elected mayor introduced into the local political landscape by the 2000 Act. It explores whether these new mayors are able to construct a new type of politics, or whether political parties are able to marginalise and out-manoeuvre elected mayors from both their own parties as well as mayors from opposing parties.

Chapter 10 concludes by considering the resilience of political parties involvement in local democracy and as vehicles of local representation. It suggests that local representation has been reduced from broad ideals of citizen empowerment and involvement to a narrow focus on party loyalty and party interest. It shows how political parties have ensured that it is the party, not the citizenry, that benefits from local democracy and representation and how it has been able to colonise localities in the name of the party. The chapter sets out an alternative view of how parties could approach local politics so as to encourage, rather than avoid, citizen involvement, and how parties may reform themselves to work alongside a range of local political actors and bodies that prefer to conduct politics outside the walls of a party.

The methodological approach

The book is a result of data collected through four separate but related formal research projects that employed a range of quantitative and qualitative research methods: questionnaires, formal semi-structured interviews, focus groups of councillors and political party members, the construction and analysis of case studies and in one project, participant observation. Of these research projects, which were conducted over the last five years, one was a regionally based study, the remainder were national research projects.

The book rests more heavily on the qualitative than the quantitative material collected, so as to give voice to the experiences of those involved in party politics and to help uncover how they go about the business of politics and the intentions behind their actions. That qualitative data were collected through formal interviews with 150 serving councillors and with focus groups that comprised a total of 120 serving councillors. The book also draws on elaborative comments and quotes collected over the years from a range of events were councillors have expressed views on the dynamics of party politics and the experiences of representative democracy at the local level. In addition, the tables presenting the results of qualitative research are based on the circulation of a total of 2,500 questionnaires throughout the four projects of which 1,470 were returned and usable for analysis, giving a response rate of almost 60 per cent. The qualitative and quantitative methods were employed across a range of county, district and unitary authorities, and were also designed to ensure political affiliation across the parties was sufficiently represented and that the urban and rural experiences of party politics in the localities were captured.

The case studies contained in chapter 6 were created as a result of research conducted specifically for the book. In each of the five authorities concerned, interviews and focus groups were conducted with councillors and party members; in all, some 67 people gave up their time to be interviewed or take part in a focus group. Repeat interviews were held where particular issues needed greater elaboration and exploration. The local press was also used as a resource base when constructing the case studies.

Whilst the use of formal research methods are vital for a robust and valid study, the book also uses material collected throughout the author's years of experience in party political activity. It also employs material collected from the author's extensive and continual contact with councillors across the political spectrum as part of day-to-day academic activity.

Such material, and its use, whilst open to challenge and criticism as journalistic or anecdotal, does, however, provide a vital insight into the world of party politics, an insight which more formal research tools cannot capture, as respondents act in more guarded and careful circumstances in completing questionnaires and responding to interview questions. What follows then, rests on both formal research methods and on the informal gathering of intelligence from the world of party politics. Such a mix helps to shine a light into the closed world of the political party in local government.

Notes

1 D. Wilson and C. Game, *Local Government in the United Kingdom*, Basingstoke: Macmillan, 2002, pp. 276–277.
2 K. Young and N. Rao, 'Faith in Local Democracy', in J. Curtice, R. Jowell, L. Brook and A. Park (eds), *British Social Attitudes: The Twelfth Report*, Aldershot: Dartmouth, 1995, pp. 91–117, particularly pp. 111–112.
3 R. V. Clements, *Local Notables and the City Council*, London: Macmillan, 1969, pp. 59–66. J. Maud, Committee on the Management of Local Government (Maud Committee), *Research* Vol. I, Report of the Committee, London: HMSO, 1967, pp. 109–110.
4 G. W. Jones, *Borough Politics: A Study of Wolverhampton Borough Council 1888–1964*, Basingstoke: Macmillan, 1969, p. 324.
5 Ibid.
6 M. Maor, *Political Parties and Party Systems: Comparative Approaches and the British Experience*, London: Routledge, 1997; G. Quagliariello, *Politics without Parties*, Aldershot: Avebury, 1996, R. Garner and R. Kelly, *British Political Parties Today*, Manchester: Manchester University Press, 1993; R. Rose, *Politics in England: Change and Persistence*, Basingstoke: Macmillan, 1989.
7 G. W. Jones, *Borough Politics*; P. Saunders, *Urban Politics: A Sociological Interpretation*, London: Hutchinson, 1979; D. Green, *Power and Party in an English City: An Account of Single-Party Rule*, London: George Allen & Unwin, 1981; A. Glassberg, *Representation and Urban Community*, Basingstoke: Macmillan, 1981.
8 D. M. Hill, *Democratic Theory and Local Government*, London: George Allen & Unwin, 1974.
9 G. Parry, *Political Elites*, London: George Allen & Unwin, 1971.
10 DETR, *Modernising Local Government: Local Democracy and Community Leadership*, 1998.
11 DETR, *Modern Local Government: In Touch with the People*, 1998.
12 DETR, *Local Leadership: Local Choice*, 1999.
13 DTLR, *Strong Local Leadership: Quality Public Services*, 2001.
14 DETR, *Modern Local Government*, para. 1.2.
15 C. Copus, 'Community, Party and the Crisis of Representation', in N. Rao

(ed.), *Representation and Community in Western Democracies*, Basing-stoke: Macmillan, 2000, pp. 93–113.

16 G. Stoker, 'Local Political Leadership: Preparing for the 21st Century', Mimeo, Strathclyde University, 1998.

17 Maud Committee, Vol.1, Report of the Committee, p. 143.

18 'Community Leadership and Representation: Unlocking the Potential', The Report of the Working Party on the Internal Management of Local Authorities in England, HMSO, July 1993.

19 C. Gray, *Government Beyond the Centre: Sub-National Politics in Britain*, Basingstoke: Macmillan, 1994.

20 J. Bulpitt, 'Participation in Politics', in G. Parry (ed.), *Participation and Local Politics*, Manchester: Manchester University Press, 1972, pp. 281–302. J. Bulpitt, *Territory and Power in the United Kingdom*, Manchester: Manchester University Press, 1983.

21 Bulpitt, *Territory and power.*

22 M. Ostrogorski, *Democracy and the Organisation of Political Parties*, Vols I and II, New York: Macmillan, 1902.

2

Representation: the party or the people?

Where there are elections within the liberal democratic model of representation, there will be political parties. Where there are elected bodies which make public policy, distribute public resources and decide on winners and losers when it comes to those resources, political parties will seek office and power. It is not surprising then that political parties have a long-standing interest in local government and in seeking control of councils, or, if that is not possible, then at least in securing a permanent presence and voice within any one council chamber.

Political party has had a fundamental impact on the way the liberal democratic model of representation displays itself locally, on the nature of local democracy and on the conduct of council affairs across the country. Indeed, within the realm of the locality there exists an important three-way tension: that between the local councillor as an elected representative, the electorate he or she represents, and the political party of which he or she is a member. The aim of this chapter is to explore that tension.

The predominant understanding of the relationship between councillors and their constituents fails to take account of the impact of party on the processes of local representative democracy. That the presence of parties has introduced new elements to local authority decision-making has long been recognised. What political parties do to local representation and wider local politics is less well understood. Moreover, the role of the party group – the cohesive organisation of councillors from a single party – has received scant attention by comparison with that given to the political party generally. Yet, it will be shown that both party and the party group play an important and discrete part in the representative processes, interposing themselves between the electors and their representatives and generating their own distinctive claims to commitment. Vital to the interplay of politics locally is the fact that party members and councillors interpret representation and democracy differently from those they are elected to represent. They also have very distinct ideas about the role of the citizen and the party in local political activity and decision-making.

To fully understand the impact of party on local politics and democracy it is necessary to move beyond the study of structure and organisation – important as they are – to focus on what might be called the dynamics of the political process. Whilst organisation and structure may say much about how parties see their activities and how they construct a set of institutional arrangements within which they speak to themselves and from which they speak to the outside world, structures often serve to mask the realities of politics, obscure the way parties conduct their activities and hide the impact they have on the politics of the locality. Whilst structures set the *theatre* within which politics are conducted and may shape and drive that politics, it is the dynamics of politics, those forces that invigorate and energise people into politics and politics into action, that are crucial to consider when exploring the impact of party. Moreover, to avoid a mere descriptive account of party politics, it is necessary to look at what motivates the *party person*, and particularly the councillor, into political action, and it is vital to understand the way he or she makes sense of the day-to-day experiences of being a 'representative' of the electorate and a party member.

The first section of this chapter explores the tensions within liberal democracy as they relate to mass participation and how the political party plays a vital role in attenuating such involvement. The section links our understanding of democracy and representation with the role of the political party within it. The second section turns to the conflicts that result when the processes of representative democracy meet with the pressures of an increasingly assertive and demanding electorate. It introduces the notion of 'event-driven democracy', recognising that local issues and events may energise the community, or sections of it, to seek an enhanced input into local political decision-making only episodically. Moreover, understanding local democracy as driven by local events, rather than local parties, provides a framework to understand the often-competing interpretations of representation held by the party politician and the citizen. The third section shows how political parties have come to play an increasing role in local politics and argues for a new focus on the part played by the party group in the processes of local democracy, and in our understanding of the world of the party. It considers the idea that it is the political party, rather than the electorate, that benefits from the dynamics of local representative democracy.

Liberal democracy under pressure

It has become a commonplace defence of party in our political system and culture to argue that the classical doctrine of democracy, in which the people are active and direct participants and decision-makers, is no longer relevant. Indeed, modern society's scale and complexity requires mechanisms of an indirect or representative democracy, to ensure the quality of political decisions and of the specialist professional politicians charged with the conduct of politics and political decision-making. Moreover, representative democracy can be seen as a system deliberately designed to reduce wide-scale citizen involvement in the political processes and even that 'representative government was conceived in explicit opposition to government by the people'.[1]

Representative democracy involves a transfer of political engagement from the citizen to the elected representative, but in so doing creates a void between the processes of politics and government and the citizenry. It is the political party that seeks to fill the void created by the expectation that citizens will step aside from politics once they have selected their representatives. Yet, as Manin points out, many of the founders of representative government saw parties as having little or no role in the system they set out to create.[2] It was men of wealth and intellect that were to become the representatives, not those that used only party zeal and loyalty to obtain positions of political power.

But, the reality of party-based government, as it displays itself, is not that parties lead to mass involvement in politics, rather they result in no more than a slight widening of political participation. Further, political parties, by securing the lion's share of elected office, at the national and local levels, serve to exclude not only those who may independently seek office, but also the expression of a range of views and opinions from the public domain that do not accord with party policy. When it comes to political decisions on very local issues, party loyalty is still held at a premium, even when those issues have little or no politically philosophical bearing. Indeed, those party members holding the office of an elected representative are so bound by party loyalty that they will act against the best interest of their electorate if the party so demands.[3] Indeed, the tendency for this to occur is far greater in British local party politics amongst council group members than in Parliament.

In an exploration of the role of the political party within representative democracy, particularly at the local level, it is vital to recognise the relationship between political affiliation and how various sets of political actors interpret both democracy and representation. Those signing up to and becoming involved in party politics – whichever party – not only sign-up to the party and its policies, but also to specific notions of democracy and representation. What, however, may appear surprising, when comparing the views of the parties towards democracy, representation and the role of the party within them, is the considerable similarity of interpretation of these factors held by party people across the political spectrum. Such common ground develops from the shared experiences of party membership and from the holding of elected office, as well as from the interactions that the holders of elected office have with those they represent. It is the common ground between the parties, about the nature of democracy and representation and the balance of input by the elected representative, the party and the citizen into the political processes, that makes political parties the glue binding the elements of liberal democracy together. It is necessary then to consider those elements in detail.

The elements of liberal democracy

The theory of liberal democracy is based on two propositions: 'the electoral presumption' and 'competitive *elitism*'.[4] The 'electoral presumption' is that a system of electorally based representative democracy is the most 'practical' mechanism for choosing 'governors' from competing *elites* and for reflecting the general priorities of the electorate. Here the people are, and can be, no more than producers of governments (either nationally or locally), being required only to make the decision as to those that 'are to do the deciding'. Indeed, democracy can be defined by the existence of institutional arrangements for 'arriving at political decisions in which individuals acquire the power to decide by means of a competitive struggle for the people's vote'.[5]

Inextricably linked to the electoral presumption is the notion of 'competitive *elitism*'; that is, the elevation of political *elites* to positions of power through the sporadic and casual input of the electorate. Indeed, within liberal democracy the political role of the citizen is restricted to infrequent electoral activity and the selection of leaders, nationally and locally. The selection of those leaders and consequently the transference of political power to them from the electorate are made easier by the mechanism of political parties. Any greater input by the citizen other than the use of elections to select rulers and produce governments (and provide legitimised opposition to them) is ruled out, for, as has been argued, the electorate lack the intellectual sophistication for wider political involvement.[6] Indeed, political parties attenuate even further this minimal citizen input, by selecting its own leadership then placing that leadership before the electorate against an opposing party's choice. The electorate need look no further than the party when it comes to selecting between competing *elites*, either nationally or locally.

Yet, the development of liberal democracy sought not only to ensure the selection of the right people to govern, a political system was required that would enshrine the protection of minority rights, specifically the rights of property ownership, from the tyranny of the majority. Theorists of liberal democracy sought to balance minority property rights with political involvement of the non-proprietor classes. Much democratic theorising has been based on reconciling support for a system of popular democracy with protecting 'the haves (a minority), from the have-nots (a majority)' and avoidance of a majority turning the 'instruments of state policy against a minority's privilege'.[7]

The fear of an irresponsible majority acting tyrannically against the interests of a minority underpinned the foundation of US democracy.[8] The answer to such a threat was to turn from notions of democracy, or any wide-scale direct involvement in political democracy, to Republicanism, or 'representation'. As Madison described it: 'in a democracy, the people meet and exercise the government in person: in a republic, they assemble and administer it by their representatives and agents'.[9] As Crick points out: the important question for the founding fathers of the United States in designing a new political system was how strong the 'democratic element' should be.[10] Furthermore, republicanism was linked to a broader set of ideals such as 'simplicity, civic virtue, and even small proprietorship as the typical estate of a true citizen' and thus protected the propertied minority from the 'majoritarian overtones of democracy'.[11]

Tocqueville identifies the success of the US experiment in developing a political system that protects the individual holding of property from the 'omnipotence of the majority'. It succeeds to such an extent that it becomes part of a broader political outlook – not simply a set of institutional arrangements and constitutional safeguards to property ownership, but a deeper belief in the sanctity of private property ownership.[12] Here is the key element in the success of representative democracy: it produces the illusion of wide-scale political involvement and control, without threatening certain fundamental political beliefs about the hierarchical nature of society.

While protection of the proprietor minority from popular exploitation and expropriation is not a central feature of British local politics, earlier periods were characterised by just such a debate. First, the local government franchise as it developed throughout the nineteenth century ensured that those exercising the vote, and the candidates from which they could select, fulfilled some property qualification.[13] The franchise and the office of councillor was restricted to certain sections of the community and even radical candidates 'tended to be small masters, shopkeepers or publicans'.[14] Young refers to mid-nineteenth-century attempts to reform county government as not a search for 'representative democracy' but the development of a 'form of ratepayer democracy'.[15] Gyford emphasises the point that the relationship between the local electorate and councillor was primarily a fiduciary rather than a politically representative one.[16] He comments that: 'the bodies which emerged from the 1835 Municipal Corporations Act were seen first and foremost as owners of corporate property'. Indeed, 'councillors as members of the corporation were trustees in a fiduciary relationship to the ratepayers within a system based upon the rights of property'.[17]

The development of municipal government as an integral part of the growth of the British State led to some titanic battles involving private commercial interests, particularly where those interests felt threatened by any number of municipal proposals for the extension of their service delivery role, such as in the realm of the public utility: gas, water electricity and transport.[18] Indeed, municipalisation and the pursuit of local redistributionary policies undermined the entire Victorian assumption that national politics were irrelevant to local government.[19] Moreover, the extension of the franchise during the Victorian period brought with it the notion that property ownership would require protection from infringement by either national or local government.[20] Liberal democracy, then, has traditionally portrayed liberalism, with its entrenchment of minority rights, both political and property, as a counterpoint to democracy.

The role of the councillor and the relationship he or she had with the electorate during periods in the development of British local government reflect central government concern with the stewardship of local taxation. They also reflect central government's view of the largely administrative and service delivery-orientated role of local corporations, and indeed of single-service sub-national bodies, such as street improvement commissions, education boards and Boards of Guardians. The role of local politics was less about responding to and reflecting the concerns and priorities of local communities, and more about the management, administration and the delivery of some service or another. Councillors during the Victorian period were expected to be elected managers just as much as their current-day counterparts.

The relationship between the centre and the locality today still rests very much on the notion that councils are responsible for spending local money, rather than developing their own unique political and public policy solutions to local needs and issues. Whilst councils do retain the ability to identify and carve out some policy autonomy and whilst councillors can, and do, bring a broadly political view to the work they undertake, the councillor as elected manager, rather than active and powerful local politician, is still very much the norm. Avoiding the development of powerful representative institutions peopled by equally powerful local politicians is at the heart of the development of British local government – if not its local politics. Not only do liberal democracy and representative government have to ensure that national government is based on and reflects their principles, so too must any local government structure.

Not all those concerned with the development of local government and politics in the local realm viewed local government and local democracy as potential threats to central political control. Rather, the concept of participation at the local level as a precursor to involvement in national politics found a particular resonance. Mill sets out the importance of local representative bodies as places where the citizen can gain experience of governing and of acting for the wider public interest, rather than being motivated by self-interest alone. He does however sound a note of caution that minority, or rather property interests must be protected by plural voting and he clearly links local representative bodies to the spending of public money thus: 'For the honest and frugal dispensation of money forms so much a larger part of the business of the local than of the national body, that there is more justice as well as policy in allowing a greater proportional influence to those who have a larger money interest at stake.'[21]

In addition to ensuring that representative bodies were peopled by those of proper standing and intellect, the proponents of representative democracy were, and still are, faced with the dilemma of ensuring the elected representative is not bound by the views of the represented. The problem here is to justify a process by which the representative becomes de-linked from the represented and is able to follow his or her own conscience and judgement when involved in political decision-making and debate. It is here that Burke and Mill lay the foundation for the freedom of the representative from the represented and in so doing ensured that the loyalty of the elected representative is transferred from citizen to party.

Burke's address to the electors of Bristol sets out the case for the freedom of the representative:

Parliament is not a congress of ambassadors with different and hostile interests, which interests, each must maintain, as an agent and advocate, against other agents and advocates; but Parliament is a deliberative assembly of one nation, with one interest, that of the whole – where not local purposes, not local prejudices ought to guide, but the general good resulting from the general reason of the whole.[22]

Whilst Burke acknowledged that the representative owes the citizen his or her unbiased opinion, mature judgement and enlightened conscience, the representative is not bound to substitute the citizen's judgement for his or her own. Indeed, the representative 'betrays instead of serves' the citizen if he or she substitutes another's opinion for his or her own. Thus, the elected representative is not a delegate of the electorate, but the party. As Eulau and Whalke state: 'above all freedom from local connections and instructions was for Burke a necessary and very practical condition to work for a Parliamentary party, be its leader, and accept the commitments of a party man'.[23]

Mill saw the role of the representative as one of a trustee of the electorate's best interests, not as being mandated to follow the opinions of the electorate. Moreover, Mill saw the representative as having a duty to correct what he termed as 'false judgement' held by the electorate. Whilst the representative should listen to the opinions and views of the electors and consider those views, the representative should be free to come to a conclusion on the matter in hand that may differ from that of his or her elector's. In this way, government is conducted by superior minds and the tyranny of an uneducated majority can be avoided. As we shall see later, the Burkean and Millsian approach to the role of the representative finds favour with the practices of current day councillors, across the political spectrum.

Notions of whether the representative has a trustee relationship with the electorate – that is, coming to a conclusion on issues based on the representative's own judgement – or whether he or she acts as a delegate – bound by the electorate's instructions – strike at the heart of liberal democracy.[24] If political parties are to have any meaningful role in the processes of political decision-making, it is essential that the elected representative has some considerable autonomy from the electorate within his or her constituency. The representative must be able to freely select whether he or she will conduct his or her duties as a 'party man, a constituency servant, or a mentor'.[25] In the vast majority of cases the elected representative will seek the maximum autonomy from the electorate, either because that is what the party demands or because the representative wishes to place party above the electorate. Representative democracy today, is more about securing the role and place of party within the political system and avoiding direct citizen control and involvement in political decisions than it is about the articulation of the views of the citizenry by those they elect. Elected representatives must ensure that the views they express and act upon are in accord with the views of the party, which is itself part and parcel of a set of institutions and procedures designed to ensure that the best intellects are in charge of governing. Even radical parties are prone to such oligarchical tendencies.[26]

The creation of any set of representational institutions, at whatever level within the state, does not imply mass participation within those institutions, or even in the elections involved in selecting representatives. Indeed, within the liberal democratic model, citizens have as much right to disengage from politics and the political system as they have to engage with it. Whilst many involved in politics may bemoan the electorate's apparent lack of interest – gauged often only by turnout levels at elections – others, however, have taken a positive view of low levels of electoral participation. Morris-Jones furnished disengagement from the political process with its own justification and rejected a general 'duty' to participate in political activity and, specifically, to vote.[27] He argued that while low electoral turnout can weaken support for local democracy, democracy remains healthy if those with little interest in, or knowledge of political issues, 'choose' not to participate.

Parties and participation: taking a more local view

Morris-Jones's view is not one that is widely held today in discussions of the quality of democracy, where electoral turnout is awarded central importance. If representative democracy is perceived as a set of institutional relationships and procedures to facilitate the sporadic input of the electorate, then electoral turnout must be an important indicator of the health of any democracy. The defenders of representative democracy often present the public vote as the 'trump card' when it comes to legitimising the role of the representative, or more often some unpopular decision it is felt necessary to make.[28] Indeed, Phillips notes that elections can be seen by some as 'virtually absolute trumps: the only legitimate method for ascertaining the will of . . . the people'.[29] If this is to be the case then low levels of turnout serve to delegitimise not only political decisions made but also the system which makes them.

Participation by citizens in the choice of elected representative takes on a premium when those they elected make such a play of the legitimate nature of their office and actions. The public vote is seen to provide representatives with the ability to act in direct opposition to the articulated views of the public and, in many cases, without even the most perfunctory assessment of what the public might think about a specific issue. Councillors particularly use the public vote that they and their party received at an election as the sanction for any actions they may take and for any decisions they may make. Yet, local electoral turnout in Britain has reached new lows, with around 30 per cent turning out in the 2003 elections. The use of the public vote and arguments about local electoral democracy therefore appears weak were it not for the link that some see between political parties and popular involvement in local elections.

The arguments to support the presence and activities of political parties within local elections fall intro two broad types: those concerned with the stimulation of public interest, and those concerned with making the selection of representatives easier for the electorate. First, election campaigning and competition between local political parties are a stimulus to public interest in political issues. Where parties actively campaign to win seats on, and control of, a council, the electorate are presented with a choice of alternative policy proposals and electoral platforms. Indeed, in many areas there are more than two serious contenders for control of the council and certainly for winning a reasonable number of seats. In these circumstances, the electorate may face a confusing array of candidates and manifestos. Serious party competition may see the electorate responding by coming out to support the 'team', that is the party they normally vote for; or, weighing up the proposals presented by the parties, considering the current administration's stewardship of local affairs, and voting accordingly. Either way the battle between parties facilitates a choice between alternative policies and encourages the electorate to vote.[30]

Secondly, political parties ease the elector's choice when selecting a representative through the simple process of label identification.[31] Without some formal way for the electorate to identify with the candidates on offer and make some assessment of the views and political preferences of those candidates, the elector is faced with the daunting task of getting to know the candidates personally and in some detail. At this point the individual profile of a candidate, and probably an incumbent one at that, would be at a premium, for to vote other than for party an 'elector must know something of the personal characteristics of the candidates'.[32] Moreover, the elector would require knowledge of local issues and concerns to be able to come to a judgement on what the candidates are saying about them. As a consequence the 'relatively disinterested

[sic] elector' may rely on the party to make local elections 'more readily comprehensible'.[33]

Party involvement in the electoral process can have a positive impact on electoral participation. But the influence of party on turnout cannot be taken for granted, as local and national turnout figures clearly undermine arguments that political party involvement in elections increase citizen participation in the selection of representatives. Rao has categorised the relationship between party and electoral turnout into three types: first, the *marginality* of the seat concerned, that is the closeness of the result last time, leading to more hard fought campaigns by the parties. Secondly, the citizen is likely to be influenced, when it comes to deciding whether or not to vote (let alone who to vote for), by the *intensity* of any election campaign. Frequent and vigorous campaigning helps bring the party and its activities to the attention of the voter and indicates that one, or a number of parties, are prepared to campaign outside the usual election period – a tactic often employed by the Liberal Democrats *Focus Teams*, but emulated by other parties. Thirdly, the notion of *competitiveness*, or the number of parties and individuals campaigning for elections, providing the electorate with more choice, may tempt more people to turn out and vote.[34]

Arguments favouring the involvement of parties in the electoral process present them as the natural corollary of representative democracy. Indeed, in many cases the involvement of political parties is proof positive that democracy exists and works. Moreover, too many elections are the sole territory of the political party and single-issue groups enter it at their peril. Yet, the electorate have a far more ambivalent relationship with the notion of party as such a vital part of representation and politics. Indeed, evidence exists to suggest that the presence of parties at the local level may lead to electoral apathy and to something deeper: cynicism about local democracy.

The Maud Committee in 1967, the Widdicombe Committee in 1986, and Young and Rao in 1994 uncovered a range of negative attitudes towards local democracy existing amongst their respondents.[35] These studies reflected an electorate often alienated from the council and councillors that they had elected to serve them; uncertain about their ability to influence local affairs or simply lacking interest in them, and displaying a sceptical attitude towards the promises and activities of political parties in local affairs. It would seem then that the involvement of political parties in local elections has little beneficial impact and may in fact work to depress local involvement and interest. Indeed, by acting as disciplined bodies, during an election campaign, parties may serve to narrow the choice available to the local electorate to one of simply accepting or rejecting a small number of competing policy packages, or, worse, using some aggregated image of the national party reflected on to its local candidates.

The arguments about the beneficial (or otherwise) impact of political parties on local elections are, however, quite distinct from those concerning their specific impact on the conduct of council affairs and on the representative process more generally. Moreover, political parties may serve to exclude citizens from local politics and from involvement in decisions about important local issues and priorities. These latter arguments direct attention to the actual working relationship between the councillor and the party group, the importance the party group has for the councillor in his or her representative activities, and the interrelationship between the councillor, the group, the wider political party and the electorate. These are matters examined in later chapters of the book.

Accountability in liberal democracy

A balanced view of what has been considered so far would be that representative democracy facilitates, via party, a choice of elected representative, but excludes the citizen, individually or collectively from any other choices. The interaction between, say, the councillor, the party group, the political party and community, which occurs around specific issues and events, exemplifies the tensions inherent in local representative democracy, which are less obvious at the national level, except in the most intense political circumstances. Such local tensions raise an important question: can the electoral process stimulate sufficient citizen involvement to ensure that councillors, as the elected representatives of the local community, are held to account for what they do?

It is in answering this question that a judgement will be reached on whether criticisms of liberal democracy add up to a case against it, or an argument for more democracy within broadly liberal democratic terms. The judgement must depend on the particular context, for the severity of the shortcomings of liberal democracy become more or less important on different spatial scales. At the local level, for example, the shortcomings in the relationship between the councillor and the community are magnified by the immediacy of a local issue, its salience to local communities and its potential impact on the quality of day-to-day life. In addition, the closeness of the councillor to those he or she represents also serves to magnify, in the eyes of the electorate, when the councillor is acting more as a party politician than a local representative.

Within local democracy the councillor confronts tensions between the role of a party politician and community representative that are generated by a system which focuses political power in the council party group. More liberal democracy would not in itself lead to a shift of power to local communities.[36] Yet, it is more liberal democracy that is precisely what is on offer from the Blair government's agenda to modernise local government and local democracy. The agenda, as it is currently displayed, does not threaten, in any real sense, the nature of local representative democracy, the role of party and the councillor within in it, or the balance of power between councils and communities, it does, however, offer opportunities for enhanced citizen input and involvement. A more fundamental shift in the nature of local democracy and power may be both desirable and demanded by today's more politically assertive local communities.

The assertive community and local democracy

It is far too commonplace today for those involved in politics to complain that the electorate are apathetic about political issues, unconcerned about political decision-making and unwilling to become involved in local affairs. Yet, it is also the case that councillors hold quite negative views about what motivates the electorate when communities do stir into action, often seeing the electorate as self-interested and fixing on only very local concerns.[37] One thing is clear, however, the basic principles of representative democracy are continually under pressure from a rising tide of political assertiveness that has participatory consequences for the way in which local democracy will play itself out and how local politics will be conducted in the future.

It is necessary when considering notions of community to recognise the difficulty involved in defining the very concept of community itself. Moreover, local authority boundaries are not attempts to reflect 'community' as such, but are artificial and administratively convenient lines on a map, to capture sufficient populations to meet technocratic and managerial criteria, rather than the needs of political representation. Community remains and will remain an 'elusive' concept.[38] Communities of place and interest, however defined, are not bound by local authority boarders, yet the dynamics of community are constrained by the fact that the political parties, with which community must interact at some point, are focused on the 'council'. The differing focus and interests held by polit-

ical parties and groups of citizens, however, do not mean that communities are politically acquiescent when it comes to the wielding of local
political power and decision-making, rather they can be assertive and
aggressive players in local politics.

A number of surveys have considered community assertiveness as
evidence both of the electorate's willingness to take action and of a
belief in the effectiveness of it when faced with unpopular governmental acts. Three surveys in particular noted similar trends: a decline in
political passivity; a growing confidence amongst the electorate in their
ability to affect the political process; and the increasing importance of
the local arena as a catalyst for enhanced citizen protest.[39] They also
noted that few people perceived the various acts of protest as effective, compared with those claiming they would take such action.
Councillors, however, were seen as an effective focus for protest.
Indeed, a number of studies found that a greater propensity to protest
exists when it comes to actions taken by local councils rather than
central government.[40]

The growing assertiveness of the electorate, most recently witnessed by the march through London organised by the Countryside
Alliance, which saw some estimated 400,000 people in attendance,
and the even larger demonstration against war with Iraq, have put pay
to any notion of British political culture as essentially deferential in
nature. Some debate has taken place around this notion of deference
with Almond and Verba arguing that that British political culture was
characterised by 'general attitudes of social trust and confidence' and
that participation had not challenged its deferential nature. Indeed,
they argued that the British 'maintained a strong deference to the
independent authority of the government'.[41] Political participation
may in this case be merely signalling to government, local or national,
that concern exists over the direction of policy or a particular decision,
rather than fundamentally challenging the right of elected representatives to govern.

Marsh, however, has challenged the idea of British political culture
as essentially deferential, providing an alternative view of a Britain that
is willing to consider a range of political protest actions, alongside a
concern for political involvement.[42] In addition, some ten years latter,
the 1987 British Social Attitudes Report noted evidence of a 'growing
self confidence' amongst the electorate, which would bring new political concerns and a 'greater wish to be consulted in the political
process'.[43] Kavanagh noted that in Britain's civic culture, where ideology and mistrust combine, there is an 'enhanced potential for protest',

thus further undermining Almond and Verba's assertion of the deferential nature of British political culture.[44]

In their 1995 survey, Young and Rao found that two in every five respondents felt they could have a real influence on politics if they simply got involved.[45] As a result of considerable evidence available to refute Almond and Verba's notion of a deferential political culture, Young has gone as far as to comment that the *Civic Culture* could be seen as 'embarrassingly naive and . . . as simply wrong' and indeed that, Britain has moved 'towards an assertive and truculent pattern of political behaviour'.[46] Such a pattern of assertive and truculent behaviour however, whilst placing pressure on representative democracy and party politics, is not incompatible with either. Indeed, representative democracy, placing, as it does, the citizen once removed from political decision-making, requires mechanisms by which aggrieved citizens can let off steam. Political protest and pressure aimed at representatives does indeed sit very well with the notion that someone else will make the final decisions. Moreover, the electorate are able to vote for a party they prefer to be making the decisions and setting policy, whilst retaining the right to communicate to that party when and where they believe it is wrong on specific issues. The latter, of course, may well strain the voter's loyalty to their party.

The implications for representative democracy

Whilst political assertiveness and willingness to protest are compatible with representative democracy and the role of party within it, implications for both arise. Gyford noted that 'a move away from a society with a large degree of consensus on interests and values, towards a more diverse and fragmented society', exerts pressure on representative democracy to take on a greater participatory form.[47] Moreover, within specific localities it is the councillor that will directly experience the tension between his or her position as a local representative and the demands from the electorate for a greater involvement in local affairs. Widdicombe reported that councillors' response to the increased assertiveness, which impinged on their activities and those of the party group, was to support 'more say' for the 'ordinary citizen in the decisions made by local government', although this 'say' need not detract from the 'proper responsibilities of the councillor'. More recent studies confirm the trend towards councillors supporting greater citizen interest, involvement and participation in local affairs, whilst, at the same time, jealously guarding their right to make political decisions.[48] Thus, citizen input can be greatly increased in the political decision-making process, without the councillor's position as the elected decision-maker being diminished.

Two questions are raised by the developing trends in political culture. First, can the system of representative democracy at the local level cope effectively with an increasingly confident and assertive electorate demanding greater participation in political decision-making – if only around the decisions that interest them? Secondly, how will councillors manage pressure for greater participation within a system controlled by the political party and, more importantly, by the party group? Much will depend on the intensity of feeling within communities around any particular local issue and whether that issue is a 'sufficiently salient matter' to rouse an otherwise 'quiescent citizenry into involvement' and intense, though intermittent, action.[49] Much will also rest on how parties and councillors view their role and the role of the community when it comes to political decision-making.

Batley provides evidence to suggest that a community's demands for involvement in the processes of political decision-making as a response to particular events and council plans, is in striking contrast to the views of local councillors.[50] The attitudes councillors' display towards their representational role, compared with the expectations of those they represent bring into sharp relief the tensions within local democracy and between differing notions of governing and 'representing'. As Batley pointed out, councillors 'did not see themselves in the main as representatives of the community's interests'. Their task as local representatives was not:

> to represent the expressed interests of the ward but to identify these interests and then 'to convince people that you know best'. This seemed to amount in practice to attempting to bring the public to terms with party (or council) policy which must often be long-term and city-wide in scale rather than short-term and parochial as local opinion was felt likely to be.

The tension generated by citizen involvement in political decision-making is that it conflicts with the right to govern that councillors assume as a result of the legitimisation of their position by the public vote. Demands emanating from the wards or divisions that councillors represent threaten not only the cohesion and unity of the councillor's political party and party group, but also challenge the notion that councillors must take an authority-wide view of representation and act in classic Burkean terms in the interests of the whole, rather than the more specific interests of the electoral area.

Yet, communities located within electoral areas will frequently demand that the councillor places the very local interest before the party and even before the interests of the whole council area.[51] Lambert *et al.* comment that councillors seem to have little interest in 'being direct representatives of the area, but rather regard themselves as elected to create and defend city government'.[52] The tension between governing and representing an area and between differing interpretations of these notions held by councillors and communities have been explored in detail elsewhere.[53] One thing is clear, political party not only expects loyalty from those elected to office under its banner when it comes to broad policy issues, but also around particular local issues and the council's response to them. Whilst parties across the country will adopt varying degrees of rigidity when it comes to expressions of party unity over the articulation of local views by its councillors, the general pattern is to act so as to maintain the integrity and cohesion of the party. Thus, the task of the *party person* is not to express and explore diversity of opinion but to seek to shape local discourse so as to reflect the position adopted by the party. The result is that any member of the community who is moved to seek direct representation of an area and its interests, may need to join political parties to use the party itself and the processes of councillor selection to influence the policies of a local authority.[54]

The mobilisation of action

Recognition of the tension between an assertive electorate and their councillors as local party representatives gave rise to the concept of 'event-driven democracy'. The term is used here to illuminate the tension that flows through representative democracy, local government and local politics. That is, between any one local community's focus on issues and events of local importance to it, and the councillors' focus on the wider notion of governing an area through the political party and the decision-making forum of the party group. It highlights the *crisis of representation* (explored in chapter 7) that is created when councillors find that issue-based demands for representation from the community conflict with the party-based demands for loyalty and a broader governing agenda based on party loyalty.

Event-driven democracy relates to the mobilisation of communities and individuals around a particular event in which they have an interest. It can be seen as primarily *reactive* and *protective* in nature: *reactive* in that communities are often roused and mobilised after a decision has been made or consultation undertaken by a council; and *protective* in that communities perceive some threat from the decision or from its consequences. Yet, it is also important to see such processes in a positive light, with events as a motivational trigger to action. Such action provides a stake in the community for those involved and offers ownership of local issues and problems to the communities concerned; it is action which has a wider educative effect on those involved.[55] Indeed, Boaden *et al.* argued that: 'people are less willing than they were to accept authoritarian styles of leadership. Action groups and public protest have become a regular feature of policy development. The receding tide leaves pools of interest where new initiatives are taken.'

Moreover, community action stimulated by local issues and events swerves around political parties. Whilst it cannot hope to avoid political parties altogether, as they will become interested in an issue as it develops, community activity and organisation do provide an alternative point of mobilisation for those stimulated into action, a point of mobilisation that does not come with the necessity of formally signing up to one party or another and an acceptance of party loyalty and discipline. Moreover, community action stimulated by local issues and events allows the community to focus on specific matters, rather than taking on board the general political interest which is the realm of the political party. Political action without party membership, as we shall see later, does not immunise campaigners on local issues from contamination by party. Party is about power and those seeking to influence power locally cannot completely avoid party, only membership of it. As local events are immediate to local communities they can serve to motivate the electorate to a greater degree than that generated by local election campaigns, the timing of which may not be congruent with an issue's lifespan. Issues do not fall conveniently into the time frame of an election. Indeed, it is not unknown for difficult and potentially unpopular decisions to be delayed by a ruling party until after an impending election.

Campaigns on issues of common concern serve to widen our understanding of local politics from a narrow set of institutions, offices and processes that are the realm of the political party. Indeed, Cochrane notes that such campaigns by 'involving the previously uninvolved for however short a time, may increase democratic activity'.[56] The vital element that local campaigns have for our understanding of local politics and political decision-making is that they illuminate the crucial point that parties and councillors and the community are motivated by different political issues and view politics from radically different perspectives. When councillors complain of the electorate's apparent lack of interest in local politics, they are reflecting these different motivations.[57] Such varying spheres of interest held by represented and representatives at the local level, and the events that drive members of the community to activity, provide arenas in which the tensions between the councillor as a representative and the councillor as a member of a party and party group, and the electorate themselves, can be explored. Moreover, local politics conducted by and through campaigning groups of one sort or another add a richness to the political arena, contribute diversity of practice, form and process to local politics and provide a dynamic and flexible outlet for local opinion that political parties cannot emulate. Parties, however, create uniformity of process, shape and style, which is driven by rules and procedures and by notions of party conformity and cohesion.

How do councillors, as elected representatives, power holders and gatekeepers, perceive and respond to the challenges to representative democracy emanating from local events and from ever-more assertive communities? How do they respond to the demands for involvement rather than representation, and balance this against the demands of their parties for loyalty and public unity? In order to address these questions it is necessary to consider the claims made on councillor loyalty generated by the political party and the party group, set as they are within local representative democracy. It is also necessary to locate the place of party within local democracy, politics and government. To do this requires an understanding of the relationship between political parties and territorial politics, set firmly within the context of a long-term process which has seen the 'nationalisation' of local politics.

The nationalisation of local politics

It is a commonplace fallacy to identify the reorganisation of local government introduced by the 1972 Local Government Act as the point at which party politics and local government became merged almost as one.[58] Whilst it would be true to say that the reorganisation saw an intensification of party political conflict and dynamics in council chambers, national parties have had a persistent presence in the structure and processes of local representation since before the 1835 Municipal Corporations Act. Fraser has described what passed for local councils prior to the 1835 Act as being controlled by self-perpetuating Tory-Anglican *elites*.[59] The first municipal elections of December 1835 were party political battles between the holders of, and contenders for municipal power with the Tory-Anglican *elites* often being replaced by Liberal non-conformist ones.

Indeed, Fraser indicates that the campaigns for incorporation under the Act also divided along party lines. Moreover, throughout the Victorian period, political party played a vital role in the election campaigns for control of local councils and in the ongoing conduct of council affairs.[60]

The involvement of political parties in local government, whilst long a source of argument, has been a recurring theme in the conduct of local politics. What was clearly seen as the intrusion of party politics into local government elections, was deprecated as long ago as 1880 by *The Times,* which, in its edition of 3 November of that year, saw councillors not as politicians but as little more than 'docile tools of party politics'. Yet, Jones notes that support existed for party politics amongst the local press of Wolverhampton in 1885, where it was held that parties as 'political organisations' contesting local elections could overcome the 'deplorable apathy' amongst the electorate as they had done 'in Parliamentary elections'.[61]

Despite the longstanding relationship between municipal power and political party involvement, and the mixed reviews that relationship has received, until very recently insufficient recognition had been given to the importance of the local manifestation of party and particularly to the organisation, activities and influence of the political party group of councillors. Political parties are often still viewed as primarily national organisations with a concern for national politics and the capture of a majority within the Westminster Parliament, and, following this logic, now also within the Scottish Parliament and Welsh Assembly.

Equally, when viewing the conduct of local election campaigns, it is all too clear that national political considerations have been allowed to transcend what is after all the highpoint of politics in the local setting. National political parties squeeze local events and issues out of local election campaigns. They use particular local councils as the worst examples of local government by their opponents, and the best examples by their own party administrations. Local elections are drawn into some national aggregate of party activity, which may be beneficial to future national election campaigns. Not surprisingly, the oxymoron that is the national, local election manifesto usually speaks more of what central government has planned for local government or what councils controlled by one party or another could be excepted to do across local government.[62] In addition, local election results are held up to portend the possible outcome of the next Parliamentary contest. This is not a new phenomenon: as early as the 1870s Sir John Gorst, principal agent of the Conservative party, used local election results 'as Parliamentary indicators'.[63]

Yet political parties and their conduct of local politics and council affairs have a fundamental impact and significance at the local territorial level, distinct from any national concerns.[64] Parkinson correctly recognised that local political parties should be regarded far less as 'creatures of the national party machine' and that local parties have a distinctive local purpose and interest. Moreover, purely local factors had an important effect on motivating party members and stimulating them into activity.[65] The impact of political parties at the local level, strikes far deeper than is widely recognised, it is at the heart of territorial politics, and is central to the conduct of politics of the local council. Political parties have a profound influence on the dynamics of local democracy, on the interactions between key political players within the locality, on the intensity of the political processes and on the way and degree to which citizens are able to become involved and have an influence on local affairs. The extent of party influence within local democracy and involvement in councils has of course progressed differently over time and place. But one thing is clear: party has taken a consistent interest in local affairs and made sure and steady progress in ensuring that local government is seen as the realm of the party.

Accounting for the rise of party

To those with anything other than the most romantic of images of a golden age of political party-free local government, one thing is by now crystal clear: party and council have had a long and enduring marriage. Gyford summarises the long-term process of what is known as the *party politicisation* of local government, identifying five distinct stages.[66] These he termed *diversity* (1835–65), *crystallisation* (1865–1905), *realignment* (1905–45), *nationalisation* (1945–74) and *reappraisal* (1974– onward). Gyford's initial stage of *diversity* was characterised as one of confusion, with local politics adopting a 'kaleidoscopic form', and being conducted by a variety of political actors and a 'bevy of personal cliques and factions'. The key factor during this period was the lack of any uniform pattern of party activity and organisation across the country. Different political bodies offered different solutions to the issues facing different towns across the country, which does not imply the total absence of party organisation and activity in local government, merely that this had not settled into a clear two-party structure. Party existed in the local setting and party label, amongst others, was used to secure the election of candidates to an array of representative bodies.

The period of *crystallisation*, identified by Gyford, saw the gradual 'solidification' of local politics into a two-party system. Whilst the use of the independent label continued in this period, the developing Conservative–Liberal competition energised the gradual absorption by the party system of independent councillors, pressurising them to adopt a party label, or membership. There was a greater tendency in this period for candidates to adopt party labels to contest elections, making it easier for councillors to act *en bloc* in conducting council business.[67] Many candidates however, for a variety of reasons, sought to disguise their national party allegiances under a range of alternatives, such as moderate, progressive or radical. Indeed, during this period the contest for the government of London saw a vicarious two-party struggle between the Conservative and Liberal parties in the guise of Moderates and Progressives. The contest here was as much about national political concerns as it was about local government.[68] During this period it was most likely to be the Labour candidate that sought office by standing on an overtly party political label, whereas 'persons of Conservative or Liberal sympathies would use labels of the citizen or progressive type' when contesting local elections.[69]

The period of *realignment* saw the gradual replacement of the Liberal Party by the Labour Party as the principal opposition to the Conservatives, in both the local and national arena. During the 1920s, for example, Labour steadily increased its representation on the London County Council, finally taking control in 1934. The rise of the Labour Party in local government, its use of standing orders and group discipline as a device to ensure councillors acted *en bloc* as coherent units, had an important impact on the conduct of council affairs and the interplay of party relationships on councils across the country. Issues of council patronage, the mayoralty, committee chairs, aldermanic seats, would often be settled during this period, by reference to party rather than to any other criteria. Whilst it is clear that the Labour Party does not bear historical responsibility for the party politicisation of local government, Conservatives and Liberals take the blame equally for that phenomenon, Labour does have responsibility for the rigidity by which the group system began to operate. As Bulpitt notes, with Labour absent from the council chamber, Conservatives and Liberals were not likely to 'adopt the same degree of organisation and discipline, or take patronage so seriously'.[70]

The distinctive element of the period of *nationalisation* was not a domination of a subordinate level of political activity by national parties, but a reciprocal acknowledgement by key political actors of the benefits of assimilating local with national party concerns. The spur to this process was the consensual atmosphere of the post-war period, the stability of economic and social development and the 'shared assumptions and values of local and national politicians', rather than the centralising tendency of national parties. The period of 'nationalisation' saw the re-emergence of the nineteenth-century trend of local voting patterns reflecting national concerns, and national party standing and local elections became overshadowed by the national contest and votes were cast according to a national preference.[71]

The period of *reappraisal* involves a 'further escalation in the spread of party politics', brought on largely by local government reorganisation. The period has also seen an intensification of party political interaction between groups of councillors and a final recognition that party is the defining element in the allocation of patronage and control as a result of the local election. Councils are clearly seen as being 'controlled' by one party or another, or by some form of coalition arrangement where no one party has an overall majority. There has also been a further drawing together of the local and national fortunes of the parties; yet, as turn-out in local elections declines, more and more local factors come into play.

This is not to say that since the 1970s political parties have had it all their own way when it comes to the realm of local politics. A number of local organisations, single issue groups, protest groups and residents associations continue to score successes by gaining seats at local elections. The most successful of which has so far been the capture of Wyre Forest Council by Health Concern, the organisation which had a spectacular success in the 2001 general election, taking the Kidderminster seat from a junior minister. In the 2003 local elections Health Concern lost its overall majority on the council, whilst remaining the largest single group. The political fortunes of this organisation display the difficulty a locally originated and based non-party political body has in maintaining political control and prominence when faced with a sustained counter-attack by established national political parties within the locality.

Overall, the stages of political development identified by Gyford, from *diversity* to *reappraisal*, represent a process of developing influence for political groupings or parties in local government. It also confirms that, since 1835, political organisations of one sort or another, whatever label adopted, have contested elections and controlled local councils. At one time or another Tory, Whig, Conservative, Liberal, Improvers, Economiser, Chartist, Citizen, Progressive, Moderate, London Municipal Society and a plethora of other labels have been adopted for the convenience of fighting elections, and, more often than not, disguising the candidates national political allegiance. Throughout these stages, whilst candidate adoption of an overt party political label was not universal, the conditions were always present for the organisation and activities of coherent, or identifiable 'groupings' of councillors conducting council affairs. Moreover, these *blocs* of councillors would have clear support from political parties and organisations outside the council chamber. The factors necessary for the party group to develop, and then to exert an influence over local representative democracy, and to influence and discipline its members, have been a long-established feature of local government.

Types of local party systems

In his seminal text on local party politics Bulpitt sets out a clear and concise analysis of the nature and functioning of political parties within local government.[72] Whereas Gyford's stages dealt with broad national trends, Bulpitt makes it clear that, at the local level, party groups themselves changed in character, corresponding to a maturation process classified as either negative or positive.[73] The main distinction between these types of party systems is the degree to which councillors act in coherent political groupings to accept responsibility for control of council policy and the settling of patronage issues (see Figure 2.1).

Moreover, these categorisations indicate that the council party group is a distinct and separate element of the political party, which developed in local government at a different pace to the wider political party. In addition, the group has its own dynamics and its own political and personal tensions and factions to deal with. As a consequence party

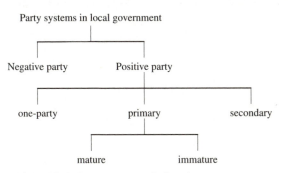

Figure 2.1 Party systems in local government
Source: J. G. Bulpitt, *Party Politics in English Local Government*, p. 130.

groups, across time and place, had differing forces influencing how they interacted with other parties and the degree of intensity with which they controlled the council. Indeed, for some majority groups the notion of control was more apparent than real. Jones argues that the Labour majority group in Wolverhampton, rather than controlling the political environment, lived merely from 'agenda to agenda'.[74]

Jones has identified four 'broad types' of local political systems. These he described as, *non-party, partially party, emergent party* and *wholly party* systems'.[75] He highlighted the importance of the political party to the process of bonding councillors together and for focusing their loyalty in a specific direction – that of the group itself. Any political grouping however, whether a formal political party or some other more informal *bloc*, can generate similar cohesive properties and act as a focus for the councillor's loyalty. Thus, the systems Jones outlined would equally exist alongside those identified by Bulpitt, within Gyford's stages of politicisation.

The contributions made by Gyford, Bulpitt and Jones to our understanding of the impact of the political party within local government throw light on the development of the party group as generating a loyalty-demanding pull on the councillor's representative activities. Indeed, Jones noted, the party group filled the vacuum left by the absence of a political executive in British local government and came to be seen as 'the place where council decisions were taken'. With political executives now a reality in local government, the party group fills the vacuum between that executive and the rest of the majority party and remains the place where council decisions are made. When it comes to acting as a representative, the councillor is confronted by at least three separate and distinct demands on his or her focus and loyalty: the party group, the wider party and the citizens of the electoral area. How councillors manage these tensions and the relationship with their party strike at the heart of notions of political representation.

The national party as the basis for local representation

In 1986 the Widdicombe Committee referred to the 'near universality of the phenomenon of politicisation' in local government, with party labels predominating in 'about 80 per cent of all councils'.[76] Whilst only 30 per cent of the Widdicombe survey's respondents could name their councillor, 54 per cent could identify their party and 61 per cent the party in control of the council (56 per cent for the upper tier council).[77] It is clear that political party has a public resonance which links local representatives to national political entities. It is not surprising that many councillors accept Newton's contention that local elections are won or lost almost irrespective of what they may or may not do. Moreover, that neither they, nor their local party, are held to account on local election day, particularly if whilst voting scant attention is given by the voter to what councillors 'have or have not been doing'.[78] Despite this widely held view, many councillors clearly believe that the electorate observe their every political, personal, social and financial move and that any action they take that displeases the electorate will see them, and possibly their party, ejected from office. Things have moved on since Newton's research.[79]

The debate concerning the impact of local and national factors and political parties on local elections remains to be settled. There is, however, widespread conviction that local government elections are a judgement on central rather than local government and local elections are fought between national parties around national concerns. Miller, however, draws the distinction between nationwide trends and local trends and variations, noting that national trends only 'explain a *proportion* of the variation in actual results'.[80] Local election results do reflect the voters reactions to a range of local concerns: taxation levels, the policies of the ruling group, variations in political style and presentation, local media coverage and candidates' personal qualities. Local impact is here understood in terms of interauthority-wide variations and political factors. What is excluded from Miller's conclusion is the impact of issues located within a single ward or a small number of wards, which in turn may affect only a small number of voters and may not be reflected in local electoral behaviour at all. But, that is not to say that these issues have not had an impact on voting patterns or influenced the result in any way. The blurring of electoral accountability however, inherent in the difficulty of disaggregating the component elements of voting, helps to maintain the view that national concerns dominate local elections.

The importance of national factors in local elections is open to exaggeration. Green identifies three specific components of voting in local elections: the national, the local authority wide and a 'truly local factor, one unique to a particular ward'.[81] The fact that local electoral swings may comprise an important local or ward-based element emphasises the representative links between the councillor and his or her electoral area. That relationship, however, is not a direct one, as the party group and political party place themselves between the councillor and the electorate – even when very local issues are concerned. Jones and Stewart have simply described the notion of local government elections as solely determined by the popularity of national government as a 'fallacy'.[82] Whatever the motivations behind the casting of a vote and whether or not the elector's political preferences transcend local concerns we are left with the question: exactly who or what does the councillor represent? Is it the political party, the council party group, the council of which he or she is a member or the ward or division from which the councillor was elected?

Confusion on the question of whom or what the councillor represents amounts to 'representative failure', and a weakening of the link between councillors and their wards or divisions. The truth is, however, that as councillors are expected to represent the interests of at least three distinct concerns they must balance these interests, arbitrate between them and act accordingly. There is an intellectual journey that party people travel which reasons thus:

> I want to secure the best quality of life for local citizens, to do that my party must win power because that will lead to policies that will result in the best quality of life for local citizens. To win power, my colleagues and I must act in such a way to best further the interests of the party, because the interests of the party are at one with the common good for local citizens. By serving my party loyally and by furthering its interests I serve the best interests of the community.

Thus, what is good for the party is good for the people and the people are best served by the councillor's own party securing electoral victory and acting as a coherent unit to pursue the policies to which the electorate have given their support. Such an approach to representation, based on party notions of an electorally sanctioned manifesto or platform, simply serves to ensure the answer to the question what does the councillor represent is: the party.

Focusing on party as the prism through which the representative views local representation makes it all the more difficult for councillors to be 'community leaders who emerge from the wards they represent'. More likely councillors generally will be those 'interested in public affairs who seek an opportunity to represent their fellow citizens wherever it may conveniently be found'.[83] Hampton's observation – based on research in Sheffield – implies that a councillor needs to have no relationship, other than a questionable loyalty, with the ward or division he or she represents, which is simply seen as an electoral convenience. As it is political label rather than the candidate's local profile that is instrumental in securing electoral success, it follows that loyalty is to the party and, more importantly, to the party group. At least in urban areas, it is only after election that the councillor may develop a local profile and area loyalty. Such loyalty may, however, be severely tested if a divergence of opinion occurs between the group and party and the local electorate over any local event, or over the general conduct of council affairs.

The rise of party in local government has seen the demise of what Lee called the *social leader*, that is the individual who secures local public office because of the position or notoriety they hold, party allegiance often being of little importance to the electoral success of the *social leader*. In such circumstances the impact of party is reduced in the face of local presence and networks of influence and contact. Whilst some areas of rural England and Wales may see the persistence of *social leaders*, their gradual displacement by what Lee termed the *public person* emphasises the importance of a councillor's relationship with party and not community.[84] The *public person* secures election on the bases of party allegiance and becomes known after, not before, the holding of office. Indeed, it is office that makes the individual a *public person*. The difference is that on ceasing to be a councillor the *social leader* will still be able to wield political influence in a broad sense, whilst the former *public person's* sphere of influence is reduced to the political party. The reality is of course that former councillors wishing to retain influence are quite capable of doing so through their party. Thus the former *public person* may not be entirely removed from political influence with the loss of a council seat. Indeed, the political party may enable the *public person* to be more influential in local politics than the social leader when both cease to hold office as the former councillor is still able to use his or her political networks to influence existing councillors.

The notion of a *social leader*, whilst developed by Lee to explore the political workings of Cheshire County Council from 1888, still has resonance today – particularly when tied to the concept of an assertive community. Those seeking election under the label of a residents association or some other non-party political local group, may not be social leaders in the same way as Cheshire's county set. They do, however, represent a potential pool of candidates that may secure election based on what they do and who they are rather than on their political party allegiances. Party does face a challenge at the local level, which could have an impact on its continued dominance of local politics, democracy and government. It is the new breed of *social leader* that ensures the expression of local diversity and variation of political practice, form and dynamics, rather than the established local political party machines.

Both *social leader* and *public person* are different constructs to the *party person*, the latter will use the party of which they are a member as the means of experiencing and interpreting the political and social worlds with which they interact. For the party person the party is not just a vehicle to secure election (although it has that potential role), it is the only vehicle through which politics can effectively and legitimately be conducted. Moreover, it is also the place where politics and representation are conducted and the only body which can genuinely claim to be 'representative'; the party is local democracy in action. The organisation and activity of political parties and the approach to politics taken by party people inextricably intertwine local democracy, representation, government and politics. Party has made local democracy, representation, government and politics its own realm, partly as a result of the strength of councillors' and party members' partisan attachment and partly as a result of the electorate's acquiescence to the dominance of political parties in territorial politics. Such acquiescence is witnessed, amongst other things, by the degree to which local electoral choice manifests itself through a party preference. As a consequence, the party and the party group are able to interpose themselves between the councillor and the community in the representative continuum. That imposition reflects a particular interpretation of politics, democracy and representation held by the party person, but recent trends have cast doubt on how adequately such interpretations currently match the needs of local democracy and local communities.

The public support for party politics

Despite the importance of the relationship between councillors, their political party and their electorate to the workings of representative democracy, there has been relatively little research on what electors think about local democracy. Major national surveys were carried out only in 1965, 1985, 1990 and 1994.[85] The findings of these surveys throw some light on the issues central to understanding the dynamics of party politics at the local level and how parties interact with those they claim to represent. The surveys illuminate public attitudes towards party politics, expectations of the councillor as a representative and trust in councillors to act up to those expectations.

In comparing electors' 'images' of what they thought their local councillors were like with what they would like them to be, the Maud Committee[86] reported that 74 per cent believed their councillor to be 'someone belonging to a political party' whilst only 40 per cent stated that their 'ideal' councillor would hold party membership. Twenty years

Table 2.1 Trends in attitudes towards party politics in local government

Which do you personally think is the better system?	*1985(%)*	*1994(%)*
The party system	34	34
The non-party system	52	33
Don't know/can't choose	14	33

Source: K. Young and N. Rao, 'Faith in Local Democracy', in J. Curtice, R. Jowell, L. Brook and A. Park (eds), *British Social Attitudes: The Twelfth Report*, Aldershot: Dartmouth, 1995, p. 104.

later the research for the Widdicombe Committee[87] reported that a little under two-thirds of respondents thought 'party politics in local government to have increased over the past decade'. In 1965, some 77 per cent of respondents agreed that voting in council elections decided how things were run locally: in 1985 this figure had declined to 60 per cent.[88] By 1990 a slight increase had occurred to 68 per cent.[89] But, 1994 saw a decline to 54 per cent.[90]

Worryingly for all of those keen to preserve the integrity and place of local government within the political system, research for Widdicombe identified a greater cynicism in attitudes towards the workings of the local electoral system than that found by the Maud Committee almost 20 years earlier.[91] To further test the electorate's feelings concerning the political party system in local government, Young and Rao asked respondents in 1994 the same question as the Widdicombe survey:

> In most areas all councillors come from one of the political parties and councils are organised on party lines. There are some areas where most councillors are independent and the council is not organised on party lines. Which do you personally think is the better system . . . the party system or the non-party system?[92]

The findings of theses two surveys in regard to that question are set out in Table 2.1.

Young and Rao noted that the 'growing politicisation' of local government brought a 'growing public acceptance of the role of party politics in local government', and that there was a striking stability in support for the party system.[93] That the party system has a resonance for the electorate is reflected in the high proportion of respondents who would vote for a party irrespective of the candidate's quality. Table 2.2 displays the responses Young and Rao received when they asked electors how they vote at local elections.

The work of Young and Rao indicates that, whilst the party system

Table 2.2 How people vote in local elections

	%
I vote for a party, regardless of candidate	52
I vote for a party, if I approve of the candidate	28
I vote for candidate, regardless of party	6
I do not generally vote at all	14

Source: K. Young and N. Rao, 'Faith in Local Democracy', as above p. 105.

Table 2.3 Most important for councillors to take into account

	%
His or her own views	1
The interests of the ward he or she represents	40
The interests of all people in the Council's area	52
His or her party's views	2

Source: K. Young and N. Rao, 'Faith in Local Democracy', in J. Curtice, R. Jowell, L. Brook and A. Park (eds), British Social Attitudes: The Twelfth Report, Aldershot: Dartmouth, 1995, p. 109.

in local government receives the support of only a third of the electorate, party affiliation is still a key criterion for electors in considering voting intention. Party is used to 'locate' a vote in accordance with political preferences, but at the same time, many using that criterion would prefer a non-party local electoral system.

Do electors, behaving in such a fashion, expect their councillors to act as party loyalists or do they perceive the councillor as having a more direct relationship with his or her electoral area? Electors' expectations of their councillors are inescapably conditioned by the prominence in local government elections and local politics of national party politics. Equally important are electors' attitudes towards the balance needed between a councillor's own personal views, those of his or her party and those of the people he or she represents. The results of what respondents thought the 'most important' influence on councillors should be (or indeed, what was their focus of representation), by Young and Rao's own admission, are 'startling' (see Table 2.3).

Whilst selecting a candidate by party, the electorate expect the focus of representation not to be that party, but the electorate themselves. The expectation that councillors should focus almost as much on their own specific electoral area as on the needs of the authority as a whole acts as a counterweight to the policy-broadening influence of the party group. Young and Rao conclude that in a system dominated by the party group: 'there is an overwhelming expectation that councillors should place local interests – either at ward level or across the local area – first. And there is also a clear indication that the public thinks there are limits to the role of party politics.'[94]

Although the public uses party as a defining point for the way in which they vote locally, after that vote the public then want councillors to be loyal to their electorate in preference to their party. Nevertheless, do they consider that councillors can be 'trusted' to place the views and wishes of the people they represent above the decisions of their party? Young and Rao inquired of respondents: 'How much do you trust local councillors of any party to place the needs of their area above the interests of their own party . . . just about all the time, most of the time, only some of the time or almost never?'[95] Less than one in three of the respondents to that question thought councillors could be trusted to place the interests of the electorate over the interests of the party, either 'all' or 'most of the time'. Fourteen per cent thought they could never be trusted to do so. The majority of respondents possessed a wary cynicism about their councillors, who could be trusted 'only some of the time'. Thus the electorate expected that for the councillor: 'their overriding concern should be the representation of local interests. That they are not widely trusted to do so betrays a degree of cynicism; that electors should then vote the party ticket regardless of the qualities of their candidates appears perverse.'[96]

Such 'cynicism' in the expectations electors have of their councillors is often reciprocated in councillors' expectations of the electorate when it comes to public involvement in political processes.[97] Such a situation would undoubtedly loosen the bonds of the representative relationship, maybe undermining it fatally. Moreover, with party placing itself between councillors and their constituents with both sceptical as to each other's motivations, the bonds of representative democracy become looser still, enabling councillors to place even more emphasis on party as the focus of their attention.

Rao (1997) presents pressing evidence of elector's concern that councillors should indeed represent their local area above the demands of party.[98] The electorate's trust in councillors to do so, however, is limited.

Clearly as Rao indicates, there are few electors that find it acceptable for the councillor to serve the party when it leads him or her to act against the local interest. Furthermore, Rao also shows that there is a

Table 2.4 Trust in councillors to put the interests of the area above party

Party identification	Almost always/ most of time (%)	Some of the time (%)	Almost never (%)
Conservative	36	49	13
Labour	29	53	14
Liberal Democrat	37	54	9
Other/None/DK	21	47	21
All respondents	31	51	15

Source: N. Rao, 'Representation in Local Politics: A Reconsideration and Some New Evidence', *Political Studies*, 46 (1), 1998, p. 33.

powerful demand on the councillor to set aside party considerations when faced with an important local issue. Yet, for the party candidate, elected with the support of a local party machine and bound to the party by numerous political, social and personal ties, the idea that he or she 'sets party aside', if only occasionally, runs counter to deep-seated notions about how representation should be conducted. Further, with the party person taking a fundamentally different view of notions of democracy, representation and politics to the interpretations held by those not involved in party politics – setting party aside – is an almost pathological act.

It is clear that the party person, whether an elected office-holder or not, has a closer and deeper relationship with his or her party than with the more amorphous concept of community or electorate. Moreover, the party person, committed as he or she is to a particular interpretation of the role of party within politics and holding definite political views, will find the boundaries of party difficult and indeed unnecessary to cross. As the link between the party and councillor is stronger than that between the councillor and the electorate, the councillor will act as a *trustee* when it comes to developing a representative relationship with citizens, but will act as a delegate when it comes to his or her relationship with the party or the party group.

The traditional tripartite relationship between the party, the councillor and the electorate should then be seen in Figure 2.2 as a four-dimensional relationship which includes the party group as a distinct and separate element of the local representative processes. In many cases the positions held by the party group and wider party will be in harmony. When the electorate are drawn into the equation, around

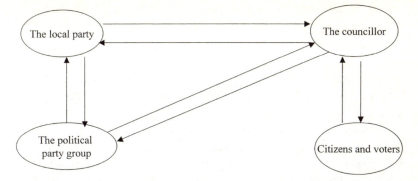

Figure 2.2 Political parties in the locality: a four-dimensional model

some important local issue, the group and party may forge a stronger relationship to defend a position against any external threat posed by the electorate. That party people will often see the actions of citizens and communities as a direct political threat to the role of party locally, means that the party becomes a valuable devise to shield the political *elite* from the electorate. As a consequence of the party playing such a role we need to rethink what we currently understand about the nature of local representation and the role of party within it.

Sir Ivor Jennings notes that J. S. Mill completed *Considerations on Representative Government* without mentioning parties, while 'a realistic survey of the British Constitution to-day must begin and end with parties and discuss them at length in the middle'.[99] The same can most certainly be said of local government today, and, whilst the importance of party is well recognised at the local level, much of our understanding of local politics focuses on the interaction between the councillor and party in the policy-making process.[100] Yet, to fully understand the role and impact of party locally we need to consider not only party and policy-making but also the role of party within local representation and how, if at all, political parties connect with those they claim to represent. Moreover, we must consider how party people view the place of the political party locally.

Broadly speaking the party person's notions of representation are caught up with ideas of good government, the wider public interest and pursuing general public well being and interest. In the narrow sense, representation is often seen in a pastoral fashion, dealing with constituent's problems with the council or some other organisation. Indeed, to many councillors such pastoral care is of vital, if not the utmost importance in what they do and of what it means to be a local a representative. Indeed, pastoral work can be seen as the 'routine way of organising local representation'.[101] Others, however, give such pastoral work little importance against policy-making, governing and party concerns.[102] Indeed, notions of representation more generally can become unattractive to some, as representation implies articulating and responding to the views of others outside the party.

Neither the broad or narrow approach to representation, taken by those active in party politics, can fully account for the relationship between the councillor, the electorate and the political party, when set against important local issues and claims by the community for involvement in political decision-making. What representation is clearly not about for the party member is the councillor, as locally elected representative, being mandated to place the views of the electorate above the views of the party. On the contrary, it is, more often than not, that councillors feel mandated by the party and more specifically the party group to pursue some course of action. If local communities go along with that course of action, then so much the better, If they do not, then the job of governing takes precedence over the task of representing. It does so because the party provides a reference point for policy and decisions that has a degree of support from the electorate and a stock of political resources to employ in the political process. Party also exerts a tremendous 'pull' on the councillor's representative 'focus', through the organisation, discipline and loyalty expected by the party and party group. The party becomes the prism through which local politics and political activity is viewed, both in a party and non-party context. Although politics exists and is conducted in a non-party form and context, and by non-party political organisations and groups of one sort or another, the party person does not distinguish between these facets of politics– all politics is party political, or can be made so by the party person. Put simply, politics can not exist outside, or without the political party.

The Blair government's modernising agenda poses political parties and party people with a challenge, and the way they respond to that challenge will decide the fate of that agenda and the notions of a more politically engaged citizenry. Modernisation is predicated on certain basic assumptions about local political decision-making and indeed about the conduct of politics. The modernising agenda's holds *a priori* a relationship between council and citizens based on openness, transparency, responsiveness and accountability, as the signs of a healthy and vibrant local democracy. Yet, these concepts are not necessarily held as positive

by all involved in party politics. Indeed, the organisation, activities, structures, process and loyalty demands made by parties and party groups are
the very antithesis of the notions underpinning much of the modernising agenda. But, if openness, transparency, responsiveness and accountability are to be achieved locally and citizens and communities to be
more engaged and influential in political decision-making, parties need
to radically rethink their role in such a way as to match these criteria.

Yet, parties are able to insulate themselves from the outside world
and to conduct politics and the politics of the council almost irrespective of external factors. The key feature which enables party to do this
and to continue to act as a coherent, stable, unified and disciplined
organisation in its conduct of politics, democracy and representation is
the loyalty granted to it by its members and its elected representatives.
What Ostrogorski termed 'regularity' or party conformity, and in
today's local politics would be party discipline, strikes at the heart of
notions of democracy and representation.[103]

Political parties do provide order and stability to the local political
system and to the complexity of political issues within various localities.
The parties also add consistency and stability to council chambers. Yet,
there is a need in the conduct of local politics today to find a bridge
between the rigidity and discipline of party politics (which serves to
exclude the citizen and to govern despite articulated local opinion) and
the more flexible, intermittent and chaotic local politics that can result
from wide-scale citizen involvement.

The local political landscape of Britain, whilst linked to the numerous layers of interconnected networks that exist in today's complex
system of governance, has its own distinctive features and existence as a
separate entity. In addition, the predisposition for the party person to
place party at the forefront of his or her loyalty, seeing the interest of
the party and the decisions it takes as axiomatic with the wider public
interest, interferes with the politically representative relationship
between the councillor and the community or communities. There is a
tension within local democracy. It is the tension between the needs of
political parties for the loyalty, discipline and unity of their membership
and the needs of non-party politics to be able to display themselves adequately and legitimately. Those involved in party politics often see those
undertaking political activity outside the party as self-indulgent and representative of small, sectional interests, unlike the party which governs
for the good of the whole. But the question we must address about
parties themselves is: are they the only vehicle for legitimate political
activity within a representative system, or are they just organisations that

themselves seek to pursue small sectional interests – those of the party itself.

Notes

1 B. Manin, *The Principles of Representative Government*, Cambridge: Cambridge University Press, 1997, p. 232.
2 Ibid., p. 194.
3 A. H. Birch, *Representation*, Basingstoke: Macmillan, 1971, p. 97.
4 D. Held, 'Competitive Elitism and Technocratic Vision', in *Models of Democracy*, Oxford: Polity Press, 1987, pp. 143–185.
5 J. A. Schumpeter, *Capitalism, Socialism and Democracy*, London: George Allen & Unwin, 1974, p. 269.
6 G. Sartori, *Democratic Theory*, Detroit: Wayne State University Press, 1962, pp. 75–78; see also, chapter 6, 'Democracy, Leadership and Elites', pp. 96–134.
7 Held, D., *Models of Democracy*, p. 66.
8 See, in M. Beloff (ed.), *The Federalist or the New Constitution*, Oxford: Basil Blackwell, 1948, pp. xvi–xvii.
9 J. Madison, 'The Federalist No. XIV', in Beloff, *The Federalist*, p. 62.
10 B. Crick, *In Defence of Politics*, Harmondsworth: Penguin Books, 1982, p. 58.
11 Ibid., p. 68.
12 A. Tocqueville, *Democracy in America* (J. P. Mayer, ed.) London: Fontana, 1994, pp. 260, 638–639.
13 For a comprehensive discussion of the property qualification for the franchise and council candidacy, see, B. Keith-Lucas, *The English Local Government Franchise*, Oxford: Basil Blackwell, 1952.
14 E. P. Hennock, *Fit and Proper Persons: Ideal and Reality in Nineteenth Century Urban Government*, London: Edward Arnold, 1973, p. 10.
15 K. Young, 'Bright Hopes and Dark Fears: The Origins and Expectations of the County Councils', in K. Young (ed.), *New Directions For County Government*, London: Association of County Councils, 1989, p. 6.
16 J. Gyford, 'Diversity, Sectionalism and Local Democracy' D. Widdicombe, Committee of Inquiry into the Conduct of Local Authority Business (Widdicombe Committee), *Research Vol. IV, Aspects of Local Democracy*, HMSO, 1986, p. 128.
17 Ibid.
18 J. Davis, 'The Progressive Council, 1889–1907', in A. Saint (ed.), *Politics and the People of London: The London County Council 1889–1965*, London: Hambledon Press, 1989, pp. 27–48, particularly p. 28, Young, 'Bright Hopes and Dark Fears', p. 17.
19 Davis, 'The Progressive Council, 1889–1907', particularly pp. 32–35; J. Gillespie, 'Municipalism, Monopoly and Management: The Demise of Socialism in one County, 1918–1933', in A. Saint (ed.), *Politics and the People of London: The London County Council*, London: Hambledon Press, 1989, pp. 103–125.

20 N. Soldon, '*Laissez-faire* as Dogma: The Liberty and Property Defence League 1882–1914', in K. Brown (ed.), *Essays in Anti-Labour History: Responses to the Rise of Labour in Britain*, Basingstoke: Macmillan, 1974, pp. 208–233.

21 J. S. Mill, 'Considerations on Representative Government', in McCallum (ed.), Oxford: Basil Blackwell, 1948.

22 Edmund Burke's address to the electors of Bristol, 1774, quoted in A. H. Birch, *The Concepts and Theories of Modern Democracy*, London: Routledge, 19⁻3, p. 75.

23 H. Eulau, and F. Whalke, *The Politics of Representation*, California: Sage, 1978, pp. 43–48, p. 47.

24 See, H. Eulau, J. Whalke, W. Buchanan and L. Ferguson, 'The Role of the Representative: Some Empirical Observations on the Theory of Edmund Burke', *American Political Science Review*, 53 (3), September 1959, pp. 742–756.

25 N. Rao, *The Making and Unmaking of Local Self-Government*, Aldershot: Dartmouth, 1994, pp. 34–35.

26 R. Michels, *Political Parties*, Glencoe, IL: The Free Press, 1949.

27 W. H. Morris-Jones, 'In Defence of Apathy: Some Doubts on the Duty to Vote', *Political Studies*, 2 (1), 1954, pp. 25–37.

28 P. Green, 'A Review Essay of Robert Dahl, Democracy and its Critics', *Social Theory and Practice*, 16 (2), 1990, pp. 217–243, p. 238.

29 A. Phillips, *Local Democracy: The Terms of the Debate*, Commission for Local Democracy, Research Report No 2, London: Municipal Journal Books, 1994, pp. 10–11.

30 C. Rallings, M. Temple, and M. Thrasher, *Community Identity and Participation in Local Democracy*, Commission for Local Democracy, Research Report No 1, London: Municipal Journal Books, 1994; C. Rallings and M. Thrasher, *Local Elections in Britain*, London: Routledge, 1997.

31 N. Rao, 'Representation in Local Politics: A Reconsideration and Some New Evidence', *Political Studies*, 46 (1), 1998, pp. 19–35.

32 J. Stanyer, 'Social and Rational Models of Man: Alternative Approaches to the Study of Local Elections', *Advancement of Science*, 26, 1970, pp. 399–407.

33 W. P. Grant, 'Non-partisanship in British Local Politics', *Policy and Politics*, 1 (3), 1973, pp. 241–254, p. 245.

34 Rao, N., *Reviving Local Democracy: New Labour, New Politics?*, Bristol: Policy Press, 2000.

35 J. Maud, Committee on the Management of Local Government (Maud Committee), *Research Vol. III, The Local Government Elector, An Enquiry Carried out for the Committee by the Government Social Survey*, by M. Horton, London: HMSO, 1967. Widdicombe Committee, *Research Vol. III, The Local Government Elector*, London: HMSO, 1986; K. Young and N. Rao, 'Faith in Local Democracy', J. Curtice, R. Jowell, L. Brook and A. Park (eds), *British Social Attitudes: The Twelfth Report*, Aldershot: Dartmouth, 1995, pp. 91–117.

36 Phillips, *Local Democracy*.

37 C. Copus, 'The Attitudes of Councillors since Widdicombe: A Focus on Democratic Engagement', *Public Policy and Administration*, 14 (4), 1999, pp. 87–100.

38 R. Leach and J. Percy-Smith, *Local Governance in Britain*, London: Palgrave, 2001, pp. 9–12.

39 K. Young, 'Political Attitudes', in R. Jowell and C. Airey (eds), *British Social Attitudes: The 1984 Report*, Aldershot: Gower, 1984, pp. 11–45; K. Young, 'Local Government and the Environment', in R. Jowell and S. Witherspoon (eds), *British Social Attitudes: The 1985 Report*, Aldershot: Gower, pp. 149–175; A. Bloch and P. John, *Attitudes to Local Government: A Survey of Electors*, York: Joseph Rowntree Foundation, 1991, pp. 36–38.

40 G. A. Almond, and S. Verba, *The Civic Culture: Political Attitudes and Democracy in Five Nations*, Princeton, NJ: Princeton University Press, 1963, p. 185; A. Marsh, *Protest and Political Consciousness*, London: Sage, 1977, particularly pp. 66–69; K. Young, 'From Character to Culture: Authority, Deference and the Political Imagination Since 1945', in S. James (ed.), *Political Change in Britain Since 1945*, Basingstoke: Macmillan, 1997.

41 Almond and Verba, *The Civic Culture*, p. 455.

42 Marsh, *Protest and Political Consciousness*.

43 A. Heath and R. Topf, 'Political Culture', in R. Jowell, S. Witherspoon and L. Brook (eds), *British Social Attitudes: The 1987 Report*, Aldershot: Gower, 1987, pp. 51–69, pp. 58–59.

44 D. Kavanagh, 'Political Culture in Great Britain: The Decline of the Civic Culture', in G. A. Almond and S. Verba (eds), *The Civic Culture Revisited*, London: Sage, 1989, pp. 124–176, particularly p. 152.

45 Young and Rao, 'Faith in Local Democracy'.

46 Young, 'From Character to Culture'.

47 Gyford, 'Diversity, Sectionalism and Local Democracy'.

48 Copus, 'The Attitudes of Councillors since Widdicombe', C. Copus, 'Re-Engaging Citizens and Councils: The Importance of the Councillor to Enhanced Citizen Involvement', *Local Government Studies*, 29 (2), Summer 2003, pp. 32–51.

49 G. Parry, G. Moyser and N. Day, *Political Participation and Democracy in Britain*, Cambridge: Cambridge University Press, 1992, p. 358.

50 R. Batley, 'An Explanation of Non-Participation in Planning', *Policy and Politics*, 1 (2), 1972, pp. 95–114, particularly pp. 104–105.

51 Young and Rao, 'Faith in Local Democracy'.

52 J. Lambert, C. Paris and B. Blackaby, *Housing Policy and the State: Allocation, Access and Control*, Basingstoke: Macmillan, 1978, p. 141.

53 C. Copus, 'The Councillor: Representing a Locality and the Party Group,' *Local Governance*, 24 (3), Autumn 1998, pp. 215–224; Copus, 'The Attitudes of Councillors since Widdicombe'; C. Copus, 'The Councillor and Party Group Loyalty', *Policy and Politics*, 27 (3), July 1999, pp. 309–324.

54 Copus, 'The Attitudes of Councillors since Widdicombe', B. Colenutt, 'Community Action over Local Planning Issues', in G. Craig, M. Mayo

and N. Sharman (eds), *Jobs and Community Action*, London: Routledge & Kegan Paul, 1979, pp. 243–252, particularly p. 246. F. Bealey, J. Blondel and W. P. McCann, *Constituency Politics: A Study of Newcastle-under-Lyme*, London, Faber & Faber, 1965, pp. 320–323.

55 N. Boaden, M. Goldsmith, W. Hampton and P. Stringer, *Public Participation in Local Services*, Harlow: Longman, 1982, p. 15 and preface.

56 A. Cochrane, 'Community Politics and Democracy', in D. Held and C. Pollit (eds), *New Forms of Democracy*, London: Sage, 1986, pp. 51–77, p. 72.

57 W. Hampton, 'The Local Citizen', *Democracy and Community: A Study of Politics in Sheffield*, London: Oxford University Press, 1970, pp. 122–152, pp. 149–152.

58 'To Whom Much is Given: New Ways of Working for Councillors following Political Restructuring', Management Papers Audit Commission, London, 2001.

59 D. Fraser, *Power and Authority in the Victorian City*, Oxford: Basil Blackwell, 1979.

60 E. P. Hennock, *Fit and Proper Persons: Ideal and Reality in Nineteenth-Century Urban Government*, London: Edward Arnold, 1973; K. Young, *Local Politics and the Rise of Party: The London Municipal Society and the Conservative Intervention in Local Elections, 1894–1963*, Leicester: Leicester University Press, 1975; D. Owen, *The Government of Victorian London, 1855–1889: The Metropolitan Board of Works, the Vestries and the City Corporation*, Cambridge, MA: Harvard University Press, 1982; A. Saint (ed.), *Politics and the People of London: The London County Council 1889–1965*, London: Hambledon Press, 1989.

61 G. W. Jones, *Borough Politics: A Study of Wolverhampton Borough Council 1888–1964*, Basingstoke: Macmillan, pp. 149–159.

62 D. Wilson and C. Game, *Local Government in the United Kingdom*, Basingstoke: Macmillan, 2002, pp. 291–295.

63 Young, *Local Politics and the Rise of Party*, p. 32.

64 J. Gyford and M. James, *National Parties and Local Politics*, London: George Allen & Unwin, 1983; C. Game and S. Leach, *The Role of Political Parties in Local Democracy*, Commission for Local Democracy, Research Paper No. II London: Muncipal Journal Books, 1995.

65 M. Parkinson, 'Central–Local Relations in British Parties: A Local View', *Political Studies*, 19 (4), 1971, pp. 440–446, p. 444.

66 J. Gyford, 'The Politicisation of Local Government', in M. Loughlin, M. Gelfand and K. Young (eds), *Half a Century of Municipal Decline*, London: George Allen & Unwin, 1985, pp. 75–97.

67 Hennock, *Fit and Proper Persons*.

68 K. Young and P. Garside, *Metropolitan London: Politics and Urban Change 1837–1981*, London: Edward Arnold, 1982, pp. 58–59 and K. Young, 'The Politics of London Government 1880–1899', *Public Administration*, 51 (1), Spring 1973, pp. 91–108, particularly p. 97.

69 W. P. Grant, 'Local Parties in British Local Politics: A Framework for Empirical Analysis', *Political Studies*, 19 (2), 1971, pp. 201–212, p. 203.

70   J. G. Bulpitt, *Party Politcs in English Local Government*, London: Longmans, 1967, p. 129.

71   J. Gyford, *Local Politics in Britain*, London: Croom Helm, 1976, pp. 125–132.

72   Bulpitt, *Party Politics in English Local Government*.

73   Ibid., pp. 123–130.

74   G. W. Jones, *Borough Politics: A Study of WolverhamptonBorough Council 1888–1964*, Basingstoke: Macmillan, pp. 175–176.

75   G. W. Jones, 'Varieties of Local Politics', *Local Government Studies*, 1 (2), 1975, pp. 17–32, particularly pp. 19–21.

76   Widdicombe Committee, *Research Vol. I, The Political Organisation of Local Authorities*, London: HMSO, 1986, pp. 25, 197.

77   Widdicombe Committee, *Research Vol. III*, p. 31.

78   K. Newton, *Second City Politics: Democratic Processes and Decision-Making in Birmingham*, Oxford: Clarendon Press, 1976, pp. 7, 17, and 223.

79   Copus, 'Re-engaging Citizens and Councils'.

80   Widdicombe Committee, *Research Vol. III*, pp. 105–172.

81   G. Green, 'National, City and Ward Components of Local Voting', *Policy and Politics*, 1 (1), September 1972, pp. 45–54, p. 45.

82   G. W. Jones and J. Stewart, *The Case for Local Government*, London: George Allen & Unwin, 1983, pp. 16–18.

83   W. Hampton, *Democracy and Community*, pp. 203–204.

84   J. M. Lee, *Social Leaders and Public Persons: A Study of County Government in Cheshire Since 1888*, Oxford: Clarendon Press, 1963.

85   Maud Committee, *Research Vol. III*; Widdicombe Committee, *Research Vol. III*; Bloch and John, *Attitudes to Local Government*; Young and Rao, 'Faith in Local Democracy'.

86   Maud Committee, *Research Vol. III*, table 27, p. 91.

87   Widdicombe Committee, *Research Vol. III*, p. 81.

88   Ibid, table 6.13, p. 94.

89   Bloch and John, *Attitudes to Local Government*, table 25, p. 34.

90   Young and Rao, 'Faith in Local Democracy', p. 101.

91   Maud Committee, Research Vol. III, p. 100.

92   Young and Rao, 'Faith in Local Democracy', p. 103.

93   Ibid., p. 104.

94   Ibid., p. 109.

95   Ibid.

96   Ibid., pp. 114–115.

97   Copus, 'The Attitudes of Councillors since Widdicombe'; Copus 'Re-engaging Citizens and Councils'.

98   N. Rao, 'Representation in Local Politics'.

99   W. I. Jennings, *The British Constitution*, Cambridge: Cambridge University Press, 1947, p. 31.

100   J. Dearlove, *The Politics of Policy in Local Government: The Making and Maintenance of Public Policy in the Royal Borough of Kensington and Chelsea*, London: Cambridge University Press, 1973, D. Green, *Power and Party in an English City: An Account of Single Party Rule*, London: George Allen & Unwin, 1981.

101 Lambert, Paris and Blackaby, *Housing Policy and the State*, p. 141.
102 A. Rees and T. Smith, *Town Councillors: A Study of Barking*, London: The
     Acton Society Trust, 1964, pp. 46–49, particularly p. 47; H. Heclo, 'The
     Councillor's Job', *Public Administration*, 47 (2), 1969, pp. 185–202,
     particularly pp. 190–193.
103 M. Ostrogorski, *Democracy and the Organisation of Political Parties*, Vols
     I and II, New York: Macmillan, 1902.

3

Local parties and local politics: a democractic necessity or a sectional interest?

Partisan differences to one side, political parties, and the people that conduct their activities, share broadly similar experiences and assumptions about the nature of local politics and the role of the party within it. Yet, there are also some very real and powerful distinctions between the three main political parties in the way they view and experience local politics, and the politics of the local council. Politics is about power; local politics is about local power too and political parties are the vehicles, through which power is fought for, captured, held and used and through which influence is brought to bear. Local parties mainly play a very narrowly defined game when it comes to local politics, with the possible exception of the Liberal Democrats, who often use a more expansive definition of the role of a political party in the local area. Political parties acting in the local realm focus on the council. Control of the 'council' becomes the main target and parties inside and outside the chamber will take on the role of either the 'government' or 'opposition', locally and act accordingly. Subsequently, it could be concluded that only power matters and the holding of power is what makes a party dominant in the local realm, but this would be an erroneous conclusion based on a very narrow interpretation of the contribution local parties have to the politics of the locality.

It is usual when discussing political parties to describe the structure and organisation of at least the Conservative and Labour parties and the Liberal Democrats. Thus, attention will be given in this chapter to a brief description of the way political parties structure and organise themselves locally. The main concern is not, however, structure for its own sake, but to explore what clues structure gives to how parties see their role within the locality. But, as parties link their own 'territorial organisation to the structure of local government', this in itself is a clear indication of where they place their political attention.[1] It is vital, however, to move beyond the purely structural and council focus if we are to understand parties within local politics and to explore exactly what local politics comprises for parties, the party person and for the electorate and community around which they operate.

When Sharpe and Newton asked the question 'do parties matter?', their analysis concerned the impact of local authorities' political characteristics on service expenditure patterns. Political parties and party systems were 'revealed as being critical determinants of local expenditure'.[2] Yet, political parties have a far greater influence within the locality, stretching beyond expenditure decisions into responsibility for local public policy, the outcomes of that policy and the degree of citizen engagement in the local political process. Thus, political parties are critical determinants of the vibrancy and health of local democracy. Political parties also have a vital role to play in 'sustaining continuity and stimulating change' within the locality.[3] They do this through political discourse and by becoming the *theatres* within which the most important political discourse on local issues takes place. The quality of private and public discourse undertaken by parties is what sustains or corrodes local democracy. The skill with which parties address public issues and stimulate debate, or the way in which they manipulate and close down debate, have a fundamental impact on the nature and conduct of local politics in any one area. It is the way in which parties, inside and outside the council chamber, construct local political deliberation and control its tone and audibility that answers the question 'do parties matter?'.

The first section of the chapter will explore how political parties view their role in the local context and how they act out that role. It will examine the way parties interact internally and the form that interaction takes. Attention will be paid here to the way parties outside the council interact with their party 'group' on the council and the dynamics of that relationship. The second section explores notions of party loyalty, discipline and cohesion as they relate to the political party within the realm of local politics, but outside the council. The focus here is to consider the impact on local politics and democracy of the way political parties approach these concerns and, as a consequence, conduct their affairs. The third section will explore the relationship political parties forge with the world outside the party but within the locality, it will consider how parties view their external environment and the relationship they construct with it.

A lead role or a bit part player: an elite corp or a spent force?

The various public and private settings, within which local politics is conducted, provide political actors with the space in which to undertake political discourse, indulge debate and undertake political activity. These *theatres of representation* are either accessible to the citizen or closed from access to all but the political *elite* (see chapter 7). The political party is an important *theatre of representation* within which the political elite conducts its business away from public gaze. Yet, it has been argued that within the local setting political parties 'represent one of the last lines of defence of pluralist democracy', resisting centralising tendencies and totalitarianism.[4] Much of what political parties do locally, however, can not be described in such dramatic and romantic terms, nor do the local branches of national parties necessarily see their role in this light – particularly if the party is in power nationally. The local and the national can be, and often are, confused when it comes to parties playing their role. Parties can conduct much local political activity with one eye on the national impact, this means parties can contribute to the diminution of local politics and aid centralisation, as much as act as a bulwark against it. What seems to be a distinctly local matter can be drawn into some national perspective and be seen to affect national party fortunes. Many party people will subordinate local to national politics. As one Conservative Party member from an urban area said: Everything we do as a party locally reflects on our ability to govern nationally and to regain power. How we behave and perform in the constituency and on the council matters to our chances of winning this seat back and it matters for us when it comes to securing a majority in Parliament.'

It is the national perspective, which sets parties aside from any local communities of place, or interest focused on some specific local concern, or the local dimension of some national public policy. Whilst the local political arena may look like some vast pluralist haven of competing and conflicting groups, where citizens and communities seek to wield influence to one degree or another, the reality is different.[5] Political parties represent a clear and organised local political *elite*; the party has in its possession a special and very clear link with its councillors and a relationship and dynamic that transcend any other body concerned with influencing council affairs. When faced with a vast and confusing array of organisations competing for the councillor's attention, wielding different resources and arguing for different priorities, it is the party and its fluctuating fortunes as assessed by the party person that provides a constant and enduring point of reference. Moreover, party rules provide for structural linkages and communication processes between the party and its councillors. It is also the local party that controls the councillor's tenure of office. Thus, the party holds a position of some considerable authority and power when compared with those whose relationship with powerholders is less direct.

The development of effective patterns of party political behaviour within the realm of local politics depend on a number of factors. Internally, parties need certain resources to be able to function: regular and reliable sources of finance, office accommodation and or equipment, research facilities and good administrative skills, all have a profound impact on the ability of parties locally to play a key role. In addition, a healthy membership base is essential to party activity, and the balance in numerical terms between active and inactive members is vital for party activity. A party locally requires a sufficient number of active members, willing to run a party and campaign on its behalf, when compared with the number of inactive members, who simply join but play no role in party affairs.

Party activity is as much influenced by factors outside party organisation and control as it is by the resources and membership concerns. Patterns of party behaviour vary across the country, depending on a number of factors: the type of council which is the focus of attention; urban and rural settings; the holding of power locally on a particular council and the potential for that power to be lost or won; and the holding of any other elected offices locally, such as the Parliamentary seat. Socio-economic factors have an influence on levels of party activity locally, changing patterns of development, population mobility or immobility, declining or increasing populations, the nature of the industrial and commercial base, levels of affluence and depravation, all have an impact on the role the party is able to play locally. One other unquantifiable and unexplainable factor also has a fundamental impact on party activity – the existence locally of that small band of people who are sufficiently interested in politics to join a party and become active within it.

Once resources required for effective party political activity are in place, the party itself provides shape and direction for the employment of those resources and provides structure and form to political interaction and a focus for local political activity. Parties are, above all else, organisations of bias and opinion that reflect both local and national concerns and interests simultaneously. The key aim of the party locally is to secure positions of power or a voice in any arena that presents itself. To do this the party must ensure its resources are marshalled and employed in a coherent fashion, both internally and externally. The internal and external dimensions of party activity are shared between the three main parties, but with a difference of emphasis. The first concern of the party is to maintain certain basic levels of organisational presence and structure locally; or, at least signal to the outside world that the party is internally in good shape. The maintenance of this image of the party as a well-resourced, structured and internally coherent institution is vital to the esteem of the party locally. Much party activity is ritualistic and symbolic rather than effective, but such rituals and symbols help generate the appearance of a robust and active party. Thus, running the party can become an end in itself.

Running the party

The organisation that is the party must be kept in a robust, healthy shape that enables it to carry out certain basic party functions. These functions are as much ritual and symbolic activity as they are of any meaningful impact – they demonstrate to the membership and the outside world that the party is present and vibrant. Equally, they help bind party people together and serve the purpose of convincing them that the party is in good shape. As such party rituals and symbolism may disguise and conceal the reality of the party as much as they present it to the outside world, particularly to party political opponents – but either way, that is just the point. As a Labour activist in the north of England said: 'We have real financial trouble at the moment and might lose our headquarters, what ever happens, we can't let the Tories find out, they'd make us a laughing stock.' Local Conservative representation on the council at the time, stood at five councillors from a total of 60.

To keep the internal structure in order, local party units must meet frequently and conduct debate, consider procedural motions, produce agenda and minutes of proceeding, deal with correspondence and listen to reports from other party units or elected representatives. The party units will select officers, normally a chair, vice-chair, secretary, and treasurer to be responsible for particular business activities. Each post can be as powerful or influential as the holder requires it to be; in party politics a position is power – or at least the potential for power and influence. As a Labour party member said in interview: 'I've held every ward and GC [General Committee] post going except CLP [Constituency Labour party] treasurer, that's a real poison chalice that one; you have to have some post if you want to do things in the party and get known outside your branch.'

The role of party maintenance and the conduct of basic procedures do more than keep the party ticking over. Such activities provide a regular focus of activities for members, a calendar of party events, authoritative bodies through which to operate and a real presence for the party at ward, constituency and council levels. They provide the party with a mechanism and structure for talking to, and communicating with itself. Political parties locally manifest themselves through structure and more than anything political parties are about holding *meetings*. Meetings produce an illusion of activity and influence, alongside some potential for real activity and influence. Most importantly, regular meetings bind a group of party colleagues together and enable them to develop a sense of unity, which is a vital asset when it come to fighting elections and general campaigning – the meeting is the basic building block of party political activity and purpose. Yet, the numbers taking part in those meetings may be quite small. More often than not it is the same people involved in an array of different meetings and events of different units and sub-units within the party structure, as well as the more informal meetings and events, where most political activity is conducted.

As a Liberal Democrat councillor confessed: 'We don't have that many members locally and I sometimes think most of us are councillors, so a group meeting is like a party meeting and we seem to be meeting together an awful lot. Wherever I go in the Liberal Democrats I meet the same people.'

A Conservative Party member stated: 'Whether it's a meeting, a social event or something else, I can more or less tell you before hand the people that will attend, unless we've got some big name speaker coming and even then, well. I see more of some people than I do my wife; she's a member, as well you know.'

A Labour Party member commented:

> It's the same people all the time that do all the work, attend all the meetings and hold all the positions; it would be nice to see a few new faces every now and then. But then you need people that know how the party works and what its suppose to do at our meetings, people need to join all the parts together – each meeting has a purpose, even if only a few people turn up.

Such regular contact between party members leads to the development of what Game and Leach have called *party networks*, which are a far greater influence on the internal affairs of the party than the formal structure.[6] Whilst the formal structure will give members the impression of a regularised route for communication and influence, it is the more informal networks within parties which wield the real power. The more active the member the more opportunities will present themselves for informal communication with other active members and the more opportunities become available to influence the party and its elected representatives.

Informal networks and contacts between party members are a powerful political tool in the hands of the skilled party person. Simply observe a group of party activists in a social setting, particularly a party social. Observe how, for example, a Member of Parliament works the party crowd at a social gathering; note who the MP talks to or ignores; how long is spent merely chatting to, or more pointedly, huddling with particular members. Watch who the MP gravitates towards or away from at any social event and you will get a pretty clear picture of who the key players are in the local party and therefore who the MP should invest time talking with. If it were possible to check the itemised phone bills of party members, you would have an even clearer view of the network of power and influence locally.

The local political party has a levelling influence on politics and political communication, whichever party is concerned. It forces holders of elected office, whether European, national or local, to recognise that they are required to justify, explain and account for actions, inaction and decisions, in some considerable detail, even if only to a very small but vocal audience that is the local party. That does not of course mean to say that party can control office holders directly, or that elected representatives do not ignore the party when its views are inconvenient. There is evidence to suggest that the political party can be ignored or by-passed when its views are inconvenient and to show that oligarchic tendencies develop within parties.[7] Yet, national and local party leaderships can not move too far from the key concerns of the membership, otherwise they risk embarrassing and potentially destabilising political discontent within their own ranks – in other words public disunity. Simply put, local parties can provide powerful politicians with a pretty uncomfortable series of exchanges, which, if nothing else, exposes politicians to a critical voice – albeit a privately heard voice.

Elections

Party has a role beyond maintaining the illusion and reality of its structure and organisation and of providing channels of political communication for the party person. It also has a role in stimulating political activity within the locality. The obvious activity for parties to engage in here, is the fighting of elections and many do this with aplomb, others, however, even struggle to provide the most basic electoral activity. Of course, more party members are willing to sacrifice time, money and energy campaigning for a Parliamentary election than a local council election. If party members take a differential interest in national and local elections, it is not surprising if the electorate do so as well.

If parties are about anything, they are about engaging in the electoral process, they represent the mobilisation of resources and energy towards the political goal of winning the seat – wherever and whatever the seat might be. It is in the fighting of elections that parties begin to speak to the world outside and to attempt to enter into a political discourse with the electorate – all be it a minimal one with a very constrained time span and objective. Today the uncontested seat is a rarity; parties will contest the vast majority of seats at local elections. Indeed, even if the party knows it has no hope of winning, then the tactic is to enter a 'paper candidate'. That is, to make a nomination with the returning officer for a candidate to stand in a particular ward or division with the simple intention of tying down the opposing party so they divert resources into their own safe seats. A simple and straightforward tactic that is always successful; no candidate worth his or her salt, no matter how safe the seat, will leave it completely undefended, even to a paper candidate.

Parties will deploy fairly standard campaigning techniques at election time: production of a local manifesto, distributing leaflets and election addresses, telephone voter identification and door-to-door canvassing, to name but a few. Canvassing of course is not about political debate however, but about identifying where the parties' supporters are to ensure they vote on election day. Canvassing has a psychology all of its own. It can become a race amongst party members to fill up canvass cards, with as many positive responses as possible, rather than identifying supporters or the supporters of other parties.

The author witnessed during one local election a particularly enthusiastic party member constantly returning from successive nights canvassing with canvass cards full of Labour supporters. On one occasion the Liberal Focus candidates had been marked down as Labour voters! On observing this individual, a friendly but rather well-built and harsh sounding Glaswegian, at work, the following exchange was wittnessed:

Canvasser in a loud voice whilst leaning in towards a voter on the doorstep: *Are you voting Labour hen?*
Voter: *Well I'm not sure I rather thought about Liberal Focus*
Canvasser, even louder: *Are you voting Labour hen?*
Voter: *Er, yes, yes, that's ok, thank you*

One more supporter for the records!

Canvassers and canvassing techniques can, however, be remarkably and surprisingly accurate. During one election in which the author was involved, the canvass returns in a single ward were correct for each candidate to within five votes. The accuracy achieved here did require four full canvasses of the entire ward, plus several call back visits to what we refer to as 'outs' and 'doubtfuls'. The party was desperate to win that particular seat and to expend the resources doing it because the only three opposition councillors on the borough held it, and they had to be stopped!

Election day itself for the party activist, and particularly the candidate, is an ecstasy of pain and pleasure, and a tumult of emotion and energy. Polling stations will have party members taking the polling numbers of voters as they enter the polling station. Not as some electors think to identify how they voted, but simply to record that they have voted. The taking of numbers enables the party to check that its 'promises' (the voters that promised to vote for the party when canvassed) have actually voted and if by the evening they still have not, then they can be 'knocked-up'. That is, a party member knocks on the voter's door and reminds them to vote – not as exciting as it initially sounds!

Throughout election day the polling numbers of those that have voted will be periodically delivered to the committee rooms so they can be marked down as having voted. The committee room is the honeypot of election day. A good committee room is a nearly empty one, which means party members are out working on the election. A very bad committee room is one that is full to bursting with party members and candidates all anxious to know what is happening, rather than being on the streets making it happen. Even worse is the candidate who will require reassuring and comforting as the long day wears on; candidates can be a nuisance on election day because they get worried, emotions run high and that is not the best time to be dealing with elector's problems or even talking to them. As one party agent said: 'If I had my way I would send all the candidates to Southend for the day and tell them to come back when the polls close. Unless, I was in Southend of course, then I'd tell them to go anywhere else.'

One thing that all party activists and candidates find difficult to understand about election day is that the electorate, by and large, do not find the election as nail-bitingly exciting as they do. It is difficult for party people to understand why what Phil Mitchell in *Eastenders* is about to do is more important than taking part in the democratic processes and doing your duty as a citizen. But that is the nub of liberal democracy – the citizen can engage and disengage as and when they want to – particularly if political parties fail to excite the citizen's interest.

A wider role

When it comes to the conduct of local political affairs, parties have a broader role than one associated with elections alone. They are the mechanism by which a political platform is developed and refined locally and presented to the electorate. Party officers, particularly the chair of a constituency or association, represent an authoritative voice on party affairs generally, and will present the party's response to local and national events when called upon by the public and the media to do so. In this regard, parties are the gatekeepers of the political landscape, providing limited access to the internal workings of the political world. They are, however, primarily defensive organisations, seeking to minimise political damage to themselves and to maximise damage to their opponents. With this approach, parties often distort much of what passes for public debate and turn issues into a question of party loyalty, rather than an exploration of alternative solutions to political and policy problems.

Political parties act as a conduit for the public to access politicians and to connect with broader political concerns. Those involved in single-issue politics, or some local campaign, can ascertain the party's position on any matter, seek support from it, or an alliance with it, and work to uncover if the party's position is different from that of the council group. Campaigners may seek support from the party that does not control the council, or may seek to influence the one that does. Political parties represent another point at which political influence may be obtained by those outside the processes of political decision-making.

It is the Liberal Democrats that as a political organisation make the greatest effort to communicate with the world outside the party. The community politics and campaigning approach undertaken by Liberal Democrats place their members in closer proximity with the community than that experienced by members of other parties. Liberal Democrat members will campaign on local issues over an extended period of time – before being elected to the council. The production of regular newsletters, setting out he activities of the local Liberal Democrat *Focus Team* helps the party connect to voters and to local concerns. Community politics is, however, not the sole preserve of the Liberal Democrats, and community politics have been emulated by both Conservative and Labour parties across the country, often, however, as a result of the emergence of a local *Focus Team* within a ward or small number of wards. The Liberal Democrats use community campaigning as an extended electioneering technique, which has had startling results in many areas. The use of community politics was adopted at the Liberal Party Assembly of 1970, which resolved: 'A primary strategic emphasis on community politics; our role as political activists is to help organise people in communities to take and use power, to use political skills to redress grievances, and to represent people at all levels in the political structure.'[8]

Whilst the *Focus* leaflets used by the Liberal Democrats have a solely local focus, concentrating on the issues in one council ward, *Focus* leaflets from across the country have a remarkably similar look, feel, style and content about them. There is a clear national direction and influence behind the tactics employed by *Focus Teams,* which often drives the other political parties into apoplexy. A Labour councillor complained: 'They simply claim credit for everything we have done or were going to do; they collect petitions demanding the council do something we've already agreed to do and then put a leaflet out claiming they were responsible for making the council act. It's just dishonest.'

A Conservative councillor echoed these views:

> They take the credit for everything we have done and just because it appears in one of their Focus leaflets, people believe them. I have one of these so-called teams in my ward and the things they say; if I lose my seat it will be because of distortion and half-truths. The Liberals hold all the executive seats on the council and the Focus leaflet still says that they have 'got onto the council' about this, or 'contacted the council' about that, or 'spoken to the council' about the other, so I got up in our last full council and asked the leader of the council [a Liberal Democrat] to remind their candidate in my ward just who it was that was running the council she keeps getting on to – perhaps she'd like to put that in her Focus leaflet.

Liberal Democrats strenuously denied accusations made by other parties about their activities, as a *Focus Team* activist responded:

> Well, they would say that wouldn't they. The fact is, until we came along nothing ever happened, people only heard from their councillors at election time, the rest of the time, they weren't bothered. We get things done and they don't like it because it shows them up and makes them work. We can win seats from Tories and Labour by local campaigning and they hate it – they think they own these seats by right.

Community politics works for political organisations, it shows a constant level of activity, a sense of purpose and determination and a dedication to a particular electoral patch. Whether the Liberal Democrats act as a stimulus to other parties adopting community politics or whether they would have adopted those tactics anyway is debatable. One thing is clear, political parties need to talk to and with those they seek to represent to a greater extent than they do and in different ways – simply canvassing for votes is no longer adequate. Communities demand a different sort of politics and representation; if they don't demand it they respond well to it when it happens.

Political parties should be placing themselves squarely into the community arena and widening the role they play in local politics generally. For every *Focus Team* that now exists, there are equally dedicated groups of party members from other parties working in a network of organisations and campaigning in new and exciting ways. Whilst initially slow to respond to community politics, Labour and Conservatives have begun to catch-up, but the approach is down to local parties and individuals and is not at the core of the organisation or its activities.[9] Communicating with the citizenry in that long period between elections, rather than the three or four week run-up to polling day, is a vital part of the role of the political party within the locality. Such an approach enriches the political processes and adds life and vibrancy to both parties and local democracy. It makes political parties more relevant to citizen's concerns rather than being seen as organisations that periodically rouse themselves from their slumber to ask for a vote. Members of any party will have heard the oft-made criticisms of political parties: 'we only ever see you at election time when you want our vote'.

But, as Stewart notes, the politics of a local authority are 'played out in a setting with its own political culture, itself a product of history and local circumstance', so too is party politics outside the council. Parties can be slow and conservative beasts, conducting their activities in ways that are familiar and conformable to the membership. Talking to themselves rather than the outside world.[10] Political parties vary across the country in the roles they play and how they play them, depending more on the traditions of party activity in the area and less on the political affiliation of the party concerned.

Political parties when conducting local politics can fall into one of five categories: *moribund, dormant, resurgent, functioning-mechanistic* and *omnipotent*. Each of these categories displays certain characteristics, which are set out below. These characteristics are of course, not static. A party within a particular locality may move between the categories and the pace and speed of its journey will vary over time, as will the period it spends in one or other of the categories. The journey will depend on a range of factors, such as: favourable or unfavourable political climate;

the size of the base of active members (which themselves may be more or less active depending on circumstances); access to resources, such as finance, equipment, technical skills, research and office facilities. In addition, the number and quality of representatives elected on that party's ticket within the council area will have a significant impact on the condition of the local party and its ability to conduct political activity.

The categories are designed only to reflect factors that affect the political party outside the council group and to record the state of that party. A distinction between the separate units of party organisation, party and council party group, is required as the two may not be in alignment with each other when it comes to organisational and operational effectiveness. Moreover, the party and the group have very specific roles to play, have their own unique dynamics and respond to different political stimulus. The categories below apply to parties irrespective of political affiliation; they are therefore generally applicable and provide a set of characteristics by which to make sense of party organisation, role and activity as they relate to local political concerns. Finally, the categories cover the entire party across a locality, rather than specific party units within a locality, thus a *moribund* party is truly moribund across all organisational aspects.

The categories of local political parties and their characteristics are as follows:

(1) *Moribund*: A moribund party is one that exists, more or less in name only. The party is inactive and lacks any infrastructure or resources that would enable it to become active in anything other than the most perfunctory fashion. Its membership base does not have an activist core that could motivate it into any continuing action or function or that could provide any voluntary contribution of finances or other resources. It can not campaign effectively at election time, although some very basic and sporadic electoral activity may take place, such as the distribution of an election address.

(2) *Dormant*: As the moribund party but with certain key distinctions evident when it comes to resources and the ability to rouse itself into action should it be required or stimulated to do so. The dormant party simply lacks the reason and motivation to activity. Partly this will be to do with the membership base and the balance between inactive and active members; partly it will be to do with either scarce, but existent resources, or an unwillingness to use an abundance of resources in case the next rainy day is a torrent. The dormant party will campaign during election time and will have a visible presence during the election,

it will not seek to influence the councillors elected under its label however, lacking the ability to conduct the continued political activity that this would require. It will be able to signal to its party group its position on any powerful and prominent issues that affect its interests.

(3) *Resurgent*: The resurgent party is one that locally is largely, but not wholly, reactive to events. It becomes active as a response to a particular local issue, the behaviour or policies of the party group, or the behaviour or policies of its party political opponents. Moreover, it will also act when it perceives itself, or its party group, to be under attack from opponents within the community that may not be organised on a party political basis – such as a pressure or community group. The resurgent party has a good membership base and sufficient members willing to carry out ongoing party administration and party maintenance and some political campaigning. The latter, however, will not be extensive and will be largely, but not exclusively, election focussed. It will always conduct a full range of electoral activity, seeing this as its prime purpose and function; considerable time and effort will go into raising finances and other resources in between elections to fight the next election. The resurgent party will not expect to control the activities of the party group but will expect it to respond when the party is dissatisfied with particular stances, decisions, policies or behaviour.

(4) *Functioning-mechanistic*: A functioning-mechanistic party is one that has the resources and motivation to be continually active and to consistently conduct a range of party political tasks. Its focus, however, is mainly on keeping the party 'ticking over' administratively rather than politically and much time and effort is put into maintaining the proper organisational functioning of the party. The functioning-mechanistic party campaigns hard during local election time, as this is seen as part of the proper activity of the party; it has sufficient resources to be able to run well-organised election campaigns. The party expects from its councillors a clear and broad allegiance to the party, the policies it fought on at the election, and expects councillors to be loyalty to decisions of the group. The party does not, however, seek to have complete control over the activities of its councillors; rather it prefers to focus on its internal activities and less on council and local affairs. The party is insular, inward looking, but well run and organised, conducting the formalities and rituals of party political activity with some influence over its councillors, but little, if any, linkage to political activity outside the party.

(5) *Omnipotent*: The omnipotent party is constantly and continually active in all facets of the political world but from a party political

perspective and for party advancement; it has plentiful existing resources, or ease of access to resources, which it is willing to use. It sees its task as maintaining a political presence, beyond the conduct of local elections, campaigning around a range of issues and events within the locality. It does this, however, to pursue the interests of the party and to reduce the space for embarrassing political opposition. It is a vocal and prominent and powerful part of the processes of political decision-making as they relate to the council and the wider locality. Wherever elected office holders conduct political discourse, or make political decisions, reference and reverence will be granted to the party and its perceived or actual views or wishes on the subject in hand. Thus, the party is always present.

The defining element of the omnipotent party is the degree to which it expects, and is able to, control the activities of its councillors and party members more generally. Party activists particularly will not be satisfied with the receipt of verbal reports from councillors about council affairs, but will seek and create avenues of influence for themselves, to ensure that councillors are receptive to the concerns of the activist core, or elements within it. Activists make much use of informal channels of communication and influence when it comes to relationships with the party group, rather than relying on formal lines of communication through party units and/or rules and regulations.

The omnipotent party is very willing and able to use the formal machinery of the party concerned to de-select sitting councillors if they are considered to have been disloyal or have given inadequate attention to the views of the party. Equally, activists wishing to stand for a winnable seat will use the candidate selection process to replace a sitting councillor, not for any infringement of written or unwritten rules but because an individual party member simply 'wants that seat'.

What these typologies of local parties indicate is just how introspective political parties are and how they concentrate effort and resources on the party itself and the council. Even the omnipotent party has little interest in the political world outside of party politics – which is why it is omnipotent not omnipresent. Political parties can play a vital role in stimulating sustained community interest and involvement in local political affairs, but they often choose not to. Rather, parties focus on the internal world of the party itself. They do this because the appropriate national political party gives them a secure and clearly identifiable shape, form and purpose around which to act. It is to that organisational shape and form we must know turn.

National form for a local purpose

Each of the national political parties seek to give form and presence to party organisations across the country by adopting their own distinctive, though broadly similar organisational structure, a structure, which has the outward appearance of a centralised organisation and set of political relationships. Game and Leach refer to the party structures as 'stratarchies',[11] that is stratified hierarchies which acknowledge that high degrees of central control are undesirable and even injurious to the party. Parties are hierarchical in structure and process, but it is a hierarchy that must respond to the realities of political dynamics and discourse.[12] Parties prefer to resolve their internal difference more by debate and compromise than by the employment of hierarchical power, although they will resort to the latter if required. The key role for the local membership is to ensure, as far as possible, that each of the party units required by the national party are formed and are operational; moreover, that they appear to the outside world to be part of a consistent and coherent national organisation. But, a closer inspection of the parties' organisation indicates more of a federal dimension to what appears to be centralised structures and relationships. National parties realise that local units are staffed by volunteers not paid employees and volunteers with a political vision – they need to be treated as such, whilst encouraged to see themselves as a vital part of a national organisation.

Wilson and Game have set out a clear distinction between the approach of the Conservative and Labour parties when it comes to organisational, structural and procedural aspects of the parties.[13] Their work provides an enlightening comparison of how the two main parties view direction from the national party; the basic units of party structure for local government purposes; the key operational unit of the local party; candidate selection; the party group on the council; relationships between the local party and council group; the development of council policy; the election manifesto; and the election of group leaders and the selection of committee chairs and executive members. The distinctions and similarities Game and Wilson provide, illuminate the practical and philosophical relationships which are at the heart of the way in which the Conservative and Labour parties approach the business of local politics within the framework of a national party (Chapter 5 of this book explores the relationship between the party group and the national party in some detail.)

What needs to be emphasised when comparing the parties structurally and organisationally is the approach each party takes nationally and

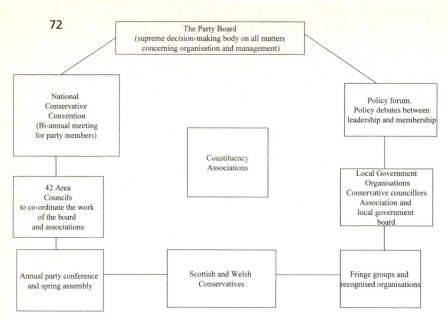

Figure 3.1 The Conservative Party organisational structure
Source: Conservative party website: www.conservatives.org.uk

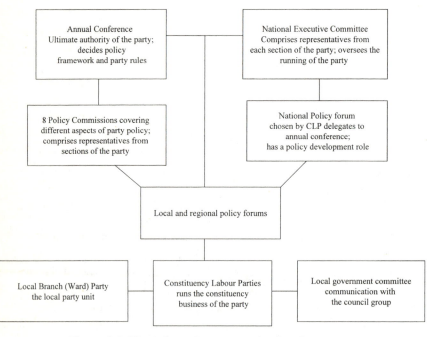

Figure 3.2 The Labour Party organisational structure
Source: Labour party website: www.labour.org.uk

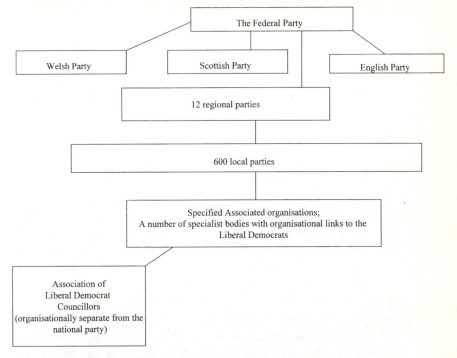

Figure 3.3 The Liberal Democrats organisational structure
Source: Liberal Democrats website: www.libdems.org.uk

locally to interpreting its structure and the degrees of formality with which structure, role and party dynamics go hand in hand. Whilst all parties will want to ensure that party units are formed and running as defined within party rules, it would be true to say that the Labour Party nationally and local Labour parties, across the country, are much more rule bound and driven, than their Conservative and Liberal Democrat counterparts.

The Labour Party's more rigid interpretation of the rules and the roles and responsibilities of party units stems partly from the history and tradition of the party and from its original conception as a vehicle for trade union politics and representation in the late nineteenth and early twentieth centuries. It also stems from a desire to protect the party and the integrity of its organisation from legal action from disgruntled party members and thus from being defined and interpreted by the courts. A rigidity of structure also comes from the fact that the Labour Party and its local organisations existed outside of Parliament and local councils before it existed inside them. The purpose of the party was to get representatives elected where there were none. As a consequence, clear structures of accountability and communication and clear organisational responsibilities were required from the outset. Structural clarity also gave the party the means to influence its elected representatives once they were in office.

The Conservative Party and Liberal Party forerunner of the Liberal Democrats did not share the same historical development as that of the Labour Party. These parties existed in Parliament before they existed in the country. It was the stimulus provided by the Reform Acts of 1834 and 1867 that energised the Conservatives and Liberals to organise in the constituencies. These organisations were originally concerned with voter registration and electoral turnout, not with controlling the activities of Parliamentarians. Although Joseph Chamberlain's Birmingham Liberal Association of the 1860s pre-dates Labours organisational structures and was a highly successful party organisation, it was by no means the norm for the Liberal Party at the time.

Whilst parties will want, as far as possible, to ensure organisational structure reflects the basic unit of local government – the ward – resources, particularly members, may be scarce. Instead of ward-based organisations, branches may be formed which encompass the membership of two or more wards and which meet together to conduct business – except the selection of candidates. Indeed, the Liberal Democrats, recognising that the party's membership base is smaller and often more geographically dispersed than that of the Conservative and Labour parties, refer to 'local parties', which may cover one or more Parliamentary constituencies. In addition, the Liberal Democrat constitution refers to the formation of branches covering defined areas of local parties, which then may comprise one or more ward.[14]

It is the local party unit – the ward or branch – that has responsibility for selecting council candidates, although each party handles this process in slightly different ways. The Local Government Committee (or Borough Party) of the local Labour Party draws up a *panel* of potential council candidates from which the ward parties can select. Recent attempts by the party nationally, code-named variously: *Projects 2000, 2001*, have aimed to tighten up the selection process and to improve the calibre of candidates available to branches from which to select. Those wishing to be accepted on to the panel must not only have party and trade union experience but also prove their worth through a series of events and tests designed to assess capability and aptitude for council work.

Once the Local Government Committee has a produced a panel of potential candidates, wards then hold a series of meetings at which they shortlist a number of candidates to interview, then at another meeting called specifically for the purpose, they interview and select. So, although the ward is supreme in the process, it can only select from the names appearing on the panel.[15] It is at this point that the robust nature of the panel formation process is at a premium. It is not unknown for ward parties to be controlled by political dynasties, or have a very small membership, that always ensures the same candidate is selected time after time. Such rotten-wards with moribund parties have proved a problem for Labour in the past, a problem which the *Projects 2000, 2001*, etc, have been designed to address. It is the nature and process of candidate selection that bind the councillor to the ward party and lead to the ward party expecting not only regular reports on the councillor's activities, but a degree of loyalty from him or her to its own decisions and policies. As one recently re-selected Labour councillor put it:

> Whenever I go to ward meeting, I am always reminded by someone that they raised the money, walked the streets, canvassed, and leafleted in all weathers, and it was they that won the seat for me. As a result they should be able to tell me what to do in the council chamber, as though I didn't do all those things myself. But, yes, the ward expects me to voice its opinions and concerns and that's only right. I've not yet had a real problem with the ward demanding I do something the group wouldn't like – it can happen but its not likely, not here any way.

Labour's council candidate selection process is far more rigorous than that used to select a parliamentary candidate. The sitting MP can be 'affirmed' by the various branches within a constituency, thus avoiding the need for a full selection process, where different candidates present themselves for consideration – the MP can therefore be re-selected without facing competition. The Labour councillor seeking re-selection must go through the full selection procedure from acceptance on to the panel of candidates to selection interview by a branch alongside at least two other interviewees. A Labour councillor facing the re-selection process for council candidates complained at the disparity in procedures thus:

> The party should not treat its councillors differently from MPs; if the branch wants to re-select a councillor without a full selection process then they should be able to do just that. If its good enough for MPs then its good enough for councillors; there is no reason why we should be treated differently, but the party always looks after its MPs.

The Conservative Party and Liberal Democrats have a variation on the Labour theme when it comes to selecting candidates for the council. Conservative Central Office publishes model rules for Conservative and

Unionist Associations which sets out a selection procedure. Sitting councillors are treated differently to new council aspirants; the sitting councillor is required to make a written application to the Executive Council for re-adoption and the decision 'should be taken in reasonable time having regard to mutual convenience'.[16] Those wishing to stand under the Conservative banner but are not already councillors, need their local branch or committee to recommend them to the Executive Council for approval; once approved a general meeting of the branch is required for the candidate to be selected and then adopted.

Conservative Party rules are produced as a guideline, so Conservative parties need not abide by them, most however do. Yet, the Conservatives, unlike Labour, are by inclination and circumstances prepared to operate around these rules. It is not unknown for Conservative Associations to advertise in local newspapers for those wishing to secure a Conservative council nomination to apply to the local party. Moreover, they are less inclined to seek a candidate that has served a Party apprenticeship; no longstanding party experience or activity are necessarily required. In this way Conservative parties locally, make available to themselves a wider pool of potential candidates. But, the longstanding party activist, with his or her own network of local supporters, is just as well placed as any Labour Party member to secure a council nomination, to the exclusion of this wider pool of potential.

The Liberal Democrat's council candidate selection process is closer to that of the Conservatives than the Labour Party. Despite what rules and procedures may say, it is also driven by the often smaller party membership available to Liberal Democrats compared with their political opponents. In many areas, the Liberal Democrats have constructed a large, well-established political machine with a considerable number of potential candidates available for selection. In other areas, however, scarce resources drive the selection of candidates, more so than party rules. The Liberal Democrats select candidates from an approved list maintained by the local Executive Committee. But, Liberal Democrats have also been known to recruit candidates on the doorstep. As a Liberal Democrat councillor recalled: 'I was canvassed by all three parties, only the Liberal Democrats came back a few times and eventually asked if I wanted to stand, so I agreed and won.'

Conservative and Liberal Democrat willingness, when seeking local candidates, to go beyond the rules, and even the party membership, finds no reflection in local Labour parties. The Labour Party with the smallest of memberships will rigidly apply the rules, albeit rather mechanistically, and certainly not look beyond the party for a candidate, although they may seek to recruit someone as a member a few months before the selection process starts.

It is on the issue of a sitting councillor's status with the party group that another interesting distinction exists between the Labour Party and its Conservative and Liberal Democrat counterparts, when it comes to candidate selection. A Labour councillor who has had the whip withdrawn by the party group for an *indefinite period* is unable to have his or her name placed on the panel and therefore cannot be selected by a branch. A time-limited withdrawal of the whip does, however, enable the councillor to be re-selected. There is no constitutional bar for Conservatives or Liberal Democrats to re-select a councillor as a candidate even if the party group whip has been withdrawn.

Thus, all three main political parties, through the production of constitutions, rules and procedures for party units, seek to give a cohesive and unified shape and form to party organisation across the country. Nationally, it is important for local party organisations to follow set procedures and process so that the party looks and operates in a broadly similar fashion wherever it is located. Moreover, these constitutions and rules act as a safeguard for the party from legal challenges by disgruntled party members. Structure, form and organisational shape provide a *theatre* within which party politics can be conducted. Parties may seek regularity of process and arrangements through these formal organisational settings, but the dynamics of party life reflect the personalities, ambitions and intentions of the membership and what individuals seek from party activity. It is the party's local membership that breathe life into dry organisational structures, rules and procedures.

A family at war? Cohesion and unity

Whilst political parties, locally and nationally, attempt to present to the outside world a unified and cohesive organisation with a single direction and purpose to which all members subscribe, the reality is far more interesting. Fundamental to being a committed party person, however, is the belief that the party must stand publicly united at all costs and that dissent and disagreement must be kept as far from the public gaze as possible. It is, of course, not always possible to keep deep division from the public, as the Labour Party learnt to its cost during the 1980s and early 1990s with the internal warfare over policy, leadership and the activities of the Militant Tendency.[17] The Conservative Party is currently experiencing a parallel process to that of Labour in the 1980s and 1990s, with public dissent over the party leadership, the division between Europhobes and Europhiles and battles between left and right over the general direction of the party.

An obsession with public party unity and the deep-seated belief that the party must avoid public dissent amongst its membership serves to rob the public political space of much debate and deliberation that would lead to an enriched and better-informed public.[18] Moreover, the public is able to tell the difference between good-natured, healthy, informed debate and disagreement over an issue and a party internally at war with itself over matters that strike at its very soul. It is a distinction, however, that party people are loath to make, at least in public and thus will seek to remove dissent and disagreement from the public arena and replace them with the image of a cohesive, united and disciplined force. Yet, parties fail miserably at this pretence both nationally and locally. Indeed, party politics is anything but united around a single purpose and, as a consequence, party politics is far more absorbing and entertaining than it may appear at a first and cursory glance.

The internal dynamics of local political parties are set by the leading players within them, more than they are set by purely party political concerns and policy issues.[19] Those leading players need not, of course, be leaders in the formal sense of council leadership or high profile and prominent councillors or party officers. They will be those party people who invest considerable personal resources into party activity and, as a consequence, are able to set the terms of any debate, the culture within which personal and political relationships take place and the intensity of party activity.

As one Labour Party activist commented in an interview:

> I've lived in a number of constituencies and branch parties over the years. The one I'm in at the moment takes the biscuit. I've never come across such a bunch of mean-spirited, self-centred, power-obsessed people in my life. The politics here are nasty, personal and poisonous and people treat the party like their own plaything for personal disputes. There are about a dozen to 15 people across the whole of the party in this area that are responsible for that. No one in their right mind would come to more than one meeting around here.

Not all parties are riven with such animosity and personal rivalry, of course; a Labour activist from another area enthused thus:

> The party is my life. Its my political and social life, I've made friends in the party here that I'm going to keep for life; we go away on holiday together and socialise outside the party. Politics here is fun, that might sound unusual but the people make the party and we've got a great bunch of comrades here (oops did I say comrades, sorry).

These two different views found their echo in both the Conservative Party and the Liberal Democrats, a Conservative Party member commented in an interview:

> I enjoy my work for the local Conservative Party; we have an extremely good social side, the people that hold us together are those looking after the social aspects you know. We still go through the rough and tumble of the political world, which can get very heated, shall we say, especially around Europe, but we can all enjoy a drink in the bar afterwards.

A Liberal Democrat expressed another view:

> Generally people get on well, some of us socialise outside the Liberal Democrats, some don't. We have two members, however, married, whenever they turn up to anything, you know there will be trouble. They just make the atmosphere nasty and uncomfortable and they do it deliberately. I can't work out if it's a game they play for the fun of it, or their way of manipulating things for their own benefit. You know, they've knocked on my door a few times and I've pretended to be out!

In one constituency in which the author was active, one particular member springs to mind for being quite and frighteningly mad. She would disrupt branch meetings with inane and pointless questions, completely away from the subject in hand. She would verbally abuse others at meetings at her fancy and thought nothing of following one down the street remonstrating on some absurd point. All of us pretended to be out if she called. I hope she found some appropriate care because we offered her none, we simply didn't know how to handle her, even with a room full of teachers, social-workers and other care professionals and caring types.

Aside from dealing with the odd eccentric, local party politics is about power and it is as much about power within the party as obtaining power for the party. Parties offer positions of power and influence within the party itself, which for some are sufficient; holding one party office or another within a number of party units becomes a purpose in itself. Whilst many positions and offices within a party are administrative, often routine, hard-work and sometimes tedious and thankless, they provide the committed and the ambitious with a platform from which to develop his or her network of influence and contacts. Moreover, such positions provide the influential party person with a source of patronage to dispense amongst supporters or to deny to opponents. Whilst one party branch may be unable to find enough volunteers to fill its officerships, in another there will be a hard-fought, well-organised campaign conducted by different sides for the most menial of party offices. In political party internal disputes winning is everything, whatever post it is that is won.

Whilst Game and Leach use the notion of informal *party networks* standing alongside the formal party structure, and *inner networks* of multiple office holders with overlapping membership of party units, acting as a foundation for consensus and conflict resolution, there are also forces at play which have far from positive consequences for internal party politics.[20] What exists within political parties are multi-layered networks, often working against each other, seeking to exploit internal differences and dissent, rather than produce consensus. There may indeed be a dominant network, but many subservient networks will exist below it, seeking to replace it when conditions allow.[21] Thus, local parties are prone to a range of divisive factors that have the potential to result in the creation of formal or informal factions or divisions amongst the membership. There is a tension within parties between the need to present a united front to the public and political opponents and the realities of internal party politics, which can be far more divisive and chaotic. Indeed, personal rivalries and political clashes serve to undermine the smooth working of the party machine and work to ensure that any ruling party *elite* does not become too confident in its position.

Whilst political parties do rest on *networks* of influence and communication, they are also the setting within which a number of what may be termed *kindreds* exist and operate. These *kindreds* consist of groups of closely associated party people drawn together by some shared political agenda or beliefs. But, they also form around other uniting factors such as geographical location, native or migrant status in a locality; social affinities such as age, occupation, class, bonds of friendship, personality clashes and character traits; as well as simple likes and dislikes of party colleagues. *Kindreds* may also form around political ambitions as individuals seek allies to further their aims to hold a certain party office or be selected for a council seat, or seek advancement on the council. *Kindreds* are the product of sources of discord and internal strife and are as powerful, if not more so, than any more positively operating *network* that may exist.

Kindreds differ from formal political factions that may be well organised and constituted and exist at a national as well as local level, in that they are the product of local circumstances and serve to disrupt the otherwise smooth working of local political parties. Equally, they can distort the processes of debate and decision-making within parties into one of seeking advantage for personality orientated, rival groupings. Moreover, the way in which *kindreds* conduct their activities, planned as well as casual, conflict with notions that parties are united around a set of core beliefs and objectives, and display the reality that party people

Table 3.1 The local political party: sources of discord and discontent

Type	Source
National organisation or grouping	Support for a cause or concern or for a political objective pursued by a nationally organised body or faction. Such groups may exist only inside or outside the party.
Ideological	A firmly held set of political beliefs that transcend party affiliation and are a yard stick by which political allies and associates are selected – a case of seeking the true believer.
Formal local organisation	Support for, or membership of, an organisation existing in the locality only and that sprang from local concerns (not the branch of a national body), such as local pressure or cause groups and community organisations. They may exist across the local authority area or be concerned with only a part of it.
Socio-economic-geographic: the politics of the personal	Age, occupation, location, length of residency, type of household tenure, class background, social interests or concerns, gender, ethnicity, sexuality, culture, religious, conscience issues
Personality politics	Personality clashes and rivalries, personal dislikes and disagreements, conflict based on the differing personality traits of the individuals concerned. Simply put, some people just don't like each other!
Ambitional	Political promotion and advancement at the cost of others; seeking to hold some office within the party or some public office obtainable only by coming into conflict with the existing holder or other contenders. Such conflict then spreads into other facets of the party's local activity.

often act so as to pursue political advantage for those with whom there is a *kindred* connection. The idea of *kindreds* as a series of feuding groups operating on the basis of political and personal vendetta, provides a different context to understanding the dynamics and interactions that occur within local political parties. Thus, the picture of local political parties that emerges is one of a complex series of groupings, that orbit around each other and continually and predictably collide and clash, but with often unpredictable results. As well as the specifically localised concept that is the *kindred,* parties divide and sub-divide for a number of reasons, which are summarised in Table 3.1.

What is clear from Table 3.1 is that the party person may conduct politics from the perspective, or membership, of a number of these categorisations of discord. As a consequence, transcendency is the defining characteristic of any source of discord within a political party; a source of discord must act as a motivating factor to action for the party person that transcends any other. That is it supersedes all other beliefs and loyalties, affiliations, affinities and connections; it is the political primal force for the person concerned.

All internally opposed party groupings, whatever their source and categorisation, operate in broadly similar fashions and have a broadly similar impact within each of the main political parties. Some may, however, operate on the basis of a formal organisation, with elected or appointed officers, and a clear plan of action; such organisations may of course not be open about their existence and activities. Other sources of discord operate in a purely informal way and coalesce around the needs, motivations and ambitions of a group of individuals in relation to their party political activity. The impact that such discordant groupings and activities have, however, is normally negative as they are based on conflict, competition and rivalry, and sometime on the artificial stimulation of internal party conflict where none had previously existed.

When the external political climate is quite, or when the party nationally and locally is securely ensconced in office or opposition, with little threat on the horizon that the situation will change, internal rivalry keeps party politics interesting and entertaining for the membership. Yet, it is problematic if these rivalries become an end in themselves and ultimately more important to the participants than some broader, but local party perspective. In many cases, the resultant impact on the local party of many internal rivalries, generated and maintained by *kindreds,* is to debilitate and demoralise the entire membership, to starve the party of committed volunteers and resources, thus preventing it from exploring and pursuing its role in the wider local polity. Such results are not necessarily related to power; parties in a minority position locally are just as likely to be riven by conflict as the party holding sway and power.

In an interview a Conservative councillor was particularly revealing of the impact of the internal disputes within the local party:

> We have ten councillors on the Borough council and as a result of personality disputes within the local association and the group we are now effectively two parties and actually two Conservative groups, official and unofficial, but both with five councillors. It was all caused by one of our members, also a councillor, pursuing her own personal agenda and shooting from the hip on every single issue. It was very tiring and time consum-

ing, but many of us were not prepared to put up with the way she was running the party and the group. Ironically for her, we are the official group. But the party has suffered locally and our ability to fight Labour and the Liberal Democrats has been drained, we can not provide a credible alternative to either; local people do not know that, but we do. What with the national situation, it's very difficult for any of us to work for the party and to ask the public to support us, so hard.

Not only has the councillor here provided a revealing and very open insight into the nature and impact of internal disputes, he has also highlighted how party people will often conduct activity irrespective of its consequences on the party locally. Moreover, the public may be blissfully unaware of such disputes; however, the public may be made be very aware of internal strife in the local party, as one Labour Party member suggested:

> It was some time ago now, back in the mid-eighties but Militant were very active in the party at the time and control of the GMC [General Management Committee, now know as the GC] was on a knife-edge. Militant supporters had been selling the newspaper on the doorstep whilst canvassing for the local elections, the party imploded. There was an internal enquiry, which condemned Militant in a report, but we were so concerned to maintain an image of party unity that, when it came to the GMC, we unanimously removed the condemnation from the report. The press got hold of the story anyway and we had a very hard time locally, it was a very unpleasant time to be canvassing for Labour.

So, whilst some may conduct internal party politics unaware or unconcerned for the impact they may have on public perceptions of the party, or believing that the public are not interested, leakage can and does occur. Parties are not completely closed organisations, as much as they work hard to be. Internal strife and the approach to the politics of the party, based on rivalries and power seeking, damage the internal coherence of the party – but they are the stuff of party politics. Yet, in conducting politics in a particular style internally, an impact is had on the way in which political parties view the outside world and conduct politics outside the party and within the locality.

Local politics: the party's realm

Local politics encompasses a far broader and richer scope of activity than that of the political party alone. Civil society within particular localities can be vibrant, robust and healthy, but its scope of activity extends beyond the political and certainly beyond the party political. When issues and events conspire to encourage non-political bodies, or political but not party political bodies to engage with the processes of local political decision-making, political parties will respond as a *gatekeeper*, or as a *bulwark* against public involvement and pressure aimed at the council.[22] They can also act as an *arbitrator* between the local community and councillor or council group when a political dispute around a local issue arises. Or, parties can choose to act as a *defender of the faith*, which is to protect and promote the party, its councillors and the decision of the group or council.

So, how does the political party locally play these roles and what is the impact of party activity on the wider political processes in the locality? The party operates at the interface between the private activities of the party machine itself and the external world comprising of a myriad of different groups and organisations, of varying resource bases and articulating different demands and interests, to differing degrees of success. Yet, party is also the provider of the local political *elite*, those holders of public office that can make public policy and commit public resources to certain courses of action. As such councillors will be subject to varying degrees of pressure, organised or otherwise, to make certain decisions, or to change existing ones. It is here that the party must choose to be an *arbitrator or a defender of the faith*. To do that, the party must first decide its position on any issue or event of importance to the local community, or sections of it. That decision will be made on a number of criteria. First, does the council party group already have a position on the issue? Secondly, does the issue cut across the entire area of the council, a substantial part of it, or is it located in a single ward? Thirdly, who are the key protagonists in the campaign? Fourthly, what is the position taken by party political opponents on the matter? Fifthly, what are the opinions of key players within the party locally? Sixthly, what is the opinion of the party units closest to the issue location? – it is on this that political parties may hold varying positions on particular issues, depending on the unit concerned. For example, the local branches closest to the issue may hold different positions from say a constituency or local government party unit, or the council group. Finally, what are the merits of the issue itself and how do they impact on party fortunes in the role of government or opposition locally? The party undertakes a careful, but privately conducted assessment of the issue itself and what it means for the party and its position locally. Once the issue has been assessed at varying levels within the party, often by the same party people acting in different party units, the party will then present a united front to the public concerned.

Political parties often face considerable difficulties in thinking about local issues in a way that does not link those issues and their outcomes to the fortunes of the party. No issue is considered in isolation and the position the party adopts is as much about party advancement and its public face, as it is about the issue itself. The role parties play locally when acting at the interface between the political *elite* and the community depends on the traditions and tightness of party loyalty and discipline and on the event or issue that has stimulated public interest. Local parties would rather avoid disputes between units of party structure over some external issue as this simply offends against the principle and practice of public party cohesion. Yet, some local parties, particularly branches or ward parties, that are in the immediate proximity of very local issues, may take a view at variance with the wider party and the group over some local concern. Here, branches will use formal party procedures, such as internal debate and the passing of resolutions, to apply pressure to elements within their own party – including their own councillors. One Labour district councillor commented:

> I would not normally go against a group decision on a local matter, unless the ward instructs me to do so, then I would feel happier debating the issue in the group. If the ward wanted me to speak or vote against the group in the council, well I'd work to avoid that happening. Most ward members understand the need for group discipline and what standing orders say, it would have to be a really important matter for them to even think about asking me to break the whip. You do have to balance what the group has decided with what the ward party wants you to do. It's a very difficult situation.

More likely, however, is that the weight of the local party will be thrown into the fray, to defend the group or local councillor, against community opposition to a particular party decision. Parties are on home ground when they undertake this role, as the issue itself for the party is not that which stimulated the public into action, rather it is notions of party unity against a political foe. Here, the tactic often adopted by local parties is to party politicise the dispute and to paint any pressure or action group as controlled and run by an opposing party; or at the very least that its members support another party.[23] When faced with community opposition, local parties will engage the enemy full on and conduct the full range of campaigning activities, using similar tactics to that deployed by any pressure group. Leafleting, press releases, speaking at public meetings and letter writing will be used to promote the party or council's position and to refute the opinions of those opposed to the party's stance. Parties and party people reserve particularly visceral responses to those single-issue groups, which dare to enter that special inner part of the party's realm – the local election. It is here that any single-issue group crosses the Rubicon and displays to party politicians that they are indeed *political*.

During what became a particularly bitter community campaign centred on opposition to the construction of a new road within a particular local authority area, a residents action group, after failing to secure any movement on the issue from the council, decided to stand a candidate in the local elections. The local Labour party sprang into action to defend its council and the decision it had taken. A party spokesperson used the local paper to accuse the residents of '*getting involved in politics*'. He explained:

> I welcome the decision of the action group to field a candidate in the local elections. We in the Labour Party believe it is vital and healthy for democracy that more people take an active part in local politics. But this decision somewhat surprises me since it was reported in this paper that they had no interest in local politics. Surely by contesting elections they become political. I am sure the electorate would also be keen to know the candidate's policies on housing or employment and on the services provided by the council.

After a public meeting held locally to consider the new road a Labour Party member interviewed at the end said 'yes we've got them now, they left the imprint off their last leaflet, I've reported it to the police. Look if they are going to get involved in elections they've got to do it right or we're going to jump on them.' For the uninitiated, like most first-time electoral campaigners with no party experience, the imprint is that part of any election leaflet that is legally required to denote the printer and publisher.

After a vitriolic election campaign the action group candidate was narrowly defeated. He did, however, come closer to unseating Labour than any other candidate during the last ten years in this annual election authority, with only a handful of votes separating the Labour and action group candidates. During the election campaign, repeated action group requests for meetings with councillors on the issue had been regularly refused, because 'there was an election on'. At the count the re-elected Labour councillor for the ward approached the unsuccessful action group candidate and the following exchange was overheard:

Councillor A: *We can have that meeting you've been asking for now.*
Defeated action group candidate: *Good, thank you, when can we meet?*

Another Labour councillor who had just been re-elected to his safe Labour seat for another ward in the district shouted, 'No we bloody well won't have any meetings and there's the reason', at which he banged on the table and pointed to the piles of ballot papers. He was later over-heard to say to a party colleague, 'bloody cheek, come that close to winning our seat and want to meet with us afterwards, and old [named councillor] agrees to it, I'd tell them to clear off in no uncertain terms and stay out of our wards'.

So, political party activity can deteriorate into a straightforward fight between the party and local campaigners, who are treated in exactly the same way as any opposing party. Similar reactions to that recorded from Labour Party members have been forthcoming from Conservatives, thus:

> I have no objections to Independent candidates, but single-issue groups should not use local elections, its about much more than any one issue in which they might be interested. (Conservative County Councillor)

> Local elections are not the place for single-issue politics or causes, local government is a very complex business and elections can not be reduced to a weapon available to certain groups – they must have a much wider plat-form to put before residents. (Conservative Party member)

Not surprisingly Liberal Democrats take a slightly different, but not massively divergent view when it comes to local elections, as one *Focus Team* campaigner said:

> I don't blame people from getting frustrated with the council, that's why I got involved with the Liberal Democrats in the first place. Yes, we cam-paign about local issues, but we also have policies about council services and wider political policies. We support action groups, but rather than standing in an election – they should vote for us. More referendums would solve the problem I expect.

Political parties can, as with any council, be in conflict with local com-munities, or work in co-operation with them to solve some local problem or concern. They can place themselves at the forefront of com-munity action and public involvement in the political processes, or can act as an antagonistic adversary to any organised attempt by citizens to enter the political realm. Party, however, raises itself above community concern and particularly single-issue campaigns, by adopting a broad political interest across a range of issues, most of which locally will be focused on the council. Parties also see themselves as the only legitimate player in the electoral game, with the exception of Independents (who themselves understand and play by the rules of the game).

Yet, by acting as though local elections and council seats are the sole property of political parties and by viewing interactions with community or action groups as party political and based on defending or promoting the party, rather than engaging with the issue, parties often force non-party groupings into contesting elections. On occasions, such groupings can have political and electoral success: Health Concern currently being the largest group on Wyre Forest District Council and has six councillors elected to Worcestershire County Council; Elmbridge residents association currently control Elmbridge District Council; the London Borough of Hounslow has three Independent Community group councillors; Sefton Metropolitan Borough Council has three councillors sitting as the 'Southport Party'; Lancaster City Council has 14 Morecambe Bay Independents; and the London Borough of Newham has a lone opposition councillor elected from the Christian Peoples' Party. These councillors from outside the three main parties represent but a few of the instances where candidates with a truly local or non-party focus have defeated candidates from the three main parties.

Political parties themselves are responsible for encouraging non-party groupings to enter the electoral fray because parties use the public vote as a mechanism to legitimise their role and place in local politics, and to de-legitimise those that seek to influence affairs from outside of an elected position. Moreover, parties do not, by and large, enter into the outside political world as much as would be expected; even community politics has politically very traditional objectives – to win seats. Parties prefer to operate on familiar territory, speaking to the outside world when they must, at election time. They also prefer to focus on internal party concerns, rather than the confusing and murky world of the local community – that is the role of the councillor. Yet, political parties remain powerful players locally, especially when the party's councillors are in control of the council. They can act as conduits to authority and as a voice of local communities, that in most areas they choose not to but to concentrate on internal party affairs, and to put party unity above public discourse, remains a key source of public disengagement from local politics.

Conclusion

British local government and politics is a party-dominated affair, and the democratic processes, as they play themselves out locally, are shaped and directed by the activities and organisation of political parties. Moreover, parties create the climate within which public engagement and deliberation take place, or are prevented from taking place. Parties are experienced in the game of politics and better resourced and organised than those from other non-party groupings seeking influence. Moreover, they are able to control access to political decision-makers as well as control the institutions of political decision-making themselves.

The very nature of the political party as a power-seeking organisation, with a broad political interest and a focus on internal affairs, produces a *party approach* to politics and democracy. That approach is more about the fortunes and influence of the party and party people than it is about creating a vibrant and healthy, yet challenging and complex local democracy. Party is about nullifying challenge from other parties or other organisations involved in political campaigning, it is also about producing certainty and consistency in party advantage and fortunes and focusing on internal party activity. Ostrogorski's description of parties as a machine, composed of a number of smaller and smaller machines, is as apt today as it was in 1902 and particularly apt in the context of British local politics. It is the machine-like quality of political parties that gives them an element of predictability in the way they play politics and how they respond to particular issues.[24]

Yet today, when conceptualising political parties in the local arena, we need to move beyond notions of machine-like quality if we are to explore fully the dynamics of political parties and the impact they have on local politics. Political parties in the local arena are organisations that mobilise, concentrate and co-ordinate political bias and which structure their activities and focus their attention on the representative institution that is the council. Whatever the internal condition of a local party, be it *moribund* or *omnipotent*, it is a multi-layered and multi-dimensional construction that merges a formal structure and identity with a set of informal processes and interactions that outwardly maintain a united and coherent public face, whilst inwardly providing a battleground for displays of often intense political and personal conflict and discontent. Parties, then, are the organisation of contradiction into a cohesive, yet fissiparous unity, held together by rules and procedures and the glue of political prejudice and opinion. Parties are also held together locally not only by what they wish to achieve but by the fact that other parties, set on achieving alternative goals also exist.

Political parties locally are inherently competitive and combative organisations, both internally and externally. The party is provided with an ongoing purpose by the very nature of conflict over the control of a

council and the ability to then govern locally and by the access to patronage, resources, support and influence that positions on a representative institution can offer. Parties also provide a *theatre* in which the
politically motivated can conduct the politics of the party as well as the
politics of the locality. But, they are closed organisations, which exclude
the outside world, unless it wants to join or can no longer be ignored.
Thus, parties have a purpose and form that often sets them in conflict
with the citizens they seek to represent and govern

Yet, political parties are the bodies through which local politics is
largely conducted and are the vehicles through which power is obtained,
maintained and used. Parties are structured and organised so as to
ensure the efficient running of the party machine and the effective
conduct of political activity within the confines of scarce resources.
Parties act to provide a distinct political identity to the outside world
and use that identity to secure political office. But, parties reduce all
political activity and concerns to party political ones; the parties party
politicise the community campaign and view with intense suspicion
those that are outside their boundaries but conducting political activity.
Moreover, the party person relates political activity (all of which is of
course party political) as fundamentally about representation and
government, and to represent and govern locally the party must secure
elected office. Once party candidates have been elected to the council
yet more facets of the political party emerge which add to our understanding of the impact of party on local democracy and representation,
it is to these aspects we now turn.

Notes

1 J. Stanyer, *Understanding Local Government*, London: Fontana, 1976,
   p. 70.
2 L. J. Sharpe and K. Newton, *Does Politics Matter? The Determinants of
   Public Policy*, Oxford: Clarendon Press, 1984, p. 203.
3 J. Stewart, *The Nature of British Local Government*, Basingstoke:
   Macmillan, 2000, p. 8.
4 J. Kingdom, *Local Government and Politics in Britain*, Hemel Hempstead:
   Phillip Allan, 1991, p. 118.
5 R. A. Dahl, *Who Governs?* New Haven: Yale University Press, 1961; K.
   Newton, *Second City Politics: Democratic Processes and Decision-Making in
   Birmingham*, Oxford: Clarendon Press, 1976.
6 C. Game and S. Leach, 'Political Parties and Local Democracy', in L.
   Pratchett and D. Wilson (eds), *Local Democracy and Local Government*,
   Basingstoke: Macmillan, 1996, pp. 146–148.

7 R. Michels, *Political Parties*, Glencoe, IL: The Free Press, 1949.
8 R. Pinkney, 'Nationalizing Local Politics and Localizing a National Party', in I. Hopton, *Directory of Liberal Party Resolutions*, London: Liberal Publication Department, 1978, pp. 143–144. p. 351. R. Pinkney, 'Nationalizing Local Politics and Localizing a National Party: The Liberal Role in Local Government', *Government and Opposition*, 18, 1983, pp. 347–358. pp. 350 and 353.
9 D. Blunkett and K. Jackson, *Democracy in Crisis: The Town Halls Respond*, London: The Hogarth Press, 1987.
10 J. Stewart, *The Nature of British Local Government.*
11 Game and Leach, *Political Parties and Local Democracy*, p. 146.
12 I. Budge, J. A. Brand, M. Margolis and A. Smith, *Political Stratification and Democracy*, Basingstoke: Macmillan, 1972.
13 D. Wilson and C. Game, *Local Government in the United Kingdom*, Basingstoke: Macmillan, 2002, pp. 286–287.
14 *The Constitution of the Liberal Democrats*, London, 2002.
15 The Labour Party, 'NEC Procedural Guidance for Selection of Local Government Candidates', The Labour Party Rules, London, 2000 (updated 2003).
16 National Union of Conservative and Unionist Associations, *Model Rules For Constituency, Branch and European Constituency Councils*, section 19 (2) (b), 'Procedure-Local Government Candidates',1993, p. 11.
17 H. Wainwright, *Labour: A Tale of Two Parties*, London: Hogarth Press, 1987.
18 D. Prior, J. Stewart and K. Walsh, *Citizenship: Rights, Community and Participation*, London: Pitman, 1995.
19 S. Leach and D. Wilson, *Local Political Leadership*, Bristol: The Policy Press, 2000.
20 Game and Leach, *Political Parties and Local Democracy*.
21 K. Livingstone, *If Voting Changed Anything, They'd Abolish It*, London: Fontana, 1987.
22 M. Steed, 'Participation through Western Democratic Institutions', in G. Parry (ed.), *Participation in Politics*, Manchester: Manchester University Press, 1972, pp. 80–101.
23 J. Dearlove, *The Politics of Policy in Local Government: The Making and Maintenance of Public Policy in the Royal Borough of Kensington and Chelsea*, London: Cambridge University Press, 1973; C. Copus, 'The Councillor: Respresenting a Locality and the Party Group', *Local Governance*, 24 (3), Autumn, 1998, pp. 215–224.
24 M. Ostrogorski, *Democracy and the Organisation of Politcal Parties*, Vols I and II, New York: Macmillan, 1902, p. 372.

4

The political party group: the *Leviathan* of local politics

Party politics in local government is often confused with what is actually party group politics. The political party group is a discrete (and indeed, discreet) unit of party organisation within each of the three main political parties and the Scottish National Party and Plaid Cymru. The party group has its own rules, procedures and organisational structures that are distinct from, but bound up with, the rules and structures of the wider party of which it is a part. The political party group is a coherent, unified and disciplined *bloc* of councillors, sharing the same political party membership or allegiance.

The unique and defining characteristic of the political party group is that it demands the loyalty of the councillors that constitute its membership to the exclusion of all other potential sources of loyalty to which the member may wish to defer, including the wider local party. The party group demands that its members act as trustees of the general public good, so that they can become delegates of the group, mandated to speak and vote in public, as the group has decided. The organisation and activities of the political party group generate a dual problem for local politics arising from the 'conduct of the group' and 'the extent of group discipline'. Indeed, Jones and Stewart noted that the approach to the question of whether, in any one party group, discipline is firm or relaxed lay 'at the heart of the democratic processes of local government'.[1]

Despite the importance of the party group to the conduct of council affairs and the intermediary position the party group holds between the councillor and the electorate, the party group has not been granted the attention it deserves in reviews of the organisation and management of local government. Part of the reason for overlooking the group system is that the group is not part of the formal political decision-making processes of local government, but it is widely recognised by members and officers as the place where council policy is set. The group, and particularly the majority group, is a vital but informal part of the way local government operates as a politically representative institution. It is not in itself an informal body however, being structured and organised by rules and procedures. Moreover, the group will elect a number of officers to conduct its own internal business, such as a chair, secretary and treasurer. In addition, the group will elect a whips office and a chief whip, charged, amongst other things, with ensuring the group retains its coherence and unity in public, and that members are aware of group policy and decisions on all issues. The party group can be accurately described as a *formalised informality*.

Prior to what might be called the 'outing' of the party group and the higher profile it now commands amongst at least academics and researchers, the party group was often spoken of by members and officers in hushed and reverent tones. Indeed, at a council meeting in which the author participated a long-standing and elderly member of the ruling group referred to the need for an issue to be considered in 'another place' – the euphemism used in one House of Parliament when referring to the other. He, of course, meant a group meeting. Whilst the group may or may not still be referred to in parodies of Parliamentary eloquence one fact is clear, the group is a *Leviathan*-like organisation that reaches into all facets of council politics and into the wider public realm.

The chapter addresses the factors that have enabled the political party group to achieve its power and influence within the processes of political decision-making, and, more generally, within local representative democracy. In so doing, it offers an approach to understanding why the political party group conducts its affairs in the way it does and how political affiliation affects the relationship between the group and its membership. The chapter looks at the dynamics of party group activity and how those dynamics create a tension within local representative democracy. Finally, it explores whether a party group's holding of majority or minority status on the council and the likelihood that the group will either lose or win power in the near future, impacts on notions of group loyalty and discipline.

The first section sets out the current understanding of the process by which councillors come together in an identifiable party group. The second section explores exactly how and why Conservative, Labour and Liberal Democrat party groups maintain a cohesive and disciplined approach to the conduct of local representation and council affairs. The third section examines how the party group, by adopting what can be called a governing and opposition approach to council affairs and local politics, can distort the councillor's relationship with the electorate.

Fourthly, the chapter explores whether a group's proximity to power within the council makes a difference to the way it conducts its affairs.

The political party group: a formalised informality

Nothing demonstrates the penetration of the political party within local political affairs and political decision-making more than the organisation of councillors into definite party groupings for the conduct of council affairs. The factor that unifies the party group across the political spectrum is unity itself; whichever party is concerned, council affairs are viewed by the councillor through the prism of the party group. Whilst differing degrees of flexibility exist across groups in the way public cohesion and discipline are interpreted, the vast majority of council chambers consist of *blocs* of opposing councillors organised around a party political – or some other – label.

These *blocs* of councillors are not just creations for the convenience of conducting council politics and acting as a government and opposition within a local setting, they are integral parts of the local political system and of the parties from which their membership springs. Gyford and James demonstrated the independent existence of the party group as an important element of political party structure in a model comprising the party at headquarters, the party in Parliament, local party units and the local authority political party group.[2] It is the existence of the group as a structured reality, yet still somehow seen as outside the formal processes of council decision-making, that provides it with its political influence. The group further entrenches its influence through its ability to generate loyalty amongst its members and by providing councillors with a closed and private *theatre* for representative activity. But, its power really stems from and the willingness of councillors, as party affiliates, to subordinate their relationship with the electorate to the one they have with their political party group.

Party group cohesion in public, and the varying reasons across the main political parties for its existence, means that councillors often act differently from the ways they would act as independent representatives. The group demands the loyalty of its members, and the councillor must either comply with or dissent from it. Thus the relationship between the individual councillor and the individual elector is not such that they interact with one another in an 'ideal representative system'.[3] Indeed, a *crisis of representation* arises when the views of the group and electoral pressures collide over specific local issues, and the group and the electorate demand that the councillor adopts a contradictory position on a local issue.[4] The ability to generate such crises is what places the group in an intermediary position between councillor and the communities and citizens he or she represents and indicates the strength and resilience of the group system.

As membership of the group entails expectations of public adherence to group policy and decisions, it exerts a pull on the councillor's representational activities, and is a powerful alternative to demands for representation made by the electorate. The imbalance between the demands for councillor loyalty made by the group and the electorate holds the key to understanding the current experiences of local democracy had by the vast majority of councillors today and indicates the outcome of any competition for the councillor's loyalty between the group and the citizenry.

Group expectations of councillor loyalty create an 'exclusive' political decision-making environment, the outcomes of which may conflict with the expressed wishes of sections of the electorate. This is a major source of tension in the representational process, a tension that need not be of a partisan nature, but related to particular issues or decisions. Even so, the councillor's election, often as a result of party affiliation alone, produces an affinity with the group, drawing the councillor away from the electorate.

Understanding the party group

The very existence of large numbers of councillors elected on a shared party political platform places pressure on them to organise to ensure their political success. Indeed, the three main parties either require or encourage their councillors to adopt a set of model rules for the party group and to organise and conduct business along set lines. As a consequence, recent studies have confirmed that the party group is now prevalent within local authorities.[5] One of the most serious attempts to understand and explain the role of the party group was conducted in 1967 by the Maud Committee. The committee considered in some detail what it felt at the time to be the largely urban phenomenon of councils operating on 'party political lines', with political discussion and decision-making taking place in groups which operated 'outside the committee structure'.[6] Indeed, Maud referred to a number of authorities (a minority by its reckoning) where political parties had a 'stranglehold' on 'day-to-day operations' and councillors followed the party line with a 'forced' and 'unnatural' regularity.

The Maud Committee noted some key distinctions in approach to the party group system between Conservative and Labour parties. Conservative Central Office were described as 'wary' of the group reducing the council to a 'rubber stamping' exercise, but felt the system desirable to attain 'co-ordinated action and to ensure that information is available to members'. The Labour Party was generally more supportive of the role of party politics and party organisation as a device to 'ensure a consistent direction of policy'.[7]

In clarifying the depth to which the party group and group system had penetrated the workings of local government, the committee noted that the political party group was 'fundamental to the influence of party politics in local government'.[8] Maud also observed that party groups had formalised their procedures to ensure the smooth running of at least the politics of the council chamber. The committee commented on group operations thus: 'almost invariably, party groups of all political persuasions meet before each council meeting, to receive information about the business and in most instances to decide on a party line (even though this may not be obligatory)'.

Reflecting on this, Maud Commented:

> Whether a party group is engaged in vetting recommendations originating in committees, or considering a line to be taken in council or committee, it is a closed organisation which the electorate may not be able to influence. In so far as the decisions of the group are 'binding' on the member he can be regarded as a delegate of the group or party organisation rather than a representative of the electorate. There is a possible contradiction between the stimulus to public interest and contact caused by the election campaigns and the appeals of party controversy on the one hand, and the tendency towards an inward-looking organisation in the party group, unresponsive to the needs of the electorate as a whole, on the other.[9]

In sum the group serves to distance the councillor from the represented. It sets itself up as the beneficiary of the aggregation of political support that flows from the processes of a local democracy. Local government and democracy may be 'impoverished by the strait-jacket of party politics', which constrains public involvement, but some defend it nonetheless as the most appropriate method of ensuring that local decisions are democratically made.[10] Moreover, secrecy establishes the group as a forum within which representative activity is conducted away from the gaze of the represented, in turn enabling the group to influence the ways in which councillors behave in more open and public settings.

Despite the many observations made by the Maud Committee on the organisation and activities of the party group and group system, it did not undertake a formal study of the work of party group.[11] It did, however, do one thing that is vital to our understanding of the nature and dynamics of the political party group and group system. The committee produced the foundations of a working definition of group politics and its impact on the representational relationship between the councillor and the electorate. The important characteristics defined were the closed and secret nature of the party group; its existence as a decision-making mechanism outside and alongside the council as a representative body; and its acceptance by Conservative and Labour parties as having a valuable policy co-ordinating role. Moreover, the ability that the party group has to transform the councillor from a community representative into a 'delegate' of the group, has a profound affect on how councillors approach local representation and democracy. Subsequently, these components were to be added to and elaborated by other inquiries.

The sources of group cohesion

Nearly 20 years after the Maud Committee's investigation and deliberation, the Widdicombe Committee considered the organisation and activities of party groups, the importance of group discipline, and the phenomenon of group members voting *en bloc* in council and committee meetings.[12] Widdicombe received advice from its researchers on the importance of these factors as an indicator of the ability of the group to direct, if not control, the activities of councillors in council and committee. They were important because Widdicombe found party label predominant in 80 per cent of councils.[13] Young and Davis, however, found little evidence to 'sustain the notion of a rising tide of politicisation beyond the obvious and trivial observation that most councillors wear a party label'.[14]

It is the party label that marks out the cohesiveness of the group in the conduct of council affairs and accounts for consistent findings that councillors display a 'marked reluctance to vote against group decisions'.[15] The party group maintains its cohesion and public unity by the adoption of varying degrees of discipline and co-ordinated action in public settings. The effect of which is to elevate the private group meeting above the formal arena of the council as the place in which political decisions are made.

Young and Davis made a judgement about the nature of group practices based on the extent to which councillors were considered bound by group decisions, and measured by the extent to which councillors vote

Table 4.1 Mandating by party: effect on members of group decisions

	1985(%)	1989(%)	Variation
Not bound	6	13	+7
Routinely bound	68	71	+3
Special issues only	26	16	−10

Source: K. Young and M. Davies, *The Politics of Local Government Since Widdicombe*, York: Joseph Rowntree Foundation 1990, figure 10, p. 46.

en bloc in council and committee meetings.[16] On this criteria and by examining how far councillors were either 'routinely bound', 'bound on special issues only' or 'not bound' by the group, Young and Davies identified an increase in group discipline in their own findings over the 1985 Widdicombe Committee results. As demonstrated in Table 4.1.

Young and Davies noted the move amongst both parties in the direction of 'routine mandating' of members on a range of issues, not just those of major policy concern or arising from a party manifesto. Some 92 per cent of Labour and 50 per cent of Conservative authorities at the time of their study adopted the practice of binding their members in public council meetings by the results of debate and decisions within a private group meeting. Looking for a more direct measure of group cohesion they examined the extent to which councillors of majority groups actually voted together at council or committee or never voted with the opposition.[17] They concluded by echoing the Maud Committee some 20 years previous, by referring to the practice of councillors being increasingly bound by, and supportive of, the group in both council and committee meetings and the whole notion of group cohesion and public unity as a largely urban phenomenon.

A distinct behaviour pattern amongst councillors is discernible from the Widdicombe research and the work of Young and Davies. That pattern is one of greater group cohesion in council than in committee, a pattern which has changed since the Young and Davis study to a situation where the coherence of party groups in council and committee, and even outside the council chamber, varies very little.[18] There are weaknesses however, in resting an understanding of the nature of party group politics on an analysis of voting patterns in council meetings alone. Such an approach may not produce a subtle enough measure of group influence on the representative activities of the councillor, nor illuminate clearly enough how the group influences the development of council policy and the taking of political decisions. Equally it says nothing about any of the other *theatres of representation* within which councillors act.

Subsequent to the work of Young and Davis, it has been recognised elsewhere that group cohesion is far from an urban phenomenon alone, but stretches across all types of councils.[19] In addition, the group not only binds its members in council meetings but also attempts to restrain and direct the speeches and potential votes of councillors in a range of public *theatres of representation*. As one Labour district councillor reported: 'the chief whip [of the district council group] reported me to the group for a statement I had made as a parish councillor at a parish meeting. He told me it does not matter where anyone speaks, or in what capacity, you are bound by the district group's instruction.'

Indeed, the reach of group discipline can be extended by the group and by group members self-discipline into meetings of the wider political party as well as public meetings and the press, radio and television.[20] Despite restrictions on whipping councillors in the new overview and scrutiny committees, those bodies are also not immune from the impact of group discipline, an issue to which we will return in detail in chapter 9.

It is clear that if we are to fully understand the nature of the party group and the group system and the impact they have on local political affairs we need to move beyond consideration of cohesion based solely on councillors' voting practices. Exploring practices such as voting in groups in council, the frequency of cross-voting or the degree to which councillors feel bound by group decisions, produce sound quantitative data illuminating how party politics is practised. It is, however, insufficiently sensitive to capture the realities of group discipline or to explain the reasons for group cohesion in public settings or to begin to explore the dynamics of the party group.

Despite recognising the enormous power of the party group and the ability it has to distort local representation and to exclude the electorate from any meaningful engagement with the political process, the group remains to be the subject of any detailed and extensive government-backed research. Whilst every other facet of local government has had one committee of enquiry or another, the party group, is relatively untouched. Even the Blair government's most recent reforms of local government political decision-making, and its attempts at local democratic renewal, make scant reference to the party group. Despite the lack of properly funded research into party group practices, the modernising agenda has at least publicly recognised the powerful position the party groups hold locally: 'Committees are often not where the real decisions are made. In most councils it is the political groups, meeting behind closed doors, which make the big and significant decisions.'[21]

And in the white paper *Modern Local Government: In Touch with the People*:

> Traditional committee structures, still used by almost all councils, lead to inefficient and opaque decision-making. Significant decisions are, in many councils taken behind closed doors by political groups or even a small group of key people within the majority group. Consequently, many councillors, even those in the majority group, have little influence over council decisions.[22]

What is missing from the government's analysis is a thorough exploration of the party group as a closed and private decision-making forum with the potential to exclude citizens from effective participation in the political processes. Further, despite concern for transparency and openness, there is no comprehensive strategy developed within the government's modernising agenda by which the role played by the party group and the group system can be brought into the open. The political party group is a body which in local government holds, and is set to retain, inordinate power.[23] Moreover, the Local Government Act 2000, and the subsequent regulations flowing from it have made no fundamental challenges to the way the group conducts politics, other than the following mention of the party whip in regard to overview and scrutiny:

> Overview and scrutiny committees are to hold decision-makers to account. To do so effectively will require a change in the way members have traditionally questioned decisions. Although this is a matter for the political parties to consider, both locally and nationally, the Government believes whipping is incompatible with overview and scrutiny and recommends that whipping should not take place.[24]

The absence of any serious and detailed public exploration of the role and influence of the party group and the group system is a gap in current government thinking about local politics and a flaw in attempts to modernise political practices. It is a dangerous omission to separate the informal practices of politics from the formal and indeed even ritualistic processes that pass for the public face of political decision-making in council chambers. It would further compound the error if we were unable to account for the depth and richness of council politics as they are conducted in and through the political party group. To do this we must look at the broad range of practices that occur within and across the party group when it comes to the conduct of council affairs, local representation and the business of the group itself.

The party group: a coherent approach to politics

In the great majority of councils across Britain, the formal and public display of democracy in action that occurs within the council chamber will have a familiar context and content to it. Moreover, it will be clear to the observer that *blocs* of councillors speak and vote as one on the majority of issues; those *blocs* will consist of councillors sharing a party label. In public, the party group maintains unity and a disciplined approach to the affairs of the council and to the politics of the territories from which it emerged. Whilst the group presents a united face to the public and political opponents, the reality can be much more exciting and dynamic than the serried ranks of councillors, speaking with one voice and voting as one. It is behind the closed doors of the group room that the tensions arising from political, ideological, geographical and demographic sources, and even arising from the size of the group concerned, display themselves.[25] Moreover, different interpretations of what it is to be a councillor and of the role of the elected representative are played out. Such interpretations are often reflective of councillors' political values and political affiliations.[26]

Putting to one side for the moment the issue of party affiliation, the party group is a product of its particular territorial surroundings and the political culture of its locality, as well as that of the council. Moreover, the pressures for change impinging on any one locality will also act as pressure on the group to develop new responses to existing and emerging problems. The group will reflect these factors in the way it conducts its internal business and the business of the council. In this regard, the party group mirrors the internal divisions within the wider party as discussed in chapter 3 and we should not be surprised to find such replication of divisive factors occurring within a group – the group is a product of the local party as well as of the electoral process. As a consequence, the group is yet another platform on which to play out the tensions that exist within the wider local party and its various *kindreds* as sources of discontent.

The party group is often dominated by various cliques and factions as well as the politics of personality, all of which will bear little, if any, relationship to political values and views. In one ruling Conservative group the author visited, it was explained that to rise to a leadership position, either within the council or within the group, one had to be at least 50 years old. Councillors judged the worth of their colleagues by age and thus by perceived experience; interestingly many councillors under 50 went along with this age-based criteria.

In a Liberal Democrat ruling group the criteria for a leadership position were to represent, or come from, wards in the south of the authority. One disgruntled Liberal Democrat councillor bemoaned her lot thus: 'It's true, unless you come from the right wards you have no chance of getting on. Not only that, but everything gets done in the south and nothing happens anywhere else. I'm trying to find another seat'. A Labour county councillor commented in a similar vein:

> After the last re-organisation [1974] the councillors that came up from the old county borough used to run this place. There weren't enough of them to do it alone, so after each election they'd furtle around to pick a few favourites from seats around the county to pad out their numbers, and then took everything. There were a lot of us not sorry to see them go back when the city went unitary – things are shared out a lot more now.

Occupational backgrounds also hold sway when it comes to the dynamics of the party group and the allocation of both council and group patronage. It is commonplace to hear councillors of all parties complain along the lines of: 'if you haven't been a member of the NUM then forget it'; 'a lot of young, middle-class professionals run this place'; 'a job in the city helps'; 'the old school tie and old boy network is what counts here', or 'the council is run for and by farmers'. Councillors will also often complain of one *Mafia* or another that controls the group, and, if that is the ruling group, then it also controls the council. What is at work here are the relationships often forged in a work environment, in close-knit communities of place, or a ready identification and empathy with a council and party colleague having similar background characteristics and accordingly expressing some shared interests. Finally, of course, councillors will also complain that, when it comes to power and patronage, 'it's the masons', or that it is 'the officers' that run the council.

Wherever one goes across the country and across party, it does not take long for councillors to identify the various factions and *kindreds* within the group, within the party groups in opposition and within the council. They will also observe similar factors at play amongst the senior officers of the council and particularly any common ground existing between small groups of officers and certain elected members. The factors that bring small cliques together within a party group also work to exclude others from the centres of power, and patronage, in much the same way as the group system excludes all those outside it from any meaningful input in to political decision-making. In addition to all this, there is the potentially explosive ingredient into the party group mix of ideology, or at very least, certain strongly held political values. The impact of ideological differences on both Conservative and Labour groups is well documented.[27] Such ideologically based differences within the same party group, will drive members to construct almost impermeable barriers around a tightly knit group of colleagues, sharing not only a party label but an ideological perspective as well. Those sitting outside the ideological faction will be viewed as implacable enemies in exactly the same way as those that are outside the party, as enemies of the cause.

Despite attempts to ensure that ideologically driven internal disputes and other sources of division within the party group do not boil over into the public arena, the intensity of feeling amongst councillors will often be difficult to contain in the group meeting alone. Back in 1996, Hackney Borough Labour group found itself disbanded in a national party attempt to restore discipline to a deeply factionalised group and to prevent the activities of a 'party within a party'.[28] To rejoin the group councillors were required to give an undertaking to abide by party rules, to accept whips approved by the national party and to accept the authority of the group leader. Similarly, a local–national party policy dispute that had arisen as a result of a deeply divided Labour group in Walsall was resolved by the expulsion of 15 councillors from the Labour Party. The move resulted in the formation of a group of councillors referring to themselves as Democratic Labour, depriving Labour of control of the council. More recently, in 2002, allegations concerning the Conservative leader of Lincolnshire County Council saw the Conservative group provide public support for him to a point, but eventually pressure from within the group resulted in his resignation. Party groups across the country and across the party spectrum, are the political play-thing for those seeking to pursue individual political grievances or a vendetta, or for those who simply want to take a job or position held by someone else.[29]

An incident experienced by the author at one of his first-ever group meetings highlights the ideological cleavage within party groups, as well as illuminating other sources of division, such as age, occupation, tenure in the locality and social class. In the mid 1980s on this particular London Borough council a change was beginning to occur in the social composition of the ruling group. At Borough elections in the 1980s, the party ruling group won all 60 council seats and a large contingent of young, well-educated, middle-class councillors, not all of whom were born in the borough, were returned to the council. There was a fine balance between the older, working-class, more traditionally orientated Labour members that had sat on the council for some considerable period. It was alleged at the time, that Masonic links and influence were at play when it came to patronage positions and power in the group generally. Moreover, that the Masonic links were particularly strong around one key spending committee and associated department.

The leader of the council, a longstanding councillor who had been a member of the predecessor county borough, born and brought up in the area and knighted for his services to local government, was faced with a large section within the group that he simply did not understand. The experience was mutual. At an early group meeting after the election the leader was reporting to the group, the author cannot remember the issue concerned, so unimportant is it to the story. But, well recalled is that during his report an old East End colloquialism was employed along these lines: 'of course the group must understand that the nigger in the wood pile is . . .', at which point the rest of his speech was drowned out as a section of the room exploded into rage, screams of abuse, people storming out, papers being thrown on to the floor, crying, rending of clothes, and pulling of hair and other expressions of disquiet. Basically all hell had broken loose; thankfully it was a private group meeting and not full council. The meeting naturally had to be adjourned while tempers were calmed and as runners went between the two factions in the group to mediate.

I remember the look of total astonishment on the leader's face as the room exploded, he had no idea what was happening, or why. At the time, being a young left of centre type, the author sided with the enraged section. But, reflecting on what occurred in this group over the next few years, the leader, in his casual employment of phraseology, had simply handed certain councillors a very, very large stick with which to beat him, which they did with abandonment and a barely concealed sense of glee. He was no racist and I now know what all the hysterics were about: a shift of power from one well established group to the new contenders for power and those contenders not missing a trick when it presented itself.

Trends in group cohesion

The historical trend in the development of the group system has been, and continues to be, towards greater and greater public coherence amongst councillors based on party affiliation alone. The use of a disciplined approach to council affairs however (notwithstanding the absence of 'disciplinary' mechanisms or procedures) can be the product of political circumstances, rather than an ideological approach to the conduct of politics based on parties and was not always welcomed by some councillors.[30] The current phenomenon of group cohesion has developed over time and place and some resistance has occurred to adopting a cohesive approach to speaking and voting, even to the extent of some councillors refusing to attend group meetings as they impinged on their rights to act as public representatives.[31] Equally some councillors have indicated a 'strong resentment against group control' and against the 'principle of obeying majority decisions'.[32]

Such literature as does exist on the development of a cohesive approach to group activity indicates its uneven progress over both time and place but also indicates a longstanding tendency for councillors to operate as identifiable groups, with varying degrees of success in maintaining councillor loyalty.[33] A prime motivating factor in the development of group cohesion was the very early recognition amongst local politicians that organisation held the key to political success in the council. Acting as a united group when it came to council affairs converts a 'collection of individual councillors elected under a common party label, into an effective political force'.[34] Unity equals political success and the successful implementation of a policy platform that has secured some degree of public support through the electoral process. Yet party group unity cannot always be guaranteed without effort or a degree of arm twisting, and it is the effort required to secure group unity that is often criticised for restricting the freedom of the individual member. Yet, councillors willingly relinquish some of their freedom to act in public as a trade-off for influencing group decisions and using the group meeting to freely express themselves, influence party policy and 'dispose of any doubts and disputes'.[35] Councillors will only be prepared to cohere in public if the group provides them with a platform for the resolution of a range of council, political and ward-based concerns. The group meeting is the place where councillors can question, challenge and criticise their own leadership, and, if in the majority group, they are confronting the leadership of the council. Group and council leaders, however, have available the resources, support mechanisms and access to officers through the council that are not available to the ordinary member. The outcomes of group meetings rest as much on the imbalances in political resources across group members as they do to the eloquence of an argument or the rightness of a cause. Despite this, however, the leadership must not 'offend the core political values and commitments of back-benchers', if it wants to remain in office.[36]

Whilst some party group meetings are hard-fought and bloody affairs, group discipline and cohesion in public ensures these battles are not undertaken in the observable and accountable public *theatres* of the council. The defining point for all party groups is the degree to which formal disciplinary mechanisms exist and are used to ensure public unity, or the extent to which discipline operates as an informal process. It is here that party affiliation has something to tell about the organisation and activities of councillors as discrete groupings. Labour groups are far more willing than their Conservative and Liberal Democrat counter-parts to publicly subscribe a legitimacy to the group as a place to conduct politics and representation. Although Conservative and Liberal Democrats do see the group in much the same light, they are simply less willing to admit to it.[37]

Once decisions are made in the private group meeting, the group expects the councillor's loyalty and public support, or at least avoidance of opposition. It is that expectation and the disciplinary mechanisms available to ensure compliance that sets the private party group up as the most important political decision-making body of the council. Indeed, the group is now the place where decisions are made that extend beyond purely council business and into the wider realms of governance and community leadership. Even when it comes to disciplining recalcitrant members, the group likes to act publicly 'more in sorrow than anger' with harsher accusations of treachery kept private.[38]

Despite all of the pressure and forces for division and dissent within party groups, and despite general agreement amongst councillors with the adage that: 'no one in local politics hates someone in the opposing party more than they hate someone in their own party', the group system displays a remarkable resilience. Groups cohere in public, dis-playing a united front to both the public and opposition parties alike, the councillor that strays from the fold, for whatever the reason, is seen as acting pathologically by his or her colleagues. So the forces that bind councillors together are a more powerful element in the day-to-day experiences of the councillor, than those that may lead to division – at least in public anyway.

Yet, party groups operate in public in united and cohesive *blocs* for reasons other than because the party rules say they must. Custom and practice in both group and council activity play a part, as they are pow-erful and comforting forces. The way in which the group has always approached its business and the business of the council is difficult, though not impossible, to challenge. The group may be fairly flexible in its expectations of group unity in public, or it may take a very firm approach. Either way consistency, regularity and the traditions of polit-ical behaviour by councillors, ensure that political activity is conducted in familiar ways and also ensure that newly elected councillors quickly learn what is expected of them as members of the group.[39]

As one former council deputy leader that moved from one council area only to be elected to his new council commented:

> It is a different world. In my old council I encouraged as much freedom amongst our members as possible; the leader wanted people to feel they could address important issues in public. But, here its like joining a new party let alone a new council. It's a very very tight ship and I found out overnight that the freedom I was used to just did not exist in this group. I got into a lot of trouble just by asking a very simple question in council about cutting the grass on roadside verges. I hadn't taken as seriously as I should the fact that group members are told in writing before every council meeting who is saying what, where and when. It's the culture of the place, plus the leadership, and us as the ruling group, are very insecure – its not because we could lose control, that's not on the cards at all. They just do not like people discussing things in public.

The cause of the insecurity the councillor refers to in this case has more to do with the internal power dynamics of the group itself, and how it sees politics, than it does with political affiliation. Moreover, it is less about a potential threat to the party's hold on power and more about an interpretation of democracy that sees members tightly bound by the decisions of the group. To the councillor, democracy is what takes place within the confines of the group meeting, not in the more public settings within which the councillor acts.

The degrees of flexibility available when it comes to councillor loyalty to the group is often open to interpretation within the group itself, with different meanings placed on notions of flexibility. In one focus group a Conservative district councillor stated: 'We have a policy where any member can get dispensation from the group to speak however they like on a ward issue.' To which one of his Conservative colleague replied: 'I didn't know that; I didn't get any dispensation, I was told to shut-up.' Which brought the retort from the first councillor 'but you did not ask for it and anyway it wasn't just your ward that was affected it was about the whole of our policy on leisure provision.'

In a focus group with Labour councillors on another authority the Labour district leader commented: 'Any member can say anything on a ward issue and they do not have to ask permission to say it. We are very flexible on ward matters.' After the focus group, not during it, a Labour councillor made a point of commenting privately: 'That was complete rubbish you know; I tried it and they came down on me like a ton of bricks. He [the leader] likes to say we can all speak as we want, but we can't.'

The reason for councillor loyalty to the group is only in part a reflection of the firmness (or flexibility) of a party (or group's) approach to group discipline, and the group's willingness to 'punish' any councillor who publicly dissents. It is clear that the loyalty councillors grant to the group of which they are a member is only in small part, a result of group disciplinary mechanisms and rules that say they must abide by group decisions, which all three parties produce. Although a certain amount of enforced loyalty through 'fear' of punishment appears to be present when it comes to group coherence, it is by no means the only source of councillor loyalty to the group. Loyalty to the party group arises at least as much from a councillor's own predispositions towards public unity as well as interpretations of what democracy means and how it is realised, alongside views about the role of the councillor, as well as political philosophy.

Councillors enter into a four-part 'contract of loyalty' with the party group of which he or she is a member, which binds the group and councillor closely together when it comes to the day-to-day conduct of politics. First, there exists an element of loyalty to the group that is born of a genuine fear of the consequences of public dissent and a feeling of intimidation, discomfort and an intense sense of unease at the unknown elements of the disciplinary processes and their outcomes. Councillors use the political discretion they have with a careful eye to the anticipated reactions of their group, alongside an understanding of how far it will tolerate public dissent and the nature of that dissent. Generally councillors are very reluctant to expose themselves to group discipline because of the uncertainty, personal disquiet and feeling of embarrassment, isolation and failure such processes would bring. As one Labour councillor commented: 'Look, I don't want to be disciplined by the group for much the same reasons as I don't want to be in a disciplinary situation at work, its just not a pleasant thing and you are highlighted as having done something wrong. Guilty before proven innocent if you like.'

A Conservative councillor added in the same vein: 'much like being cashiered from the regiment; a public disgrace, and not a pleasant experience I would imagine'.

Others see public conflicts with their own party group as a potential barrier to political promotion within the group or on the council, a fear which may be very real, or totally unfounded, depending on the group concerned. The story of one Conservative Borough councillor is worth repeating at length here.

> At the end of the day I felt I could not support [named scheme] and when a vote was taken. I, together with three of my fellow Conservative councillors, abstained and the vote was lost. All the rebels had to attend a special

meeting of the group and we were all asked individually why we had abstained and not voted with the group. We then had to wait outside while the group decided what punishment we were to receive. I felt like resigning there and then. After about three quarters of an hour we where called back in and told that on this occasion we would all be seen individually by the group leader and made to apologise. It was like being back at school and going to see the Headmaster. After that I did vote against the group but I always made sure that I gave notice.

The 'headmaster' analogy is one particular to Conservative councillors. It is as though acting against group decisions is a form of errant behaviour worthy only of a troublesome schoolchild. It would appear that the sanctions do not necessarily end there, depending on how strongly the group feel the recalcitrant members need to be taught a lesson. The Conservative councillor last quoted above continued:

> Later that year two Liberal councillors joined the Conservatives and we took control of the council from no overall control, we were already the largest party. It was decided that the group would take all the chairmanships and vice-chairmanships and every Conservative councillor except one, me, got a position. I shall no doubt again be having differing views to my party and although unpleasant at the time at the end of the day I shall have the knowledge that I did what I thought was right.

Discipline, then, can be both formal and informal, and is often more effective when councillors impose their own self-discipline when faced with acting against the group over what is seen as a local issue

Public dissent and disagreement with the group need not however always result in a block on promotion within the group or council. At his last full council meeting before the upcoming elections at which he had decided not to seek re-election, the author made the following observation to the meeting:

> Looking at the committee chairs sitting here I am reminded that the chair of leisure and recreation has before becoming chair had the group whip withdrawn; the chair of finance and deputy leader, before becoming chair, has also had the whip withdrawn; myself before becoming chair of planning and works has too had the whip withdrawn; even you [to the chair of the council], before taking up the chair of the council, has had the whip withdrawn. My advice to any newly elected councillors seeking promotion to a committee chair, can therefore only be: get the whip withdrawn as soon as you possibly can and you'll be a committee chair in no time.

These two examples indicate a slightly different attitude towards discipline between Labour and Conservative groups: Labour taking an attitude that can be summed up as 'doing the crime and doing the time' resulting in rehabilitation; the Conservatives more inclined to say 'we'll get you later'.

The second element of the 'contract of loyalty' involves a psychological element in which councillors feel predisposed to support their party colleagues, and to do so in public, particularly against an opposing party. Group loyalty is then often the result of general agreement on principles and policy and the existence of a shared set of political beliefs. Any public disagreement, even on a matter specific to the councillor's electoral area, is at best disloyal to the party's programme and ideology, and at worst a betrayal of both the group and the individual's own beliefs that sustain their membership of a party. Put simply, councillors just do not like going against their party group because they more often than not agree with it.

Public dissent raises the question of the councillor's relationship with an organisation that is a prominent part of their daily lives and challenges an individual's core value system. Thus, when the councillor finds his or herself at odds with the group on a specific issue, this must be balanced against the generality of issues on which the councillor is in harmony with his or her colleagues. The question for the councillor becomes one of deciding whether the matter causing disquiet is significantly powerful enough to override all those other factors that bind the group together. In most cases the answer will be that it is not.

Thirdly, the councillor's contract of loyalty might also contain a real contractual agreement and be seen as such by both the individual councillor and his or her party colleagues. Prospective Labour, Liberal Democrat and SNP candidates must agree to accept group standing orders before election.[40] No similar conditions yet exist for the prospective Conservative council candidate. The acceptance of candidacy, however, and election as a councillor implies an expectation of support for the party which makes public acts of rebellion seem disloyal, and this *implicit* contract may be no less real for Conservative councillors than conditions contained within the rules of other parties.[41]

Finally, a vital element of the contract of loyalty, is a predisposition amongst councillors towards mutual support amongst party colleagues. The group is seen by many councillors as a *team*, a tight-knit group of colleagues to whom the same attachment is given as to any organisation to which an individual may experience strong feelings of attachment and affinity. Councillors often explained this aspect of loyalty by reference to team sports, such as football, or to notions of family and kinship.

As one Labour councillor put it bluntly: 'I can have a go at the team I support when its doing badly but I will defend it against criticism from supporters of other teams. It's like that with the group, it's my side, and my team and I'll defend it.'

Thus, the group is to be protected against 'outsiders' or opponents and, as a consequence, any disagreements must not be publicly displayed, and that above all else and whether right or wrong the 'family' that is the group is to be supported even when internal disagreements exist. As one Conservative councillor commented, 'we all have our disagreements and spats, but I would always support my fellow Conservatives against the Socialists. Our very worst member is infinitely preferable to their very best.'

A Liberal Democrat councillor explained: 'Like being at home, you simply don't wash your dirty linen in public, all families fall out, or have skeletons in the cupboard but you keep it away from the outside world. Publicly, you play happy families don't you. Funny, because I spend as much time with my council colleagues as I do with my husband and children.'

The basis of the contract of loyalty that binds councillors together in public as coherent, unified and disciplined groups, then, is one of reciprocity and mutual support. The source of that reciprocity and mutuality is the experiences that arise from shared party membership and a predisposition towards public displays of unity. The factors that unite party groups are of a greater impact within the day-to-day business of local politics than those factors which can lead to discord and dissent within the group. That is not to say that discord and dissent is entirely absent from the conduct of any one group's affairs, or that groups will not experience some form of political factionalism at one time or another, or even over an extended period of time; it is to say, however, that those forces do not prevail over the intense desire held by councillors to avoid public displays of party dissent and disunity.

The party group in government and opposition

There is a real and powerful tension existing at the heart of local politics. It is the tension between, on the one hand, councillors assuming a governing role and mandate as a result of the local elections and the minority group or groups adopting the role of a political opposition and, on the other hand, communities, local civil society and citizens looking for responsive representation and the public articulation of views and opinions. The task of the councillor is to arbitrate between the demands of communities within the wards they represent and the broader concerns for the general well being and public good, but they do this through the political party. When the two sets of interests coincide, then so much the better, when they collide the councillor must balance the competing opinions and come down in favour of one section of interests or another. As councillors are elected from wards and divisions it could be expected that they would place the interests of those 'patches' above all else. The party group, however, will expect the councillor to take a stance based on the broad needs of council government, not the very specific needs arising from the ward. It is the impact of party that draws councillors into taking a governing perspective to their activities.

That councillors elected as candidates of a political party meet in private groups to facilitate governing an area, or acting as an opposition, is of no surprise. In the case of the majority group, its meetings are the place where council decisions are made, policy deliberated and set, information is disseminated to its membership, the council leadership questioned and challenged, potential political and policy problems identified and considered and voting strategies agreed. In many respects, meetings of the majority group resemble that of a *cabinet*, along Westminster lines, even before the Local Government Act 2000 introduced cabinets proper into local government. The meetings of the minority group or groups also have a clear and distinct role as a theatre for opposition to the ruling administration. Minority group meetings will assess political tactics, develop responses to proposals of the majority group, develop an alternative political platform to offer the electorate, devise a strategy to ensure minority views are articulated in public and plan ways in which to hold the administration to account. Minority groups need to be flexible enough to recognise opportunities and to act on them when presented, respond quickly to political events, exploit majority weaknesses and present a high and effective profile to the electorate.

One particular opposition Conservative group leader devised a tactic to outflank the majority Labour group of his council on what he called the 'green left', but the tactic boiled down more to conservation issues than green politics. As he commented:

> Labour is development mad, they think it brings jobs and jobs bring Labour votes. They are desperate and give permission for all sorts of inappropriate development in all sorts of inappropriate places. So, we back residents' campaigns when the council approves yet another industrial development. When John Prescott said 'the green belt is a Labour achievement and we intend to build on It', he must have been thinking of this Labour group, they'd build on anything.

In another piece of interesting political volte-face by both Labour and Conservative groups, the Labour majority on a council in the north-west of England proposed selling a publicly owned zoo to the private sector. The opposition Conservative group campaigned for the zoo to stay in the public sector. Thus, the party groups on that council took a classic government and opposition approach to their business and the business of the council – irrespective of the broad direction of their own political philosophies.

To ensure that the group operates effectively, either as a governing machine, or opposition *bloc*, councillor loyalty to the decisions that flow from group meetings is necessary to enhance the party's political success within the council. That means there is little space for councillors to act in public to deliberate issues, to consider alternatives and to engage in cross-party working. Such action would offend against the principle of the group operating as a government or opposition within the council chamber. Even agreeing to free votes for councillors on certain issues have the potential to cause embarrassment to the ruling group.[42]

By acting as government and opposition the party group ensures that adherence to the party line becomes a necessity for practical political decision-making. Rees and Smith, show how Labour councillors in Barking maintained their unity as a group *inter alia* their consciousness of being the 'administration or government in Barking', a government in which all members shared 'to a greater or lesser extent'.[43] Councillors acting as government and opposition is a theme also noted and explored by Jones and Bulpitt.[44] The intensity of party politics is often increased when political divisions within and between parties are exposed, and political clashes remove the possibility of consensual approaches to even the most simple of issues. Indeed, a 'party intent on governing is bound to break a few eggs'.[45]

Yet, there are advantages to the notion of the group as a competing governing *bloc* of councillors.[46] The group meeting provides a private forum where councillors can speak unguarded, and is a place where political options can be considered amongst colleagues, without enraging public opinion. The governing approach provides certainty to the outcomes of most council meetings and ensures a consistency and direction to policy making, particularly where groups cohere around a platform or set of policy preferences – even a manifesto – which they seek to implement through the council. As a consequence the opposition minority group(s) is(are) encouraged to challenge, criticise and oppose the majority. Thus, the ruling group can be clearly seen as 'in power' or forming an administration and therefore responsible for council policy and actions. Thus, they can be held to account at an election and rewarded or punished for their stewardship of the council and its affairs.

Yet, such an approach in turn reinforces the need for secrecy and a group system, designed to exclude political opposition and public alike from policy and decision-making and thus distance the councillor from the represented. Moreover, the narrowing of political focus encouraged by the group system within a governing/opposition model draws councillors' loyalty toward the need for group cohesion and thus away from representing local interests. The party group then has a fine line to walk between the demands of the general well-being of the area and specific demands and needs of local communities. It is not entirely impossible for the individual councillor and the group, to do justice to both sets of demands. But, this depends very much on how sophisticated groups are in balancing the needs of particular communities with some vision of the general good. An exchange at a public meeting between local protestors and a senior councillor puts the need for sophistication and balance into perspective:

> Councillor: we have to take the difficult decisions people don't like and it's all too simple for people like [named residents protest leader] to take the easy way out. The council has to look after the entire area and this [named development] will regenerate our economy for the general well being, for everyone's benefit.

> Residents' protest leader: Well who are these people that are going to benefit? Show me them, where are they? I can take you to hundreds of individuals and families whose lives will be devastated by this development – what about them, don't they count. The council doesn't care about people just its own image.

Is local government simply about 'government' and the making of decisions, irrespective, and, indeed, despite, community opinion, or is it about representing those views by responding to them? The party group system in its rawest form responds to the needs of government and decision-making rather than to the representation of local opinion. As a Conservative councillor succinctly put it: 'The people can tell me what to do at the election, after that its up to me to get on with things'. In a more subtle and sophisticated form the group system can merge elements of participation with Burkean notions of representation and freedom for elected representatives to make decisions. The question remains, however: Is it easier for a minority opposition group than a majority group, to represent and respond to community opinion in the strictest sense? To answer this question the relationship between the dynamics of the group and the proximity of the group to power or the likelihood of power need to be explored.

The prospects and proximity of power

The holding of political power or the possibility of obtaining political power in the near future make little difference to the way in which the party group conducts its affairs and the politics of the council. Indeed, it is whether the group has traditionally taken a firm or relaxed approach to group discipline, rather than its proximity to power that influences group cohesion in public. Yet, the discipline of power, or the possibility of obtaining or regaining power at some future point, does focus the mind of the councillor on the consequences of public displays of dissent from a party group. Councillors strongly subscribe to the notion that a divided group looses elections.

In areas with prolonged one party domination, both Conservative and Labour councillors, when in the minority, display the same degrees of reluctance to dissent from the group in public as they would if in a majority. Liberal Democrats also become reluctant to publicly display disagreement within their ranks if it appears that capturing control of the council is a possibility. But, Liberal Democrats are more willing than Conservative and Labour councillors to tolerate open deliberation amongst members, if power is a distant or unobtainable prospect.

When experiencing long periods of council control and even with a large majority, a group, and its members, will still be reluctant to see dissent from group decisions played out in public. Whilst a more relaxed attitude towards genuine deliberation in public might be expected when the party's majority would be sufficient to ensure victory in any vote, councillors remain unwilling to act in opposition to their own group. Although, it is true to say that councillors are more willing in these circumstances to speak against the group – but certainly far less likely to vote against it. The speak–vote dichotomy is a real one.[47] But, in any circumstances the tendency is for councillors to continue to act in unified *blocs* in public. As one Labour councillor commented: 'Group policy is group policy; it doesn't matter if the majority is one or a hundred and it certainly doesn't matter if the group is in opposition either – group is Caesar.'

Councillors recently experiencing the loss of council control by their political group, particularly for the first time, indicate the impact on group solidarity of a fall from political power. A temporary 'blip' can occur in group solidarity as a result of the immediate shock of the changed political circumstances, especially after a long period of control. As the group seeks an explanation for its defeat, or to understand that it and its members are now required to act in a different way, group cohesion may suffer. Indeed, internal in-fighting amongst rival leadership contenders after an election defeat can further damage group cohesion. The group may even try to ignore the fact that it has lost power and act as though it was still in control. As a council officer reported: 'For weeks after the election the former leader was still coming into the office to see the chief executive; it was really hard for him to grasp that he just wasn't in charge any more.' A councillor serving on a council controlled by her party since 1974 and which lost power for the first time in 2003 to a Conservative–Liberal Democrat administration commented: 'it was a real shock, not only did we not expect to lose we just don't know how to respond to things. The group is taking a very long hard look at the way we operate to see what has to change.' But, the general pattern in such circumstances is that after settling down to the new position and, with the prospect of regaining control in the future, little difference occurs in the expectations of group loyalty, which are brought back into line. The long-term political behaviour for councillors remains that of cohesive party *blocs* facing each other.

Councillors in marginal authorities indicate that loss of power makes very little difference, if any, to the centrality of the group and its cohesion. The temporary problem of the group reasserting itself as a centre of councillor loyalty is less likely in councils that have a tradition of change in political control. A Conservative metropolitan borough councillor commented, 'The group's attitude toward discipline did not change and has not changed one bit from when we were in power; it is exactly the same whether in power or not.' This was supported by a second Conservative metropolitan borough councillor, 'This is a highly political council, whether we are in control or not that tends to concentrate the mind on winning, whether in power or not, if you see what I mean. We have held and lost power before and that will happen again, so the group must always be ready and united.'

The politics of the hung or balanced council often present the party group's use to majority or minority status, with new challenges and opportunities for a different approach to the conduct of the group.[48] A number of possibilities arise within a hung council for cohabitation between different parties: formal coalitions, although the word coalition is normally avoided; shared or joint holding of committee chairs, or under executive arrangements the sharing out of portfolios amongst parties; or a less coherent approach of taking each meeting in turn and deciding chairs at that point. The pressure on a group within the hung council, particularly at full council is, however, towards very rigid group cohesion and discipline. The first group to blink and allow members to act outside the decisions of the group will find itself unable to achieve much political success in a hung or balanced situation. The latter is certainly true if no arrangement to form an administration has been agreed between two or more groups and no accommodation reached about the conduct of council affairs – in this case group unity becomes all. As the former Labour leader of a county council explained her position forcefully:

> It was the first chance we had ever had to run the county and we needed the Liberal Democrats on board to do it. We took all the chairs and they had some vice-chairs. But the group had to stay absolutely solid and the Liberal Democrats and the Tories had to know that. I had to be able to go to the Liberal Democrat leader and say to him, my group will be doing this, can you deliver. He could only deliver if his group understood exactly what we were going to do and did the same. That way we could run an administration and keep the Tories out. Being hung, if anything, made group discipline even more vital than it normally is.

Proximity to control of the council and the holding of power makes little difference to the way groups, across the political spectrum, view the necessity of group cohesion and discipline. Yet, some groups do allow members to dissent in public and even to vote against the group. Others, however, treat the slightest deviation from the group line as a case for disciplinary action. Political culture, tradition, personalities and interpretations of democracy and representation, that are prevalent in particular areas, count for more when it comes to degrees of group cohesiveness than proximity to control and power.

Conclusion

When it comes to the organisation and activities of the political party group and the operation of the group system, the three main parties display remarkable similarities. These similarities arise from the shared experiences of councillors involved in local politics and democracy and they are what results in the party group becoming the *Leviathan* of local politics. We saw at the end of the last chapter that political parties in the world of local politics act as organisations for the mobilisation of political bias and view politics as the domain of the party, set within a highly complex and confrontational political environment. The political party group of councillors and its organisation and procedures, coupled with inter- and intra-party group dynamics, is another dimension to the political party locally and serves to broaden our conceptual understanding of party and its place and power in local politics. The party group represents the formalisation of the political party's hold on local power, or its position as an opposition *bloc*, within the representative institution that is the council and within its political decision-making processes. Yet, it is also an informal part of those institutions and processes, if a highly visible and readily recognised part. Moreover, it is a formal, constituent element of the national and local political party outside the council and as such acts as a bridge between the activities and dynamics of both council and party, feeding into each the interpretations of local democracy and representation held by the other. Thus, the group is a mechanism by which the flow of politics and political decision-making is facilitated, from party to council and back again.

That the party group is able to demand and receive the loyalty of its membership and that notions of party unity, cohesion and integrity in public are powerful concepts for the councillor in the day-to-day conduct of political affairs, serve to produce a high degree of rigidity to the boundaries between the parties. This rigidity is maintained and promoted to signal the existence of clear political identities to the electorate, but in turn often results in a forced, artificial and highly theatrical display of political uniformity in the conduct of local politics and the politics of the council chamber. Moreover, the party group holds a special place within local politics as the manifestation of the party's local electoral success and so the group is the outward manifestation of the party's electoral legitimacy.

As far as the party group and the wider party are concerned, however, political activity is axiomatically party political activity and related to some form of electoral legitimacy. The group claims a mandate to govern an area as a result of the local election and claims public support for its manifesto or policy platform from the same source. Thus, the group and group system is a vital element of the permission political parties grant to themselves to govern a council and of the way in which they secure dominance of the local political terrain. Parties assume vicariously the legitimacy assumed by its councillors in governing an area, or in providing an opposition, to speak as the authoritative voice for the local community or communities. The binding together of party group and party is also vital to claims by political parties to provide local political leadership. It enables parties to dominate the construction of any notion of what does and does not constitute acceptable and legitimate local politics and what is or is not the business of the political processes. Thus, it is in the interest of the national parties to ensure the party group and wider party operates on the basis of a sound working relationship and a shared vision of local politics. It is this drawing together that ensures the dominance of local politics by the party is not threatened by other more participative approaches towards local politics.

Thus, we see the emergence of the third dimension of our conceptualisation of local party politics: the national dimension. It is here where we see that much binds our adversarial political parties together when it comes to approaches and interpretations of local politics, representation and democracy and the role of party within them. The national political parties have a series of expectations about the relationship between the councillor and the group, the organisation and role of the group and the playing out of local politics, which they communicate to their membership, their councillors and to the outside world. National political parties have very clear views about the conduct of local group activity and business and about the role of the group in the conduct of council affairs. Moreover, the parties are concerned to be able to regulate the shape, structure and form of local party groups to ensure the existence of clear political identities on any council and that the group sees itself as part of a wider political whole. That is the subject of the next chapter.

Notes

1 G. W. Jones and J. Stewart, 'Party Discipline through the Magnifying Glass', *Local Government Chronicle*, 30 October 1992, p. 15.

2 J. Gyford and M. James, *National Parties and Local Politics*, London: George Allen & Unwin, 1983, p. 7.

3 L. J. Sharpe, 'The Politics of Local Government in Greater London', *Public Administration*, 38 (2), summer 1960, pp. 157–172, pp. 170–171.

4 C. Copus,'Community, Party and the Crisis of Representation', in N. Rao (ed.), *Representation and Community in Western Democracies*, London: Macmillan, 2000, pp. 93–113.

5 D. Widdicombe, Committee of Inquiry into the Conduct of Local Authority Business (Widdicome Committee), *Research Vol. I, The Political Organisation of Local Authorities*, London: HMSO, 1986; K. Young and M. Davies, *The Politics of Local Government Since Widdicombe*, York: Joseph Rowntree Foundation, 1990; C. Game and S. Leach, *The Role of Political Parties in Local Democracy*, Commission for Local Democracy, Research Report No. 11, London, Municipal Journal Books, 1995.

6 J. Maud, Committee on the Management of Local Government (Maud Committee), *Research Vol. I, Report of the Committee*, London: HMSO, 1967, para. 24, p. 6, para. 33, p. 8.

7 Ibid., paras 376 and 377, pp. 110–111.

8 M. Harrison and A. Norton, Maud Committee, *Research Vol. V, Local Government Administration in England and Wales*, Chapter 5, 'Some Effects of the Presence or Absence of Party Politics on the Operation of Local Authorities', 1967, para. 27, p. 103. para. 37, pp. 105–106.

9 Maud Committee, *Research Vol. I*, para. 383, pp. 112–113.

10 P. Chamberlayne, 'The Politics of Participation: An Enquiry into Four London Boroughs 1968–74', *London Journal*, 4 (1), 1978, pp. 49–68.

11 Maud Committee, *Research Vol. I*, para. 383, p. 112.

12 Widdicombe Committee, *Research Vol. I*, chapter 2, 'The Patterns of Local Politics', London: HMSO, 1986. pp. 23–40.

13 Ibid., especially p. 25.

14 K. Young and M. Davis, *The Politics of Local Government since Widdicombe*, York: Joseph Rowntree Foundation, 1990, p. 61.

15 P. Saunders, *Urban Politics: A Sociological Interpretation*, London: Hutchinson, 1979, p. 221.

16 Young and Davis, *The Politics of Local Government*, pp. 43–50.

17 Ibid., tables 6–7, pp. 46–49.

18 C. Copus, 'The Councillor: Representing a Locality and the Party Group', *Local Governance*, 24 (3), Autumn 1998, pp. 215–224.

19 Ibid., pp. 215–224; C. Copus, 'The Attitudes of Councillors since Widdicombe: A Focus on Democratic Engagement', *Public Policy and Administration*, 14 (4), 1999, pp. 87–100; C. Copus, 'The Party Group: A Barrier to Democratic Renewal, *Local Government Studies* (special edition), 25 (4), winter 1999, pp. 77–98.

20 C. Copus, 'The Party Group, Model Standing Orders and a Disciplined Approach to Representation', *Local Government Studies*, 25 (1), spring 1999, pp. 17–34.

21 DETR *Modernising Local Government: Local Democracy and Community Leadership*, 1998.

22 DETR, *Modern Local Government: In Touch with the People*, 1998, para. 3.4, p. 25.

23 Commission for Local Democracy, Final Report, *Taking Charge: The Rebirth Of Local Democracy*, Municipal Journal Books, 1995.

24 DETR, The Local Government Act 2000, *New Council Constitutions: Guidance Pack*, 2001, para. 3.45.

25 P. Haynes, *An Islington Councillor: 1971–1992*, London: Haynes, 1994, pp. 84–87.

26 J. Bulpitt, *Party Politics in English Local Government*, London: Longman, 1967, pp. 99–103, 120–121.

27 J. Gyford, *The Politics of Local Socialism*, London: George Allen & Unwin, 1985, S. Lansley, S. Goss and C. Wolmar, *The Rise and Fall of the Municipal Left*, Basingstoke: Macmillan, 1989, H. Cutler, *The Cutler Files*, London: Weidenfeld & Nicolson, 1982.

28 *Guardian*, Thursday, 23 May, Thursday, 30 May, Friday, 2 August 1996.

29 J. Stewart, *The Nature of British Local Government*, Basingstoke: Macmillan, 2000, pp. 137–138.

30 K. Young and P. Garside, *Metropolitan London: Politics and Urban Change 1837–1981*, London: Edward Arnold, 1982, p. 61.

31 E. P. Hennock, *Fit and Proper Persons: Ideal and Reality in Nineteenth-Century Urban Government*, London: Edward Arnold, 1973, pp. 97, 145 and 249.

32 F. Bealey, J. Blondel and W. P. McCann, *Constituency Politics: A Study of Newcastle-under-Lyme*, London: Faber & Faber, 1965, p. 372.

33 K. Young, *Local Politics and the Rise of Party: The London Municipal Society and the Conservative Intervention in Local Elections, 1894–1963*, Leicester: Leicester University Press, 1975; K. Young, 'Political Party Organisation', in G. Rhodes (ed.), *The New Government of London: The First Five Years*, London: Weidenfield & Nicolson, 1972, pp. 16–49; A. Saint, *Politics and the People of London: The London County Council 1889–1965*, London: Hambledon Press, 1989; R. V. Clements, *Local Notables and the City Council*, London: Macmillan, 1969; Hennock, *Fit and Proper Persons*.

34 J. Gyford, S. Leach and C. Game, *The Changing Politics of Local Government*, London: George Allen & Unwin, 1989, pp. 172–173.

35 W. E. Jackson, *Achievement: A Short History of the LCC*, London: Longmans, 1965, p. 53. A., Rees, and T. Smith, *Town Councillors: A Study of Barking*, London: The Acton Society Trust, 1964.

36 G. Stoker, *The Politics of Local Government*, Basingstoke: Macmillan, 1991, pp. 95–98.

37 C. Copus, 'Community, Party and the Crisis of Representation', in N. Rao (ed.), *Representation and Community in Western Democracies*, Basingstoke: MacMillan, 2000, pp. 93–113.

38 R. Butterworth,, 'Islington Borough Council: Some Characteristics of Single Party Rule', *Politics*, I, May 1966, pp. 21–31, particularly 25.

39 F. Bealey, J. Blondel and W. P. McCann, *Constituency Politics: A Study of Newcastle-under-Lyme*, London: Faber & Faber, 1965. D. Green, *Power and Party in an English City: An Account of Single-Party Rule*, London: George Allen & Unwin, 1981.

40 Labour Party, *Labour Group Model Standing Orders*, London, 2000, updated 2003; ALDC, *Model Standing Orders For Liberal Democrat Council Groups*, Hedden Bridge, 2000; Scottish National Party, *Model Standing Orders*, Edinburgh, 1998 (up-dated).

41 J. Dearlove, *The Politics of Policy in Local Government: The Making and Maintenance of Public Policy in the Royal Borough of Kensington and Chelsea*, London: Cambridge University Press, 1973.

42 H. V. Wiseman, 'The Working of Local Government in Leeds: Part I, Party Control of Council and Committees', *Public Administration*, 41 (1), spring 1963, pp. 51–69; H. V. Wiseman, 'The Working of Local Government in Leeds: Part II, More Party Conventions and Practices', *Public Administration*, 41 (2), summer 1963, pp. 137–155.

43 A. Rees and T. Smith, *Town Councillors: A Study of Barking*, London: The Acton Society Trust, 1964.

44 G. W. Jones, *Borough Politics: A Study of Wolverhampton Borough Council*

1888–1964, Basingstoke: Macmillan, 1969; J. Bulpitt *Party Politics in English Local Government*, London: Longmans, 1967.

45 M. Parkinson, *Liverpool on the Brink*, Policy Journals, 1985, p. 153.
46 C. Copus, *It's My Party: The Role of the Group in Executive Arrangements*, Local Government Association, Designing Governance, Issues in Modernisation Series, April 2001.
47 C. Copus, 'The Councillor and Party Group Loyalty', *Policy and Politics*, 27 (3), July, 1999, pp. 309–324.
48 S. Leach, and J. Stewart, *The Politics of Hung Authorities*, Basingstoke: Macmillan, 1992.

5

Local party groups and the national party

As we discovered in the preceding chapters, three elements of the group system identify it as a distinct component of both the structure and organisation of the political party and of any local authority: first, the secrecy of its activities as a closed and private *theatre of representation*; secondly, the expectation that councillors will be publicly loyal to the decisions made at group meetings; thirdly, that group meetings are restricted to those councillors comprising its membership, and to a limited number of members of the wider local party. The distinctiveness of the group and the importance of close co-operation between group and local party is recognised at the national level with parties making varying arrangements for attendance at group meetings by party members. Moreover, co-operation and consultation between groups and local parties is nationally encouraged to ensure a strong and positive working relationship between the party's councillors and its wider membership.

The three elements of secrecy, group loyalty and cohesion and restricted access to meetings serve to ensure that political party groups are fundamental to the conduct of council affairs, the quality of local representation and the health and vibrancy of local democracy within a particular territory. Yet, political party groups make two other distinctive and unique contributions to the political processes within the British unitary system of government. The first contribution is concerned with how local government, as a set of institutions, and local politics, as a series of processes and dynamics, enable the reflection of local difference and diversity when it comes to identifying local needs and responding to local concerns and priorities, what Wilson and Game refer to as the *government of difference or multiversity*.[1] Here party groups add certainty and familiarity to the political processes of local government which will look and feel the same, wherever they occur, irrespective of the parties in control, or, indeed, whether there are any parties at all.

The second contribution political party groups' make is to link the politics of the territory to national political concerns and interests. Conservative, Labour and Liberal Democrat groups are creatures of a national political organisation that take varying degrees of interest in the activities of party groups and make varying attempts to bring shape, form and consistency to their organisation and its activities. It would not be correct to say that the group is a conduit into the cabinet or shadow cabinet, or even that a council party group has any discernible and direct links to Westminster.[2] Yet, political party groups are an integral part of the national party machine, being its local manifestation as either a local *government* or *opposition*, irrespective of national position in Parliament. Party groups are a linkage between national and local party organisations and concerns and are, as a consequence, also a link between the low politics of the territory with the high politics of the centre.[3]

The relationship between council party groups and the national party are rather more complex and intriguing than mere membership by councillors of a national party may imply. In each of the three main parties there is a continuing tension and dynamic between the national party and party groups and their councillors. That dynamic plays itself out differently in the three parties where councillors place their own meanings on concepts of representation, democracy, politics and the very notion of party itself.

The chapter will explore the way in which the three main political parties deal with the dynamic between local party groups and the national party and also the differences and similarities between them. The first section will explore the nature of the linkages and relationships between national political parties and the local party group. The second, third and fourth sections will look at the distinct relationships between the national Labour, Liberal Democrat and Conservative organisations respectively. The fifth will explain the differences and similarities found between the parties and explore the impact of political affiliation and value systems on the dynamics of national party and local group relationships.

Party groups: a national party in a local setting

Each of the three main national political parties produce model *standing orders* or rules for party groups, the purpose of which is to ensure that party group cohesion rests on more than the voluntary acquiescence of group members to majority decisions. Game and Leach point out that the national parties forward these documents to party groups in 'the expectation or hope of compliance', rather than as instruments they must abide by.[4] Compliance, or for that matter a positive accep-tance of such models drafted nationally, is more a product of political affiliation and belief in the use of rules to regulate political behaviour than any expectation or hope generated by the national party. Equally, the councillor's national party will have its own expectations of the rela-tionships between group and councillor and of loyalty to the group. These in turn, shape how national political organisations interpret the party group as an entity within the political processes and how it sees its relationship with the national party.

When it comes to Labour groups there is no alternative but to operate under the model standing orders produced by the national party; however the Conservatives and Liberal Democrats approach this matter rather differently. In addition, the national parties display varying degrees of willingness to act when local party groups fail to meet expec-tations or hopes of compliance with model standing orders. Indeed, national parties may react differently depending on the individual council party group concerned when it comes to ensuring how model documents are adopted and implemented.

The purpose of any model standing orders or rules produced by the national parties is to bring consistency to the group system and to the organisation of councillors. They also provide a clear structure and set of procedures for internal political decision-making by the group. Thus, party groups across the country – of the same political affiliation – look, act and organise in a broadly similar fashion and thus act as a force for conformity and uniformity in the conduct of local politics. Moreover, across the party spectrum, groups are structured, conduct business and undertake political affairs in a broadly similar fashion and organisational context. Yet, there are also crucial differences between the parties in the way in which political affiliation has a bearing on the relationship between the councillor and party group of which he or she is a member.[5] Political affiliation also has an important bearing on the party group's expectations of its relationships with the wider local party, to the extent that Game and Leach concluded that the structure of local party net-works were a reflection of differences in political ideology and culture.[6] In addition, the dynamics of the relationship the central party forges with its party groups in the localities reflects the deeply felt history and traditions of the party concerned. It is as much a statement of party phi-losophy and belief as any policy pronouncements from the central party.

Political parties nationally are living histories of political experience and statements of past victories and defeats; these are echoed in the local party group. The group, of course, brings to the dynamic its own political experiences, and past victories and defeats; it may of course never have experienced victory, or defeat, depending on the electoral inertia of the area concerned. Moreover, the tenacity, resilience and ideological direction of a particular party group, or individual councillors mean that varying interpretations of the relationship between the national party and the local group will exist and change over time. All this means that the relationship between the central party and local party group is not as clear cut as the party's organisational structure chart would have one believe.

Despite the power of the central party as a rule-generating body, and its extensive resource base compared with the local party group, the relationship between the two facets of the party is not one of dominance of the centre and subservience of the local group. Councillors, establishing themselves into a party group, are the products of the electoral process; they may be the governing party, managing large and complex political problems and developing public policy solutions to them. In this position, or even holding the status of an electorally sanctified opposition, the group acquires a moral and political authority. Whilst this does not distance the group from the central party, such moral and political authority has a balancing effect on the dynamics that develop between the two.

The party group can carve out for itself some degree of autonomy from the central party, which enables it to develop a unique political role within its own territory. That autonomy can, however, be stretched to limits beyond which the central party is willing to tolerate. Much depends here on the public behaviour of the group concerned as well as any policy initiatives it may develop and implement. But for national parties diversity of form and procedure amongst groups is fraught with danger. As a consequence parties use national rules to ensure conformity of shape and purpose to political organisation and thus serve to remove diversity and uniqueness from the political system, a process in which party affiliated councillors are, by and large, happy to collaborate. It remains now to explore in some detail the similarities and differences between the main political parties, when it comes to the organisation and activities of the party group, and to consider what these tell us about the impact of political affiliation on the conduct of local politics.

The Labour Party and the political party group

Traditionally, the Labour Party has been the most rule driven of the three main parties when it comes to regulating the organisation and behaviour of the party group and councillors. The first model standing orders for Labour groups was produced by the national party in the 1930s, some 40 years before the Conservative Party produced a wholly voluntary *terms of reference* for its party groups to adopt, adapt or ignore. The Labour Party's model standing orders provide a prescriptive framework of rules that Labour groups are expected to adopt and abide by. The model can be amended to suit the political circumstances existing on a council, but only by securing a two-thirds majority at a special meeting of the group convened to consider the proposed changes; such amendments also require the approval of the party's National Executive Committee.

The Labour Party nationally and Labour groups locally, place great emphasis on the importance of standing orders as a means of ensuring coherent and disciplined action by Labour councillors, and for avoiding displays of public dissent and disunity. Moreover, the view is that political success, as either a local administration or opposition, is dependent on co-ordinated and consistent action and policy. In addition, there is a clear link made in model standing orders and the *Labour Councillors Handbook* between the actions and behaviour of Labour councillors and groups with the national electoral success of the party.[7] The lessons of the 1980s, when the behaviour of a small number of Labour controlled councils was employed by the national media and Conservative Party to damage Labour's general electoral performance, have been well and truly learnt.

Prior to the advent of the Local Government Act 2000, the Labour Party nationally produced a single version of its standing orders designed to fit all types of council and all the political circumstances with which Labour councillors could be confronted. The Local Government Act 2000, which introduced the 'political executive' to British council chambers in the form of directly elected mayors and indirectly elected council leaders, meant that the party's existing standing orders became redundant in the face of these new political decision-making arrangements.

As a result of the 2000 Act, the Labour Party now has four separate sets of Labour group model standing orders for councillors operating under each of the executive options available and the slimed-down committee system of alternative arrangements. Each of the model documents set out the expectations placed on Labour councillors individually and on groups collectively, when operating under specific political decision-making structures. Whilst the documents are broadly similar in content, style and tone, they also deal with the different structural arrangements of each decision-making option available under the legislation. Labour, leaves little, if anything, to chance.[8]

Despite the existence of different model standing order documents, the concerns of the party for public discipline, unity and cohesion and the avoidance of public argument and dissent, remain the same. Ensuring common practice, organisation and behaviour amongst Labour groups across the country are key elements of the model standing orders and the documents focus on how such uniformity is to be achieved. In each of the documents Labour councillors must agree in writing to abide by the group standing orders and become members of the Association of Labour Councillors, keeping their subscription payments to the ALC up to date. The documents also set out the group officers required and the procedure by which they are to be elected. In addition, the process for nominations for civic offices and appointments and for selecting membership of the executive and overview and scrutiny committees are clearly displayed. Finally, they make provision for observers from the local party to attend group meetings with the right to speak, but not to vote.

In a new departure for Labour Party model standing orders, councillors now have defined within a preamble to the document a specific requirement to engage with the wider local community; the Labour councillor 'shall be outward looking and active in local communities'. Prior to the most recent versions there was no recognition, within model standing orders, of a representative relationship between the Labour councillor and the community – only the recognition of the relationship between councillor and the party group. Labour, nationally, now expects its councillors to work in partnership with 'community groups, tenants and residents' associations, business groups, trade unions, the voluntary sector, ethnic minority groups, and all other relevant interests'. In addition, Labour acknowledges that, in fulfilling their representative duties, councillors may speak and ask questions in council on behalf of their constituents or some other community interest. If such questions conflict with group policy, however, the appropriate lead councillor must be consulted.

Representation is clearly seen by Labour nationally to have a wider focus than simply concentrating on the business of the council alone and this pushes notions of representation beyond those linked simply to the processes of governing and taking governing decisions through the party group. Representation is also about the councillor acting as a conduit for the views of the public and sections of the community into the policy-making processes. It also reflects, not surprisingly, the government's concerns with greater public participation and involvement in local government. Yet, there are tensions here which conflict with councillors' attitudes towards representation and the proper input of the councillor and citizen to the processes of political decision-making, where councillors clearly see themselves as the final arbiters of local affairs.[9]

The key concerns of Labour's model standing orders are: the determination of group policy; action taken by individual members; and the requirements for responding to a breach of group rules by a member. It is here that Labour councillors' knowledge of standing orders is widespread and encyclopaedic. The author has never encountered, in either his political experience or any research project, a single Labour councillor that does not know and understand the contents of standing orders when it comes to policy determination and group discipline.

The group itself is responsible for developing the policy strategy and political framework for the 'Labour agenda' on any council and it is expected to do this in conjunction with the local party, but to finally determine policy at an appropriate group meeting. The group then becomes responsible for pursuing the implementation of its policy agenda, or for presenting an alternative policy platform to the ruling group if in opposition. Loyalty to group decisions is underpinned by an emphasis on democratic procedures and a deliberative environment conducive to the maximisation of member participation. Group meetings are to be conducted in such a way as to promote maximum involvement and to avoid 'aggression, rancour, sexism and racism'. In other words, if all councillors can participate freely in private group meetings, none should need to publicly dissent from the result of that process. Thus, inclusivity and involvement are the key approaches to the work of the party group – which itself is an exclusive and exclusory organisation.

Discipline

Under the group standing orders Labour councillors are required not to 'speak or vote at meetings of full council' in opposition to group decisions. Moreover, they are precluded from acting on resolutions at any council meeting without prior group approval, but councillors can ask questions which do not conflict with group policy. Labour members must be clear that the intention of any question asked is not to criticise the group. The emphasis in normal circumstances is on group loyalty, and on the councillor seeking permission to dissent. All issues are whip issues. Change has however occurred in the way Labour nationally views the activities of its groups under new political management arrangements. The Labour chair of a scrutiny committee, for example, is able to speak and ask questions on matters relevant to their scrutiny work.

Again, if the tendency is that such action conflicts with group policy the lead member for that subject area must be consulted. A regular feature of past Labour model standing orders has been, and continues to be, the Labour councillors right, enshrined within standing orders, to abstain on 'conscience issues', such as religion or temperance. The matter, however, must first have been raised at a group meeting. Finally, Labour councillors are not whipped when acting in a quasi-judicial capacity, such as on licensing and planning matters, where councillors cannot fetter their discretion.

The introduction of overview and scrutiny committees into the work of the council has resulted in a second major change for Labour when it comes to the requirements of its model standing orders. The rules specifically mention that when acting in overview and scrutiny councillors shall not 'be subject to binding group decisions' and this represents a major departure for Labour and recognises that there needs to be some limits to group discipline. Moreover, it introduces an element to the political processes that Labour has long sought to avoid – the prospect of uncertainty of action by Labour councillors in the public domain. Yet, it would be impossible to carry out scrutiny without open public deliberation and investigation amongst councillors and the public. What is seen here, whilst a sea change in approach to group cohesion in public for the Labour Party, is more a reflection of the Labour government's intentions for scrutiny than a fundamental shift by Labour councillors in the way they approach council business. Yet, it must be seen for what it is: a relaxation of rigid group discipline in specific circumstances and an opening up of opportunities for Labour members to engage in genuine public debate. It represents a breath of fresh air for many council chambers. Some Labour groups, however, have experienced problems in the relaxation of the whip in overview and scrutiny. A Labour councillor from a particularly faction-ridden group reported that: 'Some are just using scrutiny for a second bite at the cherry on issues they lost at group; it's causing a lot of problems here for the leadership.' The Chief whip put it down more to 'teething problems with the new system' rather than a 'total break down in group discipline'. But, it is one thing to change the rules and procedures, quite another to change deeply ingrained approaches to politics and firmly held convictions about how politics should be conducted.

It is in cases where a Labour councillor is alleged to have breached group rules, or acted against group policy, that the model standing orders are very clear. In such circumstances the chief whip investigates the matter, reporting to the group and local party. As a result of any breach of rules a member may have the whip withdraw for up to six months or for an indefinite period. An appeal system operates on request from the member concerned. The effect of the withdrawal of the whip is to prevent the councillor from attending group meetings, but he or she is still bound by the outcome of meetings. A memorandum attached to the model standing orders does encourage flexibility when it comes to disciplinary issues; it is the choice of the group concerned as to how flexible they wish to be.

One Labour councillor who tried to use the memorandum's exhortation to flexibility, reported that he was informed at an appeal meeting to consider his indefinite group suspension (over a ward issue), that: 'It is standing orders that matter, not the memorandum, or national policy. The memorandum is not standing orders and it was standing orders you broke.' Thus, there is a danger that organisational procedures alone become ends in themselves.[10]

One potentially problematic issue for Labour groups is their relationship with a directly elected Labour mayor. The mayor will have been elected on his or her own platform, which in reality will have been developed with the local party and so reflect the party's manifesto for the council elections. Thus, group and mayor should experience few policy differences. But, local politics is rarely that simple and policy and personality clashes could well develop between a directly elected Labour mayor and the Labour group. A clash of policy between the mayor and Labour group would normally be thrashed out in a group meeting. If a dispute spills over into the public arena it is unlikely that disciplinary mechanisms will be able to resolve the issue. Labour may have to get use to experiencing something it has always attempted to avoid: a public difference of opinion between its elected representatives. The solution is simple: accept that the group and mayor have a different mandate and should act accordingly, view the relationship in the same way as that between councils in two-tier areas. The potential for mayors and their party groups to entertain public disagreement may add a new and exciting tension to council politics. But, it may also see the national party taking an even greater interest in internal disciplinary matters than at present.

It would be difficult to see how the Labour Party nationally could become even more involved in the business of its party groups under the party rules than it is already. Party rules give the National Executive Committee (NEC) power to suspend councillors from group membership and oversee councillors' adherence to group standing orders and wider party rules, and Labour nationally has shown little reticence in using these powers to discipline councillors. The seriousness with which the Labour Party investigates councillors and party groups indicates that what Labour councillors do in local government is seen by the Party, to reflect on its ability and rectitude to govern nationally. Labour is concerned that its councillors not only act as cohesive and disciplined groups but that they also act with probity and integrity. This is as true for Labour in power as in opposition.

The Labour Party uses its model standing orders to avoid public division and disagreement being displayed by Labour groups and to act as camouflage to the reality of group dynamics. In this, they are no different to their Conservative and Liberal Democrat counterparts. Yet, viewing party groups as adjuncts of the national party has the effect of dislodging public deliberation of important local issues into the privacy of the group meeting. Traditions of loyalty, discipline and cohesion in public are part of the Labour psychology of politics, coupled with a majoritarian interpretation of democracy. The majority decision is therefore binding, but it is a decision taken in private without the benefit of public debate.

The production and employment of model standing orders by the Labour Party are not conducted in some faint expectation that groups will go along with the rules, but requirements for both Labour councillors individually and collectively to organise and behave in a set fashion. Whilst flexibility is encouraged, it is often difficult to achieve, by councillors, groups and the national party. The loyalty of the Labour councillor is clearly to the Labour group, but, importantly, also to the national Labour Party and thus Labour locally govern, rather than represent.

The Liberal Democrats and the political party group

Model Standing Orders for Liberal Democrat Council Groups are published by the Association of Liberal Democrat Councillors and are an amalgam of best practice in group organisation and operation from across the country.[11] In the traditions of Liberal Democracy the model standing orders draw on the experiences within party groups, rather than impose solutions from above. That this document emanates from the Association of Liberal Democrat Councillors, rather than the national Liberal Democrats, reflects an organisational separation within the predecessor Liberal Party that occurred in 1978. The separation arose because local parties at the time felt the national party was indifferent to local government and to the struggles experienced by its then councillors.[12] Moreover, it reflected a belief prominent amongst Liberal activists at the time that the Liberal Party was unwilling or unable to learn nationally from the activities of Liberals in local politics.

Although not emanating from a national 'party' in the same way as Labour group model standing orders, the ALDC's model is a clear and positive attempt to construct a unified and cohesive approach to group activity and organisation. Moreover, it concerns itself with very similar areas of concern to that of the Labour Party: group organisation; regulating meetings of the group; the election and duties of group officers; party observers at group meetings; policy development; executive arrangements; and group discipline.

The ALDC does not produce separate versions of its standing orders to deal with the various executive and non-executive political decision-making arrangements under the 2000 Act. The standing orders are, however, written in such a way as to take account of the different political arrangements Liberal Democrat groups may face and sets out the relationship between Liberal Democrat executive members in relation to the group. It sets out the role of portfolio holders, or group spokespeople where the group is in control, and of course makes allowances for balanced councils or circumstances where the Liberal Democrats may be in control but do not hold all executive portfolios, or, where Liberal Democrats are in opposition with no executive portfolios.

The model contains a clearly stated expectation for Liberal Democrat councillors to support publicly all group decisions. Moreover, the standing orders note that despite the fact that some Liberal Democrats think 'there should not be group discipline and group lines, this is simply not the case'. The importance of loyalty and discipline for political success is emphasised.[13] Moreover, every candidate should agree to the standing orders at the time of approval, a similar condition to that exiting for Labour candidates. The Liberal Democrats do add an element of sophistication to notions of group loyalty by identifying three facets of the decision-making process that emanate from the group. Decisions can be *organisational*, that is issues concerning council patronage – who chairs what; *policy issues;* and, *ward*-based concerns. In all events, however, the Liberal Democrat councillor is expected to abide by group decisions. Liberal Democrat councillors unable to support the group should inform the group leader or whip in advance and refrain from speaking or voting against the group. When failing to attend group meetings, or to make their intentions known on matters before the group, they are expected to abide by its decisions, and indeed, not abstain from voting in public. Liberal Democrat model standing orders make none of the provisions about the freedom of the councillor from the dictate of the group that might be expected when speaking to Liberal Democrat councillors or when observing them in action.

The Liberal Democrat's approach to disciplinary procedure varies somewhat to that used by the Labour Party, although not as significantly as might be expected. If a Liberal Democrat councillor breaches standing orders, brings the party into disrepute or is accused of serious misconduct, the group leadership, including the whip, meet with the member to discuss the matter and report to the group their findings. The following results may flow from the group meeting that considers the report: find no fault, issue a verbal warning, or issue a written warning. A simple majority is required for any of these recommendations to come into play.

If either type of warning has been issued in the last four years, or the matter is so serious as to warrant special consideration, officers of the group and the local party executive, and a party member from the councillor's ward must meet to consider the matter. Witnesses and representations are to be heard and a report produced for the group. In addition to issuing warnings of one sort or another, the group may require a written contract of behaviour to be agreed between the councillor and the group: or the councillor may be suspended from the group for up to one year.

If the matter is so serious, or the councillor persistently acts in a manner 'seriously in conflict' with group aims, or in breach of the rules, councillors can be permanently excluded from the group, on a two-thirds majority vote. A stark contrast between the approach of the Liberal Democrat and Labour Parties to the issue of discipline is indicated by this two-thirds requirement, Labour members can be subjected to the withdrawal of the whip on a simple majority.

The model standing orders produced by the ALDC somewhat conflict with the Liberal Democrats' popular image as community politicians and can compromise councillors when involved in community politics by its requirements for group loyalty. There is a rule-generated tension for the Liberal Democrat councillor between the demands of group cohesion and unity and the Liberal Democrat's national commitment to community politics. Liberal Democrats do recognise the tension between local representational concerns stemming from particular wards and issues of group policy and discipline. Indeed, all Liberal Democrat councillors are expected to keep in constant communication with the community through the production of regular *Focus* leaflets. Pressure of political, community and council workload notwithstanding, *Focus* newsletters are a vital part of the Liberal Democrats' community politics armoury. As Ballard noted in a warning to all Liberal Democrat councillors and groups: 'Practically everywhere, the more councillors you get the slower the focus leaflets go out and the fewer campaigns! Reverse the trend and retain your seats.'[14]

Yet, despite the freedom from the group required by any councillor conducting community politics if he or she is to be a genuine representative of community opinion, the expectations that are placed on Liberal Democrat councillors in model standing orders are similar in tone, and to a large extent content, to those that exist for the Labour councillor. Both parties, for example, require the group to be informed by the councillor of any act which may conflict with a group decision. The parties also have similar provisions for dealing with matters of 'conscience', but the expectation on both the Labour and Liberal Democrat councillor is of group loyalty and disciplined coherent action in public. The expectation on the councillor in conflict with the group is also clear: they neither speak, nor vote, against the group in any public place. Indeed, Liberal Democrats have shown themselves willing to adopt the group system, irrespective of the size of the group concerned. Stoker and Lowndes noted in their study of a Tower Hamlets neighbourhood, that Globe Town's Liberal Democrats 'found it necessary to maintain group discipline through pre-meetings prior to committees'. The Globe Town area committee consisted at the time of only five members, four Liberal Democrats and one Labour.[15]

Whilst model standing orders enable Liberal Democrat groups to discipline their members and have set in place a series of procedures that are employed in disciplinary cases, the question remains whether Liberal Democrat groups in practice act on the expectations of group loyalty, so explicit in standing orders. It is here that a striking difference emerges with the normal practice of Labour groups and councillors when it comes to discipline. Despite exhortations contained within the ALDC's model standing orders that group loyalty is not inimical to the Liberal Democrats, the reality is somewhat different. Liberal Democrat groups are generally reluctant to have recourse to formal disciplinary procedures and many do see agreed group lines and whipping as restricting the councillors freedom of speech and action.

Some Liberal Democrat councillors are even blissfully unaware that a model standing orders document has been produced by the ALDC, a Liberal Democrat county councillor commented: 'No sorry, you're getting confused we don't have anything like that, I've not seen any model standing orders, that's not how we do things.' Interviews uncovered that such a response was not uncommon from Liberal Democrat councillors to the revelation that the ALDC have produced a set of standing orders for them to employ in their political and council affairs. Further, some Liberal Democrat councillors have doubted their group's ability to discipline its membership, or even to want to do so. One Liberal Democrat Borough councillor commented when she was asked about the withdrawal of the whip: 'Er, I don't think we can do that can we? That's more Labour than us isn't it?'

However, some Liberal Democrat groups across the country have shown themselves as willing as any Labour group to run a tightly disciplined and publicly cohesive party group. A Liberal Democrat portfolio holder spoke in these terms about his party group:

> We have to keep the group together and our councillors need to support group decisions both in what they say and how they vote. If some members have problems with decisions the place to deal with that is in a group meeting, we can normally come to some accommodation. But, if we can't, then I expect all Liberal Democrats here to go along with the group.

Another Liberal Democrat councillor, this time a county councillor in an opposition group said: 'The group has to pull together in public. We should not have to go a far as disciplining people, that's all a bit silly, but members need to know what's expected of them when it comes to being in the Liberal Democrat group and to act accordingly.'

Nationally the Liberal Democrats have shown themselves willing to take action against councillors in a similar fashion to the Labour Party when it comes to party and councillor integrity. A Party inquiry in 1993 into the conduct of Liberal Democrats in Tower Hamlets considered, amongst other things, allegations of the publication of 'racist' election literature. The inquiry identified evidence since 1990 of Party awareness of, but inaction over, problems in Tower Hamlets. Moreover, it concluded that no effective, concerted action had been taken to resolve the problems and that there had also been a lack of party guidance and firm action in the situation.[16] The Liberal Democrat inquiry team, including an independent member nominated by the Commission for Racial Equality, criticised activities seen to have brought the party into disrepute and councillors it felt had 'failed to co-operate' with the inquiry. It recommended the party membership of those concerned should be revoked and appropriate disciplinary action to be taken against the councillors that had failed to co-operate with the inquiry. Whilst finding no evidence of any action based on 'racial prejudice' it made pointed reference to 'misguided populism' and a belief that ends justified means. Importantly for local Liberal Democrat campaigners, the report defined community politics as an 'ideology' and not simply as an election-winning technique or tool. Thus, confronting how many Liberal Democrat Focus Teams had previously used community politics, the report attempted to bring community politics back to its original position of using power with and alongside local communities, rather than just to win seats.

The production of model standing orders by the ALDC provides Liberal Democrat groups with a recognisable and consistent form, shape and set of procedures by which they can conduct their activities and local politics. Moreover, Liberal Democrat groups have a rule-granted power to expect and receive the public discipline and loyalty of their members. That this may generate a tension between the organisation and running of a Liberal Democrat group, and some Liberal Democrat councillors' interpretations of liberal democracy, is a reality with which many groups are struggling. The resolution of that struggle comes with the careful use, rather than over use, of disciplinary procedures, alongside attempts to resolve disputes by compromise and debate. In addition, there is a greater willingness amongst Liberal Democrat groups than Labour groups to tolerate public dissent and debate, yet just as much concern to avoid it.

Finally, it must be stressed that for both the parties model standing orders are as much about ensuring the smooth running of the group and successful political action, as it is about restraining councillors' discretion. Too much emphasis placed on discipline by groups undermines the organisational cohesiveness of the group and damages its potential for success by restricting political action. Yet, by adopting a rule-driven approach to group organisation, Liberal Democrats make it possible to ensure a clear, separate and distinct political identity, whatever the political circumstances that may face a party group. Ensuring this alone, in the circumstances many Liberal Democrat groups still find themselves, is an achievement in itself.

The final word on Liberal Democrat standing orders goes to a long-standing councillor who knew of their existence but denied the need for them and commented:

> The ALDC produces standing orders based on its own experience of dealing with northern Labour Party groups and they are a reaction to the political circumstances the people that put them together have had. We haven't had those experiences so we don't need the standing orders – thank you very much.

The Conservative Party and the political party group

The Conservative Party nationally has long been faced with a unique problem when it comes to shaping the relationship between the national party and council party groups. The problem experienced by the Conservatives is for the national party's need for a clearly identifiable Conservative voice and form in local government to be made compatible with the often fiercely minded independence of Conservative councillors from interference by a central party organisation. As Young noted, the task of those seeking to forge a united Conservative voice locally is to recognise the ordinary Conservative's 'values of localism . . . emotive symbolism of the values of the smaller place, fear of strong central institutions, and a distaste for the presence of nationally orientated and controlled parties in local affairs'. In addition, they must overcome the view that Conservative leaders have colluded in the 'subordination of local government to central authority through the medium of party'.[17]

Managing the tension between Conservative visions of localism and local councillor freedom of action, and the role of a national party, which requires the existence of cohesive and recognisable Conservative groups, involves a political balancing act not required of the Labour Party or Liberal Democrats. The latter see strong central and local institutions in a very different light to the Conservatives, that is, as agents for empowering the locality and local politics, rather than dominating and subjugating them to national pressures. Conservative political antecedents make it difficult for the Conservative Party nationally to attempt any kind of co-ordination of party group organisation and for some considerable time the localist view has held sway in the relationship between the local and central party. Until very recently, the last serious attempt by Conservative Central Office to balance the philosophical rejection of central control and party interference with the need to promote a cohesive and recognisable form to Conservative groups came in 1977. The publication of a *model terms of reference* for Conservative councils groups, as a guide to organisation and the conduct of council business, was still a victory for localism, as adopting its provisions was advisory not compulsory. Conservative groups did adopt, adapt and ignore its contents. The 'terms of reference' provided the more ideologically inclined Conservative with a framework in which to conduct council affairs and with a tool to encourage more localist inclined Conservative councillors to pursue clearly recognisable party policy and objectives.[18]

Yet, the existence of a model terms of reference for Conservative groups produced by the national party, was not an effective tool for central party intervention into the activities of Conservative groups. Conservative group organisation remained, as it was, very much a product of local circumstances and political traditions, handed down, developed and evolved, rather than the creation of the national party. The existence of the model terms of reference since 1977, however, meant that it was often incorporated, in part or in whole, and over time, into the terms of reference, rules and procedures of many Conservative groups. Yet, such adoption is just as likely to have been accidental or unintentional as it was a ready acceptance of the role of the national party in structuring group organisation and activity. The terminological difference, terms of reference, as opposed to Liberal Democrat and Labour use of standing orders, implies a difference of emphasis in the way rules are constructed and applied to regulate the relationship between the councillor and the group. In much the same way as Liberal Democrat councillors are not always aware of the existence of model standing orders produced by the ALDC, Conservative councillors were often blissfully unaware of the existence of the model terms of reference. Or, if they were, it was seen as a purely voluntary document, which they could accept or reject.

Circumstances have changed for the Conservative Party; today the Party nationally clearly intends for Conservative groups across the country to adopt a national standard package of rules and procedures and operate within a nationally approved framework when it comes to council politics. The national Conservative Party has undertaken an extensive consultation exercise with its councillors on a new document entitled 'Rules of Conservative Party Groups on Local Authorities'. After the 1997 and 2001 general election defeats the party adopted a new national constitution and organisational structure in an attempt to revitalise its political base and restructure the party within a clear and distinct framework. Yet, the business of Conservative Party groups remained outside the remit of even that new constitution, which was a testament to the ability of Conservative groups to carve out an independent existence from the national party, but it is a situation the national party wants to rectify by bringing groups firmly and squarely within the remit of that constitution.

The saga of how the Conservative Party has approached the delicate manoeuvre of securing agreement from its groups to a nationally developed set of rules and procedures indicates the continual tension at the heart of the Conservative Party. Council groups, by and large, reject the notion that they are subservient units of the national party, and can and should be organised on a nationally recognised basis. Whilst some Conservative councillors see the benefits of integrating the party group into the national party as providing a national focus and a distinct Conservative voice in local affairs, others remain to be convinced that such a national (or as one Conservative councillor commented, *nation-alised*) set of arrangements is necessary. Many view national interference in group organisation as not just unnecessary but as an anathema to deeply held political beliefs about local independence; linked of course, as these notions are, to councillors acting as members of a national polit-ical party.

The process of obtaining agreement between national party and local groups to new model standing orders has been continuing, in one form or another, since 1997. It has generated opposition amongst many Conservative councillors, not only unhappy at certain provisions within the new rules, but also concerned at the very nature of a document that gives the national party oversight and involvement in local party group business. As one Conservative councillor said of the process: 'I am not concerned about how extensive or responsive the consultation is; I'm concerned it's taking place at all. We run our group here as we think fit and should not be dictated to by the Party in London.' Another Conservative councillor took a slightly different view, she explained:

> There are some issues, shall we say, with some of the provisions of the con-sultation document, and we are ready to fight London over these; they will not receive a ready agreement from us unless certain issues are resolved. Our group does agree, however, that there needs to be stronger guidance and direction from Central Office in the way Conservative groups operate. It is very important we have direction in how to deal with these new exec-utives the Government have forced upon us.

At the moment the political circumstances may not be ripe for Central Office to seek greater direction and control over its party groups. Two consecutive and convincing general election defeats and a continuous internal tension concerning the leadership of the party do not enamour localist sentiment to national dictate. The party is in better shape locally than nationally, winning at the 2003 local elections around 650 extra seats and control of an additional 30 councils to become the largest party in local government. Moreover, as with Labour during the 1980s, Conservative councillors are locally experiencing political control, power and leadership, unlike their national counterparts. Yet, for exactly the same reasons, some party groups and Conservative councillors are surprisingly receptive to exhortations, emanating from the national party, to party unity and cohesion at the local level. Guidance, direction and even rules, which signal a clear and recognisable Conservative presence, and or control at the local level, could pay dividends in Parliamentary elections. The localist view may be voluntarily willing to subordinate itself to the need to return to power at the national level and so regain the role it sees for itself as the natural party of government.

The recent consultation by Central Office represents a genuine attempt to reverse consistent localist victory over national party requirements when it comes to the local political arena, and more specifically to council politics. It is not surprising that the relationship between the local and the national in Conservative politics has been constantly updated and revisited. The party has had to construct a carefully negotiated settlement that reflects local fear of centralised power with recognition of the need to yield some local freedom to export Conservative values nationally. In addition, relationships between the central party and party groups have needed to reflect tradition and custom and practice at the local level, yet draw it in to some national focus on local politics and government. It simply will not do, in the conduct of Conservative politics, to impose a national settlement on the organisation of Conservative Party groups and the role they play in local politics.

The party nationally has long wished to establish a route that enables it to intervene in inter-group disputes, to be able to provide a binding interpretation of group rules and to prevent occasions where Conservative groups split in two to operate as separate groups, or for some Conservative councillors to form alliances with Independent councillors against former party colleagues. Moreover, the national party has long wanted to ensure that groups are not run locally in a way that would be contrary to the party's national interests. Yet, they must still recognise and cater for the fiercely independent attitude of many Conservative councillors that dislike overpowering notions of the role of party. The central party, however, has allies in the campaign to provide a national stamp on the conduct of party groups amongst the more ideologically and politically intense Conservative councillors, a fast-growing phenomenon since the 1980s.

There is a factor that has been at the heart of the relationship between the national Conservative Party and local groups, that is in stark contrast to the approach taken by the Labour Party: voluntarism. Whether party groups should be able to voluntarily accept or reject national rules, or parts of them, or whether they should have them forced upon them, in part or in whole, remains central to the development of a cohesive Conservative voice at the local level. If the national party is able to secure the agreement from its membership that group rules will be mandatory and are to be employed by all party groups, the centre would have won its battle over the forces of localism in Conservative politics. Conservative councillors would finally have accepted nationally what they have long accepted locally: coherent and regularised party organisation is essential to political identity and success for parties and party people.

So, what are the Conservative model rules attempting to achieve in the organisation, conduct and activities of Conservative Party groups? They are attempting to provide a set of rules for procedure, form and group discipline that are recognised, accepted and acted upon by councillors, with little if any question or doubt as to their voracity, purpose and legitimacy. What is striking when exploring the draft rules that the party are currently consulting over, is the similarity of content, purpose and concern they have with the model standing orders produced by both Labour and the Liberal Democrats.

The model is concerned with defining a Conservative councillor as someone elected as an authorised party candidate, or someone that, whilst standing as a candidate for another party or independent, has been accepted into the membership of the Conservative group by a vote of the group. Councillors are expected to maintain membership of the Conservative Councillors' Association. In a provision similar to the Labour Party and Liberal Democrats, Conservative councillors will in the future be required to sign up to an agreement to abide by group rules before election.[19]

The model rules set out the officers of the group, and the way in which they shall be elected at a group annual general meeting. Whilst members of the group can hold more than one post at a time they are prevented from jointly holding those of group leader and deputy leader and group leader and chief whip. The model rules also carefully and clearly set out the duties of the group leader, deputy leader, secretary and chief whip. They also provide for a motion of no confidence to render any of the offices vacant if supported by not less than half of any group's total membership; the vacant post being filled at the next group meeting. The rules provide for the group to decide upon the holders of positions of group spokesmen, cabinet or shadow cabinet members, chairs of scrutiny committees and ceremonial positions. The holders of these posts can either be appointed by the group leader or elected by the group – depending on which provision of the new rules the group adopts. So groups that are used to strong, almost autonomous group leadership can continue that tradition if they wish – or if the leadership tells them to.

The appointment of councillors to executives or chairs of scrutiny are the only recognition the new rules provide to the executive arrangements introduced by the 2000 Act. Conservative councillors must not take part in a multi-party executive without having first received the approval of a group meeting. The existence of a directly elected mayor as the political executive of a council is dealt with in a proposed amendment to the draft rules on which the party is consulting. It provides groups in such circumstances with the ability to apply to the Board of the party (its new managing body) for a variation of the mandatory rules, thus maintaining the tradition that local circumstances can still shine through in the way Conservative groups organise themselves and conduct business, at least in some limited circumstances.

The draft model rules set out the way in which group meetings are to be conducted and how they are to deal with group business. Groups will meet before each full council meeting and hold other meetings as necessary. As with the other parties, non-councillor members of the Conservative Party can attend its meetings and speak, but not vote. The list of potential attendees is quite considerable: Association chairmen and agents, any Conservative MPs, Greater London Assembly members, Welsh Assembly Members, prospective Parliamentary candidates, or prospective Welsh Assembly candidates; relevant Area chairmen and the Area campaign director; and prospective council candidates. How members of any Conservative group, in many cases, respond to the attendance at their meetings of such a potentially large group of outsiders will be an interesting experience.

Another major departure from traditional Conservative practice in party group activity comes with the provisions concerning loyalty to group decisions and issues of discipline. The model rules expect all Conservative councillors to 'support decisions taken at group meetings on *all issues* [my italics] other than matters of conscience'. The councillor will be required to abide by group decisions in council and committee, other than scrutiny committees, or where the council is acting quasi-judicially. In a massive step to ensure group discipline the model rules go further than anything produced by the Labour Party in issuing a specific requirement for Conservative councillors not to speak against the group in the media or at any other public meeting. A massive and wholly surprising step this, and one which Labour has overlooked, but only because so many of its councillors operate under a self-imposed whip when it comes to the press and public meetings anyway – the rules do not have to tell them to abide by the group as councillors happily do that for themselves.

The availability and use of disciplinary mechanisms open to Conservative groups to employ against recalcitrant councillors, is set to be formalised and a short, sharp, shock applied to errant councillors, rather than the *liase faire* approach that has traditionally been open to Conservative groups. Indeed, Conservative *liase faire* in group management led one flabbergasted Labour councillor to report of a ruling Conservative councillors activities: 'He spoke at committee and at full council on more than one occasion, against what the Tories wanted to do, he actually stood up and did it. The Tories did nothing, just let him get away with it; they took no action at all. How can you run a council like that?'

The new draft rules for consultation provide for the group leader to investigate any initial complaints that a councillor has breached the rules or acted against the group, and to refer the matter to the group if a serious breach has occurred and disciplinary action is required. If the original complainant is unsatisfied with the outcome of the leader's investigations the matter may be raised by that member at a group meeting with a set of proposals for action. After consideration of the matter by the group, it can, on the support of two-thirds of the members present, but not less than half the total group membership, suspend a councillor from membership of the group for up to six months, or expel a member from the group. The two-thirds vote for disciplinary action exists with Liberal Democrats also, but not Labour groups. It is a safeguard against heavily factionalised groups, or groups riven by personality disputes, from using group rules to remove from group meetings opponents in another faction. A safeguard, which Labour would do well to consider for its own party groups.

The new draft model rules are far less reflective of the underlying political philosophy of Conservatism and ideals of independence emanating from the 'localism' of its local representatives, than past attempts at bringing national cohesion to local groups. Moreover, the party nationally draws less of a distinction between its councillors as elected representatives, and as local party members, than has hitherto been the case. The national party is concerned publicly with regulating local party groups, via some national model rules and organising councillors into cohesive groups to which loyalty is owed. Whilst this is not a new concern, the Conservatives are trying to move from the position of being the party with the loosest of impacts on the structure and functioning of the party group of the three main parties, to at least on a par with Labour. Yet, at the same time, running the show with as much voluntarism as the national party can tolerate and local party groups demand – a fine balancing act this one, and one that also reflects the tightrope the Liberal Democrats must walk in the approach to group public unity and discipline.

Whether the central party is able to minimise voluntarism in group organisation and behaviour, or whether councillors will be successful in fighting off, in part or in whole, central attempts to control local groups will indicate where the balance between centralism and localism lies within the Conservative Party. One thing is sure, however: if party groups acquiesce with, or are defeated by this present attempt to bring them into line with Labour and Liberal Democrats and to control the shape, form and activities of the group, the battle will be over for good. If, on the other hand, party groups beat off the attempt by the centre to direct and organise them and their political activity, the battle will be far from over.

The parties' approach to the group compared

The three main political parties produce model rules or standing orders as a mechanism by which to bring form, cohesion and a clear political identity to the activity and organisation of their party groups. These model documents provide a framework within which *blocs* of councillors, sharing a party allegiance, can conduct political business and are designed, not only to regulate group meetings, but to set-out a context for those meetings and, importantly, to regulate the relationship between group and councillor. They are a mechanism by which the party group can discipline its members and ensure public adherence to group decisions, which is preferable for the national parties to relying on councillors' voluntarily acquiescence to decisions with which they might have considerable political or moral conflict. It can be clearly seen that model standing orders suit the needs of a central party machine for well-behaved, well-organised, coherent, identifiable and politically effective *blocs* of councillors within each council. Thus, such documents can be seen as a way in which the national party puts its stamp on the conduct of council politics for a national political purpose, well beyond local politics alone.

These nationally produced models grant to diverse *blocs* of councillors across the country, but sharing a political affiliation, the certainty required when operating under conditions where internal disputes, factionalism or over powerful *kindreds* may exist, that may disrupt the otherwise smooth running of the council political party machine. In addition, any party group of any affiliation knows it is conducting its affairs, the affairs of the council and local politics generally, within its territorial space, in a similar fashion to colleagues elsewhere, thus binding them into a common political purpose and process. They are a way of empowering party groups when it comes to governing local diversity; councillors, wherever they are, or whatever party they represent, prefer certainty and consistency, over political chaos and confusion. These models provide them with the former and allow them to avoid the latter.

The issues covered by nationally produced rules for party groups, and the nature, tone, content and structure of them not only regulate group business and relationships between councillor and group, but also set the context for their own interpretation.[20] That interpretation will be based on political culture and tradition, attitudes towards democracy, representation and political decision-making more generally, and the way the individual councillor interprets the role and purpose of the office he or she holds. Whilst the model standing orders from the three main parties contain similarities and distinctions between them, they will be subject to differing interpretations and usage, depending on the political affiliation of the councillor concerned.

Table 5.1 sets out the key structures and procedural functions addressed by each party's standing orders and the similarities existing in content, across the party spectrum. As is clearly and starkly demonstrated, there is far greater common concern and shared approaches between the parties, in the issues dealt with by model rules, than differences between the parties. Standing orders are an important generator of party group loyalty, discipline and cohesion in public, but they are not the be all and end all of the story. Indeed, when it comes to the content of model rules and the organisation, behaviour, political activity and internal coherence of the party group, political affiliation is not a powerfully discriminating factor. As a result we must look elsewhere to understand the influence of the national party through model rules when exploring the differences in the way parties go about council politics, governing locally, engaging with the citizenry and undertaking political decision-making.

It is in the history, traditions and political beliefs of the party, taken alongside the tone of model rules, that some consideration can be given to how each party's documents encourage a firm, flexible or loose interpretation of the councillor–group relationship. Groups can interpret their standing orders in either a firm or flexible fashion; traditionally Labour groups have taken a firm, if not rigid approach to the employ-

Table 5.1 Structural and procedural concerns addressed in model
group standing orders

	Labour	Conservative	Lib Dem
Model standing orders/rules			
Purpose and aims of the group	✓	✓	✓
Loyalty clause	✓	✓	✓
Restrictions on councillors' action	✓	✓	✓
Disciplinary procedure	✓	✓	✓
Sanctions for breach of group rules/decisions	✓	✓	✓
Election of group officers	✓	✓	✓
Role of whips	✓	✓	✓
Role of other group officers	✓	✓	✓
Meeting frequency	✓	✓	✓
Conduct of group meetings	✓	✓	✓
Ward role	✓	✗	✓
Communication with the electorate	✓	✗	✓
Conscience clause	✓	✓	✓
Party observers	✓	✓	✓
Executive and scrutiny arrangements	✓	✓	✓
Executive controlled by another party	✓	✓	✓
Confidentiality clause	✓	✓	✗
Ethics and probity (standards of behaviour)	✓	✓	✓

ment of standing orders. However, Conservative groups have been
rather more flexible in interpreting their rules, whilst Liberal Democrats
have been considered to take what can only be described as a very loose,
even caviller approach, to the employment of group rules.

Yet, within such an explanation of interpretation of the role and
flexibility in the implementation and use of standing orders, there is
plenty of room for deviation by groups from their assessed approach.
Flexibly inclined Labour groups and firm Liberal Democrat and
Conservative groups do exist, operating at variance with the norm for
their party. There is by no means an exclusive approach taken by any of
the parties when it comes to the use of model rules.[21] Indeed, any one
party group's usage of its rules will vary as the group's personnel
changes with an influx of new members and an exodus of longer standing councillors. Moreover, some groups will have amongst its membership those more willing to use structure and procedure, rather than
deliberation and argument, to win political battles. Again, not a tendency that is the sole property of any one party – knowledge of the rules
is power for any involved in local politics.

It is because councillors within the three main parties see the group as a legitimate theatre in which to conduct representation, make political decisions and bind their colleagues to a set course of action in public, that model rules, produced by national parties, are accepted and employed. Until, of course, a time occurs when the employment of such rules becomes inconvenient, in which case a more flexible usage may be developed; alternatively a firmer approach can be taken should the needs of political power and group control dictate.

The dynamic between national party rules for the group and the group's willingness to accept and employ them, develops simply because councillors from the three main parties view the group and group system as an integral part of the processes and conduct of local politics. As the group is the natural habitat of the councillor, rules and structure provide a way of ordering the affairs of a closed and private, yet powerfully dominant facet of the local political elite. Or, for those of a more pluralist theoretical approach, the group is but one of many groupings competing for political space and influence, but a powerful one that has access to resources beyond the norm of the community. Whichever theoretical framework one adopts, the party group is a rule bound and driven political organisation. It is able to use its rules to act in such a way as to change the landscape of the local political territory, or act as an organisation dedicated to maintaining the political status quo within the local polity. At this point how model rules for groups, produced by national parties, relate to the government's agenda to modernise local political decision-making is worthy of brief consideration.

Political modernisation

The white paper *Modern Local Government: In Touch with the People* sets out a strategy to enhance the accountability and transparency of local political processes.[22] A clear identification of elected executive responsibility, separated from a body of councillors with a wider representative and scrutiny function, is a major challenge to the way that party groups do business. Whilst each of the three main parties model standing orders make varying reference to these new arrangements, the traditional group values enshrined in those standing orders – secrecy, private debate and public unity – are threatened by proposals to open up political decision-making to the public view.

It is the operation of overview and scrutiny committees that poses the greatest challenge to the traditional drafting and employment of group standing orders. Councillors acting in overview and scrutiny committees are charged with holding new council executives publicly to account. The process may place councillors in the position of critically questioning and challenging colleagues from their own party, and doing so in public. It may call for councillors to act in public in such a way as to contradict or even oppose private group decisions. Whilst new standing orders from the three parties have catered for this eventuality, the culture of local politics has not yet transformed sufficiently for such open debate between party colleagues to become a reality.[23] Doubtless party groups will want to maintain private debate and decision-making, and public unity, when holding an executive to account, or acting as an executive giving political lead to the authority.

New political management models weigh the public cohesion of the party group against open deliberation and decision-making. To prevent the party group using the rules as a barrier to a more open, deliberative and inclusive political culture, political parties must further adapt group standing orders to create the conditions for effective scrutiny to emerge.[24] What is now required of the three parties is an even greater sensitivity to and admission about the way in which the group can and does employ standing orders to stifle public debate and to dilute the probing of difficult and politically contentious issues.

It is not sufficient to rely on the group to act flexibly or to interpret standing orders in a generous fashion. Indeed, even an explicit recognition within group rules that overview and scrutiny should operate without a whip needs to be underpinned by enabling councillors to act in any forum in scrutiny mode, rather than just in a scrutiny event. Councillors will no doubt wish to pursue lines of inquiry opened up in scrutiny at full council; as the three parties standing orders currently exist, this would be a perilous passtime. By careful and judicious drafting of model standing orders, these documents can become part of the dynamic of political change and progress and help improve the health and quality of local democracy and politics, or by dint of drafting and interpretation, they can act as a barrier to public engagement and deliberation.

Conclusion

The commonplace adoption by candidates and councillors of a party label clearly links locality with a national party. Thus, what the party group does locally is important to the national party and as a result national parties attempt, to one degree or another, to direct the organisation and activities of their party groups. Model standing orders give both form, and continuity of action, to council groups but they are insufficient to enable national parties to control all their activities. Where they prove insufficient to protect national party integrity, because they do not provide the national party with direct control over the actions of individual councillors or groups, then other national party rules and procedures come into play, or the rules will be changed. Standing orders in turn, provide party groups with the ability to discipline and direct their members in their representative activities and local politics more generally. Thus, such rules and regulations mean that councillors come to be seen more and more as representatives of the group, rather than the communities from which they were elected. In turn, this indicates a lack of sophistication and subtlety in those models and moreover, they can become barriers to responsive, open and deliberative local politics.

When exploring the model standing orders produced by the national parties a striking thought occurs as a result of the remarkable similarity between them. One could be forgiven for thinking that there was some continual communication between the local government offices of the Labour and Conservative parties and the ALDC, and that copies of drafts had been exchanged between the parties and commented upon. Surely not, as this would undermine the image of self-confident political institutions correct on every issue, with no need to indulge ideas from their political opponents. It would pose a much more cosy and corporate relationship between the main parties and emphasise their stranglehold on both local and national politics. At the same time, however, it would indicate that parties could speak to each other, albeit privately, about internal management issues and reach some form of accommodation about how politics should be structured and conducted. That alone could, in turn, lead to more positive relationships in other policy fields and plant the seeds of a less confrontational style of politics.

The construction by the national parties of rules and procedures for the organisation and activity of council party groups, and the varying degrees of willingness within and across the parties to interpret and employ those rules, add to the developing conceptualisation of party politics in local government that has been a theme of the previous chapters. Such nationally produced rules are part of the process by which local political practices and dynamics lose diversity and uniqueness to political conformity and regularity. Thus, local political parties are uniform structures, which contain within themselves a uniform set of constraints on party political dynamics that are common across the parties and the wider local political landscape. Whilst political philosophy does display itself in the structure of the party machine and the rules it adopts locally, the three main parties are very similar constructs driven by very similar concerns and procedures.

In part, political parties are a reflection of the liberal democratic representative framework existing in Britain as it displays itself locally. Political parties in turn, however, influence the structure and dynamics of liberal democratic representative local government and politics. The mutuality of influence between liberal democracy and political parties comes together in political concerns about power, political decision-making ability, accountability and a range of multifaceted political goals, which parties cannot and will not confine to localities alone. Thus, we can view political parties locally as multi-layered organisations with an overarching concern for the integrity and coherence of the organisation. The organisation that is the political party is a body of rules and structures designed to provide a *theatre* within which political dynamics, of a shared kind, can be shaped into some overall political purpose or objective – even if that purpose is simply the wining of power or representative office. However, political objectives may be based on very broad policy or philosophical concerns that can only be enacted by the obtaining and maintaining of positions of political power within local councils. Yet, when parties conduct politics locally, they do not see a specifically local dimension to political activity and processes, only a set of local circumstances that are to be resolved within a very precise framework of activity understood to be party political. Parties then are forces for constraint and conformity within the localities and are constructs that serve to remove diverse approaches to local concerns and attempt to shape and direct all local political activity within and through themselves.

Finally, on a more positive note, it is worth commenting here, that the willingness with which each of the parties make their model standing orders and draft consultation documents, available for academic study, is a testament to their commitment to a more open approach to local politics. It is something which should be positively recognised, complimented and encouraged, as it is only by public consideration and comment given to internal party rules that party politics becomes more accessible, relevant and understandable to the public. The parties have much to gain in being open and honest in the expectations they have of their councillors and the loyalty they demand from them to group decisions. Moreover, local government, local citizens and politics have much to gain from understanding how and why parties operate in the way that they do. As at the moment there is little if any clear view of how party groups conduct their business and that of the council. It may help repair some of the damage that an overly secretive approach to party activity and decision-making has had on public faith in the probity of local government and local politics, and lead to greater public deliberation of political concerns. We shall see in the next chapter, however, just how political parties serve to separate themselves from those they represent and how, for the party person, the interests of the party, supersede all other interests.

Notes

1 D. Wilson and C. Game, *Local Government in the United Kingdom*, Basingstoke: Macmillan, 2002, p. 40.
2 R. Rose, *Politics in England: Change and Persistence*, London: Macmillan, 1989; R. Garner and R. Kelly, *British Political Parties Today*, Manchester: Manchester University Press, 1993.
3 J. Bulpitt, *Territory and Power in the United Kingdom*, Manchester: Manchester University Press, 1983.
4 C. Game and S. Leach, 'The Role of Political Parties in Local Democracy', Commission for Local Democracy, Research Report No. 11, London, 1995.
5 J. Brand, 'Party Organisation and the Recruitment of Councillors', *British Journal of Political Science*, 3 (4), 1973, pp. 473–486.
6 Game and Leach, 'The Role of Political Parties in Local Democracy'.
7 Labour Party, *The Labour Councillors Handbook*, London, 1999.
8 Labour Party, *Labour Group Model Standing Orders, b,c,d*, London, 2001.
9 C. Copus, 'The Attitudes of Councillors since Widdicombe: A Focus on Democratic Engagement', *Public Policy and Administration*, 14 (4), 1999, pp. 87–100.
10 J. Gyford, *Local Politics in Britain*, London: Croom Helm, 1978.
11 Association of Liberal Democrat Councillors (ALDC) *Model Standing Orders for Liberal Democrat Council Groups*, Hebden Bridge, 2000.
12 R. Pinkney, 'Nationalizing Local Politics and Localizing a National Party: The Liberal Role in Local Government', *Government and Opposition*, 18, 1983, pp. 347–358.
13 ALDC, *Model Standing Orders*.
14 J. Ballard, *Running A Successful Council Group*, 2nd edition ALDC, 2000, p. 11.
15 G. Stoker and V. Lowndes, *Tower Hamlets and Decentralisation: The Experience of Globe Town Neighbourhood*, Luton: Local Government Management Board, 1991, pp. 22–23.
16 'Political Speech and Race Relations in Liberal Democracy,' Report of an Inquiry into the Conduct of the Tower Hamlets Liberal Democrats in Publishing Allegedly Racist Election Literature between 1990 and 1993', Liberal Democrats, London, December 1993, p. 3, pp. 58–59.

17 K. Young, *Local Politics and the Rise of Party*, pp. 219–221.

18 J. Bulpitt, *Party Politics in English Local Government*, London: Longmans, 1967; A. Glassberg, *Representation and Urban Community*, London: Macmillan, 1981.

19 Conservative Party, *Conservative Council Groups: Draft Model Rules*, London, 1998, revised 2001.

20 Bulpitt, *Party Politics in English Local Government*.

21 S. Leach and G. Ben-Tovim, *It's our Party: Democratic Problems in Local Government*, London: Local Government Management Board, 1998, p. 32.

22 DETR, 'Modern Local Government: In Touch with the People', 1998.

23 S. Snape, S. Leach and C. Copus, *The Development of Overview and Scrutiny in Local Government*, ODPM 2002.

24 J. Stewart, M. Clarke, D. Hall, F. Taylor, R. Hambleton and G. Stoker, 'Practical Implications: New Forms of Political Executive', Local Government Management Board, London, 1998, pp. 40–42.

6

Party political exchanges

The framework developed in the preceding chapters, for exploring the dynamics of party group politics, indicates the profound effect parties have on the activities of councillors as local representatives. In conceptualising political parties within local politics we can see them as multi-dimensional, multi-purpose, rule-constructed organisational settings, designed to inwardly constrain and shape divergent, and often conflicting, political dynamics (but with a shared ideological underpinning), and focusing those dynamics on some external political goal. Of course, party people are also bound together by the notion of the party itself, as a coherent political organisation and are tied by a form of *esprit de corps* and devotion to the party, which transcends, if only temporally, and only in public, any ideological purpose, belief or disagreement. That parties are bound together by more than ideology is partly displayed by how members in any party are able to point to a colleague and exclaim that he or she would be in an opposing party if that party were locally in political control. For some, then, the party represents a route to political influence and power and no more; but, such individuals are as bound to the party, its fortunes and well-being in the same way as any of his or her more ideologically inclined colleagues.

As a result of the magnetic pull of political parties on those seeking local political power and influence, parties become a force for regularity and conformity in the processes and practices of local politics. Parties ensure that party people approach political concerns, seek political solutions to problems and pursue a range of policy options that are multi-locational in nature (that is that issues exist at different spatial, temporal and cultural levels), within a distinct set of organisational arrangements – the party. Moreover, that they do so from a concern with the integrity, well-being and repute of the party and its future political advancement. But, parties are not just dry, organisational settings that dominate political practices and power. Parties contain within themselves a wide range of competing, conflicting and even mutually hostile forces, bound together not only by ideology, but by a shared knowledge that the political fortunes of all involved in the party, rest on the fortunes of the party itself.

A form of mutually assured political destruction emerges that produces a balance between competing party interests and ensures that the party maintains a publicly united local face, whatever the internal state of affairs and balance of power between the conflicting interests within the party. Such unity is, however, strained to breaking point in politically exceptional circumstances, or in cases when an individual suffers a personal political defeat – in such incidences party people will turn from the party to join another or to continue political activity as some form of independent. Parties in liberal democracies, can not force their members to stay members as they are after all voluntary organisations, the members of which join and disengage from the party as circumstances and experiences dictate.

Whilst displaying the outward signs of a mechanistic set-up, parties have a more organic nature. Parties learn from experience (though not always quickly) and develop and change within set confines that are physical, emotional and practical. Parties grow, diminish, exist in various states of health and display an inherent desire to survive. The purpose of that survival is to secure power and office as well as some more broadly defined set of political objectives. Local parties, then, focus on local political offices and share a concern with their councillors, organised in party groups, for acquiring those offices and in using the influence and power associated with them to govern or to oppose a governing administration. Once the party moves into the council chamber, party group organisation and activity clearly display the unique and powerful impact parties have on the conduct of council politics and on the intra- and inter-party group dynamics that occur within council chambers.

The party group and wider political party is the most prominent feature in the councillor's experiences of politics and political activity. Parties demand that their councillors organise and act in particular ways, with the purpose of providing a clear party political identity to the electorate, interest and stakeholder groups and to their party political opponents. Political parties and their members make it clear that it is the councillor's task is to protect the integrity of the party's identity and to ensure that a coherent and united front is presented when conducting politics in public. Yet, the executive political decision-making arrangements, introduced by the Local Government Act 2000, have placed a strain on notions of maintaining a united party approach to council politics by the introduction of a separate executive and the overview and scrutiny function. Party groups are, however, displaying considerable resilience to these changes.

Set out in this chapter are five case studies taken from councils across the country. The case studies explore the patterns of political behaviour existing within those councils and the way in which the organisation and activities of the political party group influence councillor activity. The patterns of political behaviour display the resilience of the party group when faced with changing political structures, as well as the intensity of the relationships councillors have with the group. It is that relationship which places the group at the centre of political decision-making and policy development within local government. It explains the nature of the inter- and intra-party dynamics existing in any one council and how councillors view the world of politics outside the council chamber in the wider local community. The case studies were constructed as a result of a series of semi-structured interviews with key political players in each authority and through a number of focus groups with councillors and party members. The research was designed to ensure that all the three main parties were represented. In each of the case studies below the council has adopted the leader and cabinet executive arrangements.

Case study one: northern Labour

Local authority A is a northern Labour controlled council where the long period of undisturbed Labour hegemony is beginning to be diluted. The party has seen its majority slowly reduced over the last few years and, whilst still retaining a comfortable majority, the loss of seats, some in previously safe Labour wards, has served to heighten tensions within and between the parties. The Conservatives provide the largest opposition group with 10 seats and there are two Liberal Democrats.

Labour has formed a single-party executive, taking all the portfolio positions; the Conservatives were offered the chair of one of the overview and scrutiny committees, but rejected the offer, preferring as one councillor said: 'to stay in opposition proper'. The relationships between the parties are cordial on a personal level and the intensity of the party political interactions is low with theatrical displays of party loyalty and grandstanding the norm. Labour and Conservatives, however, often aim their fire at the Liberal Democrats and, whilst the two seats they hold were former Labour seats, the Liberal Democrats' community politics machine has been brought into action in a number of other Labour and Conservative held wards. Thus, both parties feel threatened by the Liberal Democrats and both have much to gain from marginalising and opposing the Liberal Democrats' particular brand of politics, inside and outside the council chamber.

Before the introduction of the council executive, under the committee system, the full Labour group met before each committee and imposed a whip on every agenda item. Thus, all members of the group, including those not on the committee were provided with the opportunity of agreeing the way in which their colleagues on the committee would speak and vote. The group also met before each full council meeting and again imposed a whip on every agenda item. The Conservatives also met before each committee, but, unlike Labour who met three or four days before, the Conservatives met an hour before and considered a line of action; Conservative members were free to disagree or pursue alternative courses of action but largely the group spoke and voted as one and took the line of simply opposing what Labour wanted to do. The Liberal Democrats admitted to a 'quick chat over the phone before full council', rather than any formal meeting between the two councillors.

Since the introduction of the leader and cabinet option the Labour group has met every three weeks, with emergency or urgent meetings being called by the leadership or members if necessary. The meetings serve a number of purposes. First, they bring Labour members together on a regular basis to discuss broad policy issues, something not done under the old system, where group meetings were driven by council agenda. Secondly, they provide Labour councillors with a theatre in which to question the leader and executive members about decisions they have taken or are about to take. It is here that the group has taken on the scrutiny role and explains why the council's scrutiny process is yet to develop a robust approach. Thirdly, the group meetings provide the council leadership with an early warning signal of any potential trouble within the group about executive activity or other political issues. The leadership is then able to take remedial action to prevent a major political disagreement affecting the group's cohesion. As the leader said: 'We now get much clearer and earlier signals in the group about trouble brewing; in the past this was often picked up too late.' Fourthly, Labour councillors use their group meetings to indicate to the leadership the direction the executive should follow and to raise specific political and policy concerns the executive should address. One councillor stated:

> I don't like this new system, but our group meetings have changed and
> I think for the better, we are speaking about policy much more clearly
> than we did in group before. We have separate meetings about specific
> policy concerns and about what the executive is doing; I still don't feel
> as though I'm as in touch as I was before, but the group meetings are
> better.

One of his Labour colleagues put forward a very different view:

> There's no point in being a councillor any more; we have these long
> winded, airy fairy debates in group about this policy and that policy and
> then the leadership goes and does what they want and there's really not a
> lot we can do about it. I've no idea what's going on in the council any
> more. Some times you could come to the group meeting and you'd know
> exactly what was happening even if you weren't on the committee. If you
> were on the committee and couldn't get to the meeting because of work,
> then you would still know because you'd been to the group meeting.

Despite the obvious change in the nature of group meetings, group
coherence and discipline had not changed, if anything it had become
slightly more rigid. No whips are imposed on Labour councillors
serving on overview and scrutiny committees and, until very recently,
there was no need, as Labour members saw their role as proceeding
through the business in much the same way as in a traditional committee. In addition, they used the overview and scrutiny committees to
protect the executive from critical challenge by opposition councillors –
not that there was a great deal of such challenge anyway. In one
meeting, however, a Labour councillor had asked what she felt to be a
fairly innocent question about the Public Finance Initiative funding of
a new school. The question had sent the portfolio holder into apoplexy
and he considered the intervention an attack on his integrity and com-
petence as well as criticising agreed group policy.

Despite the wording of Labour Party standing orders, the chief
whip was asked by the portfolio holder to investigate and report to the
group. The chief whip, adhering rather more closely to the rules, spoke
to the member concerned, but did not issue a formal report to the
group, rather convened a meeting between the member, portfolio
holder, leader and the whip himself. At the meeting the member maintained her question was not a challenge or criticism but merely a question seeking to clarify funding for the project. The portfolio holder
maintained that the question had undermined his position, embarrassed
him publicly and cast doubt on his ability to manage council business.
The issue between the two members was left unresolved, but the leader
delivered a long 'lecture' to the Labour group on the importance of

group unity on overview and scrutiny and the need, as he saw it, not to give the 'Tories or the press' a 'stick to beat us with'.

Labour group discipline and coherence in this council has normally operated on the base of members adhering publicly to group decisions and where uncertainty about the group position exists or where no formal decisions have been taken, but discussion held, then a form of self-whipping operates. Labour councillors do not disagree in public. The chief whip reported that in his 20 years on the council there had been only one case where the whip had been removed from a member, and that was on an increase in council house rents some 12 years ago. Group members had not deviated in public from any agreed position once in the intervening period, despite the chief whip describing some group meetings as 'terrifying affairs and not for the feint-hearted'. One other factor had recently affected the coherence of the Labour group and that was the loss of previously safe seats at the last election. Many group members felt threatened by the losses and four councillors facing a challenge from Liberal Focus Teams were particularly edgy about the need for group discipline, as one said: 'We mustn't let the cracks show or that lot [the Conservatives and Liberal Democrats] will have a field day.'

The Conservatives, however, had not taken a formal approach to group discipline and the leader of the group could not recall a single occasion on which a Conservative member had been disciplined. That was not to say that the group did not cohere in public, it did, particularly when attacking Labour proposals or policy – it simply allowed its members to devise their own lines of attack, or to say nothing. The leader admitted: 'Half our group hasn't said a word in council for the last four years.' He was looking forward to a few seat gains at Labour's expense at the next election, but admitted to be worried by the Liberal Democrat challenge in two Conservative held seats. It was possible over time that the Liberal Democrats could replace the Conservatives as the largest opposition group and there did not appear to be a strategy to prevent this, save more of the same type of tactics in council meetings – focusing on what was seen as Liberal Democrat unfair campaigning. The Conservatives cohered in public because they faced two political opponents: the vastly larger Labour group and the smaller contender in the Liberal Democrats. As a Conservative councillor commented: 'Nothing concentrates the mind of this group like being replaced by the Liberals.'

The Liberal Democrats made few interventions in either council or overview and scrutiny, but were, as one of their number admitted: 'keeping our powder dry until there are a few more of us – and there will be'. They were more inclined to speak up on issues affecting the wards they represented; Liberal Democrat energy was going into winning more seats whilst maintaining a small foothold on the council. The Liberal Democrats were very aware that their presence on the council and their campaigning in certain target wards was leading to an increase in tension between the parties. But, they were relishing the 'jumpiness' that a few of them had caused in the Labour and Conservative ranks: 'sometimes you can almost feel how much they hate us', said one of the two councillors.

On this council there was a well-established pattern of interaction between the parties and within the groups themselves, which had not been disturbed by the introduction of a council executive. The party groups understood their individual roles: Labour provided the governing *bloc*, the Conservatives a clearly identifiable opposition grouping, with the Liberal Democrats challenging, at least electorally, if not in the council, the Conservatives for the title of opposition. Labour are in power, with little real challenge to their dominance, only a perceived threat of what may, or may not come as a result of any future local elections. The Labour leader linked the future of the group more to the national fortunes of the Labour government than to any action or inaction by his group: 'We are bound to lose seats the longer we are in government, it always happens, its up to Blair.' The Conservatives and Liberal Democrats in particular were more inclined to see cracks in Labour's defences as a result of local concerns, although giving a grateful nod to the affects locally of the Blair government's fortunes. The Conservative leader said: 'There is a shift in Labour support, but much of it is because they've run the council for so long people want a change; what happens to Blair will help us of course.' He went on to say: 'Some of us are even fanaticising that we could run the council one day – as long as the Liberals don't spoil things.' Whilst a Liberal Democrat councillor commented: 'We know that in the wards there is a lot of discontent about Labour, people never see their councillor when they need them, only when they're needed to vote for them; enough people are getting fed up for us to eventually make a real break though and Labour are doing nothing about it.'

Outside the council chamber it was the Liberal Democrats that had a small but active party and that saw its community activity as providing the mechanisms by which council seats would be captured. The local Conservative Party was dormant, and the Labour Party locally was functioning-mechanistic. The parties were not engaged in constant political competition and conflict, rather focused their activities on the election – with the Liberal Democrats running what one Labour activist called 'a year long election campaign'. There was little activity by the Labour and Conservative parties or any attempts to out-manoeuvre the Liberal Democrats by indulging a community politics approach; the focus was on party maintenance and developing the resources of the party, rather than constructing an on-going deliberation with the electorate. As far as the voter was concerned the parties sprang into action at election time only and then in a fairly perfunctory fashion. Only a small number of voters in those wards targeted by the Liberal Democrats would have noticed any on-going party-based public activity.

In this authority party politics had reached a situation of stasis, largely undisturbed by the introduction of executive arrangements. It was more unsettled by the arrival of two Liberal Democrats into the council chamber and the prospect, real or imagined, of them being joined by others. The Labour group saw itself and its meetings, as the place where council policy was deliberated and decided upon; the Conservatives used their group meetings to devise an issue-by-issue opposition to Labour proposals and considered how to embarrass the Labour administration. Politics here are certain, set in their ways, unconventional, centred on the activities of the ruling group and of medium intensity. They are firmly based on the cohesion of the party groups, particularly the Labour group; the task of Labour and Conservative councillors is to maintain that cohesion at all costs.

Case study two: Midlands Conservative

Local authority B is a West Midlands Conservative controlled council with a comfortable majority over the minority Labour group. The Conservatives had controlled the council until 1994 when they finally saw a gradual haemorrhaging of seats, ending in the loss of council control. They have since regained a working majority. Political relationships between the party groups are intense, strained and difficult, arising from the shock of defeat, which still echoes with the Conservatives, and the brief taste of power Labour enjoyed, with Liberal Democrat support (the Liberal Democrats having lost all their seats). The Conservatives have all the executive portfolios and have given Labour the chair of one scrutiny committee and the vice-chair of another. Labour took some time to consider the offer when it was made, but after a delay, when the issue was considered and voted upon in a group meeting, agreed to take the positions offered.

The Conservative council leader was a member of the council (though not leader) before and during the period of Labour control. His political attitudes and approach to politics hardened in and after that period, not, as he admitted, as a result of anything in particular Labour had done, but simply because they had been able to take control at all. He commented: 'This is not a Labour borough and will not be again, I shall see to that.' The Conservative group held regular meetings under the committee system and continues to hold fortnightly meetings under the new executive arrangements. It initially began holding group meetings monthly, but found that members were unaware of what was expected of them in scrutiny and full council. The fortnightly meetings take the format of a report by the leader and cabinet members with a general question and answer session and discussion then ensuing. The Conservative group also meets formally, outside of these fortnightly meetings, immediately before full council, when the council agenda is agreed and a whip imposed on members. It is, however, unusual in this particular group to hear the term 'whip' used – but members know what is expected of them and act accordingly.

There have been no occurrences where Conservative members have criticised or challenged the executive in overview and scrutiny, but a few occasions where the Labour chair has been openly criticised for being too 'political' in overview and scrutiny meetings. In other word she had challenged the executive. As one Conservative overview and scrutiny councillor commented:

> Many of my colleagues were not at all happy about Labour having the chairmanship of this committee; it took the leadership a long-time to convince us it was the right thing to do. I remain unconvinced and if I feel she [the Labour chair] is acting politically or trying to score points I will say so loud and clear. We have re-gained control of the council and should not be providing the opposition with perfect opportunities to take pot shots at us.

The Conservative group coheres rigidly in council and also responds vociferously to Labour challenges and taunts; councillors in both parties attested to the tension that pervades some, but not all council meetings. The parties use council and to a lesser extent overview and scrutiny, to aim criticism at each other and to indulge party political grandstanding and point-scoring. One Labour member gave the following example of party political exchanges in the council:

> At the council just after the Countryside Alliance march through London the Tories obviously smelt blood. We had this great tirade from [named council leader] about Labour letting the countryside down, about freedom of choice and liberty and how the countryside was collapsing around our

ears and how it was all the Government's fault. So we responded in kind, I told them, none of their lot said anything when the mines were being closed and communities destroyed, oh no, that didn't matter; they all supported Heseltine in that. It gets a bit like that in council sometimes and it can be a bit touch and go with them in the scrutiny committee; they're out to get [Labour chair] because most of them didn't want her to chair it in the first place.

A Conservative councillor also gave an example in a similar vein:

Labour managed to raise in an overview and scrutiny committee the future of Ian Duncan-Smith as party leader. It was after Portillo had criticised Duncan-Smith and the rumours that if we did not perform well in the local elections (2003) he would resign. Labour were making a big fuss and bother about the leadership of the Conservative Party, what on earth that has to do with the health and social care overview and scrutiny committee one can only but guess.

The Labour group hold group meetings before each council and impose a whip on members as a result of group decisions, it also holds policy meetings on an *ad hoc* basis when contentious issues are facing the council. The Labour group does not whip its members on overview and scrutiny committees, although members of such committees do hold pre-scrutiny meetings without their colleagues that are not members of the committee. No whip is imposed but the very nature of a group of colleagues from the same party discussing overview and scrutiny business before the committee is likely to lead to a self-imposed whip.

Labour recognise that it is very unlikely to regain control of the council, unless the unusual political circumstances of the mid-1990s return. It has not completely resigned itself to a position of permanent opposition but the group is moving towards accepting that as a political reality in this borough. That has not, however, dampened Labour's enthusiasm for a united and disciplined approach to the business of the council and the conduct of politics. Political successes as opposition rest just as much on disciplined and united public action as they do for the majority group. In addition, the Labour group adhere to the letter and the spirit of the party's model group standing orders, and act publicly as a solid *bloc* of members on each and every issue.

The Labour and Conservative groups are not internally factionalised as a result of ideological differences, although clearly there are a number of *kindreds* existing in each group. These *kindreds* appear to only disturb the internal harmony of the two groups and have no impact on public group cohesion, particularly when the two groups confront each other in a council setting. As a result of the lack of internal dissent and the drawing up of very public and clear battle lines between the two groups, the conduct of council politics is indicative of the very real differences over policy that exist between the parties. Moreover, there is recognition in the conduct of council politics that there are two competing teams of councillors, the members of which simply want to see their team win and are willing to support it in all cases. It is fortunate in this authority that there are few intense personal animosities between councillors in the two groups. Such personality clashes would make any already tense set of political dynamics all the more tense and would damage the interactions between the parties further still.

In this authority the introduction of executive arrangements has made no difference to the interactions between and within the party groups or to the intensity of that interaction. Whilst the Conservative leader and executive members have considerable freedom to act individually and collectively, the relationship between the executive and the rest of the group is, in Conservative terms, very close. The group and council leadership are very keen to keep their group colleagues on board with executive activities and to keep them informed of decisions and the general running of the council. The approach to the group taken by the executive has its formation in the period of lost control; most Conservative leaders expect and receive greater freedom from the group than in this case. Yet, members of the group are clearly happy for the executive to act largely as they see fit, as one Conservative councillor commented: 'The executive knows we will support them against Labour, in fact they could have no group meetings at all and we'd still back them against Labour; I'm not advocating no group meetings by the way.'

Politics in this authority are intense, party oriented, driven by real political differences between the groups and by the view that councillors have of their parties as in constant competition with their opponents. There is little room for compromise and even less desire to do so; Labour would rather lose on issues than seek compromise with the Conservatives; the Conservatives are happy for this situation to continue as they simply see no room for compromise or genuine deliberation with Labour. The outside observer or the concerned citizen would see party politics dominate all facets of the activities of this council and be able to observe two party *Leviathans* charging into each other on every possible occasion.

Case study three: Midlands Labour

Local authority C is Labour controlled and has been since 1974, except for a brief period in the 1980s when the Conservatives and Liberal Democrats controlled the council on the casting vote of the mayor. The Labour group claim they gave power to the opposition to enable it to make mistakes, which it duly did and lost seats massively, being reduced to single figures for both Conservative and Liberal Democrat groups, with the Conservatives loosing all their seats in the mid 1990s. Whether this was because of the Labour-held folklore of the mistakes the Conservative and Liberal Democrats made when in control, or, more likely, as a result of shifting national political fortunes matters little, the controlling Labour group subscribe heavily to the former version of events.

Labour has seen its majority again slip back to that of nine seats over the combined opposition Conservative, Liberal Democrat, Independent and Residents' Association groups. A member of the Residents' Association group is a former Labour councillor who was de-selected and a member of the Liberal Democrat group is a former Labour member who changed parties. The Conservative group has amongst its membership a former Liberal Democrat who also changed parties. These changes of sides and the reasons for them add to an intense and heady political mix on this council, which is a product of not only deep party political animosities but also personal clashes and dislikes.

The politics of this council were described by one Labour councillor as: 'very, very unpleasant', but he added, 'They [the opposition groups] deserve it'. A Conservative councillor commented: 'I was on this council up to 1992, when I lost my seat, it was always unpleasant, political, personal and antagonistic; I was re-elected in 2000 and all I can say is its much, much worse. Labour is threatened again and they don't like it.'

A Residents' Association councillor said:

> I can't believe it sometimes, the smallest thing will lead to a huge party political row; they're all as bad as each other. The Conservatives deliberately bait Labour, you can see them doing it and Labour just respond in kind; the Liberal Democrats are just as bad. I'm not standing next time I just hate it.

The Labour group has taken all the executive places and all of the chairs of overview and scrutiny committees, as one Labour councillor discussing the sharing of overview and scrutiny chairs put it: 'I didn't fight this lot and beat them [in the election] to give them power. If they ran the council we'd get nothing and I tell you we wouldn't take it even if it was offered, they could get ****'.

To add to the already tense political dynamics of this council is the element of insecurity amongst members of the Labour group. The Labour group is anticipating future losses at local elections, but the group places the responsibility for these losses firmly at the feet of the government, rather than its stewardship of the council. Moreover, it firmly believes that it will remain the largest group on the council even if it loses its overall majority, a situation that could last for a few years because of the seats to be contested at annual elections. It reasons this because of its traditions of rigid group discipline. As the largest party, faced with three opposition groups, of varying sizes and with varying degrees of coherence within the groups and across the groups, Labour feels confident its united voting strength will give it all the executive posts. In addition, it believes it can hold all overview and scrutiny chairs; although they are less concerned about losing one or two of those, they will work to avoid this happening. The Labour group's political antenna tells it that the political and personal animosities across its three opposition groups, are more powerful than those groups' desire to unseat Labour from power. Thus, with Labour voting as one, and the opposition groups not, Labour will be saved, until the electorate return it to majority control.

The Labour group relies in all circumstances on its tradition of iron discipline and expectations of absolute public unity amongst group members, not only in council but also in the press, public meetings or anywhere else its councillors may act. Indeed, this group has a reputation within the midlands for harsh discipline and with every public deviation by Labour members being dealt with by the indefinite withdrawal of the group whip from the member concerned. As a Labour councillor on another council said of this Labour group: 'They only have one penalty for breaking group whip – it's the death penalty.'

The Chief whip of the Labour group reported that over the last four years five Labour members had been disciplined and the group whip withdrawn for a variety of misdemeanours. None of those concerned had gone as far as voting against the group; two had spoken against a group decision in full council; two had spoken against a group decision in committee; and one had been quoted in the local press as criticising the council's decision on a particular local issue.

The Conservative group had not been without its own disciplinary problems and in the same four-year period admitted to expelling two members from the group, one for voting with Labour in committee and the second for speaking against the Conservative group's agreed line in full council. Indeed, the group leader admitted to *'leaning very heavily'* on the Conservative Association and the branch party to ensure that the councillor concerned was not re-selected as a Conservative candidate. As a result, the councillor concerned had stood against the official Conservative candidate as an Independent Conservative and Labour took the seat. The Liberal Democrat's also had cause to discipline a member, but he was arrested and left the council of his own accord before the disciplinary process was complete.

An intense party political atmosphere exists on this council, coupled to this is the personal loathing that several members within and across the parties have for each other. These feelings of personal hatred (which is the word used by several councillors on this council) add a dimension to the politics of this council which extends beyond the party political. Allegations of treachery are often made by former colleagues against those councillors that have changed parties; other personal dislikes and clashes add an additional twist to the party political exchanges. In this council the adage that no one hates someone in another party more than someone in their own party is also very acute and clear. All of which means that councillors retreat into their party groups, including the Residents' Association councillors, and nothing happens on this council without the groups considering their position first.

The local Labour Party could be categorised as *omnipotent*; it was well resourced and maintained its internal activities and integrity. It did not see its role as constructing a political deliberation with the electorate, but was focused very heavily on organising and campaigning for the annual council elections. The local party expected its councillors to be active in the party and to reflect the decisions and policy of the party when conducting council business. The party had a history of de-selecting councillors that had strayed too far from the party's position on various issues, local and national.

As the Conservatives had been slowly but steadily increasing their numbers on the council, it is surprising the local Conservative Party was *dormant*. The membership base of the party was low but well resourced; the party was prevented from becoming *moribund* because of the annual elections held for this council, without these the party would lack any reason to stimulate itself into action. The party had a very distant relationship with its councillors, expecting them to get on with the job once elected.

The Liberal Democrats as a party were *moribund*, lacking resources, membership and the basic material that would enable it to conduct a serious local election campaign. The Liberal Democrat electoral successes were due to the community politics conducted by those individuals that were councillors or those potential candidates that were targeting a small number of wards. These individuals lack party support and as one potential candidate stated: 'I have 5,000 Focus leaflets to deliver each month and I do it all by myself, sometimes the children help if they've finished their homework'. It was the Residents' Association that had the most robust, healthy, outward looking organisation well integrated into the community within the area it represented. It held three seats in one ward but had no organisation across the authority. The councillors were discussing forming an authority-wide residents organisation and were beginning to make contacts with Associations in other wards; the councillors, however, were more concerned with the interests of their own ward, rather than governing the authority.

Within the council it was the politics of the party group that became the politics of the council. The Labour group was disciplined, organised and publicly united; Labour members knew that their responsibility was to ensure that the executive was defended, the opposition groups attacked at every opportunity and that overview and scrutiny posed no problems for the executive or for the party group. The Conservative group was similarly well organised; its members spoke and voted together in council and in overview and scrutiny. The latter was seen as a prime place for the opposition to score points at the expense of the ruling administration. The Conservative group was the main opposition to Labour, partly because they were the largest opposition party, but significantly because they acted as such and as a coherent and disciplined group.

The Liberal Democrats also acted as a united party group, but had yet to experience any deep difference of opinion between members over some policy or decision of the ruling group – or generated by some local issue. They acted together in council because they agreed, rather than as a matter of political tactics. The Residents' Association councillors had between themselves, spoken and voted differently on policy issues, but not on matters arising from their ward or when they saw a policy matter directly affecting that ward. They clearly recognised that they were part of the opposition groupings and were inclined as individuals to vote against Labour taking the executive seats if it became the largest party at a future election but lacked an overall majority. Each councillor would base his vote on the individual Labour candidate standing for any portfolio but would not vote for a Labour executive slate.

Politics here are very intense, driven completely by the decisions of the ruling Labour group and lacking any room for compromise or genuine public political deliberation. Everything is a party political issue for each of the three party groups and is recognised as such by the Residents' Association group. Indeed, Labour councillors refer to the Residents' party, rather than Association, and as one Labour councillor said: 'They stood for election didn't they; then they're political and a party.' The Conservatives are a bit more charitable referring to Residents' councillors, but their view was summarised by one Conservative councillor who commented: 'They are councillors, they stood for election on a form of manifesto and will stand for re-election – that makes them like us, they are a party, no mater how much they deny that.' Councillors in the two main parties take a deeply suspicious view of any community group or organisation that attempts to influence, in one way or another, council policy – seeing them in the same light as the Residents' Association: a party political threat. There is little evidence in this council of the political atmosphere changing; rather the local election results are set to intensify an already poisonous political dynamic.

Case study four: southern Conservative

Local authority D has always been Conservative controlled and remained so during the mid to late 1990s when the Conservatives were losing control of councils deep in their political heartland. Whilst the Conservatives lost seats their continued control was not seriously threatened. The Labour and Liberal Democrat groups have seen their numbers increase dramatically only to fall back again to what is considered to be their natural levels for this council.

The Conservative leader for the past four years dominates his group and expects and receives from them complete public loyalty. The Conservative group meets infrequently and meetings are convened at the leader's request, although two groups meetings have been held as a result of backbench members' insistence on considering certain issues arising from the council's budgetary process. The group does not meet as a matter of course before full council meetings. Yet, the Conservative group holds together in council by taking its leader's direction as issues come up; there have been instances of confusion on the part of some Conservative councillors as to which way to vote, but the party's considerable majority is not threatened when such confusion arises. Such accidentally disciplinary hiccups are ignored. The Labour and Liberal Democrat councillors have both openly admitted that they occasionally call for named votes in council meetings to trip up one or two Conservative councillors who are not sure how to vote until after the leaders name has been called.

The Conservative group currently have all the executive seats, however the leaders of the Labour and Liberal Democrat groups were given a cabinet seat without portfolio and had speaking and voting rights. The operation of a multi-party cabinet came to an end by mutual agreement between the groups, with Labour and Liberal Democrat cabinet seats being replaced by the chairs of an overview and scrutiny committee for each of the group leaders. The arrangements appear to be working well as the two opposition group leaders are well ensconced in the overview and scrutiny committee process and with the running of their respective committees. Moreover, they have been able to bring their party groups along with them into supporting the sharing of chairs and the new political arrangements. As the Liberal Democrat leader commented: 'We can have some impact through overview and scrutiny when we weren't getting any through having a seat on the executive.' The Conservative leader was very happy with the arrangements saying:

> Councillors [named Labour and Liberal Democrat Labour leaders] felt it was their duty to be awkward and cause trouble sometimes. Indeed [Liberal Democrat leader] could be very political sometimes, far worse than [Labour leader]. Now they chair overview and scrutiny they really do behave themselves and are much quieter politically; it's all working rather well at the moment.

The Liberal Democrats meet before each full council and before the scrutiny committee which their leader chairs. The group does impose a whip on major issues facing the council and by and large Liberal Democrats speak and vote as a coherent group in council. Some members have acted against group decisions, more on tactical than political reasons, but, in the two most recent cases, no disciplinary action was taken. The Liberal Democrat leader said: 'I'd rather we worked together as a group because we wanted to not because people were forced to.'

The Labour group is the smaller of the two opposition *blocs*. It holds regular group meetings and always meets before full council; Labour councillors cohere as a disciplined and unified *bloc* in public. Whilst there have been some internal discontent over the tactics of the group leadership when it comes to opposing the ruling administration, these have not resulted in any Labour members speaking or voting against the group in the last four years. The chief whip for the group commented: 'We operate by standing orders and I expected all our members to support group decisions in council; the jury is still out on how our people on overview and scrutiny operate but we've had no problems so far. It's a pretty sensible group and we all understand the need for group discipline.'

The political and personal interactions between the three groups are cordial enough on this council and reflect the well-established patterns of political dynamics that exist between them. The ruling group will remain so and the opposition groups are neither challenging the ruling group for control, or challenging each other for the prize of largest minority group. There are a few personal animosities that affect the relationships between some of the backbenchers in the Conservative and Liberal Democrat groups but the group leaders work to keep these in perspective and out of sight of the public. The Conservative leader said: 'Its all a bit unseemly when people start calling each other names in public, especially as its nothing to do with council business.'

Despite the generally cordial relationships between the parties and between individuals and the fairly easy going relationships between the groups, the politics of the council are not consensual, neither do the party groups specifically seek consensus. The parties see themselves as parties, opposed on political doctrine, direction and value systems. The Conservatives are in control but are not too ideologically driven and take a managerial and business-like approach to the running of the council, but with identifiably Conservative policies and direction. The Labour group respond in kind, and whilst displaying a very clear political identity do not oppose for oppositions sake. The Liberal Democrats, as the largest opposition group attempt to improve the quality of council policy and decisions, rather than radically change them. All in all, the conduct of politics in this council suit all those involved very well.

All groups admit to things becoming slightly more tense in the run up to the four yearly elections for the council. As a Conservative councillor commented:

> It gets a bit touchy and there is a little bit more point scoring going on than normal, usually it's the Liberal Democrats [the Liberal Democrats denied this charge and levied a similar one at Labour and the Conservatives]. Its not as though we will lose control of the council, but from our point of view some one could lose a seat and that makes all councillors jumpy.

A Labour member added: 'Elections make all councillors uneasy and tense. We know we're not going to run this council and if we did it would be with the Liberal Democrats I suppose. But, elections do things to you; the last full council meeting before an election can be a right bit of knock about, then its business as usual.'

The local Conservative Party had a close relationship with the council leadership; the chair of the local Association was the council leader's son. Indeed, the leader was more inclined to confide in some members of the Association than members of his own party group when it came to aspects of council business. Although he admitted that the group was always informed of any discussions he had with the Association. The local Conservative Party was *functioning-mechanistic;* it was extremely well resourced, held regular meetings of all party units and had a continual stream of income from party social activities and donations, that enabled it to maintain a comfortable existence, with elections proving no strain on the party's resources. The party did have a close relationship with the council group but did not expect to control its councillors. The Association chair commented: 'As long as they follow Conservative principles and are good Conservatives that is what we expect. We expect them to be able to get on with council business without interference from the Association.'

The local Labour Party was *moribund* with few active members and very strained resources. It was able to conduct electoral activity but this was supported financially by councillors themselves paying their own election expenses. Although party units met regularly it was on the basis of branches formed from a number of wards and a small gathering of members for meetings of the constituency party. Here the continual existence of the Labour Party was based on a small number of individuals holding positions and offices at all levels of the party; councillors played a vital role in keeping the party going at all.

The Liberal Democrats had a much healthier party base, which could be described as *resurgent*. It met regularly, had sound finances and put much effort into raising and maintaining its income; it had a good base of active members that attend party meetings and had no shortage of volunteers for various party offices. Liberal Democrats here saw themselves as political activists and party people and were committed to the principles of liberal democracy and the notion of the Liberal Democrats as a political party. Although the party did engage in community politics it did not see this as its only political role, indeed for some members community politics had distinct drawbacks, although they recognised the election-winning potential of this approach. The party membership supported councillors in delivering *Focus* newsletters throughout the year and not one councillor was in the unenviable position of the Liberal Democrat in authority C who had to deliver all his own leaflets.

The politics of this council are relatively benign but are conducted with reference and reverence to the notion of political parties and party groups as distinct political identities with a clear party political purpose and set of objectives. Councillors do not engage in open and genuine political deliberation with councillors of other parties, they have an agreed or accepted group line to follow and broadly that line holds. The cordial nature of political interaction somewhat disguises the nature of variations of political views and values systems that are expressed in council meetings. As with all the case study authorities so far, the parties and party groups in this council are organised to conduct political combat, to advance a political view and objective and to undermine and defeat political opponents – they just do it very nicely.

Case study five: southern Liberal Democrat

Local authority E has been controlled by the Liberal Democrats with an overall majority since 1995 having been captured from the Conservatives. There are no Labour councillors on this council. The Liberal Democrats saw their strength grow slowly but steadily for a period when they concentrated on a Focus community politics tactic in targeted wards. By the mid-1990s they were beginning to win seats without employing that tactic and soon recognised that they were seen as a viable political alternative to the Conservatives as they lost favour nationally.

The dual journey to the council available to Liberal Democrats here, community politics or party political alternative to the Conservatives, has resulted in two distinct types of Liberal Democrats sitting on the council. First, the community politicians elected through the Focus route. These members have a very loose attachment to the notion of party and were either Liberal Democrats that chose the community politics approach, or were active in the community in some way or another and were approached by the Liberal Democrats to stand under their banner at an election. The second group within the Liberal Democrats consists of long standing party members, ideologically committed to the principles of the Liberal Democrats and to the notion of acting as a party with a distinct political identity – not driven by community politics. There is a tension within the Liberal Democrat group on the council between these two types of councillor, but they are all deeply determined to keep control of the council.

The Conservative group has recovered from the shock of losing control of the council and has certainly not resigned itself to a position of permanent opposition. The group and local party are determined to win back control of the council, which they perceive as having been unfairly snatched from them by a mixture of unfair campaigning and political opportunism. One Conservative councillor summed things up by stating:

> They [Liberal Democrats] made some absolutely outrageous claims in their leaflets about the council when we were in control and about what the Focus people had achieved in wards where they didn't even have councillors. They were claiming to have had successes where even a councillor could make little or no difference to a matter – so how did they do it. We think some of the officers were deliberately helping them out.

A Liberal Democrat councillor responded to allegation of this kind thus:

> They [the Conservatives] always come out with this nonsense, the fact is some problems can be cured by a few quick phone calls to the right officer and following up progress. That's exactly what we do and then we tell people what we've done; if the councillors can't do that themselves in their own wards then they deserve to lose their seats.

The Liberal Democrats have all the executive seats but have allowed the Conservatives to chair one overview and scrutiny committee. The Conservatives took some time in agreeing to accept the offer and then did so with private and public reluctance. Indeed, the offer was held up as an indication that the Liberal Democrats could not run the council without Conservative advice. A claim, which almost resulted in the offer being withdrawn, save by some deft political footwork by the Liberal Democrat leader. Some members of the Conservative group were adamant not to be seen to be co-operating in any way with a Liberal Democrat administration by taking the chair offered. The Conservative group also made its opposition to the new executive system publicly very clear and as a consequence did not want to co-operate with either the Liberal Democrats, or the new decision-making structures.

The politics of the council chamber are conducted on strict party lines with little compromise or genuine deliberation between the groups. Group meetings are held by both Liberal Democrats and Conservatives and a whip is imposed on all issues. Local Liberal Democrat councillors have been allowed to speak at variance with the group on issues affecting their own wards but have been expected not to vote against the group, rather to abstain or absent themselves at the point of voting. The Liberal Democrat leader insists on rigid group discipline and commented thus:

> We have our group meetings and I expect every Liberal Democrat to attend
> and to stick together in the council. I run a very tight ship and I expect dis-
> cipline, that is the only way we can run this council and continue to run it,
> the alternative is that we are all over the place and allow the Conservatives
> to out vote us in council. If we looked to the public like a bunch of mave-
> ricks all doing what they wanted then they would pretty soon put the
> Conservatives back in control. I was the first Liberal Democrat councillor
> here and saw how they [the Conservatives] treated the council – like they
> owned it. I do not intend to let that happen again and my people must
> understand that.

The Liberal Democrat council leader spoke openly about the tensions
in his group; he recognised that some of his members placed the ward
they represented above all else, whilst others saw their role as governing
the authority. He also recognised that some members of his group were
far less driven by political ideals and commitment to the Liberal
Democrats as a political organisation than other members. Managing
this tension when it displayed itself took considerable time and energy
and some of the less ideologically committed members of his group
were inclined to follow their own instincts on some policy matters. The
leader commented:

> It is very difficult on occasions and this is what comes of recruiting people
> to stand as candidates before they are members of the Liberal Democrats.
> We no longer need to do that anymore but we have a number of council-
> lors that would just as happily be Conservatives or Independents if I didn't
> manage them properly. But I will not be blackmailed and I've had to call
> one or two people's bluff; we have disciplined a member and I would not
> hesitate to do that again. I've made sure every member and every candi-
> date has a copy of the ALDC's standing orders and I make it clear at most
> group meetings that I expect people to stick by our decisions. It works 99
> per cent of the time.

The Conservative group displayed more rigid internal and external
cohesion than the Liberal Democrats did, with the group leader revel-
ling in some of the problems he had observed his Liberal Democrat
counterpart struggling with. 'They can be a rabble some times, an awful
bunch and we just wait for that to happen and make the most of it', he
admitted. The Conservative group was bound together by the deep-
seated desire to regain control of the council and to remove what one
Conservative councillor referred to as 'the usurpers' from power.
Conservative group meetings before full council are events where political tactics are considered and agreed as well as decisions about what
position the group will take on each issue. Indeed, the group also consider the agenda for each overview and scrutiny committee and, whilst

it is not clear if a whip exists, committee members are very clear as to the feeling of their group colleagues.

The Conservative leader is proud of the discipline, loyalty and public cohesion of the group, and that in his 23 years on the council he could not recall a single incident where any Conservative members spoke, or voted against the group. 'We have one aim now', he said, 'to remove them [the Liberal Democrats] from control and to show the public what a shower they are.' Conservative councillors echoed his comments and were clearly bound together by strong feelings of party loyalty and by a clear allegiance to the Conservative Party as a political entity. Councillors here often referred to the national Conservative Party and had tied their success in regaining control to regaining office nationally – what they did in this council to return to power would be a lesson for the national party.

The politics of the council are party political and two *blocs* of councillors face each other in each council event determined to hold the line against their opponents. The Conservatives, could rely on absolute and rigid party discipline in public, the Liberal Democrats were on occasions slightly less certain, but had a majority that could overcome an individual member or two taking umbrage at a group decision. They simply disliked intensely the public embarrassment this caused, and the opportunity it provided for the Conservatives to make political capital. There was an absence of any obvious personal animosities, but the intense party political dynamics resulted in many heated public exchanges; personal relationships remained as cordial as could be expected under the political circumstances. The Liberal Democrat group is the place where council policy is decided and is clearly recognised as such by all councillors; a change in political control if it comes, will simply see the policy-making forum of the council shift to the Conservative group and it's meetings.

Conclusions

The common theme that runs throughout each of the case studies is that the politics of the councils are conducted within the political party groups before it reaches the public domain. Whilst the groups in each council cohere publicly with varying degrees of rigidity, they do cohere and are identifiable as distinct *blocs* of councillors with a clear political identity and set of objectives. What varies between the cases is the intensity of the relationship between the groups, and the degrees of political and personal animosity that shape the political dynamics.

Political affiliation makes little difference to the way councillors approach council politics and to how they interact with councillors from the same party and from other party groups. Council politics, and politics outside the council, are a team sport and members back the team in public. Internal dissent finds little outlet and where it does occur it falls broadly into two categories: that concerned with ideology or policy and that related to issues steaming from the ward or division the councillor represents. Whilst Labour members are the least likely to allow these internal disputes, of either kind, to spill over into the public arena and Liberal Democrats most likely, it is a rare occasion for this to occur in any case. When it comes to the conduct of council politics Conservative groups share the approach to public discipline and loyalty taken by their Labour counterparts. They are simply less inclined to want to admit to the rigours of group discipline and the use of disciplinary mechanisms to secure that cohesion.

Party groups manoeuvre for advantage, seek opportunities to exploit the weaknesses of their council opponents, party politicise local issues that could remain outside the scope of party politics, seek positions of patronage and reject such positions for party advantage and merge the activities of the council with some national party focus. Yet, they also serve to indicate to the electorate that one group of councillors or another is the political administration of the council and thus responsible for the stewardship of the council and for polices adopted. Party politics also signal to the electorate the existence of clear political alternatives to the ruling administration, and opposition groups, no matter how small, have vital roles to play in ensuring the existence of political choice.

The advent of council executives and overview and scrutiny committees has introduced a new element to the internal and external cohesion of party groups. The executive acts as a focus for party loyalty for the ruling group and, whilst willing to question the executive and to challenge its decisions, ruling groups do this at a group meeting not in overview and scrutiny. Yet, overview and scrutiny provides councillors with a new forum in which to explore and deliberate political issues and opens up a potential for party groups to indulge more cross-party deliberation than the old committee system. It does this because overview and scrutiny does not make decisions, but can develop a series of recommendations to be considered by the executive or full council. Even so, it is clear that some opposition groups see overview and scrutiny as an arena to criticise and challenge the ruling group from a purely party political perceptive and, as a consequence, have simply transferred a set of political behaviours from one forum to another. Correspondingly, the ruling group feels duty bound to protect its executive from party political inspired attack and does just that.

What is clear from the case studies is that despite geographical location or type of council, party politics is conducted in a very similar fashion. It is only the intensity of relationships between and within parties and individuals that varies not the conduct of party politics, the nature of party political exchanges or the relationships between the parties. Yet, such party political dynamics as do occur are not set for all time, never to change, as the Labour and Liberal Democrat party leaders on one council, long in no overall control, agreed with the Conservative leader's analysis of the flux of party political relationships:

> A few years ago the relationships between the groups was absolutely poisonous, we hardly had a civil word to say to each other and council and committee meetings would degenerate into slanging matches. We would agree on nothing and if one side suggested something the others would automatically disagree, whatever the issue. Then, over a few years some people stood down, others lost their seats and things changed. Now we get on very well, we can agree and disagree in public and do so in the right spirit; council is a much happier place. We still want our side to win and will go all out at election time, but the council is just far more pleasant than it was. Who knows it could all change again in a few years – it just depends on who's here.

Thus, party political interaction is driven as much by the way individuals interpret party politics, political circumstances and what is and is not appropriate party political behaviour as anything else. It is just that party membership and coherence encourages a certain approach to political behaviour that sees an adversarial interaction as the more natural state of affairs.

Political decision-making at the local level is party-based political decision-making, and party politics can not be divorced from the activities of the council as a representative institution. It is because the parties see themselves as national organisations playing out their role in a local setting that partly ensures that *blocs* of members cohere around a party label when conducting council business. It is also because parties provide the foundation for the political control of a council and are the basis of opposition to a ruling group that council politics becomes the politics of the parties. It is the domination of local politics and council chamber politics by national parties that prevents any distinct carving out of a specifically local dimension to governance in Britain. Parties have nationalised the experience of local politics and the very way in which local politics is conducted. Moreover, parties have contributed to the construction of a very narrow definition of what is meant by any *local dimension* to politics and political processes. Whilst council chambers deal with issues that specifically relate to a sub-national geographical area, the parties do so in a way that contributes to the subordinate role that notions of locality and a local political dimension have within British political culture for the national and local political *elite*. Local politics is prevented from having an independent existence from national politics, not only by the structure of British governance, but by political culture and the role played at the local level by political parties.

7

The councillor, the citizen and the community: crises of representation

Amongst the most compelling and convincing arguments for any form of sub-national, territorially based structure of representative government is that it brings political decision-making closer to local communities. As a consequence of elected local government, decision-making by local elected representatives has a local democratic mandate; and, by being more immediate to local communities, can, in turn, be far more responsive to local wishes than national government. Thus, local citizens can be assured that the views they articulate will be heard by councillors, and that councillors in turn, will be concerned not only to respond to, but also to anticipate the reactions of the electorate to the polices they develop and decisions they make.[1]

What such normative arguments for local democracy ignore is the way in which local political parties generally, and the party group specifically, act as a filter between the views of the citizen and the councillor. Indeed, the party group system serves to ensure strict party political boundaries are maintained within British councils and that the councillor's primary loyalty is focused on the group and the party rather than the electorate. Moreover, the councillor is expected to publicly acquiesce, or actively support, the group – irrespective of his or her own views and how he or she may have spoken or voted in a group meeting, and irrespective of the views of those he or she was elected to represent. Group loyalty – and the reasons for it – has a profound affect on the health and responsiveness of British local democracy and a fundamental impact on the representative relationship between the councillor and the citizenry.

The chapter explores the tension between the councillor as an elected local representative and the electorate he or she represents, generated by the political party group and its demands for councillor loyalty. The first section develops some of the arguments set out in chapter 4, which explored group cohesion and loyalty. It considers how councillors can adopt a different focus, or interest priority in their work as a representative and how they can balance the needs of the ward or division with the party group's demand for loyalty and its concern for governing an area. The second section explores the concept of a *crisis of representation*, when the demands for group loyalty collides and conflicts with demands for representation made by the electorate. It looks at how councillors, across the political spectrum, respond to solve a crisis of representation. The third considers the various settings or *theatres of representation* within which councillors can act and what it is they can do to 'represent' local interests. It considers the choice strategies available to councillors to select between *acts of representation* and the various *theatres of representation* within which to employ them. Finally, the chapter considers the different interpretations of local representation employed by councillors of different political affiliations.

The councillor and the scope of representation

The very fact that councillors are elected from wards or divisions serves to generate some concern for the needs of the ward and an interest in the views articulated by communities within those electoral areas. The boundaries of council wards or divisions, are not, of course, drawn only to reflect notions of identifiable communities existing in a specific geographical area, although these are considerations in the design of ward boundaries.[2] Rather, they are primarily an administrative creation designed to capture appropriate numbers of electors to warrant the allocation of a councillor. If the boundaries of the electoral area coinside with some identifiable community, so much the better, but that is not their purpose.

The geographical basis of local electoral representation does bring with it expectations on behalf of the voters, that the interests of that 'patch' will be promoted and defended by the councillor. Councillors, however, display varying degrees of connection to the concept of representing an electoral area, rather than some other focus of loyalty and interest.[3] Part of the reason for this is the party group's vision of itself as governing an area, a vision based on group cohesion and public unity, and a singleness of purpose that risks considerable disruption by what Widdicombe referred to as 'elements of territoriality', and 'long established localist sentiments'.[4] Indeed, some councillors do focus very heavily and deliberately on the particular ward or division they were elected to represent, seeing themselves as its defender or tribune.[5]

Others, however, have only a passing loyalty to the ward or division from which they are elected, a loyalty which is very easily transferred to another area if the councillor changes his or her seat.[6]

The ways, in which 'localist sentiments' are perceived and responded to by the councillor, and his or her party group, of course go to the heart of the issue of local political representation. Despite the general spread of party politics in local government, Widdicombe found that local loyalties could persist and occasionally 'run counter to party solidarity'. Councillors in these circumstances are 'well entrenched in their communities' and their role is primarily one of 'defending their local interest regardless of party considerations'. More recently, Goldsmith noted that large numbers of elected officials 'derive their greatest satisfaction from representing local and community interests'.[7] For much of urban England, however, this is not the case, and whilst councillors may go dutifully about the business of case work for individual constituents, articulating and reflecting the views of the wider public, or sections of the community, is not seen in the same light. Indeed, it is the views of the political party and the party group that councillors are expected to articulate in public settings, even if these conflict with the opinions of his or her electorate, and, in some cases, even if they conflict with his or her own opinions.[8] The extent to which the party group can contain within itself any localist sentiments, or the expression of public views that may clash with those held by the group, reflects the power that is held by party groups across the country.

The party group is able to ensure localist sentiments are expressed within the confines of its own meetings, and so serves to eliminate their expression from the public theatres of representation. The expression of 'localism' may be tolerated internally within the group but when issues affecting localities, or wards and divisions spill into the public arena, the councillor is faced with making a choice. He or she can focus on either the ward or division before the party, and thus express dissent from the group, or conform with its decision or policy, so giving priority to the views of his or her group, or party colleagues, before notions of community representation.

What is it then that drives councillors to focus on either their relationship with the ward or division before all else, or to focus on the party group and its broad policy-making and governing role? Eulau *et al.* explored the concept of representative 'focus', that is where the representative will concentrate his or her attention when it comes to the political processes. Or, more simply, what it is that the representative sees as deserving of his or her loyalty. Eulau *et al.* show that representatives will focus their attention on the needs of 'a geographical unit, a party, a pressure group or an administrative organisation'.[9] In the British local context Jones noted that, as well as representing a 'geographical' area, the councillor may also act as a representative of a broad section of the community, a particular organised group, another local authority or individual citizens.[10] Heclo saw the councillor as focusing their activity as a *committee member*, specialising on the business of the council, a *constituency representative* focussing on local concerns, or a *party activist* who approaches the work of the council and representation with the interests of the party at the forefront.[11]

Yet, the councillor's attachment to his or her party group will vary in intensity and purpose, just as it does with the electorate, or any other focus of loyalty. Corina developed five typologies to explain the nature of the councillor's relationship with the party group.[12] His party politician, ideologist, partyist, associate and politico-administrator varied in the connection and closeness they have with the group and in how they interpret its role and purpose within the conduct of council affairs. Simply put, some councillors are more inclined to place party and ideology above all else, whilst others see the group as assisting them in some aspect of council work.

Since Corina's work the intensity of party group cohesion and discipline has increased across all parties, providing less space for councillors to develop a relationship with the group that may rest on their own terms. Councillors may wish to have a loose attachment to the group and to carve out different spaces in which to act, but the rigidity with which groups conduct business and act in public settings means that such space is all but non-existent. However, councillors are still free to have a very loose attachment to the ward or division from which they were elected, creating in turn a representative vacuum between councillor and community represented. That vacuum is filled for the councillor by the party group, which employs calls for group loyalty and appeals to party and principle in order to ensure that all issues faced by the councillor, at some point, will come to the group for consideration or to be solved by it.

Rao argues that, for the councillor, his or her focus tells us whether he or she is more a 'party man, a constituency servant, or a mentor'. She also reported earlier that the majority of councillors place dealing with constituents problems above policy and decision-making.[13] Young and Rao found that a majority of councillors gave 'first preference to dealing with individual problems . . . while ward commitments came a close second'.[14] Yet, there is an important distinction between the advisory, supportive, almost pastoral nature of casework, and the councillor focusing on an electoral area as a political representative. Providing pastoral care to a patch is very different from political representation and the articulation of views and opinions held by communities and other interests within the electoral area represented, particularly if these views are in conflict with those of the party. Simply put, for the councillor the choice is stark – loyalty to the party or loyalty to the patch – the overwhelming majority choose the party.

Councillors experience another tension when it comes to what Glassberg identified as the councillors' 'scope of representation', that is the extent to which councillors see the borough, or their ward as the main focus of their attention.[15] Those with a ward scope he classified as 'classic parochials' or 'localists'. The parochial simply saw the ward as the only factor of importance in conducting council affairs. The localist, on the other hand, approached ward representation in a broader political context than the parochial, to make sense of and understand local issues within a national framework. Here, the ward has distinctive interests to be articulated and met at the same time as serving in borough-level politics. Glassberg's approach toward representation is useful for understanding the ability of the party group to draw the councillor toward an authority-wide perspective, or at least containing within the group meeting the activities of the ward-focused councillor. Indeed, in a party political system of local government, the party group may be the only theatre in which local issues are seriously considered and in which the 'critical tension' between city-wide or ward-based representation is resolved.[16]

It is a norm in British local government, identified by Glassberg, that councillors adopt a broad authority-wide focus of attention and to their role as an elected representative, finding their parochial colleagues little better than a nuisance. As a Labour councillor commented of a party colleague in an interview: 'he thinks the world starts and finishes at the ward boundary, we're running a council here not one ward'. Add to this the role of the group which places councillors in a governing rather than representing context, and it is clear how the views of communities within wards or divisions can be silenced and squeezed out of the political process. Indeed, councillors will experience pressure form their party colleagues to put council-wide programmes and policies above the interest of their own wards or divisions or local issues emanating from them.[17]

In exploring the link between broad political representation and government and the pastoral nature of ward-based case work, it is useful to consider the five distinct role types of councillor developed by Newton: the *parochial* is the councillor concerned with the problems experienced by individuals within the ward; *peoples agents* are also concerned with problems of the individual constituent but also see themselves as trustees of the whole council area as well as their own wards; the *policy advocate's* interest lies in governing the authority area from a political perspective or through the implementation of a manifesto; *policy brokers* are less ideologically inclined than the *policy advocate*, seeing themselves as an arbitrator over policy matters; and *policy spokesmen* focus on constituents but from a broad policy perspective.[18] Newton's work not only categorises the role types and approaches of the councillor, but also clearly indicates that an orientation towards *policy* in one form or another is prevalent to the extent that it requires distinctions between the type of policy focus taken. Those taking a ward-based focus, however, are simply parochials. The question remains: How do the case work councillors and those more orientated towards policy deal with the issue of responding to the articulated views of communities of interest or place and how do they 're'-present those views in council – if indeed they see that as their role at all?

Many attempts to categorise the roles councillors undertake, whilst separating out what they do and where they say they place most priority, or gain most satisfaction, have failed to adequately account for what councillors mean by representation or for the role of the party group within it. Attempts to categorise councillors' relationships with the group itself have, in turn, been clouded by some assessment of the different facets of the councillor's job. Any form of role analysis and categorisation of councillors, whilst an attractive exercise, needs to place its findings into the context of inter- and intra-group politics and to recognise that the party group and its members are at the centre of the councillor's day-to-day experiences of politics. That is, all facets of the job, even those that do not on the surface appear to need the sanction of the group, will be conducted by the councillor with both reference and reverence to the group as a political entity and to the wider political party and its fortunes. Whilst researchers may separate out what councillors do into neat bundles, councillors themselves see the world as much more of a chaotic political mess. It is constant reference to the group and the nature of its organisation and activities that provides some clarity to that mess.

The party group provides the councillor with a theatre within which to conduct all facets of his or her role and somewhere to explore and develop an understanding of his or her relationship with the electorate, and the party. It is a place where the councillor can separate out a polit-ically deliberative role in regard to the electorate, from the processes of conducting casework and dealing with individual problems as a facet of the representative role – something much role analysis overlooks. The group meeting is also a place where councillors can explore their own reactions to policy issues, or policy preferences. Thus, it is a deliberative theatre and as such a powerful alternative for the councillor to public deliberation and a mechanism to resist pressure towards a more delib-erative style of democracy.[19]

The view of democracy as a set of deliberative processes is one which sits well in the local context, but is often not addressed by councillors as a specific role or role preference. Deliberative processes are also dis-tinct from ideas of councillors giving 'voice' to local communities and issues.[20] Giving 'voice' need only be a one-way process and, indeed, a theatrical and artificial process at that, where a councillor repeats, without conviction or enthusiasm, the views of some section of the com-munity. Genuine deliberation involves a multi-layered approach to debate and discussion and one that has few preconceived ideas about the outcome of the deliberative process in terms of a decision or policy solution. The danger for councillors and the party group in a deliber-ately based local democracy is that it challenges the position of the coun-cillor and the group as the political *elite* charged with a governing responsibility. Indeed, deliberation rests on active local citizenship, rather than the citizen as a passive recipient of policy and decisions made elsewhere.[21]

It is in the lack of genuine deliberation, as a vital element of the politically representative processes, that the seeds are sown for a *crisis of representation* for the councillor, the party group, the citizen and com-munities. Councillors conducting local representation disengaged from the electorate but fully engaged with the party and party group, are acting in a classic Burkean framework which intensifies the likelihood that a significantly salient local issue will arise, that motivate commu-nities, or sections of them, into some action. As a result the councillor will be faced with citizens demanding a local focus and the party group demanding loyalty to the group. How councillors respond to local con-cerns, and the communities that are stimulated into action by those con-cerns, strikes at the heart of the way in which representative democracy is conducted at the local level.

Yet, the question still remains what exactly is a local issue? An issue of significance to the community, to the councillor and to his or her party group can exist on a number of associated levels within and across

Table 7.1 The importance of issue location

Representational focus	Issue location
Party group (loyalty) Ideological commitment Policy	Supra-local, local authority wide
Community/electorate	Two or more electoral areas/single electoral area

a local authority area. Thus, some distinctions about local issues and concerns need to be made. Local issues can be distinguished in the following ways: the *supra-local,* extending beyond the local authority area (often nationally determined issues); *authority-wide,* across the area of the authority; *local,* that is internal to the local authority but affecting less than the entire local authority area; and *electoral-area only,* that is arising in a particular ward or division. How the councillor views issues so located depends on whether he or she focuses on a party, ideology or policy or on some rather more local focus or interest. The process is represented diagramatically in Table 7.1.

Councillors with a focus on the group, an ideological commitment, or those interested in broad policy concerns, will view all issues, no matter where they are located, as though they are supra-local or local authority wide. That is, the issues require a governing perspective to be taken in dealing with them. The councillor of a more parochial focus will see issues arising from specific wards or combination of wards as of prime importance and will analyse all policy pronouncements for the impact they have on a specific locality (or community of interest). Issues of course can be made to fit any of those perspectives. Yet, the truly local issue, the issue that has no connection to some broader policy concern, is held by many councillors to be a rarity. A school closure may for the local councillor be a local issue, but for his or her colleagues in the group it is a matter of the reorganisation of education across the borough and thus a policy matter. The building of a factory unit for the ward councillor is a local issue, for his or her group colleagues it is an integral part of a wider economic development initiative. Although the councillor may focus on an electoral area, the pull of the group will demonstrate itself by creating tensions for that orientation and seek to draw it into a broader governing concern. If the councillor's orientation is towards policy, he or she will attitudinally focus on the group rather than the community; if focusing on the community is the centre of attention, any demands placed on the councillor to respond to calls for group loyalty could place him or her in conflict with the electorate.

Citizens, communities, councillors and the group: confronting a crisis of representation

A *crisis of representation* occurs for the councillor when a number of very distinct political factors coincide. First, there must be a specific local issue, problem or reaction to a council policy pronouncement or decision that stimulates the interest of the community, or sections of it, and motivates them into action. The issue may or may not be related to the council, but local communities seek the assistance and support of the councillor. More likely, the issue will emerge as a result of council action or inaction or be generated by a decision of the ruling group and thus by what is council policy. Secondly, the issue itself must be of significant salience for the community, or sections of it, to mobilise and to begin to articulate, in one way or another, a clear and discernible position or reaction to the issue. Thirdly, inherent in the first two stages is a difference of opinion between council and community on how the issue should be addressed, or, indeed, if it should be at all, and that the electorate look to their councillor to protect its interpretation of a very specific interest. Fourth, and of crucial importance to the generation of a crisis of representation, is that the councillor agrees with the views of the electorate on the matter. Fifth, the party group demands the loyalty of its councillors to decisions it has made and requires them to not only acquiesce to the decision publicly, but to actively support it. Sixth, the electorate, or sections of it, expect the councillor to oppose the council decision and work in support of their position. Finally, both the group and electorate expect the councillor to act in a demonstrable fashion in a public and observable setting.

When the above factors come into alignment the councillor experiences a tension between the issue-based demands for representation from communities located within the wards or divisions from which they were elected, and the party-based calls for loyalty from the group. The electorate, by demanding a say over the resolution of the particular issue and by making use of a range of participatory and protest mechanisms available to them, can expose the ruling party group to continuous criticism and organised opposition.[22] Councillors from council minority groups are not immune from such public pressure, particularly if they support the ruling party on a particular initiative, or if the community see the political opposition to the majority group as somehow colluding in the decision, as often happens with economic development schemes.

In a *crisis of representation* the councillor will agree, or have common ground, with the views articulated by the community, but is

constrained by feelings of loyalty to the party group, and group discipline, in how and where to act on the matter. Membership of the party
group entails expectations of public loyalty and adherence to group
decisions. In this way, the group exerts a pull on the councillor's focus
of representation and is a powerful alternative to the electorate's
demands that the councillor act in response to articulated community
opinion. Thus, the group prevents the councillor from acting on behalf
of his or her constituents and in accordance with his or her own views.
Whilst any party group will anticipate the reactions of the electorate, the
group will also be prepared to ignore those reactions. It does this
because it sees itself governing in the best interests of the wider community and not in deference to what some councillors see as sectional
and parochial interests within wards or smaller communities.

A defining feature of a *crisis of representation* for the councillor is
the expectation placed on him or her that some political action will be
taken on the issue, in a public setting. It is these expectations of demonstrable support from the councillor, for either the group or the community, that more than anything increases the intensity of the crisis as
experienced by the councillor. Both protagonists, group and citizens,
expect the councillor to act on their behalf in public. That expectation
will be greater on behalf of the electorate, as citizens will operate in the
belief that their views should be articulated where they believe it
matters: in the council chamber. The councillor and the group, of
course, work on the basis that it is the party group meeting that makes
the decisions. So, a *crisis* is further intensified by two different sets of
assumptions held by representatives and represented. Whilst the group
meeting is the decision-making forum, the group itself will still expect
the councillor to publicly adhere to the decision or policy that is the
cause of public concern. Moreover, the conflicting expectation held by
the group and citizenry that the councillor will publicly act on its behalf
reduces the councillors options. Absenting oneself from any public
setting in which the matter is considered or attending but abstaining
from speaking or voting – thus avoiding the crisis altogether – are no
longer tenable in a *crisis of representation*.

In attempting to resolve the crisis situation, the councillor must give
attention not only to the issue itself, but also to balancing and arbitrating between the conflicting expectations of the group and the electorate as to how he or she should act and where. To do this the councillor
must give greater weight to the views of either his or her party group,
or to those of his or her ward electorate. When balancing these considerations, councillors use their discretion to weigh up the cost of dissent

from the group in terms of discipline, against the electoral retribution that may be meted out by the voters. The disciplinary mechanisms available to the group and the possible block, or even ending of a councillor's career that may arise from disciplinary action, weighs heavily against any electoral retribution the voters may choose to dispense. The latter is a blunt instrument, which requires a critical mass of voters to shift from past voting patterns, or to vote when previously they had not, before a councillor faces losing his or her seat as a direct or indirect result of some specific local issue. Moreover, that issue must be of such local salience as to transcend for the voter all other political and electoral concerns and other criteria that the voter employs when casting his or her vote.

The common bond of councillors operating in a party group system and the problems all councillors suffer in a *crisis of representation* is experienced irrespective of party affiliation. The ability to generate a crisis for councillors of any party places the group in an intermediary position between councillor and the electorate. It is this position which indicates the power and strength of party within British local government. When faced with a contentious, locally orientated issue, which has the potential to impact negatively on the quality of life of a geographically distinct area, yet, we are told, will positively benefit some wider common good, councillors remain reluctant to publicly oppose the group of which they are a member. Councillors generally recognise that the responsibility of representing the interests of an electoral area, will, on occasions, involve conflict with the group, particularly over a very sensitive local matter. In such situations, councillors of all parties prefer to contain acts of dissent to private settings and particularly the party group meeting itself, rather than to act in a public theatre. Or, if an issue is to be voiced in a public theatre, then it is done in ways that the group finds acceptable, such as through the presentation of a petition to council. Although petitions are often derided as 'unrepresentative' in themselves, they are seen as an acceptable way of transmitting the views of an area, without the councillor needing to commit his or her self in public.[23] One Labour councillor commented on the use of petitions:

> Look I could go down one side of the street on Saturday and collect signatures demanding that the council does such and such or doesn't do so and so. Then, on Sunday I can go down the other side of the street and collect the same number of signatures for the complete opposite to happen. But, I'll hand a petition into council because you're seen to be doing something and it's a traditional act to let the council know about a current of opinion.

Another Labour councillor stated:

> What [named councillor] did was clever, we all know where he stands on the matter [local issue], and he handed in this petition. Some of us at the group meeting expressed an opinion that he had probably organised and collected it, but we didn't really know if he had. He had made his point, through the correct channels you might say, and that was that. If we found out he had organised and collected it then there would be trouble because that's going against group policy

If councillors do address in public an issue that is the subject of a *crisis of representation*, particularly if they speak in council, they must tread a very careful path. One Conservative councillor commented that:

> I cleared the matter with the leader first, he knew the feeling in my ward and that I had to be seen to be doing something. His advice was 'just be careful, stick to the point, don't criticise the council or your Conservative colleagues and above all do not say that the protestors are right'. It didn't really leave me much to go on, but I set out the stall so to speak and everyone seemed happy. Nothing happened mind you; it was all a bit pointless really, because we are not going to change our mind.

Thus, party political sensitivities mean that councillors of all parties, are expected to act in ways acceptable to the party when responding to those sections of the community that are opposed to a group policy or position. The best way for the councillor to act is to keep dissent within the confines of the group, but as the group meeting is a closed and private affair, this does not resolve a crisis when the public want demonstrable representation from their councillor(s). It is at this point that any one party group's flexibility or strictness in interpreting group loyalty, discipline and cohesion have a contribution to either solving or exacerbating the crisis for the councillor. Many party groups, of all political persuasions across the country, attest to an understanding of the awkward and unenviable position a councillor finds him or herself in when confronted with a *crisis of representation*. Moreover, they often record a willingness to allow the local member concerned to express in council the views of the community, done carefully and acceptably of course. A councillor speaking in council on an issue can play safe by prefacing a statement with the comment 'some people in my ward think', or 'some are of the opinion that' but go on to finish the statement with support for the group line and a willingness to adhere to it in public.

Other groups will be less willing to display even the slightest crack in the party group's public unity over any local concern emanating from a ward or division. In these cases the group will expect the councillor to publicly adhere to the group decision, but, if the councillor's attendance is not required to secure a majority, the group may invoke the time-honoured method of abstention by popping to the toilet. At an appropriate point in any council meeting the whip will tap a member on the shoulder and politely suggest: 'Isn't it time you went to the loo?' As a result of the many occasions on which this tactic was employed on the author, the group whip involved was referred to as the chief urologist, concerned only with the state of the group's collective bladder. Eventually, I ended up telling him, 'No thanks, I went before I arrived.' Of course, absenting oneself from an event at which the issue is to be considered is only a solution for the group; the public demand public action by the councillor – thus the crisis remains.

Another way in which the councillor may seek to resolve the crisis is to change the group's decision. Again, however, this is a closed process, which involves private debate within a group meeting and private negotiations between councillors. It does not lead to public deliberation, which is still shunned as a way of resolving matters. It is a gamble to attempt to change the group decision, if this fails the councillor is still collectively bound by the group and by its expectations of loyalty. Indeed, the situation may be made worse by failure to change the group's decision. Generally speaking, such inflexibility is one of the most damaging effects of the group system on local democracy and representation. Indeed, it damages the fabric of local politics to the extent that communities may become even further disengaged from the political process as a result of the actions of intransigent party groups.

Solving a crisis of representation: representative theatres and acts

In responding to a *crisis of representation* the councillor must make a series of decisions about which actions to take and where to take them. As an elected representative the councillor is able to act in a wide range of settings, or *theatres of representation*. Table 7.2 sets out the various theatres of representation available to the councillor and the acts that can be employed within them.

These different settings have varying levels of secrecy and transparency attached to them and councillors can and do act in a number of ways in each place. Indeed, they may act differently in a closed setting when compared with a more visible and open place. Most councillors conduct most of their business in more private and closed settings and go as far as to express a preference for acting beyond the gaze of the public.[24] The councillor's willingness, or otherwise, to articulate and act

Table 7.2 Theatres of representation and representative acts

	Speak	Vote	Abstain	Absent
Open theatres				
Council	✓	✓	✓	✓
Committee	✓	✓	✓	✓
Public meeting	✓	✗	✗	✓
Local press	✓	✗	✗	✓
Electronic media	✓	✗	✗	✓
Closed theatres				
Party group	✓	✓	✓	✓
Local party	✓	✓	✓	✓
Private meetings	✓	✗	✗	✓

upon the interest of an electoral area need to be considered in the context of such *theatres*. Councillors can either act within closed and private settings such as the party group meeting, the local political party and in a range of other private meetings held with other councillors, the public, or other agencies. Or, councillors can act in publicly accessible and open settings, where representation becomes a visible process. Places such as a council meeting, or overview and scrutiny committee, a public meeting or other public event, or the press and radio or television, present opportunities for the councillor to act in front of the electorate. Councillors use their discretion to select between various acts of representation – votes and speeches – and between the various *theatres* within which to employ those acts. The discretion available to the councillor translates into a choice between loyalty to the party group or to some manifestation of local community opinion – or simply to the ward represented. For the most part, such choices do not need to be made, and most councillors would certainly hope to avoid being placed in a situation where they had to choose between the two competing and conflicting centres of loyalty – or hope the party would protect them from external pressure.[25]

Central to understanding the influence of the group within local democracy is whether councillors display a preference for it as a place in which to act and as a body to which they will be loyal. Tables 7.3 and 7.4 display the responses from councillors when asked to indicate how likely they were to speak or vote against their party group if it faced community opposition and where they would be more or less prepared to act.

When considering what action to take and where to take it the councillor must weigh up the political cost of dissent from the decision

Table 7.3 Likelihood of dissent: closed theatres of representation

Theatre	Labour % likely	Lib Dem % likely	Con % likely
Party group			
Speak	93	99	93
Vote	77	91	79
Party meeting			
Speak	92	95	88
Vote	79	87	76
Private meeting			
Speak	65	78	78

Table 7.4 Likelihood of dissent: open theatres of representation

Theatre	Labour % likely	Lib Dem % likely	Con % likely
Full Council			
Speak	25	59	62
Vote	10	43	32
Committee			
Speak	38	66	72
Vote	17	50	43
Public meeting			
Speak	40	56	60
Local press			
Speak	21	44	45
Electronic media			
Speak	19	37	35

of the party group or from a refusal to articulate the views of the electorate, and that price will in turn be related to the theatre in which the councillor acts. The more open and public the setting the greater the cost to the group; the more closed and private the setting the greater the cost to the electorate, who remain unaware as to whether their councillor is acting at all. Moreover, the cost of dissent can vary depending on whether the councillor speaks, votes, or speaks and votes and of course what they say and how they say it, let alone how they vote.

The tables show that a clear pattern of representative behaviour is discernible from councillors across the political spectrum when faced with demands from the public that they act in a way that is at variance with the decision of their party group. That is, the councillor prefers to act within the more closed and private settings, hoping to avoid the matter spilling over into more a public arena.[26] Not surprisingly, it is in the meetings of their own political party group where councillors are most willing to act when it comes to dealing with any form of political conflict that places them at odds with their party colleagues.

It is the preference for more private settings for deliberation and action which has a profound impact on the processes of local representative democracy. A preference for privacy when it comes to political action also fundamentally undermines public engagement with the political processes and dilutes attempts to achieve greater citizen involvement. If political representation is conducted in private, and the tendency is for just that to occur, then the quality of representation offered to citizens in more public settings is flawed and local politics remains deeply opaque.

Yet, councillors will seek to use a series of more private settings in an attempt to resolve a *crisis of representation*. A range of meetings can be held where the councillor brings political pressure to bear in order to develop a solution to the crisis. The dynamics of such events, the selection of participants by those arranging the event, and the processes of negotiation involved mean that the political processes remain exclusive rather than inclusive. Indeed, the conduct of politics operates on two levels: the privately negotiated use of power and the more theatrical and artificial display of political representation that takes place in the open. Indeed, the Commission for Local Democracy went as far as to comment that 'the council and committee chambers become little more than a political theatre where decisions are given formal effect'.[27] In such circumstances it becomes truly impossible to identify exactly who governs.[28]

Such private political interplay, however, is the most effective when it comes to developing solutions to complex political problems, or to clashes of opinion between councillors and their parties and the citizenry. Small, less formal settings are far more conducive than more pubic events to negotiation, compromise, the brokering of deals to be later reneged upon and to a sharing of views and opinions in an unheated fashion. Yet, unless the wider public can become involved to one degree or another, as participants or observers, to such political interaction, politics and democracy will remain the realm of the political party and the party person. The use of a range of participative and deliberative mechanisms available to councils to involve the public are one way in which the processes of negotiation and compromise can be opened up, not necessarily, however, to a wider participant group, but certainly to a wider audience.[29] Even so, it is the party group meeting, where councillors meet only with other councillors of the same party, that provides the environment most conducive to political negotiation, yet, at the same time, the least practical for such debate to take place.

What is also clear from research amongst councillors, is that they not only distinguish between the various public or private theatres in which they can act, they also distinguish between the acts of speaking and voting.[30] There is a real dichotomy for the councillor when it comes to selecting whether to speak or vote, or to do both in a *crisis of representation*. Councillors are far more willing in public settings to give voice to the opinions of the electorate than they are to vote in favour of them if they conflict with the policy of the party group. Voting, particularly voting against the group, is a highly charged symbolic and emotive act of defiance that will result in largely expected retribution by the group. As one Labour councillor commented:

> I knew exactly what I was doing, I was simply just not prepared to ignore what people in my ward were saying. I voted against the group, intentionally and at a full council meeting, the worst possible place. The group withdrew the whip, as I knew they would, and I didn't' appeal because I'd done the crime so I should do the time.

Speaking, however, in a public, rather than a private setting, need not signal defiance in such an overt and symbolic fashion. Indeed, any council debate can be seen as little more than a theatrical raising of an issue or placing it before some wider audience for consideration. Speaking actually requires no debate or discourse or attempts at persuasion as such, and need certainly not amount to 'a process of realising the public interest'.[31] Unlike genuine deliberation, speaking need be no more than a symbolic act of representation, the stating of a position, which may or may not be shared by the councillor, but which, when voiced in public, fulfils some representative obligation felt in relation to the electorate.

To resolve a crisis the councillor is required to undertake a series of actions: first he or she must seek to consider the issue with those sections of the public that are articulating a particular concern; secondly, he or she must use a range of informal and, yes, closed settings to bring the decision-makers and the public together to explore the issue. Third, the councillor must use the group meeting to either seek compromise or to secure an understanding that he or she must eventually act in public if no compromise can be found. Fourth, the councillor must be prepared to use a range of public settings to articulate the views of the public, and/or vote in conjunction with them, irrespective of how the group may react. The fifth point, is a corollary of the last, that is the councillor must be prepared to accept that some disciplinary action may flow from his or her actions and be prepared for the consequences of it.

It is clear that councillors across the party spectrum allow the group to fetter their discretion when it comes to acting as a representative and deciding where to act. They do not, however, allow the electorate to fetter that discretion to a similar degree. That the group is the key facet of local representative democracy is demonstrated by the fact that a *crisis of representation* can emerge as a result of its activity and decisions. Such crises would not be possible if the councillor saw his or her linkage with the electorate as stronger and more durable than that with his or her party or party group. Some councillors resolve a *crisis of representation* by failing to recognise it in the first place – there is no crisis as it is the group which always commands and receives loyalty. For others, the journey is a rather more tortuous one and councillors of different political persuasions take different intellectual journeys when resolving a crisis or when simply making sense of the day-to-day experiences of being a councillor.

The ideological link: notions of what it is to be a local representative

Councillors from different parties use different philosophical and political concepts to determine how they will operate as an elected representative and the nature of the relationship they will construct between themselves, their party and their electorate. Yet, the different political perspectives taken on these issues are firmly set within the context of representative democracy and politically representative institutions. It is because councillors are above all else party people that they become anchored to notions of a very specific type of representation and specific approaches towards it, that enables the party to interpose itself between the councillor as a representative and the community as the represented. The party provides the councillor with a constant and stable reference point from which to make sense of the complex array of political, personal, social and psychological pressures and challenges they face.[32]

As a consequence of deeply held political value systems and political beliefs sustained for the councillor by the certainty provided by party membership, the way councillors act and react to local political events becomes predictable. Once the affiliation of the councillor is known, how he or she perceives representation, politics and democracy becomes clear; whilst all councillors across the spectrum take a broadly similar view of their role and of the political world, they do so for different reasons. So, how does the councillor's political affiliation affect how they view the political world and the role of the representative and impact on the relationship they develop with their electorate?

Labour councillors: interpreting politics, democracy and representation

Labour councillors adhere primarily to a theory of representation based on the notion of a mandate received from the public, but granted to them through their membership of the party. In addition, by voting for Labour councillors, the electorate has shown support for the manifesto produced locally by the party. As a consequence Labour councillors are bound to the general objectives of the party and to the specifics of a manifesto mandate.[33] The notion of a mandate also fits well with the idea of local politics and representation as a governing process. The electoral mandate of the Labour councillor is a dual one: first, support for a specific governing platform contained in the manifesto; second, support for the councillor to govern generally when issues arise that were not covered in the manifesto. The latter also provides cover to the Labour councillor when faced with a *crisis of representation*; the councillor can make decisions – unfettered by sectional-based citizen protest or pressure – because the general electorate have granted the party power through an election. Finally, by the act of voting the electorate have given the party a right to govern and so respond to issues not covered by the specific mandate given to the manifesto.

Yet, Wolman and Goldsmith have called the manifesto theory a 'fiction at all levels of British politics, and particularly so at the local level'.[34] Indeed, whilst Labour councillors display a firmly held belief in the veracity of manifesto theory and the granting of a right to govern by the electoral support given to a manifesto, the author, in 25 years of canvassing experience, has been led in another direction. In that time, not one voter has been encountered who maintained the argument that they were originally planning to vote for my party, but, after a careful and assiduous reading of the three main parties local manifestos, coupled with close questioning of the main candidates, and then going on to discuss the merits and demerits of the three sets of proposals with family and close friends, he or she was now voting for another party. It would have been a remarkably pleasing event to experience.

As a result of subscribing to a manifesto-based approach to local politics, Labour councillors place the party group at the forefront of their attention. The group is the mechanism through which the manifestos is implemented and by which Labour councillors are bound to its contents. The group, being the recipient of the collective mandate through the public vote, can deal with issues not included in the manifesto and still expect and be granted the councillor's loyalty. It is not surprising that Labour councillors subscribing to a collectivist approach to solving local problems, also subscribe to a collectivist approach when making decisions and developing policy.

The Labour councillor exists in a corporatist political world in which the task of the local politician is to balance competing sets of interests that cut across the entire local authority area. Those interests, whether they are social, economic or political, will be filtered through the deliberation that takes place within the group in order to develop a collective and corporate response or solution. The group is the key corporatist institution in the local setting and represents what could be called the local state in negotiation with the interests of business and labour.[35]

It is the subscription to a manifesto theory, coupled with notions of a corporatist approach to governing and representing locally that enables the Labour councillor to focus on the group (and group meetings) as a body with a legitimate right to govern and to expect the loyalty of its members. The group is thus a comprehensive and coherent decision-making body with a clear concern for the general public good and wider well being. The group could expect and is entitled to loyalty, as it represents the mechanism by which the party political policy supported by the councillor and the electorate can be implemented. The group system is underpinned by an expansive interpretation of 'collectivism', not only, as a method of meeting collective needs but also as a unifying force for decision-making. It is also similar in interpretation to democratic centralism, or collective ministerial responsibility. The consequence is the same: a high degree of loyalty to the group at the expense of other interests.

The easy combination of manifestoism and corporatism achieved by Labour councillors and Labour groups, does not, however, result in a uniquely Labour approach to the conduct of local politics and political decision-making. Many facets of Labour councillors' approach to representation and political decision-making are shared by Conservative and Liberal Democrats. What is unique to the Labour councillor and Labour groups though, is the way in which group loyalty and discipline is made a virtue, even at the expense of the councillor's relationship with his or her own electorate. Labour councillors ascribe legitimacy to the group meeting as a sovereign local political body, to a degree that is not shared by their Conservative and Liberal Democrat counterparts.

Local politics, representation and democracy, for the Labour councillor, are all centred on the party group and all take place within it. Whilst it is the electorate that place the councillor in office, that is secured though adherence to a party label. Once office has been achieved the electorate are served by continual and steadfast adherence to that label on all local issues – whatever the electorate think. Thus, it is the party to which loyalty is owed, as it was the party for which the electorate voted. Labour councillors will openly articulate the view that they are representatives of the party first and foremost, but that means that they also represent the electorate through the party. As one Labour councillor bluntly put it: 'I represent the party, if you want to represent the electorate then stand as an Independent.' A view that has a resonance for many Labour councillors.

Conservative councillors: interpreting politics, democracy and representation

It is not surprising that the conduct of representation and local politics by Conservative councillors finds expression through concepts of liberty, personal freedom and responsibility, as well as freedom from interference by state authority. These concepts, for the Conservative, have a dual applicability in that both the electorate as a whole, but also the councillor, should benefit from them. The councillor is just as entitled to liberty and freedom from interference by local citizens when acting as a representative, as the citizen should be free from state (including local government) interference or any action by authorities that have the effect of diminishing individual responsibility.

There is a clear and unsurprising wholesale acceptance by the Conservative councillor of a Burkean approach to representation. That is, the elected representative requires freedom from those he or she represents, to be able to carry out the business of representation properly and effectively. A Conservative district councillor summarised the representative relationship thus:

> I believe wholeheartedly in the work of Edmund Burke. I am an elected
> representative with the interests of the entire area to defend not just one
> small part of it. Of course, I will be available to my constituents, but they
> would not thank me if I keep going back to them and asking them what
> they think about particular matters of concern. They elected me to get on
> with it. They can cast a judgement on the value of my work as a councillor
> every four years at the elections.

The freedom from the represented that is particularly cherished by the Conservative councillor, is, as Burke intended, then transferred into a focus on the 'party' as the body through which representation is conducted, unfettered by the electorate. For the Conservative it is the party group, rather than the council chamber, that constitutes a 'deliberative assembly . . . with one interest, that of the whole'.[36] Conservative councillors are just as prone to using the party group as the place in which to conduct the business of politics, undertake deliberation, make decisions and bind colleagues to those decisions as the Labour councillor. They are also just as inclined to want to do this without undue influence and input from the electorate – save in some very general way. But, the intellectual journey that brings them to these conclusions is a different one, but one with the same destination – group cohesion and loyalty.

Just as for the Labour councillor, Conservatives transform loyalty to the electorate into loyalty to the party group, but see this as the way in which the electorate are served and represented. It is in the justifications for group loyalty that clearer differences emerge between Conservative councillors and their Labour counterparts. It is here, also, that even more distinctly Conservative approaches and philosophies become obvious. When it comes to the business of local politics and political decision-making, Conservative councillors link the Burkean ethos to ideas of voluntarism, responsibility and discipline. As one Councillor explained succinctly: 'As it is in life so it is in politics: you have to have order and discipline.'

The party group is for the Conservative councillor, a point of reference for legitimate decision-making. Once a decision is made, notions of discipline and loyalty are not far behind as a way of binding Conservative groups together. The Conservative can combine representation based on individual responsibility, freedom and even suspicion of authority, with support and respect for authority once the group has legitimately made a decision. Individual responsibility implies the obligation to accept decisions, but this is granted voluntarily, so providing Conservatives with a philosophical justification for the councillor as decision-maker, free from any local interference by citizens, but bound to a party group.

It is rather a tangled and tortuous intellectual journey undertaken by the Conservative councillor, reflecting a potent mix of notions. It is a journey made all the more difficult by a general reluctance on behalf of Conservative councillors to grant the party group the open acknowledgement as a legitimate decision-maker and focus of loyalty, that comes so much more easily for the Labour councillor. It is also a journey that conflicts with somewhat more sentimental images of the Conservative as the defender of localism and the protector of the interests of the ward or division and the electorate and community within it.

For many Conservatives today, localism lies not so much in a relationship with the ward represented, but in the idea of promoting the interests of the wider local authority and protecting it from an overbearing central state – of whatever political colour. Localism means local authority not local area. Yet, there is now emerging in some urban areas a new type of Conservative activist and councillor. A Conservative distinct from the more ideologically driven types of the now somewhat dated idea of the new right.[37] A new type of Conservative, one with roots firmly planted in the traditions of the party and that sees the office of councillor as linked to the community through more than social and business ties, but through political activity.[38] That is what can be called the urban *community Conservative*.

The urban *community Conservative* combines voluntarism with political activity in a broadly similar way to that of the Liberal Democrat, but with the uniquely Conservative twist of seeing this as a voluntary service to individuals rather than community empowerment. The *community Conservative* is not concerned with only the issues raised by the more affluent sections of the authority,[39] rather, and like the Liberal Democrat, the *community Conservative* sees such activity as first a route on to the council and secondly as an extension of case work. But this does involve the Conservative working closely with sections of the community, or with more deprived groups, than would be seen as normal Conservative territory. Yet, they do not see this as responding to some populist ideal. Quite the opposite, as many of the Conservative councillors that ground themselves in communities expressed considerable divergence from what they perceived to be the 'populist' approach of the Liberal Democrats. A Conservative metropolitan councillor criticised the Liberal Democrats thus:

> The trouble with them is that they think they invented community. We have been working in our ward for ages on what you could call a community approach, that is how we originally won this seat and why my colleague and myself were re-elected with an increased majority in what was once a safe Labour seat. The Liberal Democrats say anything to anyone, they say what they think people want to hear and go public on things straight away without thinking of the consequences six months down the road. Then even before the issue is dead, they move on to something else.
>
> We work in the community and we are very forthright in our opinions, we will say in a leaflet we are going to crack down on this estate on rent arrears, prostitutes, or whatever, but we don't say anything that we haven't

considered in group, or with the group leader and we don't say anything that we could not repeat anywhere in the borough. The Liberals just look for causes to use and say what people want to hear.

Such community Conservatism sees the Conservative councillor with an active role within the area represented but one which is also reflective of the dominant position within local democracy held by the party group. The community activity undertaken is in some cases sanctioned by the group or at least notified to its leadership and is not contradictory of any decision or policy taken by that group. The same Conservative council-lor recalled attending a very difficult public meeting within his ward, to defend the council's policy (then, but not now, Conservative con-trolled) of contracting the laundry service on a council estate to a private company:

> It was a very difficult meeting, but I agree with the policy. The people did not want it privatised, I stuck to the group decision, had a rough time on the night, but now two years later everyone had forgotten about it and was happy with the service. Then we lost control of the council, but I held my seat in what was a Labour ward.

Yet, such community Conservatism tends to ebb and flow as Conserva-tives win and lose seats in less affluent areas; the party locally is far less wedded to this as a political tactic than are the Liberal Democrats. What we see from the Conservatives when it comes to the dynamics of local politics is a rather eclectic mixture. That mixture consists of principles fundamental to Conservatism, with a view of the party group as a legit-imate source of decision-making and focus for loyalty, a linkage to notions of community and localism but a desire to distance oneself from being fettered by community opinion, and where suitable political con-ditions exist then community Conservatism flourishes.

Ultimately the Conservative approach to local politics and repre-sentation is a pragmatic response to changing local political circum-stances. Thus, we should not be surprised to find different patterns of Conservative activity existing across the country, but united by the desire to provide an identifiable political presence through the party group and wider party. As one Conservative cabinet member on a hung council commented:

> We have our basic principles and approaches, but we have won seats here from Labour, not because of a national swing, but because we changed how we did things in the wards. So you have to be prepared to take the cabinet without a majority otherwise the changes you make elsewhere have no point.

The art of good Conservatism is to change whilst you stay the same.

Liberal Democrat councillors: interpreting politics, democracy and representation

Since the 1970s Liberal and then Liberal Democrat activists and councillors have carved out a unique niche in local politics, a niche firmly rooted in liberal traditions of individualism and social justice. Indeed, Liberal Democrats articulate a very individualistic political ideology and philosophy but one which is linked to ideas of community and community involvement and of the need for politics and representation to stem from individuals needs, but based on community concerns.

The community politics that Liberal Democrats appear to have made their own invoke, however, an affinity of concept with the Conservative councillors' approach to representation outlined above, that is a community orientation to representation but of community built on the concept of the individual. For the Liberal Democrat, unlike the Conservative, it is individual needs, rather than individual responsibility that matter and it is free individuals who comprise a community. As community consists of individuals, Liberalism can place the individual at the centre of its philosophy. Communities for the Liberal Democrat are not collectivist or communal identities to be dealt with as groups, as for the Labour councillor; they are simple collections of individuals and Liberal Democrats represent them as such. By focusing on communities consisting of individuals and conceiving of, and working with, community as a collection of individuals, the Liberal Democrat rejects the extreme individualism and responsibility of the Conservative councillor and also the corporate/collectivism of Labour councillors.

Yet, Meadowcroft has concluded that community politics has not had a dramatic impact on representation in the United Kingdom and that Liberal Democrat councillors do not behave any differently to their constituents when compared with councillors from other parties.[40] He does, however, link community politics to a transfomative political force by quoting Hain: 'Our goal is nothing less than a total transformation of society. In place of the competition and authoritarianism which characterises contemporary society we wish to see mutual aid and mutual co-operation.'[41] Yet, in the day-to-day practice of politics Liberal Democrats, particularly when in power, come to revise the focus on community and community politics. Liberal Democrat councillors feel the tension between governing for the whole of an authority area and representing their own electoral area more so than their Labour and Conservative counterparts. They often have difficulty in making the transition from that of an individual representative focusing on a ward

or division, to member of a governing (or opposing) *bloc*, making political decisions from a wider remit.

Part of the problem is that there exists two distinct types of Liberal
Democrat councillor: those that are motivated by political ideology and
purpose and that employ community politics as an election-winning
technique, and those individuals or residents that emerge from local
communities. The latter are motivated less by party political concerns
and far more by local concerns or just a casual interest in 'the council'.
One Liberal Democrat councillor summarised the feelings of many of
his colleagues thus:

> I would never have thought of standing for the council. But, at the last elec-
> tion each of the parties knocked on the door and I asked them what they
> stood for and what they were going to do. The only ones that came back
> a second time to chat were the Liberal Democrats; I had another chat with
> the chap and later he came back with a colleague and asked me if I wanted
> to stand as a Liberal Democrat candidate. I did and won the seat from the
> Conservative, who was also the county councillor – I'm having a crack at
> her at the county elections as well.

Another Liberal Democrat recalled a similar experience:

> I was chair of our tenants association and was very active for the tenants
> and went to meetings at the council that sort of thing. I had a phone call
> from the Liberal Democrats one day and they asked if they could come and
> speak to me, which they did, and asked if I wanted to stand for the council
> as a Liberal Democrat. I told them that my mum and dad had always been
> Labour and I'm wasn't sure what they would have thought about it. But
> they said I was doing the sort of community work that meant I should stand
> for them, so I did and got elected very easily and in my second year on the
> council I'm chair of a scrutiny committee.

Many Liberal Democrat councillors recount similar recruitment histories
and passages on to the council. For the more ideologically and politically
committed Liberal Democrat the more casual acquaintance with the party
that some of his or her colleagues may have, can cause problems when it
comes to group unity. The more party politically inclined Liberal Democrats are required to hold the ring when it comes to the cohesion of the
group and in drawing representation away from a very specific focus on
community, whilst at the same time adhering to community politics.

There is very much a tension at the heart of Liberal Democrat
groups generated by the very nature and approach to politics that the
party has carved out for itself, which makes notions of party often difficult to maintain. At the same time community politics is also difficult to
sustain, not only because of its focus on the very local, but also because

of the commitment of resources it requires, and because, as more than one Liberal Democrat has reported, it can be simply exhausting. Finally, many of those Liberal Democrats that commit themselves to community politics do see it as a technique to win seats and possibly power, rather than a fundamental shift in power towards communities that was the original intention of the community approach. It is for these reasons that community politics has failed to change the nature of local representative democracy in Britain, alongside the fact that many Liberal Democrats share the same views about politics and representation as their Labour and Conservative counterparts.

An interesting footnote to any consideration of community politics is how it can appear to work for candidates of any or all parties. An element of the recent success of the British National Party in winning council seats has no doubt come from the adoption of a form of community politics; regular newsletters published by the BNP take up local grievances, such as cracked paving stones, dumped cars and traffic congestion. Surely though, the development of community fascism must be a political oxymoron.

The impact of political affiliation

Councillors, of each of the three main parties, understandably and expectedly express clear political differences of belief and approach to representation between themselves and their political opponents. But they also emphasise a striking similarity of views when it comes to making sense of representation and democracy. Moreover, they hold very similar views about the role and importance of parties and of the party group in local government as a focus for political decision-making.

Labour corporate/collectivism and Conservative individualism provide sets of beliefs by which Labour and Conservative councillors can justify shifting their focus of attention away from the represented and thus enhance the freedom of the representative to focus on the group. The Liberal Democrat mix of individualism and communitarianism does not provide such a strong justification for representation being focused away from the community. It is all the more interesting then that Liberal Democrats largely support the need for group loyalty and for an element of group discipline. It is only the lesser degree to which they carry such loyalty and discipline when faced with a *crisis of representation that* distinguishes Liberal Democrat councillors from their Labour and Conservative counterparts. Councillors of different parties simply use political concepts relevant to their party affiliation to effectively de-couple themselves from the represented as and when it is required.

The key shared concept to which councillors across the political spectrum adhere is the need to signal to the electorate a clear party political identity and a very strong recognition of the importance of group discipline and cohesion when faced with political opponents, whatever the organisation, size and capabilities of those opponents. Councillors recognise that unity is the key to political success both inside and outside the council chamber. Indeed, group unity has become even more important under new council executives: either to support the party's cabinet or to oppose one consisting of councillors from another party.

What started out as an exploration of what it means for the councillor to be a local representative and the relationship between the councillor, the community and the party, concludes on a concern with parties governing an area or providing a clear opposition role. Such a conclusion should not be a surprise, as parties are about power, and power, in any representative democracy, even within the local arena, is about government and opposition. What this means, however, is that representation as an expression of community opinion, on important local issues, is filtered through the prism of party and its broader political focus of attention.

Party interferes, quite clearly and deliberately, in the relationship between the councillor and the community for the convenience of government. It does this in a systematic way, so as to transform local democracy from pluralistic chaos, into a more ordered system heavily influenced and directed, if not controlled, by the party-based *elite*. That *elite* then sets about running the council and employing political and economic resources to govern the area.[42] Yet, the structure within which the process of governing an area and making political decisions takes place has changed radically as a result of the Local Government Act 2000. The provisions of the Act have disturbed the already complex and delicately balanced dynamics of council politics and added a new element for political parties to contend with – the council executive. How political parties and in particular party groups have responded to these changes to ensure the continued dominance of party within local politics demonstrates the resilience and primacy of political party within local democracy and it is this aspect of local politics we must now consider.

Notes

1 R. Gregory, 'Local Elections and the Rule of Anticipated Reactions', *Political Studies*, 17 (1), 1969, pp. 31–47.

2 C. Rallings, M. Thrasher and J. Downe, *One Vote, One Value: Electoral Re-Districting in English Local Government*, Aldershot: Ashgate, 2002.

3 C. Copus, 'The Councillor: Representing a Locality and the Party Group', *Local Governance*, 24 (3), Autumn 1998, pp. 215–224; N. Rao, *Reviving Local Democracy: New Labour, New Politics?*, Bristol: Policy Press, 2000.

4 D. Widdicombe, Committee of Inquiry into the Conduct of Local Authority Business (Widdicombe Committee), *Research Vol. I, The Political Organisation of Local Authorities*, London: HMSO, 1986, p. 82.

5 J. Gyford, *Local Politics in Britain*, London: Croom Helm, 1978; K. Newton, *Second City Politics: Democratic Processes and Decision-Making in Birmingham*, Oxford: Clarendon Press, 1976.

6 W. Hampton, *Democracy and Community: A Study of Politics in Sheffield*, London: Oxford University Press, 1970.

7 M. Goldsmith, 'Representing Communities: Who and What?' in N. Rao (ed.), *Representation and Community in Western Democracies*, Basingstoke: Macmillan, 2000, pp. 10–23, p. 19.

8 C. Copus, 'Citizen Participation in Local Government: The Influence of the Political Party Group', *Local Governance*, 27 (3), autumn 2001, pp. 151–163; C. Copus, 'The Attitudes of Councillors since Widdicombe: A Focus on Democratic Engagement', *Public Policy and Administration*, 14 (4), 1999, pp. 87–100; C. Copus, The Councillor, pp. 215–224.

9 H. Eulau, J. Whalke, W. Buchanan and L. Ferguson, 'The Role of the Representative: Some Empirical Observations on the Theory of Edmund Burke', *American Political Science Review*, 53 (3), September 1959, pp. 742–756.

10 G. W. Jones, 'The Functions and Organisation of Councillors', *Public Administration*, 51 (2), summer 1973, pp. 135–146, particularly p. 142.

11 H. Heclo, 'The Councillors Job', *Public Administration*, 42 (2), 1969, pp. 185–202.

12 L. Corina, 'Elected Representatives in a Party System', *Policy and Politics*, 3 (1), September 1974, pp. 69–87. For a consideration of Corina's typologies see, B. Barker, 'The Operation of Bristol Labour Party: A View from the Edge', School of Advanced Urban Studies, Working Paper 27, Bristol University, 1983, pp. 9, 20–22.

13 N. Rao, *Managing Change: Councillors and the New Local Government*, York: Joseph Rowntree Foundation, 1993, p. 29; N. Rao, *The Making and Unmaking of Local Self-Government*, Aldershot: Dartmouth, 1994, pp. 34–35.

14 K. Young, and N. Rao, *Coming to Terms with Change? The Local Government Councillor in 1993*, York: Jospeph Rowntree Foundation, 1994, pp. 24–27, particularly p. 24.

15 A. Glassberg, *Representation and Urban Community*, Basingstoke: Macmillan, 1981.

16 J. Lambert, C. Paris and B. Blackaby, *Housing Policy and the State: Allocation, Access and Control*, Basingstoke: Macmillan, 1978.

17 D. Muchnick, *Urban Renewal in Liverpool*, Occasional Papers on Social Administration, the Social Administration Research Trust, London: Bell & Sons, 1970, pp. 105–107, particularly p. 106.

18 Newton, *Second City Politics*.

19 J. S. Fishkin, *The Voice of the People: Public Opinion and Democracy*, New Haven: Yale University Press, 1995.

20 J. Stewart, *Further Innovation in Democratic Practice*, The Institute of Local Government Studies Occasional Paper No. 3, May, 1996; J. Stewart, *More Innovation in Democratic Practice*, The Institute of Local Government Studies Occasional Paper No. 9, May, 1997.

21 J. Stewart, *From Innovation in Democratic Practice Towards a Deliberative Democracy*, The Institute of Local Government Studies Occasional Paper No. 27, April 1999.

22 G. Parry, G. Moyser and N. Day, *Political Participation and Democracy in Britain*, Cambridge: Cambridge University Press, 1992.

23 C. Copus, 'Re-Engaging Citizens and Councils: The Importance of the Councillor to Enhanced Citizen Involvement', *Local Government Studies*, 29 (2), Summer 2003, pp. 32–51.

24 C. Copus, 'Community, Party and the Crisis of Representation', in N. Rao (ed.), *Representation and Community in Western Democracies*, Basingstoke: Macmillan, 2000, pp. 93–113.

25 A. P., Brier, 'The Decision Process in Local Government: A Case Study of Fluoridation in Hull', *Public Administration*, 48 (2), summer 1970, pp. 153–168.

26 Copus, 'The Councillor'; C. Copus, The Councillor and Party Group Loyalty, *Policy and Politics*, 27 (3), July 1999, pp. 309–324; Copus, Community, Party and the Crisis of Representation.

27 Commission For Local Democracy, *Taking Charge: The Rebirth Of Local Democracy*, Final Report, Municipal Journal Books, 1995.

28 R. A., Dahl, *Who Governs?*, New Haven: Yale University Press, 1961.

29 V. Lowndes, G. Stoker, L. Pratchett, D. Wilson, S. Leach and M. Wingfield, *Guidance on Enhancing Public Participation*, DETR, 1998; V. Lowndes, G. Stoker, L. Pratchett, 'Trends in Public Participation: Part 2 – Citizens' Perspectives', *Public Administration*, 79 (2), 2001, pp. 445–455.

30 Copus, 'The Councillor'; Copus, The Councillor and Party Group Loyalty, Copus, Community, Party and the Crisis of Representation.

31 D. Prior, J. Stewart and K. Walsh, *Citizenship: Rights, Community and Participation*, London: Pitman, 1995.

32 J. Barron, G. Crawley and T. Wood, *Councillors in Crisis: The Public and Private Worlds of Local Councillors*, Basingstoke: Macmillan, 1991.

33 D. Judge, *Representation: Theory and Practice in Britain*, London: Routledge, 1999, pp. 74–75.

34 H. Wolman and M. Goldsmith, *Urban Politics and Policy: A Comparative Approach*, Oxford: Blackwell, 1992, p. 140.

35 C. Cockburn, *The Local State: Management of Cities and People*, London:

Pluto Press, 1980; D. Held, *Models of Democracy*, Oxford: Polity Press, 1987, p. 215.

36 Edmund Burke's speech to the electors of Bristol (1774), in A. H. Birch, *The Concepts and Theories of Modern Democracy*, London: Routledge, 1993, p. 75.

37 G. Stoker, *The Politics of Local Government*, Basingstoke: Macmillan, 1991.

38 J. Dearlove, *The Politics of Policy in Local Government: The Making and Maintenance of Public Policy in the Royal Borough of Kensington and Chelsea*, London: Cambridge University Press, 1973.

39 P. Saunders, *Urban Politics: A Sociological Interpretation*, London: Hutchinson, 1979.

40 J. Meadowcroft, 'Community Politics: Ideals, Myths and Realities', in N. Rao (ed.), *Representation and Community in Western Democracies*, Basingstone: MacMillan, 2000, pp. 114–137, particularly pp. 134–135.

41 P. Hain, *Radical Liberalism and Youth Politics*, London: Liberal Party Publications, 1974, p. 19.

42 G. Stoker, *The New Politics of British Local Government*, Basingtoke: Macmillan, 2000.

8

Political executives in local government: a challenge to the primacy of the party group

The Local Government Act 2000 has the potential to have an impact on the landscape of British local politics beyond that of any piece of local government legislation of the twentieth century. Most legislation dealing with restructuring local government tends to concern itself with how local government looks, what shape it will be, how and where its territorial boundaries will be, or how many tiers will operate. The 2000 Act, by contrast, sets out fundamentally new ways of making political decisions at the local level and strikes at the heart of the traditional patterns of political behaviour by party groups and councillors. Whilst past reorganisations saw councils abolished and new ones created, the scope and conduct of party politics was left untouched.

As a result of the 2000 Act all councils with populations above 85,000, must introduce one of three options for a political executive: an indirectly elected council leader and cabinet; a directly elected mayor and cabinet; or a directly elected mayor and council manager. In the first two options, the cabinet must consist of more than two, but no more than ten members, all of whom must be drawn from the council; under the third option, the executive (cabinet) consists of only the directly elected mayor and council manager, the latter being an appointed officer not a politician.

Each of the options for political executives contained within the Act, has the potential to disrupt long-established political processes as well as the dynamics of the political relationships existing on any one council. The purpose of this chapter is to explore how one of those options – the indirectly elected leader and cabinet – has been developed and employed and the impact this executive option has had on party group cohesion and discipline. The directly elected mayor is the subject of the next chapter.

The first section of this chapter will consider the purpose of the shift to executive arrangements and what it is that an executive is expected to bring to local political decision-making. The second section turns its attention to the new overview and scrutiny committees and explores the way in which they are operating alongside the party group. The third provides a number of models to explore how groups have responded to the challenge to their political dominance, levelled by the introduction of political executives and overview and scrutiny committees. Finally, the chapter looks at the modernising agenda's expectation that councillors will become advocates for the communities they represent in their wards or divisions. It considers the implications for this enhanced community role of the governing–representing dichotomy.

A new kind of political leader, or old wine in new bottles?

The shift to an indirectly elected leader with a cabinet has been the overwhelmingly favoured option of the vast majority of the local government establishment. Indeed, it is the executive option, which also finds favour amongst great swathes of party members and activists across the political spectrum. As such, despite government declarations that no change is not an option when it comes to executive arrangements, the indirectly elected leader and cabinet, if not no change, is as close to the status quo of previous political decision-making processes as makes little difference. Which, in turn, is what explains its popularity amongst councillors and political parties generally.

Yet, it is true that, with the indirectly elected leader and cabinet, we are dealing with new political offices and a new set of emerging political dynamics between cabinet members and their party colleagues outside the cabinet, let alone with councillors from other parties. It is widely recognised, however, that this type of executive represents the institutionalisation of the informal cabinets, consisting of council leaders and committee chairs, that often operated prior to the 2000 Act.[1] Even so, the formal separating out of an executive from the rest of the council has consequences for the ways in which party groups have traditionally gone about council politics.

It is the very notion of a clear and powerful distinction from the wider body of councillors, of a small group with executive responsibility, and holding clear and visible leadership positions, that begins the separation of powers within council chambers considered in the first chapter. Moreover, it is this separation that also begins the slow process of opening up a second major fault-line within council chambers and within the conduct of council politics. The first fault-line that is clearly observable in all council chambers is, of course, the political party group; the second is now that between a political executive and the wider body of councillors. It is whether the latter can transcend the former to radically change the nature, culture and dynamics of political decision-making that will be the testing point of the success of the 2000 Act and any of its executive options.

A number of criteria are available to assess whether executive arrangements are successful in transforming the conduct of local politics and not only the way the council approaches its business but the way in which party groups conduct the business of the council. It can be asked quite simply whether the new arrangements have enhanced:

Transparency: where it is clear to people who is responsible for decisions.

Accountability: where people can measure the actions taken against the policies and plans on which those responsible were elected to office.[2]

To which could be added for the success of executive arrangements:

Clear political leadership: that the public is made aware by the council of the individuals holding executive office, their responsibilities, the tasks they are expected to perform and when the holders of those offices change, either as an outcome of the local election or as a result of a decision by the ruling party group.

Openness: The processes of political decision-making should be open to examination by members of the community. Those decisions that can be made in a public setting are genuinely made in a public setting.

Community leadership and responsiveness: The political parties and councillors provide, through the mechanisms of the council, a clear and consistent leadership role, irrespective of changes in political control. Different communities of interest and place across the council, look to the political processes to provide leadership based on a vision of the area developed and shared by politicians and the public.

Within the articulation of any success criteria for executive arrangements, can be seen the challenges that exist for the way in which politics has traditionally been conducted by councillors and their party groups. Of the executive options available, however, the indirectly elected leader and cabinet has the greatest potential for the group and wider party to maintain the same level of political influence and coherence to that held under the old committee system. The reason for this is that the majority party group continues to form the electoral constituency for the political leader of the council, and for his or her cabinet. It is within the group that the various contenders for cabinet office will have to campaign, making use of existing alliances, factions and *kindreds*, in order to secure majority support for cabinet office and the post of council leader.

It is an unfortunate truism in the allocation of political leadership positions that the best person for the job is not guaranteed success. At any group meeting called to appoint leadership positions, it is the candidate that can achieve the highest attendance of supporters and friends, when compared with his or her opponents, that will secure the office available. It is a corollary of this truism, that councillors use a number of criteria when deciding which candidate to support for leadership office, only one of these criteria, may or may not be, ability for the post in hand. Indeed, when casting a vote for or against those standing for leadership positions the councillor may use criteria as diverse as political ideology and the contenders' past stance on various issues, to simple personal likes and dislikes. As a consequence, many poor leaders are re-elected and many good leaders removed from office, not because of the way in which they carry out their leadership role, but because of the dynamics and vagaries of the party group concerned and the various rivalries, personal animosities and factions that exist within it.

Little has changed in the allocation of positions of political leadership by the introduction of the indirectly elected leader and cabinet option. Even though it is possible under the new political arrangements for the council leader to appoint his or her cabinet, the party group is not entirely removed from the equation. Some party groups have reported the use of informal leadership slates in cabinet elections, which group members are asked to support if they are voting for a certain candidate for leader. Other groups report that whilst the leader may select the cabinet members, these are approved by a group meeting; others have given the leader a relatively, or even completely, free hand when it comes to appointing members of the cabinet. Conservative-controlled councils are where the majority of leader-appointed cabinets are found, with Labour and Liberal Democrat groups much more inclined to elect the leader and then go on to elect the cabinet as well.[3]

Once a cabinet has been put into place by a majority group, councillors are generally unwilling to see the executive operate without continual and close working between the executive and party colleagues in the group; executives prefer to operate with a looser bond between them and their group colleagues. The executive, however, must govern through the council and so through its own party group. It must secure and ensure a majority within the group, not only for it as an executive collectively, but also for the proposals and decisions it makes. Thus, the voting strength and public coherence of the group is vital to the successful operation of the leader and cabinet model.

The voting strength and public coherence of the group can also come into play when the executive member (or portfolio holder) faces an overview and scrutiny committee. There is a tendency emerging for majority group councillors to see their role as one of defending the executive from being badly mauled by overview and scrutiny or being subject to criticism and challenge by councillors from other parties. Moreover, some majority groups have already shown themselves unwilling to scrutinise in public an executive, that they themselves put into place and whose political policies they support. Indeed, some councillors see loyalty to the executive as inextricably tied up with party and group loyalty and set out to positively protect the executive from challenge by overview and scrutiny committees. As we shall see later in the chapter, however, the experience of overview and scrutiny is not always based on notions of group loyalty.

Labour and Conservative groups, more so than Liberal Democrats, are beginning to report that group meetings can come to resemble a battleground between the executive and the rest of the group, with each vying for supremacy over the other. In such circumstances, notions of group discipline are being used to ensure that the executive, or the rest of the group, acts to support the policies of the other in council, and to some degree in overview and scrutiny. Such battles are not a new political phenomena, merely a different dimension to the way in which groups have previously conducted political affairs, undertaken debate, made decisions and secured group discipline. Rather, what is occurring is a reshaping and realigning of political dynamics to fit the new circumstances and, in turn, to make the new arrangements fit existing political practices. It also indicates that executives are being scrutinised and challenged within the confines of the majority party's group meeting, rather than in the open, much as occurred under the committee system.

So, the leader and cabinet option, far from posing a challenge to existing group practices, relies heavily on them for its ability to provide political leadership and carry out executive decision-making. Yet, there are some tensions beginning to emerge from experiences with the leader and cabinet option for the traditional demands of group cohesion and loyalty that dominate council politics. Councillors that are members of an executive under this option are both the political leaders of the authority and constitute the leadership of their party. Some executive members are reporting that they have been faced with decisions to which there was little or no alternative but were decisions that conflicted with manifesto commitments or some other group policy. A Labour metropolitan executive councillor complained:

> We were faced with a real dilemma about community centres and simply started to explore how we could reduce our budget by selling them. The group went ballistic and tried to stop even the slightest consideration of that as an option. We had to ignore that and weigh-up all the options. We brought some time by saying we would try and negotiate with community groups and parish councils first off, but that was a tactic for managing the group. The decision will probably be called-in [to overview and scrutiny] when we come to it and probably by one of our own councillors.

His comments reflect the experiences of many council leaders and executive members that are faced with managing their groups but also armed with the knowledge they can act without the group's agreement, or acquiescence, so long as they keep within the existing policy framework of the council. It is possible then that in some areas traditional party group cohesion could begin to fracture as executives seek to manage or manipulate the group and the group seeks to reassert its dominance over its, and the council's leadership. Such tensions are occurring in a few ruling party groups, and they simply add to the range of tensions that already exist and that lead to dissent and a loss of group cohesion. Yet, the general trend emerging from the experience of leader and cabinet executive arrangement is of the group meeting continuing to be a place in which a range of political and policy issues are considered and decided upon and the place where the leadership is challenged, questioned and criticised. Moreover, despite some examples where notions of group cohesion are beginning to become blurred, the general patterns of party group discipline and unity in public have largely been undisturbed. Indeed, despite executives being able to act without constant reference to the group, executives prefer to maintain a close relationship with it, thus replicating the group dynamics of the committee system. Executives, whilst generally seeking compromise with the group, have shown themselves willing and able to act in a way that may generate discontent from group members if a compromise can not be found – executives are flexing their muscles, but gently.

There is a further, and not wholly unexpected tendency arising for the new executives and that is the holding of private executive group meetings, before the executive proper, and in some cases before the full group meeting.[4] Such meetings, of course, exclude officers, the press and public and the wider group membership. Such a development is of no surprise, taking into account the general preference that exists amongst councillors of all parties for conducting certain business and debate in private. Executive members faced with complex day-to-day issues, as well as broader strategic concerns, will seek small and exclusive settings to consider some items of political business. We may be seeing the start of a dual group system within council politics, with executives and the remainder of the group meeting separately and privately before they meet together. Of course, model standing orders produced nationally by the political parties will either discourage or prohibit such a dual system emerging, yet that will not stop it happening where the interplay of personal and political dynamics of inter- and intra-party group relationships result in such a necessity being perceived. Ultimately, such a development would have enormous consequences on the way in which political parties maintain a united front in the conduct of council business and local political affairs more widely.

The question of responsibility and accountability

Yet another source of tension for the maintenance of both public and private group cohesion and unity arises from the possibility of a transference, from its Westminster setting into town hall politics, of the doctrines of collective and individual ministerial responsibility. Indeed, group discipline has always worked to establish collective responsibility amongst councillors, or, of course, the collective *avoidance* of reasonability, so even this notion will not be particularly new. Yet, what will be different is the potential for a sub-set of councillors – the cabinet – to be constrained by the notion that they are not only bound by their party group but also by, and to each other, so that each member of the executive must publicly support all executive decisions. These are not difficult issues for councillors already schooled in the demands of group discipline to respond to, but contextually very different to the current circumstances where groups face no real competition when it comes to securing councillor loyalty. Thus, if such a doctrine develops there is a potential clash with overall party group cohesion.

In addition to collective responsibility, the introduction of executive arrangements has set the conditions for executive councillors to take political responsibility for the performance of their portfolio areas. Such individual responsibility will be a far more powerful force on the individual executive councillor's activity, than that applied to the chair of a traditional style committee. Indeed, as decisions were the collective property of the committee it was difficult to hold any individual responsible and to account for what the committee did or did not do – including the chair. Whether a doctrine of individual executive responsibility for particular portfolios develops within our council chambers depends on a number of factors. First, opposition groups need considerable sophistication and political skill in exploiting political problems arising from any poor performance by individual portfolio holders: reports from various government inspectorates on council performance would provide some ammunition to fire at a particular portfolio holder. Yet, opposition groups alone would be unable to ensure that executive members were held politically responsible for the failures of their areas of responsibility. Majority party groups would have to accept that an individual cabinet member should fall on his or her sword because of a policy or service failure within the council. There is of course something to be gained here for majority groups from individual executive responsibility. Groups can claim that the failure was that of an individual, not of an administration or the entire party group, or of the wider political party. The conditions are therefore more favourable to councillors' individual responsibility developing than party groups accepting publicly that the cabinet should be collectively responsible for council affairs, as distinct from the cabinet's relationship with the group.

Finally, for the doctrine to apply, individual councillors must themselves be prepared to take responsibility for failures or problems and be seen to do so in public. Individual responsibility has arisen in local government in the past, less from policy or service failure and more from the personal failings and peccadilloes of individual councillors. Scandals, such as the Westminster homes for votes affair, or the problems suffered at Doncaster MBC in what became known as Donnygate, have revolved around individuals or collections of individuals. Responsibility arose in the past in conditions where councillors had either acted illegally, immorally or in some other way behaved in an ethically unsound manner. All this is a far cry from an individual councillor accepting political responsibility for the failure of his or her portfolio area and the actions of council officers in managing it. Perhaps it may seem fanciful to consider such a doctrine developing in local government at the very time it is collapsing within Parliament. When government ministers are forced to resign not because of matters related to their departments, but more because of matters of a personal nature, financial, sexual, or because the press has said nasty things about them, it seems unlikely councillors will take a higher moral stand. Or is it perhaps that the opportunity exists for local government and councillors to show their moral fibre, and, like representatives should, take responsibility for their actions or inaction and be held to account for what they do or do not do when in office. The advantage of them so doing is that the ruling party group is able to claim the moral high ground and also to evade overall responsibility. This, more than anything, may lead to executive members being required, far more than committee chairs ever were, to be clearly responsible for political decisions. A resigning executive member can claim all responsibility for a policy or service failure and thus relieve any political pressure on his or her group.

The group undiminished

The resilience and robustness of the party group system and the degree to which it is rooted within council and local political affairs, are such that it faces few real challenges from executive arrangements based on the indirectly elected leader and cabinet. The key issue here is that the group remains the electoral constituency for the leadership of the council. Thus, the option does not encourage outward-looking political leadership, focused on the community. Rather, it maintains the need for leaders and leadership contenders to focus inwards towards the needs and demands of the party group and for leaders to see the group as the focus of their leadership and political efforts.[5] It is this alone that will see the continued dominance of the group within local politics under this executive arrangement. The opposition group or groups are also relatively unaffected by the indirectly elected leader option. To provide effective political opposition, and to be able to exploit an executive's political mistakes or problems, will require coherent, disciplined, unified and well-targeted political activity. The majority party faced with such an opposition will redouble its efforts at public unity; in hung councils the drive towards the maintenance of group discipline will be even greater so as to cope with the uncertainty produced by a formal administration, but one not based on a single party majority.

The indirectly elected leader and cabinet serve if anything to intensify, rather than diminish, the need for cohesive, disciplined and united public action by groups. As a consequence, little immediate change has been obvious in the nature or context of the conduct of local politics for the public observer, or the citizen seeking to be involved in and to make an input to political affairs. Thus, a rather cautionary conclusion can be drawn about the likelihood that the indirectly elected leader and cabinet, acting as a political executive, will result in any powerful changes in the nature of party politics. The culture of party politics will not change over night in the way that the structure of decision-making can and does. As one north-eastern Labour councillor commented: 'We don't have any trouble with this executive business, we just call them to a group meeting and tell them what to do.' The reality of that 'telling' and what the executive go on to do may of course not be so straight forward, but the point was made.

It is not the indirectly elected leader and cabinet that has the potential to change the nature of local politics and challenge the dominance of the political party group, rather that challenge comes from the advent of overview and scrutiny.

Overview and scrutiny: a new way of conducting politics and a new role for the party

The introduction of a political executive into local government was a relatively easy task when compared with the development of the overview and scrutiny role. Councillors and political parties understand the notion of an executive; political parties themselves have executive committees consisting of party members charged with the detailed running of the party machine. It is a commonly understood term and concept. Overview and scrutiny, however, is not only a new term and concept but to operate effectively it relies on the application of a set of principles that are not grounded in current party political practices. Neither is it grounded in the practices of the traditional committee system. As a consequence, councillors and party people have had little experience, through their parties, of what is involved in overview and scrutiny. Indeed, party practices do not operate in a way that resembles the skills and processes necessary to make overview and scrutiny work.

At the outset of the modernisation of local government political decision-making embarked upon by the Blair government, the focus was clearly on the role, purpose and processes of the political executive. By comparison far less early attention was paid to what was initially referred to simply as scrutiny, other than to enthuse that it would provide councillors with 'a new, enhanced and more rewarding role'.[6] Indeed, the continued and clumsy reference throughout the detr modernisation publications to 'backbench councillors', relegated the role of scrutiny into something far less influential and rewarding than executive membership; a second-class councillor appeared to be emerging.

As a consequence, *Local Leadership: Local Choice* explored in some depth, what had become known by then as: overview and scrutiny.[7] Overview and scrutiny was to have a policy focus to its work as well as being the prime check and balance on the work of the executive. Moreover, it would be far freer than the old committees to conduct its activities in an innovative and flexible fashion and to bring to bear on complex policy problems a range of different ways of working. Overview and scrutiny would:

- consider and investigate broad policy issues and report to the executive or council;
- consider the budget plans, proposed policy framework and other plans and make reports to the executive or council;
- provide advice to, and review the decisions of, the executive.[8]

In addition, overview and scrutiny was to examine cross-cutting policy issues, reach out to external agencies and individuals when exploring policy options and provide an influential policy development platform for councillors. One of the most exciting aspects of overview and scrutiny, and the factor that distinguishes it from traditional committees, is that it can take an external focus to its work and is not confined to the council itself. Overview and scrutiny can negotiate with, and influence the policies and decisions made by the entire range of private and public bodies and agencies that impact on the quality of life of local communities. Indeed, it is external scrutiny, where members are exploring areas not necessarily related to council activities, that provides a politically powerful ground for scrutiny to cultivate.

The government did not see fit to give overview and scrutiny committees the power to subpoena witnesses to attend scrutiny events; scrutiny by councillors of external agencies will have to be a voluntary and negotiated affair. Yet, the Health and Social Care Act 2001 did give county and unitary authorities the power to scrutinise local health authorities and opened the door to other such powers being extended over other bodies should scrutiny prove successful. It is the process of democratically elected councillors, exploring and influencing the activities of other organisations, which ensures councils and councillors do become community leaders in a way that the previous inwardly focused committee-based system neither expected nor enabled them to. In addition, councillors, as active members of their political parties, are primarily political animals and motivated by a wide range of political concerns, yet the committee system largely restricted the issues in which councillors could become involved to those of managing the authority.

The political journey undertaken by many councillors to council office did have a rather a perverse outcome for many, transforming them from politically interested and motivated candidate into an elected manager. A politically motivated and concerned individual, driven by a set of values and beliefs, joins the appropriate political party. They undergo a form of apprenticeship, taking on officerships of the local party, becoming involved with the wider party across the constituency, and even taking on party officerships at that level. They put themselves up for selection as a council candidate, and get selected. They then undertake the political task of fighting an election campaign: canvassing, leafleting, press releases, talking to the electorate on the doorstep and in various other public settings, occasionally even coming across their political opponents. They fight the election day, attend the counting of votes, perspire as the piles of votes stack up and try to work out where they stand in relation to other candidates; they feign some interest in what is happening to their colleagues in other wards, whilst all the time keeping an eye on their own count. They hear the returning officer read out the words, 'I do hearby declare (name) duly elected to serve as councillor for the said ward', but it is not until they attend their first committee meeting that they realise they are confronted with the minutiae of service administration and management and have become an elected officer and manager.

Overview and scrutiny provides the opportunity for a much more suitable and satisfactory outcome to the set of political processes undertaken on the journey to election and to ensure councillors are not elected officers. Indeed, overview and scrutiny provides the opportunity to repoliticise the role of the councillor and to provide a forum in which elected local politicians can engage with the issues and concerns of representation and governance that first motivated them into political activity. But, how can it do that and what has been the response so far of the political party groups to the advent of this new policy orientated overview and scrutiny role? The conduct of overview and scrutiny is based on a set of principles that reflects broad political processes and behaviours, rather than a managerial agenda.[9] To be an effective policy monitoring, developing and initiating body, overview and scrutiny must be a deliberative forum with an investigative and even inquisitorial edge to its work. It must be a far more inclusive process than the old committee system, involving citizens, communities, stakeholders and experts in a detailed exploration of policy problems and possible policy solutions. As overview and scrutiny does not make final decisions in the way that committees would, it provides fertile ground for cross-party and non-partisan-based deliberation.

What is presented here, of course, is a normative argument of what overview and scrutiny *should and could* be, not what it is and how it is working. Yet, some theoretical consideration is necessary from which to mould, understand and shape the practice of this new approach to council politics, especially as councillors have little experience of scrutiny, save for the questioning and challenging of group – and possibly council – leadership in a private group meeting. In developing the overview and scrutiny committees and configuring their work and relationships with the rest of the council, many in local government look to the conduct of scrutiny at a Parliamentary level to gain an insight into what is required of them. Parliamentary select committees have long been integral features of the checks and balances on the executive at national government level. In the light of the introduction of cabinets (or executives) in local authorities, which (in many respects) mirror the operation of the cabinet in Parliament, then the insistence on a 'select committee' equivalent (the 'overview and scrutiny' committees of the Local Government Act 2000) seems a logical step.

Scrutiny as conducted by Parliament has had, however, a chequered history; the nineteenth-century practice of parliamentary specialist select committees, investigating major social problems, declined in the early twentieth century,[10] thus robbing Parliament of a process by which to contribute to policy development. The departmental select committees introduced in 1979 have received mixed reviews, being described as little more than 'Parliamentary lobbyists for the departments and interests' they sponsor or to argue for more departmental money.[11] Indeed, select committees have been seen as having 'limited impact' and as revealing the strength of the executive over Parliament.[12] Whilst Norton (1991, pp. 74–75) shares the view that select committees are 'limited bodies' he sees them as a most 'significant Parliamentary reform' as 'important scrutineers of government policy and departmental administration' and as 'contributing to the erosion of the Government monopoly of information provided to Parliament'.[13] Adonis accepts the select committees as having an 'appropriate and necessary role' in equipping Parliament with the tools to scrutinise the executive but he identifies executive dominance over the business and mentality of the Commons as a major source of weakness for select committees as tools for scrutiny.[14] In addition,

Parliamentary committees fail in the task of holding the executive to account as a result of adversarial party politics which means they 'pose no real threat to executive supremacy, nor offer the backbencher any real taste of power'.[15] Adversarial party politics is a problem that has very loud local echoes in the conduct of council affairs and the processes of local political representation.

There are, however, some important differences between scrutiny at the local and central levels. First, 'scrutiny' in local government has been given a more ambiguous role than its central government equivalent. It is required both to help the executive in its work and to hold it to account, hence the title – overview and scrutiny.[16] It is anticipated for example, that the executive will regularly commission an overview and scrutiny committee to carry out policy development work for them. Such an approach certainly would not take place in parliamentary select committees, whose role is much more exclusively that of holding the executive to account.

Secondly, there is a clear division of support responsibilities at Westminster, which does not apply in local authorities. Select committees are not supported by the mainstream civil service, whose responsibility is exclusively to the government of the day (i.e. the cabinet). Select committees are serviced and supported by a detached group of civil servants and by specialist advisers. By contrast the unified officer structure in local authorities is expected to support both executive and scrutiny functions equally, unless separate scrutiny and executive support units are formed within a local authority. Thirdly, the tradition of aggressive questioning of ministers and civil servants, which is an established characteristic of parliamentary select committees, has not been given the same emphasis at local level. Indeed, there is little evidence to date of practices equivalent to the 'grilling of ministers' in overview and scrutiny committees.[17]

In other ways, however, there are marked similarities between the two systems. There is the same attempt to generate all party support for the scrutiny process, and to emphasise the role of evidence and analysis (rather than party politics) in the proceedings. It is a requirement that the group whip should not be applied in 'overview and scrutiny' committees, but making such a dramatic change to current patterns of political behaviour and practices is far from easy. There is the same emphasis on influence: overview and scrutiny committees cannot require an executive to change a decision or modify a policy, it can only attempt to persuade them to do so. The same limitation is true of select committees. Both elements are vulnerable to an executive that chooses not to be influenced, even when a persuasive alternative case is made. Both mechanisms provide an opportunity for backbenchers of all parties to influence decision-making, and stand to enhance the role of non-executive members. In both cases, such role enhancement will only become a reality if political influence actually takes place and policy changes are clearly demonstrable as a result of scrutiny work.

Yet, returning to our focus on local party politics, it is the case that the party system in British local government is far more entrenched and far more rigid in its expectations of councillor loyalty and discipline than the party system in Parliament. Although the Parliamentary whips' office can and does apply considerable pressure on MPs to tow the party line, and MPs can have the party whip withdrawn, they have opportunities to veer from the agreed line, when speaking and voting, that are simply not available to their councillor colleagues. None of the model standing orders produced by the three main parties, for example, has the sophistication of a graduated whip system of one, two, or three line whips as exists for their Parliamentary counterparts.[18]

It is the adversarial nature of much local party politics and rigidity of the group system at the local level that pose a threat to the development of the scrutiny process and could neutralise its ability to effectively hold the executive to account. The most recent research indicates that councillors are struggling with overview and scrutiny and finding it difficult to give it a meaningful role. Indeed, overview and scrutiny has simply failed so far, to have 'engaged the hearts and minds of those involved'.[19] The reason for the failure is that overview and scrutiny places councillors in unfamiliar political territory where they are expected to conduct activities previously reserved for the privacy of the party group meeting. They are expected to publicly deliberate political options and to explore complex issues, without the safety net of a previously decided group line to pursue in public. Moreover, for those councillors in the majority party, or in the parties forming part of the administration of a hung council, they are expected to question, challenge and criticise their own party colleagues, and to do so in public. It is the dual expectations of public deliberation and of challenging one's party colleagues that represent a fundamental change in the normal conduct of political interaction and challenge notions of group loyalty and cohesion on which party politics in local government has long been based.

Recent research has uncovered a mixed response from councillors to the challenge overview and scrutiny poses to traditional political behaviour and to the primacy of the party group as a theatre for political decision-making. A study for the DETR[20] took the following view of the relationship between party group discipline and the overview and scrutiny function:

> The relationship between the role of the group and the development of overview and scrutiny appears to be crucial. In particular, where the majority parties are still in control of the overview and scrutiny committees and the whip appears to still be in place then overview and scrutiny committees are not living up to expectations. Even in those authorities where the whip is clearly off, the members do not seem to have fully adjusted to the concept yet and remain unwilling to challenge executive members of their own group in pubic.[21]

The way in which party groups across the political spectrum have responded to the development of overview and scrutiny and the new ways of working has varied. But one thing is certain, party groups retain a desire to ensure that their overview and scrutiny councillors act within the confines of agreed group policy. Moreover, that any issues coming to overview and scrutiny, which have not been considered in detail by the group, receive its sanction at some point. But the way in which this is achieved varies depending on a range of factors, such as the quality of the relationships between the party groups and key political players on the council and beyond; the fragility or strength of the ruling group's position; the internal coherence of the group and the absence or presence of entrenched internal factions; and the degree of commitment from councillors on any council to making the new system work, or seeing it fail.

A Conservative county councillor and overview and scrutiny member from a ruling group summarised the views of many councillors across party when she said:

> At first I was opposed to the new system, we were all use to committees and what they did and my colleagues and I felt change was unnecessary and undemocratic. But, I have grown into scrutiny; we have had some fascinating projects to work on, our recent studies of winter pressures in the health service was a real eye opener for all of us, and we simply would not have done that with our committees. There is still along way to go to get scrutiny working as well as it can, but I want to see that happen. The Liberal Democrats and Labour people did not take well to it at first, either, but it certainly seems to me that they have positive views on how it is working now.

A Labour scrutiny councillor, from a controlling metropolitan group, summed up many of the opposing views when he commented:

> It's just not working [overview and scrutiny], none of us know what's going on any more and that means Labour councillors, not just the opposition. We don't get told anything; the cabinet makes all the decisions and

there's nothing we can do about them; there's too much power in the hands of the executive.

When we had committees we knew what was happening, we could ask questions, get things changed; we had some real rows in group, but we were in control. I used to get piles and piles of agendas and reports every week, now, hardly anything. Officers won't tell you what's happening because they say: 'that's the cabinet's job'. Scrutiny can't do anything and there are a lot of us who feel like we're second-class citizens, and that's how we're treated.

In addition to views of the nature of those expressed above, about the working of the overview and scrutiny function, much councillor concern has been aimed at the tension it generates for the role of the party group. All members will be concerned about these issues, but particularly group and council leaders. Some group leaders have expressed concerns about the effect on public group unity raised by the very language of scrutiny: challenge, question and criticism. Moreover, the title scrutiny itself suggested an inquisitorial and adversarial process that could potentially pit executive and scrutiny members, from the same party, against each other and, worse, do so in public.

As one District Labour leader said:

The group is the place to express disagreement and to have your arguments, not in public, and overview and scrutiny has got to accept that. You can't have Labour members criticising the executive in overview and scrutiny; I don't care what the new standing orders say. Argue in group all you want, but stick together in public.

A Labour leader from another district authority was far more sanguine:

It could be awkward to be criticised by your colleagues in public, but it is also healthy to have some debate in public. Its more a case of how you say things, rather than what you say. A carefully worded question or comment that raises an issue is the way to do it, not screaming abuse at me or my executive colleagues.

Where overview and scrutiny is seen as a major threat to the dynamics of inter- and intra-party group relationships and where it is seen to pose a fundamental challenge to a ruling group's continued smooth control of the council, certain sabotage strategies have been developed. In many councils, even those which do not deliberately set out to undermine overview and scrutiny, the allocation of resources is a constant theme of complaint from overview and scrutiny councillors.[22] Lack of officer support and financial resources seriously hampers the work of overview and scrutiny, especially when holding an executive to account. Some majority group overview and scrutiny councillors have deliberately contributed to keeping the new processes under-resourced out of a misguided sense of party loyalty: if overview and scrutiny cannot do its job properly, the party's grip on power is not threatened. Yet, as overview and scrutiny councillors, and those outside the executive will always be in the majority, the simple solution is to vote the resources for overview and scrutiny.

Overview and scrutiny has received mixed reviews from the results of research and from the experiences of councillors grappling with its demands and the new set of dynamics it introduces into council affairs. Party groups, of all political affiliations, have had to come to terms with the potential disruption overview and scrutiny could generate for the smooth political control of the council and for the smooth running of the groups themselves, affecting minority as well as majority groups. Certain trends have emerged in the way in which party groups have developed and manoeuvred as a result of the development of executive arrangements generally and overview and scrutiny particularly.

Such trends display how the group system is accommodating the new structures and processes and whether it is encouraging their effective working or whether it is undermining the new arrangements to maintain the primacy and supremacy of the party group within council politics and local political affairs. Indeed, it is not only resources or the lack of them that can pose a problem, but also differing interpretations of the role and power of scrutiny can see it hampered in its work. In a metropolitan council, where in 2003 the ruling group lost its overall majority for the first time ever, the new two party administration was advised by officers that overview and scrutiny did not have the 'power' to insist that executive members should attend its meetings and consequently that the new executive members should not attend overview and scrutiny meetings when they were called. Whilst this advice may have been offered to provide a new and inexperienced and potentially fragile ruling administration with a temporary breathing space, rather than serve to create a permanent political relationship between overview and scrutiny and the new executive, it could distort the development of relationships between the parties, as well as being at odds with the spirit of the new arrangements.

Models of party group behaviour: new executive arrangements

Set out in this section are four models exploring the way party groups have begun to respond to the new political dynamics introduced in council chambers by the advent of executives and overview and scrutiny and a new and developing role for the full council meeting. These relationships are presented here in the form of the party group acting as *partner, arbitrator, filter and Leviathan*. In acting as *partner* to the executive, overview and scrutiny and full council the group works in ways that are mutually supportive to and co-operative with the new arrangements and processes. Under the second model the group sees itself as an *arbitrator* between the new set of political decision-making arrangements and their new roles and responsibilities, helping to solve problems and remove blockages to decision-making and the development of policy. In the third model the party group sees itself as a *filter* of the interactions between the executive, scrutiny and full council, with each reporting to the other through the group. Here the group's role and position is more prominent than under the first two models and by acting as a *filter* the group seeks to prevent political problems arising or to deal with any that do within the confines of its own meetings. In the final model, the group system not only retains, but expands on its current position of a *Leviathan*, where all aspects of the council's political decision-making processes are undertaken in the party group before being ratified at the executive, in scrutiny or full council.

The main distinctions between these models are: the degree of group coherence in council, and overview and scrutiny committees; the degree of group coherence in other public settings, such as public meetings, or in the press and electronic media; the readiness of the group to impose a whip on council affairs and to use disciplinary mechanisms against councillors acting outside the policy and decisions of the group; the number of group meetings; and the balance between open deliberation and closed decision-making. Groups also distinguish themselves by the nature of the relationships they develop with the full council, the executive and overview and scrutiny, and the primacy they give to the party group as a decision-making body when compared with elements of the new arrangements. Finally, the models set out the extent to which party groups wish to control the political behaviour of members in any setting – public or private.

Model 1: the group as partner

The group as *partner* operates with an almost complete relaxation of group discipline and on the basis of voluntary public cohesion amongst its membership. The group does not apply a whip to its members and makes no use of disciplinary mechanisms, other than in the most exceptional circumstances, and normally for actions that would bring the

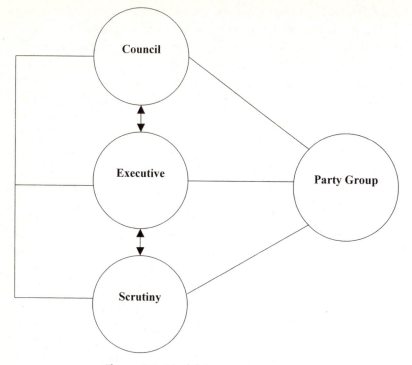

Figure 8.1 Model 1: group as partner

party into disrepute, rather than for speaking and voting against the group. Taking this approach, the *partner* group has become a deliberative and advisory body only, where councillors consider issues in a single party setting, but are not bound by expectations that they will automatically support decisions arising from the group meeting. The group acts as a *partner* to the new political decision-making arrangements because councillors are able to conduct the new roles of executive members and overview and scrutiny without being bound in those settings to a pre-decided course of action. Thus, the new processes and dynamics are able to flourish, unrestrained by past patterns of party group behaviour.

Meetings of the *partner* group are infrequent, held only on major policy issues or the budget. Councillors, however, generally cohere publicly in identifiable party groups around the outcomes of previous group deliberation because they simply agree with them and not as a result of disciplinary mechanisms or a whip. The *partner* group meets before full council to debate important policy matters or those relating to a manifesto commitment or issues of party philosophy; it does not consider all items before full council. The purpose of such meetings is to offer advice to members and provide them with a forum in which to express ideas and exchange views. There are no pre-scrutiny group meetings at all. Occasionally the group meets to consider contentious issues arising out of the business of the executive; again the results of such meetings are not binding. The *partner* group acts as a deliberative and not a decision-making body and councillors speak and vote in public without reference or reverence to the outcome of group meetings.

Model 2: the group as arbitrator

When acting as an *arbitrator* the group sees its role as making the new arrangements work and as dealing with disagreement, disputes and conflict between the executive and overview and scrutiny, or as a place for identifying possible future areas of political problems that may arise. As a consequence the group considers major issues and applies a whip to certain decisions, but only sparingly, and on issues which make the relationship between the executive and scrutiny, easier.

Overview and scrutiny is conducted by members with knowledge of the group's position, but is not bound by it and, as with the *partner* group, there are no pre-scrutiny meetings. The group meets before full council and, where no whip is applied, advice and suggestions as to what line to take are considered. If there is disagreement between the executive and overview and scrutiny, the group considers how members

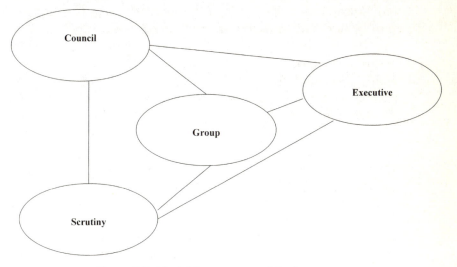

Figure 8.2 Model 2: group as arbitrator

should act in full council and tries to resolve the differences or seek some solution. Overview and scrutiny is, however, fully recognised as the body which holds the executive to account, and the group acts in accordance with this principle. The group sees itself as having a legitimate decision-making role but acts mainly as a deliberative body. It will normally confine its use of a whip to major policy issues, the budget and manifesto commitments or contentious matters where some degree of public cohesion is required as a political tactic. The latter will, however, be applied sparingly and with some subtlety to enable members to voice alternative concerns in public.

Model 3: the group as filter

The *filter* group positions itself between the various elements of the council's political decision-making process, executive, overview and scrutiny and full council, and deliberately *filters*, or interferes, in the communication and interaction between those elements, acting as an informal but important part of the decision- and policy-making system. The group expects a high degree of public loyalty and discipline from its members. The *filter* group meets before all full council meetings to consider most matters, policy issues and the budget and a whip is applied, or expectations of public agreement and support made clear to members; a positive decision is needed on free votes. The *filter* group is prepared to use the disciplinary mechanisms available to it for any breaches of group decisions by its members.

Unlike the two previous models, the *partner* and *arbitrator*, the *filter* group holds some pre-scrutiny meetings when requested by members but still does not apply a whip in scrutiny. These meetings are to enable members to express opinions and to consider issues of contention before scrutiny, not to bind members to a course of action. Scrutiny members are, however, expected to abide by the whip in full council – whatever the recommendations of the scrutiny committee. Councillors may therefore find themselves in a position where they have spoken or voted one way in scrutiny but are expected by the group to speak and or vote another way in full council. Moreover, as the group has considered an issue and expressed an opinion, scrutiny members may experience an implied 'whip' and impose self-discipline on their actions in scrutiny. Meetings of the executive, scrutiny and full council are conducted with the knowledge of the group's position; there is even some binding of executive members by the group in executive meetings. The *filter* acts as a deliberative and decision-making

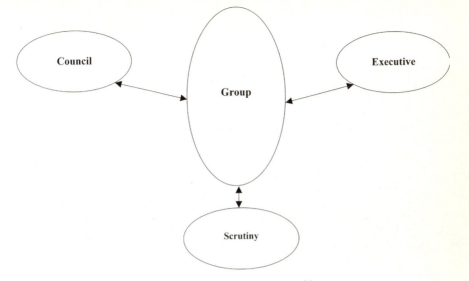

Figure 8.3 Model 3: group as filter

body, which expects high levels of loyalty to the outcomes of its meetings.

Model 4: the group as Leviathan

The *Leviathan* largely reflects the way in which the party group system has previously played itself out in the majority of councils prior to the introduction of executive arrangements. That is, all decisions are group decisions and all groups, irrespective of political affiliation, expect their members to one degree or another, to abide by those decisions in public, with disciplinary action being taken against errant councillors. Since the introduction of political executives into local government, party groups across the country and the political spectrum have shown themselves willing and able to retain this approach to the conduct of council business and political affairs more widely. Indeed, in some councils, where the *Leviathan* tradition operated, it has been maintained, and in even strengthened.

The *Leviathan* group holds meetings before selected executive meetings depending on the issues to be considered or decisions to be made. The executive is expected to report to group meetings on all its actions and seek retrospective approval, or to alter a particular course of action if this is felt appropriate. Moreover, the executive places before the group issues it will need to deal with and involves the group

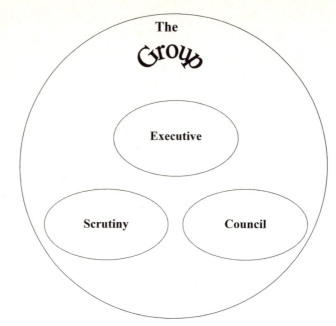

Figure 8.4 Model 4: group as Leviathan

membership in the consideration of those issues. The full group meetings of the *Leviathan* are often a hard-fought political battleground between the executive and scrutiny (or political factions and *kindreds*) with each attempting to have the other bound in public to decisions that favour one or the other element of the new political arrangements.

The *Leviathan* group meets before overview and scrutiny committees, and members are expected to support the outcomes of those group meetings, irrespective of what the standing orders of the party concerned may say. In cases where the group can not use disciplinary mechanisms against councillors acting in overview and scrutiny, because the rules do not permit that course of action, other more informal disciplinary actions have been reported, such as removal from committees or other positions, removal from group offices, reporting to local party branches and other informal pressures or sanctions being employed. The *Leviathan* group has no truck with any dissent or deviation from the group – even in overview and scrutiny. As a result, only symbolic scrutiny is undertaken in public, real scrutiny takes place in group meetings.

The *Leviathan* group meets before each and every full council and every item is a whipped item, unless a free vote is positively agreed – and these are few and far between. The *Leviathan* group choreographs full council meetings, deciding on speakers, the order in which they speak and what they say, permitting no members to speak in full council other than those previously agreed. All members are expected to vote in support of the outcomes of the group meeting. Members are also expected not to act against the group in public meetings, the press, party meetings or in any other setting where council business or political matters are discussed or considered. The group imposes the strictest interpretation of discipline possible and takes action against any and all members for the mildest of deviations or breaches of decision or policy – all disciplinary matters are dealt with by suspension from the group. The *Leviathan* group is a deliberative and decision-making body, which demands absolute loyalty and obedience to all its decisions in any council or wider public forum.

The way, in which party groups have responded to the challenges to traditional political behaviour, levelled by executive arrangements and overview and scrutiny, has had a fundamental impact on the way in which the new system has developed. The structure, processes and dynamics of the new political decision-making set-ups needed to be made compatible with the role and power of the party group as an entity and the group system as an integral part of council affairs. Moreover, it needed to be compatible with the position of the majority group or groups as providing a political administration, and with the role of the minority group or groups in providing a political opposition. Whilst party groups could alter their own organisation, processes and degrees of public coherence to accommodate the new system, most have simply carved out a position for the group alongside the new arrangements, maintaining past patterns of political behaviour.

Political affiliation does come into any analysis of how party groups have responded to the modernisation agenda and which model of polit-ical behaviour a party group will most closely resemble. The *partner* and *arbitrator* models require a greater shift in traditional behaviour and concepts of what politics are and how they should be conducted for Conservative and Labour councillors than for Liberal Democrats. Moreover, the majority of groups displaying the characteristics of the *partner* or *arbitrator* are mainly Liberal Democrat; whilst there were Labour and Conservative groups which displayed these characteristics, the majority reflected the mode of operation of the *filter* and *Leviathan*. When, however, political circumstances require it Liberal Democrats can adopt *Leviathan* tendencies. In some cases, the long-held Liberal Democrat individualistic approach to the relationship between the group and councillor has come under intense pressure, as Liberal Democrats face the reality of power and being returned to power as a majority and when they are seen locally as the ruling administration with some longevity.

There is an emerging pattern which shows that political party groups are beginning to cluster around two of the models particularly, the *filter* and *Leviathan*, as these two models match political practices that existed before the advent of executive arrangements. If this trend continues, then the new system will have been largely absorbed by the traditional ways in which councillors have conducted politics. Yet, because of the nature of council executives and the frequency with which many have found themselves meeting, executive councillors will be required to act without the group being granted an opportunity to consider and express a view on executive business. Thus, they will be some dislocation of executives from the rest of the group as a consequence of the new arrangements. Ironically, as executive members will also be the group leadership, they are exactly the councillors who will require the group to act in a cohesive fashion – particularly in overview and scrutiny.

Early signs are that party groups have experienced only a few minor problems in maintaining discipline and cohesion in public amongst the membership. Where problems have occurred, they are endemic, rather than epidemic. Only certain councils with particularly faction-ridden groups have found the new arrangements result in public displays of dissent and open political conflict between members of the same party, but this is a rarity and could well have occurred anyway under the committee system. The new system has not yet disturbed the power and position of the party group or the group system, nor has it led to any new relationships and expectations developing between councillors and the group. The dynamics of the political arena may have taken on a different context and texture under the indirectly elected leader and cabinet option, but the infrastructure of the group system remains intact. The new system has not fundamentally transformed the conduct of council politics, or the way in which councillors generally interpret their role as political representatives and notions of who or what it is they are elected to represent.

The councillor as community advocate

The government's changes to political decision-making arrangements place emphasis on councillors, not serving on the executive, developing the role of promoting and defending the interests of the wards from which they were elected. Executive councillors, of course, are not released from the responsibilities they have for dealing with constituents' complaints, or wider ward-based matters. The difference being, those councillors outside the executive will see their role much more specifically as a conduit for the views of their constituents into the council policy-making processes. The government's intention was for the focus of the councillor to be firmly on the ward represented:

> Backbench councillors will spend less time in council meetings and more time in the local community, at residents meetings or surgeries. They will be accountable, strong, local representatives of the area. They will bring their constituents' views, concerns and grievances to the council through their council's structures. Their role will be to represent the people to the council rather than to defend the council to the people.
>
> Each councillor will become a champion of their community defending the public interest and channelling the grievances, needs and aspirations of their electorate into the scrutiny process. In-touch local councillors, aware of and responsive to the needs of those they represent, will have a greater say in the formulation of policy and the solving of local problems than they could have within the committee structure.[23]

Aside from the clumsy use of the term backbencher, which appears to relegate councillors outside the executive to a lower status, and aside from rather labouring the point about representing a ward, there are other problems with this analysis. The role expectations as set out above are not new; councillors already serve the needs of the ward they represent as we considered in the last chapter. Holding surgeries, dealing with individual cases and problems and defending the interests of the ward are all aspects of representation that councillors have long undertaken. Whilst some councillors are far more assiduous than others at these ward-orientated tasks, doing more of the same is unlikely to compensate a councillor feeling excluded from decision-making because he or she is not a member of the executive.

In addition, this enhanced connection to the area represented intensifies two already existing tensions for councillors as political representatives, those between governing a council or representing a patch, and those between representative democracy and participative pressure or public involvement. The interpretation of the role of the councillor as a local representative taken by the government is very different to that taken by most councillors, the latter seeing themselves as the final arbiters of local affairs with a clearly defined decision-making role that can not and should not be abdicated to the general public. Moreover, councillors distinguish between acceptable and unacceptable forms of communication and involvement with and by the public, when it comes to responding to local opinion and governing an area.[24] Councillors need to conceptually elevate themselves above that of ward servants, or delegates, into a broader governing perspective, as, without that, they have little to distinguish themselves from ordinary citizens. Moreover, their position is weakened perceptibly when it comes to dealing with officers, other public and private agencies and the government itself if they can not act based on notions of having a governing mandate, rather than simply being a conduit for the views of others. Quite frankly, it is demeaning to be tied so tightly to the task of a ward servant. As one Labour councillor commented:

> You have to get away from this ward thing. When you're elected, you're elected to the District council, as a District councillor; you have to think about the District. That's what being a District councillor means. You are not on the District to do what the ward tells you – you have to go beyond the ward.

Championing the needs of a ward and acting as an advocate of communities from within is a role more readily acceptable to and identified by the Independent councillor, rather than the councillor from a political party. An Independent councillor from a party-controlled authority summed up her view on the councillor as a representative thus: 'The ward comes first, that is what I'm there to serve. I'm not worried about the rest of the council; they have their own councillors to fight for them. I'm elected by my ward and that is what I'm interested in above everything.'

This is not a view that that finds resonance with the vast majority of party political councillors.

Even the government's insistence that the policy role of the overview and scrutiny committee is a place where the views of the community can be channelled into the political processes offends against the principle of the councillor as an elected representative. It also offends against the interpretation councillors' hold of their role, as being first and foremost a representative of the party. Councillors confronted with views articulated within their wards with which they disagree, and which they interpret, rightly or wrongly, as party political opposition, respond accordingly and engage the party political battle, rather than channel these alternative views to overview and scrutiny or anywhere else for that matter. As a Conservative councillor pointed out: 'I won my seat as a Conservative, I'm not going to start arguing for the other side in scrutiny.'

In the one simple phrase describing the councillor's ward role as to 'represent the people to the council rather than to defend the council to the people', the government displays the fundamental flaw in the analysis of the councillor as a representative. It is not the council that councillors defend to the public; it is the party group that they defend to the public. Even for minority group members, it is defending the position of the group to the public and in council, rather than channelling the views of the public to the council, that takes precedence. Altering the relationship councillors have with the council and the citizen or local communities, means altering the relationship they have with their party and party groups. It requires serious questioning of the nature of local representative democracy and the role played within it by political parties and party people. Further, changing the nature of the representative relationship demands far more than exhortations to councillors that they must base themselves more firmly within a ward and must grant the communities within it equality with, or even primacy over, the council as an institution and by implication the party group.

With the indirectly elected leader and cabinet executive arrangement, the majority party group continues to be the electoral constituency for the council leader and, as a consequence, any attempts to place the councillor in a closer representative relationship with the electorate are immediately and fundamentally weakened. Such weakening occurs because majority councillors are clearly responsible for and supportive of the political administration of the council, which they put into place. Thus, majority councillors will defend to the electorate the executive as the council's political leadership, when needs be, rather than exposing the executive to critical analysis at the ward level and by local communities. Minority councillors, however, will have to balance a ward perspective with the much wider and more difficult task of providing a broad party political alternative to the existing administration; an alternative which they must publicly maintain and simultaneously campaign for at ward and council levels.

The indirectly elected leader option serves to draw the councillor further away from notions of representation based on a ward focus. It intensifies the personal dynamics between group members and draws councillors into patterns of political behaviour that are far more focussed on the dynamics of the party group than community interests. It does this because majority group members are now faced with selecting, and subsequently defending a political leadership with powerful executive responsibilities, that they put in place, or with seeking to undermine it if they constitute the political opposition. The same interactions between councillors will take place when it comes to selecting the leader as did under the previous system and the same political and personal considerations will be drawn upon. The basis by which the indirectly elected council leadership is put into place does not provide the motivation for a new type of representative relationship between citizen, community and the councillor to develop. Neither does it serve to loosen the ties of party, or resolve the governing–representing dichotomy. Moreover, it ensures that the council leadership will look inwards to the needs of micro-managing the party group and its internal factional machinations, rather than outwards towards the needs of community leadership and governance. Simply put, an indirectly elected leader and cabinet that want to stay in office must spend considerable time running and managing the party group – time that could be invested elsewhere.

By providing for the direct election of the political leadership of the council, through the new office of elected mayor, the government has offered a partial solution to the tensions between governing a local authority area and representing the interests of a ward and its communities. It has also offered a partial solution to the problems of accountability generated by the maintenance of the group as the electoral constituency for the council leadership. Further, it is the mayoral executive, rather than the indirectly elected leader, which poses the greatest potential challenge to the continued dominance of party politics and the party group within local democracy. Whether that potential challenge will be realised is the subject of the next chapter.

Notes

1 J. Stewart, M. Clarke, D. Hall, F. Taylor, R. Hambleton and G. Stoker, *Practical Implications: New Forms of Political Executive*, London: LGMB, 1998.

2 DETR, Local Leadership: Local Choice, 1999.

3 G. Stoker, P. John, F. Gains, N. Rao and A. Harding, *Report of the ELG Survey Findings for ODPM Advisory Group*, Department of Government, Manchester: Manchester University Press, 2002.

4 S. Leach, *Starting to Modernise: Reviewing Leader and Cabinet Models, a Practical Guide*, London: NLGN, 2001.

5 S. Leach, and D. Wilson, *Local Political Leadership*, Bristol: The Policy Press, 2000.

6 DETR, *Modern Local Government: In Touch with the People*, 1998, paras 3–40.

7 DETR, *Local Leadership: Local Choice*, 1999.

8 Ibid.
9 S. Snape, S. Leach and C. Copus, *The Development of Overview and Scrutiny in Local Government*, ODPM, 2002.
10 P. Riddell, *Parliament Under Pressure*, London: Victor Gollancz, 1997.
11 Ibid., p. 208.
12 D. Judge, *The Parliamentary State*, London: Sage, 1993.
13 P. Norton, 'The Changing Face of Parliament', in P. Norton (ed.), *New Directions in British Politics? Essays on the Evolving Constitution*, Aldershot: Edward Elgar, 1991, pp. 74–75.
14 A. Adonis, *Parliament Today*, Manchester: Manchester University Press, 1993.
15 G. Drewry, 'Select Committees and Back-bench Power', in J. Jowell and D. Oliver (eds), *The Changing Constitution*, Oxford: Clarendon Press, 1985.
16 S. Leach and C. Copus, 'Scrutiny and the Political Party Group in Local Government: New Models of behaviour', *Public Administration*, forthcoming.
17 S. Snape, S. Leach and C. Copus, *The Development of Overview and Scrutiny in Local Government*, ODPM, 2002; Leach and Copus, 'Scrutiny and the political Party Group in Local Government'.
18 C. Copus, 'The Party Group: A Barrier to Democratic Renewal', *Local Government Studies* (special edition), 25 (4), winter 1999, pp. 77–98.
19 S. Leach, *Making Overview and Scrutiny Work*, Local Government Association, 2001.
20 S. Snape and S. Leach, *New Forms of Political Management Arrangements*, IDeA/DETR, 2000.
21 Ibid., p. 27.
22 Snape *et al.*, The Development of Overview and Scrutiny.
23 DETR, *Modern Local Government*, paras 3.42 and 3.43.
24 C. Copus, 'Re-Engaging Citizens and Councils: The Importance of the Councillor to Enhanced Citizen Involvement', *Local Government Studies*, 29 (2), summer 2003, pp. 32–51.

9

Directly elected mayors: a new political dynamic or a tired party hack?

The Local Government Act 2000 introduced a political office unique to British local government – the directly elected mayor. For the first time, voters were able to choose for themselves the individual they wished to hold executive political office, rather than having that choice made for them by existing politicians. In May 2002 electors in Doncaster, Hartlepool, Lewisham, Middlesborough, Newham, North Tyneside and Watford elected the first mayors to office outside of the already existing office of Mayor of London; these areas were followed in October 2002 by the voters in Bedford, Hackney, Mansfield and Stoke-on-Trent.

Another unique factor has emerged from England's experiences with mayors so far: under the provisions of the Act a referendum is required before the office of directly elected mayor becomes a part of the structure of local democracy within a council area. Thus, voters were able to decide for themselves whether they wished to be represented and governed through a particular set of political institutions. Voters were able to select the shape and context of council politics, rather than have it imposed upon them by central government, as is the usual approach in Britain. A new democratic trend may have been put in motion for citizens not only to choose who they want to govern and represent them in an executive capacity, but also to choose how, and through what structures and processes, they want to be governed and represented in the first place.

The introduction of directly elected mayors into the territorial politics of Britain is worthy of study and consideration for these two unique factors alone. The advent of directly elected mayors, however, has the potential to radically reconfigure the dynamics of local politics and to fundamentally alter the nature, context and texture of party politics and the power of the political party group. As a result, this chapter will consider whether, based on very early experience, that potential will be realised and if, for the time being in only 11 councils, a reinvigorated local democracy will emerge as a result of the adoption of this new political office; or whether that potential will be diluted and dissipated, as political parties and party groups seek to ensure that the conduct of local politics continues to maintain the primacy of the party above all else.

The first section of the chapter will explore the potential impact of elected mayors on the conduct of local politics and on the role and influence of political party groups. It will consider the arguments for and against elected mayors within the context of party politics. The second section will look at whether the mayoral office as it is constituted outside of London, is able to transform political decision-making and leadership and the quality of local democracy. The third looks at how political parties could respond to the new dynamics introduced into local politics by the arrival of elected mayors and considers whether political parties will be able to neutralise any challenge posed by the mayoral office to their influence and position locally.

Elected mayors: politics, party and political leadership

A number of factors need to be carefully considered in any discussion of directly elected mayors in the context of local politics and these factors form the basis of the discussion in this chapter. The first, is the balance of power between the mayor as a political leader and the other representatives elected to form the council. The terms weak and strong mayor are often used to indicate whether power lies with the mayor or the council. But these terms are unhelpful, as they imply that the holder of the office, rather than the office itself is in some way the strong or weak component. Whilst personality and strength of character no doubt have an impact on the ability of any mayor to carry out his or her policies, the structural location of power and the ability to make certain political decisions are what tips the balance in favour of either mayor or council when it comes to political power and leadership. Stoker *et al.* use the terms 'concentrated' and 'de-concentrated' political leadership, rather than weak or strong mayors, terms that are more helpful when considering issues of power location and balance.[1]

Secondly, the nature and rigidity of the party political system that the mayor inhabits and what role the party plays in selecting, electing and directing the mayor once in office, will have a significant impact on the development of mayoral politics. Moreover, the relationship between the mayor and his or her party group of councillors will either work to restrict mayoral freedom by attempting to bind mayors to some shared approach with the group, or may work to ensure maximum mayoral freedom when it comes to political leadership and decision-making. Simply put, is the mayor a creature of party or an individual able to pursue his or her own set of broad policy objectives with varying levels of disconnection from his or her party. In any mayoral model the question is one of who governs. Is it the mayor as an individual, the mayor as a party affiliate (if indeed, he or she is associated to a party or other organised political body), the mayor through the party, the party through the mayor, or the party. There is also the question of what role or influence does any opposition party grouping have that is represented on the council but does not hold the mayoral office?

Thirdly, how, if at all, does the holder of office of elected mayor fuse a governing responsibility with a representational role; are they subject to the same tension as that of the local councillor, between governing an area and some representative or responsive relationship to the electorate. Fourth, the balance between policy and personality becomes far more blurred when directly electing candidates to executive office and personality has a powerful impact on the conduct of business by individual mayors. Party affiliation alone may not tell the voter enough about the policies of the mayoral candidate or whether he or she is assiduous, sagacious, honourable, virtuous and wholly worthy of the office of mayor. Thus, the merging of personality and political policy, with each being as important as the other when it comes to voting decisions and judgement of a candidate's or incumbent's worth, adds a new dimension to party political dynamics. Placing the personal qualities of the mayor and mayoral candidates so high for the act of voting means that the public spotlight falls on the individual and any fortunate or unfortunate personality defects or character traits that exist in a way far beyond that experienced by councillors. For the elected mayor, the political party will provide less of a hiding place than it has for the councillor. In turn, this importance given to personal qualities offends against a representative democracy based on party as the vehicle through which representation is provided and conducted, and the mechanism through which political power is transferred from the electorate to the elected representative. It is not surprising, then, that the vast majority of councillors oppose the introduction of elected mayors into British local politics.

For and against a new form of politics

The reaction from councillors of all parties and none, to the office of directly elected mayor as a form of political executive and local political leader is overwhelmingly hostile. Councillors articulate very specific arguments in opposition to the introduction of elected mayors into local government, which reflect their own concerns over the potential disruption of existing power and personal relationships and damage to the political status quo. They also see the mayoral office resulting in a reduction of political influence for councillors and as posing a threat to the position of the party group as the most powerful political decision-making forum within local politics. Moreover, the views councillors express on the issue are often incongruent with the views of the public.[2]

The arguments often set out by councillors in opposition to elected mayors are reactionary in nature, based on resistance to change that levels a specific challenge to existing power-holders, political structures and relationships. Moreover, it is resistance to change that would see a transference of the ability to select the political head of the council, from councillors and party groups, to the wider electorate, that is a change that opens-up the decision-making process about political leadership and takes progress along the political career path of a council out of the hands of councillors when it comes to the top post. Councillors, by and large, oppose the extension of the franchise when it comes to deciding on the holders of executive political office, preferring to keep that decision to themselves. The arguments displayed against the office of elected mayor by councillors link directly to the relationship councillors have with their political parties and into the conduct of council politics through the political party group. Yet, many of these arguments are disguised in the language of democracy and political accountability and are firmly rooted in notions of a Burkean approach to local representation. Moreover, such arguments are not unique to councillors from a single party; rather they find a resonance across the political spectrum.

The arguments maintained by councillors opposed to elected mayors, fall into three broad categories of concern: undermining local party politics; allocation of power and use of patronage; and misuse of office by the individual mayor. Local democracy and party politics is seen as under considerable threat from the arrival of an elected mayor and concerns here fall into two sub-categories: relationships with a mayor from the councillors own party and relationships with a mayor from another party, or worse, from no party. A genuine unease exists amongst councillors that the elected mayor can and will act without reference to his or her party colleagues on the council. Indeed, the mayor may stray from manifesto commitments made by the group, or respond to political circumstances without consulting or involving the party or group. Such concerns are more prevalent amongst Labour councillors, although, Conservative and Liberal Democrats also expressed similar unease. Councillors, with a tradition of selecting the political head of the council, see the ending of that right as a fundamental attack on the position they hold and on the way in which the party group relates to its leadership.

A Labour borough councillor commented:

> Mayors are a travesty of democracy, it is almost impossible for the party to ensure a mayor sticks to party policy and doesn't go off and do what ever they feel like. They're in for four years and can do what they like; all we can do is de-select them afterwards. A mayor could make a mockery of the party and there's nothing we could do in the short term.

A mayor popular with the public but who had, however, fallen out of favour with his or her party may seek sources of support from coalitions and alliances formed outside the party to fight for re-election. Indeed, de-selection may prove to be a blunt instrument for the party and not provide the stimulus to party loyalty and discipline for mayors in the way that it does for the councillor.[3]

A Conservative county councillor commented in a similar vein to the Labour councillor quoted above:

> As a Conservative I don't expect to be able to tell the leader or in this case the mayor, what to do, I know that's what upsets Labour councillors. But, I do expect to be able to ensure the mayor supports Conservative policies and acts as a good Conservative. We have our share of mavericks and if one of these types became a mayor they would be very difficult to handle and could damage the party. Best we [the group] select the mayor rather than have someone else do it.

When the mayor comes from another party, or is independent of party, the response is far more intense, as a Conservative Borough councillor simply explained: 'We would be completely out of it; an awful lot of power would rest with the mayor and we would have no influence at all'; this is a view echoed by Labour and Liberal Democrat councillors. It would appear that councillors have forgotten that under the old committee system if in the minority group they were also *completely out of it*, with only an illusion of influence granted to them by committee work.

It is with the potential for a candidate independent of party to be elected as mayor that councillors reserve their most intensive fire. The common concern was that some local notable or worse a sport, film or music celebrity would decide to seek mayoral office and use the seemingly unfair advantage of an existing high profile to trounce a party candidate. The example most often and tediously cited by councillors for the likelihood of this happening is Clint Eastwood, the one time mayor of Carmel in California. It is in the use of these types of arguments where the sanctity of party as the icon of politics and local elections is most clearly advocated by councillors. The logic runs: if an actor can become a mayor, then the system is wrong as elected office is the property of party and of the political insider who knows about local government and knows what is needed to make decisions about policy and services – those outside the system of the party lack that basic knowledge.

A Labour councillor summed up the views of councillors across party when she said:

> You could have anybody standing and being elected as mayor whether they know anything about local government or not. What if David Beckham wanted to be mayor of Manchester; people would vote for him because of who he is, not what he believes or what he would do, or what he thinks about care of the elderly for example. You have to understand politics and local government to be a councillor, yet film stars and pop stars might just want to have a go as a publicity stunt and they'd win, its obvious isn't it. You wouldn't know what they stood for or what party they supported or voted for, how could people make a proper decision when all they've got to go on was the last goal for England or the last number one record.

The tirade continued in the same vein for sometime, but the above extract provides the gist of the message: high profile, popular and independent, bad; unknown, safe, party hack, good. She also mentioned Clint Eastwood along the way and suggested the political slogan 'go ahead make my election-day'. David Beckham, of course, could not stand as mayor of Manchester as he neither lives in, nor has his principle place of business within Manchester City boundaries; a case of not letting the facts get in the way of a good pro-party argument. When discussing with councillors the idea of elected mayors there is an almost tangible fear amongst them that some well-known public figure, outside the world of party politics, could snatch away what was rightly the prize of the party – the mayoral office. Somehow, a local personality from the world of entertainment, or indeed anyone outside party politics, putting themselves forward for mayoral office, and wresting the prize from a party candidate, was not seen as *democratic* or fair. With the party allegiance of some high-profile individuals unknown, notions of democracy and politics as the territory of political parties would be undermined – perhaps fatally.

Taking a surprising second place to fears of celebrity mayors are mayors from the political extremes. Councillors of all three parties mentioned the possibility that the British National Party might win mayoral office as a reason why mayors should not be introduced into British local politics. It now appears that not liking the result of an election is a sound enough reason not to have one. Whilst the BNP have already secured election to 16 council seats across the country and in Burnley were the second largest party group on the council, no councillor interviewed suggested that the office of councillor should now be abolished in case the BNP won anymore seats.

A second constant category of concern for councillors is what they perceive to be the concentration of power into the hands of a single individual, elected by the public. Here, the power held by the mayor is often distorted beyond the realms of fantasy. Yet, councillors express little concern that the indirectly elected leader has broadly similar powers to the elected mayor, because it is they that select the leader. It is not so much the power of the mayor that concerns them, but that the electorate decide on the individual granted that power. But, in the responses from councillors about the power of the mayor one could be forgiven for concluding that the office holder would make decisions over life and death. Comments like: 'too much power for one person', 'centralisation gone mad' 'dangerous to have all that power in one pair of hands' and 'the road to an elected dictator' abound. Careful probing uncovers, however, that councillors are more concerned that power is not concentrated in the hands of political rivals, both within and outside the party, rather than the principle of what they see to be centralised power *per se*.

Not only does the office of directly elected mayor mean an end to the party group's power to select the political head of the council, it also means the loss of power to appoint the entire political leadership of the council. It is the mayor, not the party group that appoints the cabinet, and, whilst a mayor will want to balance his or her cabinet from amongst the factions within his or her the group, or even across the parties on the council, the mayor has an otherwise free hand. The selection of cabinet members by the mayor represents a departure from past patterns of political behaviour when it comes to putting a council leadership into place. As one elected mayor commented:

> The group had re-elected [named councillor] year after year to the cabinet and to the chair of [named committee] before that and he was useless. The department was badly run and the services were just not doing what we needed to be done in such a public and high profile area. But, I was stuck with him, he had supporters in the group that liked his politics despite his lack of ability and I couldn't shift him. The first thing I did as mayor was to call him in and sack him and to put someone in the job I knew could do it, it was worth it just for that.

Opposition to elected mayors is also rooted in concerns about the individual holding the office that extend to issues of wrong-doing and the fear most expressed by councillors about elected mayors is that of corruption. Indeed, one Labour councillor stated at a public meeting that: 'They have elected mayors in America and every single one of them is corrupt.' A comment, which displays remarkably assiduous research and detailed personal knowledge of thousands of individuals; or, more likely, political bile and prejudice, and an over excited imagination fed on a diet of the Hollywood depiction of mayors, and brought on by a fear of loosing personal power and influence. Corruption it seems goes hand-in-hand with political centralisation and, for councillors, elected mayors will just be more corrupt, and or corruptible, than the holders of the office of councillor or indirectly elected council leader. There is no evidence provided to substantiate this claim, coupled with a convenient oversight and forgetfulness of instances where councillors themselves have been accused and convicted of wrongdoing of one sort or another. Yet, it is not any inanimate political institution that is inherently corrupt or corruptible, but the holders of political office; wrongdoing can occur in any political model and is not confined to one type, structure or culture, as the case histories of wrong-doing amongst councillors themselves indicate.

New challenges to party dominance

The introduction of elected mayors into the local political landscape poses a fundamental set of challenges to the role and place of party in local politics and democracy. It has the potential to undermine the political party as the vehicle through which political representation is provided, as does any direct election to executive office; yet realising that potential is another matter entirely. The challenges posed to party dominance of local politics are at the heart of the reaction against the new political institution articulated by councillors as party people. Not only does the mayoral office transfer selection of the political head of the council to the electorate, and so provide uncertainty as to the outcome, it also loosens the ties between party and mayor in a way that does not occur for the indirectly elected leader. The leader can focus entirely on the needs of group management, whilst the mayor must look beyond the group and the party to the needs of the wider electorate and community. Moreover, the party may be sidelined by a mayor searching to create alliances and coalitions of interest around specific mayoral initiatives or polices. Some mayoral authorities are already experiencing this

new phenomenon, as party mayors seek to develop policy and communication networks that extend beyond the party group and local party.
To the independent mayor the need to construct such *issue coalitions*
within and beyond the council chamber, is a common political experience; for the party person, schooled in group discipline and cohesion,
this is a wholly new and unfamiliar experience, but not one that is totally
unwelcome, amongst mayors at least. As one Labour mayor commented: 'The group must realise I can do things without asking them
first and I want to talk to far more people about certain issues than just
the [Labour] group.'

An additional concern for political parties to the potential loosening
of ties between mayor and the party is the high public profile mayors will
be able to develop. A high public profile whilst not beyond the grasp of
an indirectly elected leader, is easier for a mayor because direct election
across the whole of an authority area gives mayoral candidates a head start
when it comes to public recognition. As a mayor commented when comparing levels of public recognition and public contact with his previous
experiences as a council leader 'As leader I got 30–40 queries a day. As
mayor I get 100–120 a day . . . people can see one person in charge, even
though I'm not responsible for it all'.[4] Such public profile and high levels
of public recognition are a potential that exists for all elected mayors, but
are only high by comparison with council leaders and other councillors.
Moreover, high public profile brings with it party political dangers. It is
the notion that politicians from a particular party will have a profile over
and above that of other councillors and the party, which causes friction
between the mayoral office and the party and party group. Councillors
often display a suspicion of their party colleagues who assiduously nurse
the local media and develop a somewhat higher profile than is felt decent.[5]

Media focus and attention on the mayor as an individual will inev-
itably feed personal and *kindred* jealousies and rivalries that are a part of
the dystopian world of local party politics. But, worse than that, media
attention on the mayor could also lead to suspicions within the party
that the mayor has developed a greater profile as an individual political
office-holder than as a party representative and member. By and large,
when it comes to the world of local party politics, high public profile
and media attention are not a valuable currency as they produce the view
that the party has been relegated in the eyes of the public. As one
Conservative councillor said of a colleague:

> He is always in the press about one thing or another. If it's a quite news
> week I pretty sure they phone him up and ask him to give a quote or
> comment on the weather. I never trust some one who's in the press that

much. I rather think this is all about some parliamentary ambition and nothing to do with being a councillor.

A Labour councillor was even more forthright about media attention.

> You have to be careful, they [the press] are only looking to trip us up; I'd say nothing to them about anything. We do have a media prima donna and its all about him, he never mentions the party in the press at all; even the leaflets he puts out in his ward hardly mention Labour. No, if you can't use the press to publicise the party then don't use them at all.

Liberal Democrats took a different view of using the press when it came to local campaigns and publicising *Focus Team* members that would then go on to be council candidates. For the Liberal Democrats the press and wider media are other tools for political advertisement and campaigning, with resultant electoral payoffs. They were, however, concerned about mayors using the media to gain a personal profile, which contradicted notions of councillors using the press for similar reasons. The contradiction, however, simply stems from a dislike of elected mayors.

Much of the debate amongst councillors and their parties concerning mayors has led to a polarisation of opinion and the subject becoming a shibboleth of the belief in the right of party to govern locally. Indeed, little has changed in the quality of the debate since Hambleton identified elected mayors as the source of yet more 'pro' and 'anti' camps serving to obfuscate public deliberation and consideration of political leadership.[6] Yet, it would be wrong to suggest that all councillors are firmly lodged within the 'anti' camp. Councillors have played a particularly visible, innovative and imaginative role in many of the referenda campaigns fought on the introduction of an elected mayor. Securing high profile and popular support for the 'Yes' campaign from West Ham United was particularly valuable to the Newham 'Yes' Campaign organised by some of the Borough's Labour councillors.[7] Clearly, in those areas that now have elected mayors, existing councillors and political parties provided the intellectual, political, financial and campaigning resources and experience needed to win a referendum campaign. In contrast, in the areas where referenda have been lost, councillors and parties would be expending similar resources to secure a 'no' vote.

The 'pro' mayor councillor is in a small minority amongst his or her colleagues. They are just as inclined, however, to place as much priority on the role and place of party in local politics than the 'anti' mayor councillor. What often distinguishes them is a realisation that the rigidity, with which party conducts the politics of the local territory, can act as a barrier to effective political leadership, serve to deter citizens from engaging in the political processes and unnecessarily party-politicise all aspects of local democracy. Party politics need not result in such deleterious impacts, but its very nature and the relationships between party and power at the local level encourage a certain kind of political conduct and behaviour amongst parties and party people. Thus, a self-fulfilling and circular political dynamic is generated with party structure and processes resulting in a specific interpretation of politics and particular types of political behaviour and conduct, which in turn serves to reinforce the nature of party and the party person's relationship to it. Some see elected mayors as a way of breaking this circle of political inertia.[8] But, many councillors remain fearfully unconvinced of the need for such radical surgery to the local body politic.

The elected mayor model, whilst raising the prospect of the relegation of party within local democracy and within council chamber politics, does provide an opportunity to revitalise territorial politics rather than serve to de-politicise the democratic processes. The office can achieve such re-vitalisation and a realignment of political processes and conduct because it removes local politicians from the trap of becoming fixated on issues of service delivery and management at the expense of political leadership and the development of a political vision. Bullock notes a major pitfall for mayors and indeed all councillors when he states:

> If we define ourselves by the way our councils deliver services there will be little opportunity to exploit our new role. I am not just the mayor of Lewisham Council I am the mayor of the whole Borough of Lewisham and the added value of the new system will come as much outside the Town Hall as it does inside . . . Neither must I neglect my role as a politician. Elected mayors will be seen as the leaders of their local parties to an extent that leaders of party groups rarely were.[9]

The group or the wider party of course, may not share the last comment, but he is right in identifying the challenge for parties to see themselves and elected representatives in a new light and to see local political leadership and party leadership in the same light. His notion that mayors should not be defined by council services also stands for councillors under mayoral arrangements. Not only will they be required to hold the mayor to account, they will need to rise above the minutiae of service delivery and management into a much more politically representative role. A role with a far broader focus on political leadership and policy development than previously, and far broader than their role under an indirectly elected leader, where the pressure to focus on service minutiae will be magnified.

Achieving such a transformation in the context and texture of local politics and political leadership requires a new set of relationships and dynamics, between councillors, parties, communities and citizens. Which in turn rests on the office of elected mayor stimulating public interest and engagement not just with local government, but with local democracy and politics. Stimulating such interest is a tall order for a new political office and set of office holders, but an order to which we now turn.

Mayors: re-vitalising local democracy or pursuing party politics

The Local Government Act 2000 required councils to consult the public about the three options for executive arrangements: indirectly elected leader and cabinet, directly elected mayor and cabinet and directly elected mayor and council manager. Those councils proposing to move to either of the mayoral options would be required to hold a binding referendum on the matter. Councils are also required to hold a referendum on the introduction of an elected mayor if 5 per cent or more of the local electorate sign a petition to that effect. Elected mayors, of either type, are to provide high-profile and visible political leadership to the local community and, in the government's eyes, come to that task with a greater legitimacy, both actual and assumed, than that held by the indirectly elected council leader.[10]

Direct election would enable the mayor to act on behalf of the whole area, promoting and protecting its interests far beyond the council boundaries. Indeed, the mayor would be the embodiment of the area he or she served, speaking on the same level as ministers; acting as the focal point for major projects; and linking territorial politics, where appropriate, into a national, European and even global network. Moreover, the mayoral office would be the first port of call for those seeking to apportion praise or blame for the success or failure of some local initiative. All of this could be achieved because the mayor held a direct mandate from the entire electorate. Yet, despite the high hopes that elected mayors would spark a blaze of public interest in local political leadership and ignite wider public involvement in local democracy, the response from the public to the possibility of being governed by this new political office, has been less than enthusiastic.

Thirty mayoral referendums have been held so far under the provisions of the 2000 Act and Table 9.1 sets out the results. The mayoral

Table 9.1 Results in mayoral referendums 2001–2

Council	Date	Result	For	%	Against	%	Turn out (%)	Type
Berwick Upon Tweed	7 June 2001	No	3,617	26	10,212	74	64	Poll with GE
Cheltenham	28 June 2001	No	8,083	33	16,602	67	31	All Postal
Gloucester	28 June 2001	No	7,731	31	16,317	69	31	All postal
Watford	12 July 2001	Yes	7,636	52	7,140	48	24.5	All postal
Doncaster	20 Sept. 2001	Yes	35,453	65	19,398	35	25	All postal
Kirklees	4 Oct. 2001	No	10,169	27	27,977	73	13	Normal
Sunderland	11 Oct. 2001	No	9,593	43	12,209	57	10	Normal
Hartlepool	18 Oct. 2001	Yes	10,667	51	10,294	49	31	All postal
LB Lewisham	18 Oct. 2001	Yes	16,822	51	15,914	49	18	All postal
North Tyneside	18 Oct. 2001	Yes	30,262	58	22,296	42	36	All postal
Middlesbrough	18 Oct. 2001	Yes	29,067	84	5,422	16	34	All postal
Sedgefield	18 Oct. 2001	No	10,628	47	11,869	53	33.3	All postal
Brighton and Hove	18 Oct. 2001	No	22,724	38	37,214	62	32	All postal
Redditch	8 Nov. 2001	No	7,250	44	9,198	56	28.3	All postal
Durham	20 Nov. 2001	No	8,327	41	11,974	59	28.5	All postal

Council	Date	Result	For	%	Against	%	Turn out (%)	Type
Harrow	7 Dec. 2001	No	17,502	42	23,554	58	26.06	All postal
Plymouth	24 Jan. 2002	No	29,553	41	42,811	59	39.78	All postal
Harlow	24 Jan. 2002	No	5,296	25	15,490	75	36.38	All postal
LB Newham	31 Jan. 2002	Yes	27,163	68.2	12,687	31.8	25.9	All postal
Shepway	31 Jan. 2002	No	11,357	44	14,438	56	36.3	All postal
LB Southwark	31 Jan. 2002	No	6,054	31.4	13,217	68.6	11.2	Normal
West Devon	31 Jan. 2002	No	3,555	22.6	12,190	77.4	41.8	All postal
Bedford	21 Feb. 2002	Yes	11,316	67.2	5,537	32.8	15.5	Normal
LB Hackney	2 May 2002	Yes	24,697	58.94	10,547	41.06	31.85	All postal
Mansfield	2 May 2002	Yes	8,973	54	7,350	44	21.04	Normal
Newcastle-under-Lyme	2 May 2002	No	12,912	44	16,468	56	31.5	Normal
Oxford	2 May 2002	No	14,692	44	18,686	56	33.8	Normal
Stoke-on-Trent	2 May 2002	Yes	28,601	58	20,578	42	27.8	Normal
Corby	3 Oct. 2002	No	5,351	46	6,239	53.64	30.91	All postal
LB Ealing	12 Dec. 2002	No	9,454	44.8	11,655	55.2	9.8	Combination postal and ballot

Source: The New Local Government Network Website, April 2003: nlgn.org.uk.

experiment in England has clearly not succeeded in stimulating wide-spread public interest or excitement or motivated greater public engagement in local politics. Only six of the 30 mayoral referendums so far held have resulted from public petition; the opportunity to decide on the structure of local political leadership and to take control of the shape and nature of how the area should be governed has meet largely with national indifference. All but one of the non-petition generated referendums have been council initiatives and not all the councils supported the mayoral option, rather saw a referendum as a way of removing the issue from the public agenda, at least for five years – the legal period to expire between referendums. One referenda, held in the London Borough of Southwark, was imposed on the council by the Secretary of State as public consultation appeared to favour a mayor yet the council opted for an indirectly elected council leader. The resulting 'No' vote in the referendum indicates more the power of local politicians to campaign for, and achieve, a result they want from an electoral process, rather than the inaccuracies of public consultation, as councillors and parties are able to employ all their political resources and skills to secure a favourable result from a referendum.[11]

The way in which parties have fought referendum campaigns has fallen into four broad types. First, all three main parties have combined to seek a particular result; secondly, the dominant local party has controlled the campaign, with minor parties sidelined; thirdly, parties have agreed to disagree internally and 'pro' and 'anti' groups within parties have campaigned separately, either in alliance with other parties or groups that share a position, or worked without alliances. Fourthly, a strong independent, normally 'pro' mayor group has emerged to challenge the domination of the referendum campaign by political parties: the 'Mayor 4 Stoke' and Bedford and Mansfield campaigns are notable examples. Whichever type of political campaign is fought, one thing is clear, the role played by political parties is crucial. But, the referendum campaigns and results so far have also demonstrated one other startling fact: despite the local political monolith that is the political party, a strong, well-resourced and organised independent campaign can brake the stranglehold on local democracy held by political parties. Moreover, such independent campaigns as have occurred, have built on existing political and social organisations and have acted as an umbrella group for those within the local civil society concerned to influence the dynamics of local politics.

As for the results of the mayoral elections themselves, they speak volumes about the fragility of the hold that party has over local politics. Table 9.2 sets out the results of the mayoral elections held in 2002.

Table 9.2 Mayoral election results, May and October 2002

	Winning candidate	Political affiliation	Elected on 1st or 2nd count	Electorate	Turnout
Council May 2002 election					
Doncaster	Martin Winter	Labour	2nd	216,097	58,487 (27.07%)
Hartlepool	Stuart Drummond	Independent	2nd	67,903	19,544 (28.78%)
L.B.Lewisham	Steve Bullock	Labour	2nd	179,835	44,518 (24.75%)
Middlesbrough	Ray Mallon	Independent	1st	101,570	41,994 (41.34%)
L.B.Newham	Robin Wales	Labour	1st	157,505	40,147 (25.49%)
North Tyneside	Chris Morgan	Conservative	2nd	143,804	60,865 (42.32%)
Watford	Dorothy Thornhill	Liberal Democrat	2nd	61,359	22,170 (36.13%)
Council October 2002 election					
Bedford	Frank Branston	Independent	2nd	109,318	27,717 (25.35%)
L.B.Hackney	Jules Pipe	Labour	2nd	130,657	34,415 (26.34%)
Mansfield	Tony Egginton	Independent	2nd	72,242	13,350 (18.48%)
Stoke-on-Trent	Mike Wolfe	Mayor 4 Stoke	2nd	182,967	43,985 (24.04%)

Source: New Local Government Network website: nlgn.org.uk.

Independent candidates, or candidates of no political party, have been successful in six of the 11 mayoral contests outside London, with London Mayor Ken Livingstone included in the figures, then seven from 12 mayors are independent of party politics. Of the six Independent mayors outside London, four are faced with councils where no party has overall control, in which two see Labour as the largest party and two the Conservatives/Conservative and independents; and two independent mayors are faced with Labour controlled councils. In contrast, four Labour mayors are installed with Labour controlled councils; one Liberal Democrat mayor operates with a council in no overall control. A Conservative mayor was elected to work with a Labour majority on North Tyneside council but he subsequently resigned, and on 12 June 2003 North Tyneside held the first mayoral by-election since the 2000 Act introduced the new office. The Conservative candidate was elected after second preference votes were counted and the political situation in this authority remains the same.

In a number of cases, voters have used mayoral elections to inflict damage on the party that has had an iron like control of the council for many years – so far it has been the Labour Party that has suffered in this way. If anything, the mayoral experiment has enabled some change in political leadership to emerge, that the election of councillors and their choice of indirectly elected leader would not have allowed. Moreover, voters have been able to vote for the party they prefer to provide them local representation in the ward, and for a candidate from another party or none, when it comes to political leadership of the council. Whilst these results may be monumentally inconvenient for political parties, they are empowering for the electorate and it is simply fun to observe the political fall out as parties find that local politics are not entirely their own realm to do with as they please, as they once believed.

An ushering into local politics of a new uncertainty for political parties and a realisation that a 'party' may not win every mayoral contest destabilise not only the conduct of elections, but also local politics more generally. Parties are now faced with reconfiguring the relationships they have with their own voters and supporters, the wider electorate, other parties and with the individual that holds the mayoral office and forms the political leadership of the council and its area. Potentially the advent of elected mayors demands a different response from political parties to the business of campaigning, selecting candidates and conducting the business of the party to that required for the indirectly elected leader, where parties are certain of their role and influence. Indeed, parties will have to be far more energetic and sophisticated when it comes to fighting elections. Different campaign tactics, approaches and skills will be needed when filling the office of mayor to that of councillor, and for that matter a different type of candidate will be required from the party. The new political office of directly elected mayor demands that parties view the local political world outside, in a wholly new way and not as the sole property of political parties.

Potentially, then, the office of elected mayor could, if not replace party as the dominant force in local politics, certainly provide it with stiff competition from independents or other non-party political organisations. If nothing else, local politics becomes more uncertain and exciting, local democracy becomes more encompassing and inclusive and representative democracy takes on a slightly different meaning. Yet, as Table 9.2 indicates and as Game shows, the turnout figures for mayoral elections indicates much of this potential remains far from realised. Indeed, the contests so far have failed to turn any enhanced awareness of political candidates and leaders into a 'greater readiness to vote, let alone participate in other ways'.[12]

If mayoral elections continue not to stimulate increases in turnout compared with non-mayoral elections, then little will have changed when it comes to voter engagement in the electoral process. What would undoubtedly have changed, however, is voter recognition of the successful contender. If more people are simply aware of the individual that is now the political head on the council, even if they did not participate in the election of that individual, then some success in achieving a more visible local political leadership will have been secured. That alone is an improvement on the past patterns of voter recognition, where voters could often name the party in control of their council, but not their councillors or council leader.[13]

As one mayor commented in interview: 'There is no doubt that I have a very high profile locally, people know my name and how to contact me; I don't know of any council leaders with a similar profile locally. I certainly get stopped by people in the street far more than I use to as a councillor, the difference is marked.'

Once mayoral elections have been fought and the voters have decided the holder of the mayoral office and political composition of the council, the parties and party groups must adjust themselves to a new set of political dynamics and relationships under a mayoral regime compared with those that went before. Yet, new circumstances do not always lead to new patterns of behaviour. There is much in the mayoral models that encourage councillors to continue to display the worst excesses of the group system in a struggle for political dominance set within the context of a new political experience. Political parties will be confronted with power, responsibility and accountability resting in the individual holding the mayoral office, and that office in turn becomes the personification of local politics. The mayor, on the one hand, is an individual with a separate political mandate to the party group on the council, but, on the other hand, will be faced with a party group or groups seeking to pursue a particular political direction and objective whilst maintaining the crucial public cohesion and discipline that are the hallmark of the group system. The mayoral election may have made clear the candidate the electorate wished to see in office, but the parties on the council will continue to clash in order to decide if being a mayor in office also means being a mayor in power.

Party politics and mayoral power

Party groups grappling with the distinctions between a specific mayoral mandate and the collective mandate given to the group of councillors, whether sharing the mayors political affiliation or not, will be a constant theme of politics in mayoral authorities. The mayor does not owe his or her position to a vote of the group, but the public vote; there are many dimensions to how this new political fact will play itself out within council politics and how parties outside the council chamber respond to mayoral policy and initiatives. Mayors may be faced with a council controlled by their own party, by another political party, or with a council with no overall political control. A mayor independent of party may find him or herself confronted by a council where there are no fellow councillors also independent of party, rather a number of political party groups seeking to regain the political power they lost at the election by political manoeuvring within the council chamber.

The independent candidates elected so far as mayors have experienced mixed reactions from the political parties on the council to their election and to the new political office. These reactions have ranged from outright hostility and obstruction to a willingness to work co-operatively and alongside the mayor, accepting the new political realities that have emerged from the mayoral election. It is in the formation of mayoral cabinets that independent mayors start to get a flavour of the possible reaction the political parties have to the mayor's election and mayors have been faced with parties displaying varying degrees of willingness to co-operate in the cabinet-making process. Independent mayors faced with hostile party politics on the council may of course seek to support the election of independent candidates, or candidates from some local non-party organisation as a way of removing the frustrations of office, solving unpleasant political dynamics, or breaking political logjam in the council. In one instance a mayor frustrated by what he considered to be: 'the extent to which some councillors regard petty politicking as the whole point of being on the council', rejected what were seen as attempts by political parties to control or at least direct his mayoralty, and supported candidates for the 'Better Bedford Party' at the local elections.[14] The mayor himself had been previously elected on this ticket and now has six 'Better Bedford Party' colleagues on the council, five as a result of councillors crossing the floor from other parties and one as a result of the 2003 elections.

After his election in 2002, the Independent mayor of Mansfield received co-operation from councillors in the political party groups, which enabled him to form a cross-party cabinet, but, paradoxically, the mayor views party politics as inappropriate for local government. Labour had controlled the council with a substantial majority since 1974. In the 2003 council elections, the mayor backed Independent candidates as a way of breaking the dominance of party politics on the council. The success of the Independent candidates in taking an overall majority of seats resulted in the Labour group declining places in the new cabinet, preferring to take up the position of a political opposition. The mayor's cabinet in Mansfield is still cross party, but lacks Labour representation.

The issues faced by independent mayors when it comes to cabinet formation and their relationship, with party groups stem from the fact that mayors must form issue-by-issue coalitions and that party groups operate on the basis of certainty of *bloc* support, or opposition, across all policy issues. Party groups seeking certainty and consistency of support for their manifesto commitments will continue to clash with independent mayors over specific issues and policies. It is the intensity of that clash and the willingness or otherwise of councillors to seek political compromise that will dominate mayoral politics for some time to come.

In mayoral authorities political circumstances may increase the pressure on party groups to intensify the practices of group cohesion and discipline, rather than seek a political accommodation with a mayor from another party or from none. If the mayor is from the same party as the council majority group there will be a pressure on parties to minimise any potential and public disagreements between the group and mayor. Thus, much political deliberation and scrutiny will remain a private affair, conducted between councillors and mayor in closed group meetings, not more open, public settings. Yet, if the mayoral office is to act as a clearly identifiable point of political leadership and accountability, mayors will require more freedom and flexibility in their relationships with the group than has ever been enjoyed by party political councillors. Moreover, some public displays of the tension that have already emerged between mayors and his or her own group will be required, if a completely artificial public image of a quite, serene and wholly theatrical local political discourse is to be avoided. Whilst, elected mayors have the potential to make local politics more exciting, those elected on a party ticket may place loyalty to the party over and above good governance when faced with a council on which his or her own party has a majority. Alternatively, when faced with a council majority from another party, or a hung council, they may be tempted to use the mayoral office to seek party advantage.

The potential tussle over who governs an area, mayor or majority party, is complex and difficult when an independent mayor faces party councillors on the council. It is all the more acute when a mayor from one political party is faced by a council controlled by another. Here the potential for conflict is intensified by the existence of party political considerations and dynamics. Whilst the legislation makes it clear that the mayor is the political head of the council, the party political dynamics of a council, where the mayor's own party is in a minority, do not make the matter of political leadership and control as clear cut as the legislation suggests. As the former Conservative mayor of Labour controlled North Tyneside council found, securing political leadership may not simply come with winning election to executive office, rather it is a constant struggle to assert the role and responsibilities of the mayoral office against a council majority party deprived by the electorate of the mayoralty. The Conservative mayor faced opposition from the majority Labour group over certain key aspects of his mayoral manifesto. He claimed, however, the right to pursue his manifesto by dint of his direct election; the Labour majority claimed a similar right to pursue their policies and to oppose the mayor by dint of being elected to a majority of seats. In such circumstances political deadlock could occur if political maturity is absent. For the former North Tyneside mayor the issues were about his right to govern and to get on with the tasks for which he saw himself as being elected. He saw his policies as being unnecessarily 'picked over' by his political opponents seeking to find ways in which to obstruct him from achieving his political objectives. The mayor was insistent, however, that his direct election as Conservative mayor, supported by a Conservative cabinet drawn from the council minority group, but faced with a Labour council majority, was not the same political circumstances as the traditional definition of a hung council. He claimed leadership and political responsibility from direct election, thus conceptually relegating the council majority to a subservient political status – one that they should recognise and work appropriately from as a consequence. Such a notion, however, is one that a council majority party is unlikely to accept.

A senior Labour councillor rejected emphatically accusations that Labour were obstructionist or were using the council's constitution to prevent the mayor from taking action. She saw the majority group's role as probing and exploring mayoral policy proposals and the broader executive agenda and seeking out weakness of substance and process that required improvement. She also saw the group's role as holding mayoral policy up to public, critical scrutiny and challenge and although this may frustrate the mayor it was clearly the responsibility of the council to undertake such action, particularly in the unique political circumstances of this council. Challenge was all part of making the new arrangements work.

What is clear in this council is that a previously dominant political party has been deprived of the mechanisms of power, but still remains in a position to act as though it were in power. Moreover, the nature of the relationship between the party groups prior to the election of a mayor account for the current state of inter-party relationships. Changing institutional arrangements is only a small part of changing party political dynamics, as political power is hard fought for by parties and they do not give it up easily. Yet, in North Tyneside, despite current uncertainties and the nature of the party political interchange (which is little different form most non-mayoral councils), there is the political will amongst both members and officers to move the council forward and to improve the quality of governance offered to local citizens. Time is needed for the parties to adjust to new political realities and dynamics and to new institutions, and these factors are at the heart of the way in which the mayor and cabinet executive will develop here, as it will anywhere else.

The crucial test for elected mayors, and particularly those elected on a party ticket, is to bring a fresh dynamic to the politics of the council chamber, to the wider political and local community. Yet, the party mayor will have to balance the dual pressures of responsiveness to public opinion (or representation) and the demands of party and group loyalty, in just the same way as fellow councillors. The mayor holds his or her office by virtue of the public vote not as a gift from the party group. The demands of party unity and fear of public disunity between mayor and party colleagues on the council place very real pressure on the mayor to attempt to minimise the potential for disagreement, at least from being expressed publicly. Yet, party groups and wider local parties are set to lose to the mayor some of the influence they have in the past been able to wield. The party mayor must develop and maintain a considerable degree of independence from the council group, if they are to fulfil the objective of providing a clear, visible and accountable point of political decision-making. If mayors see loyalty to the party and party unity as their prime concern then political deliberation and decision-making will remain, as at present, confined to small collections of councillors and party members, with the wider public allowed to play only a minor role.

The three main parties want their mayors to remain as close to the council group as possible. Whilst mayors may not be bound by the group in the same way as councillors, when acting in council, or on a wider political stage, parties will naturally seek harmony between mayor and group and mayor and local party. By and large, shared party membership will provide much of that harmony as mayors and party will agree on major issues, where disagreement exists party loyalty will serve to confine the exploration of that disagreement to private meetings. Yet, the very nature of the direct election of the mayoral office-holder will see party groups lose some influence, how much will depend on the individual party candidate elected as mayor and how determined he or she is to govern the authority.

The dilution of the party group's control of the council as a result of the introduction of an elected mayor will be problematic for all of the main political parties, but for Labour groups and local parties in particular. The traditional rule-driven practices of Labour groups to one side, Labour councillors place a greater premium on public unity than Conservatives or Liberal Democrats, which could potentially restrict mayoral initiative. Conservative and Liberal Democrats, of course, seek unity through means other than rules, preferring to rely on shared political principles to generate public loyalty. Such shared principles coupled with the desire prevalent amongst all party people to avoid public deliberation and disagreement will see Liberal Democrats and Conservative mayors just as keen to pursue notions of group and party cohesion as any Labour mayor – but for intellectually different reasons. Thus, it is unlikely that the mere existence of elected mayors will have much of an impact on intra-party dynamics and practices, or, for that matter, on inter-party dynamics. Party is too resilient a local construct to allow new political offices to undermine its position, coherence and role within the institution of local representation – the council. Yet, mayors can potentially pose a fundamental challenge to the continued certainty of the dominance of local politics by political parties, both because non-party mayors can be elected and because party mayors are faced with playing the game in a different way.

The mayor and council manager

Whilst only Stoke-on-Trent City Council has so far introduced the mayor and council manager option contained within the Local Government Act 2000, the option represents a similar challenge to party group systems as that presented by the mayor and cabinet. The electorate of Stoke City chose an independent candidate as their mayor, defeating the sitting MP who was selected as the Labour candidate. The mayor, elected on the 'Mayor 4 Stoke' ticket, unlike his mayoral counterparts, was not faced with negotiating with councillors from political parties in the formation of a cabinet and the inevitable compromises this involves. The mayor and the appointed council manager are the executive; there is no cabinet of councillors in Stoke. Yet, it is the council, not the mayor, that appoints the council manager; consequently there is a potential shift of power from the mayor's office to the council. But, under the mayor and manager model, senior politicians from the council, and specifically the council's largest or majority group, do not have an executive position from which to operate. The lack of a cabinet also deprives the mayor of a bargaining tool from which to secure support and agreement from party groups that do not share the mayor's political affiliation or his or her non-party status.

So far in Stoke the mayor's experience in operating with the council has been mixed and so to has the reactions from councillors in coming to terms with both a new political office and the election to it of a non-party candidate. The mayor was not tempted to campaign in the 2003 local elections for independent candidates or candidates sharing the mayoral agenda and policies so as to ease the processes of governing the city, a testament to his very different experiences of the mayoralty to those mayors operating with a cabinet. Indeed, the mayor took the opportunity provided by the election period as the opportunity for a holiday. As a result of the 2003 elections Stoke has: 27 Labour councillors, seven Liberal Democrats, five Conservatives, 18 Independents, one British National Party and two others. These results provide a complex and potentially flammable mix of party political interactions. Yet, the key change to the political dynamics of this council generated by the new mayoral office is that 'doctrinaire decisions based on party politics' no longer drive the council.[15]

Yet, the mayor and manager option remains one that political parties could colonise in such a way as to maintain their dominance of local politics. As with the mayor and cabinet much depends on the individual elected to the mayoral office and, in this case, the individual appointed as council manager. With these two individuals forming the council executive even greater pressure will be placed on any party mayor to work closely with his or her party group as the latter will be completely absent from the formal executive. Thus, group meetings and other formal and informal channels of communication between mayor and group and mayor and local party take on an enhanced importance for party cohesion and unity.

Under the mayor and manager option, the leader of the council majority group is potentially able to wield some power and influence. The mayor will often need the support or acquiescence of the majority group for the development and implementation of his or her polices and the latter will be in a position to grant or withhold just that. The majority leader will be able to guarantee, through the group system, the support of a coherent and unified *bloc* of councillors to be delivered or withheld from the mayor. Thus, the majority leader will be able to provide an alternative source of political direction to that given by the mayor and the relative political skills of mayor and leader will be crucial to the way in which the dynamics of this option play themselves out. Such influence will, of course, be informally developed and employed by individual majority group leaders. Moreover, crucial to the relationship between the mayor, council manager and majority leader will be the coherence of the majority group, which becomes a powerful lever in influencing mayoral policy.

Similar political relationships to those described will be on display between the mayor and majority leader under the mayor and cabinet model. But the presence of councillors in the mayor's executive provides a more direct route into mayoral policy development, a route missing from the mayor and manager model. As a consequence, there is greater potential under the mayor and manager model for a break down in party cohesion and for more deliberation and debate to take place in council meetings than under either the mayor or leader and cabinet options. But, there also exists the mechanism by which parties can continue to dominate the council, even if the mayor is from another or no party. The ironic thing about the mayor and manager model is that it enhances party cohesion and public unity rather than diminishes the need for it, even when the majority group holds the mayoralty.

Finally, the mayor and council manager option introduces into British local government a form of super chief executive; an appointed officer serving as part of a political executive, only held to public account indirectly by the mayor and the council. Whilst the elected mayor as a political office is unpopular amongst councillors, it does not totally lack supporters amongst councillors and political parties. The council manager, by comparison, finds little, if any support amongst party councillors, who view the elevation of an appointed officer to a position within a political executive as an anathema to deeply held notions of democracy, accountability and the role of the party and the councillor in controlling the council.

As a Labour councillor commented:

> Officers already have far too much power that they are able to use to control things without officially giving them more power. It confuses things; makes an officer into a politician and one the public can't elect and can't get rid of. Its hard enough keeping an eye on them as it is and hard to make sure they do what they are told to do by councillors. Council managers will be able to walk all over the mayor and all over the council. It's just not democracy.

A Conservative councillor commented succinctly and in a similar vein: 'It [council managers] just institutionalises officer control and detracts from the role of the councillor, even more than mayors.'

The mayor and manager executive option challenges both the role of the party and the role of the councillor in local government to a greater degree than the other two executive options and, as such, it is condemned by councillors as undemocratic and unrepresentative. Councillors, by and large, would rather avoid any mayors, with or without council managers, and from the results of referenda held so far they are winning that argument and thus successfully protecting the dominance of local politics by the political party.

Conclusions

The chapter has considered the impact the new political office of directly elected mayor will have on the dominance of local politics by political parties and whether it can bring a new approach to the politics of the council chamber. Whilst currently only a minor feature of the political territorial landscape, the office of elected mayor has a *potential*, by no means fully realised, but certainly recognised, to pose a fundamental challenge to the primacy of political parties. A challenge, however, that political parties are well resourced, organised and determined to meet.

Elected mayors challenge party dominance of local politics on two levels: first the office can loosen – but not sever – the ties between the mayor and the party group of councillors and wider party, as the group is no longer the electoral constituency for the council's political head. Moreover, the mayor must turn outwards towards the community represented and governed rather than inwards towards the needs of group management and control. Whilst the local party selects the mayoral candidate, a popular mayor, with strong local connections, tempers the power of de-selection and provides limited freedom from party control for the party mayor. That is not to say mayors will forget party membership – they will not, as membership of the party is a deeply felt personal experience – it simply means the mayor can act with reference to a wider group of contacts than merely the party alone.

Secondly, the mayor, particularly if faced with a council controlled by another party, will need to seek issue-by-issue alliances and forge coalitions around specific policy proposals, both within and without the council, rather than rely on automatic support from his or her party group. Such alliance building, particularly with interests and groups outside the council chamber, places a strain on notions of party dominance and even public unity and coherence. Moreover, it forces party people to deliberate issues, outside the confines of the party, and with citizens that are not party members. Enhanced involvement and public deliberation are, however, not automatic results from mayoral politics and mayors are equally as able and willing to surround themselves, and their administrations, with party colleagues and others that agree with them in order to avoid public disagreement and dissent.[16] It will be the individual holder of the mayoral office and how he or she interprets political representation and governance, rather than the office alone, which will ensure whether or not elected mayors can facilitate a more inclusive local politics and one less dominated by party politics than has hitherto been the case.

It is not for nothing that the chapter is entitled: 'Directly elected mayors: a new political dynamic or a tired party hack?' Much rests on mayoral elections being won by non-party candidates or party candidates with a radically different vision of the conduct of party politics locally, to that held by the vast majority of their colleagues. Political parties have ensured that, and will continue to attempt to ensure, that future referenda on elected mayors return a resounding 'No' vote.

Where they are unsuccessful in this, they will seek to colonise the office of elected mayors, if not for the direct benefit of the party, at least to ensure that its dominance of local politics is maintained. Above all parties will want to avoid unnecessary public deliberation and certainly avoid displays of dissent and disagreement between mayor and party, or sections of the party and the mayor. Whilst internal party factions and *kindreds* will seek to select their favoured candidate for mayoral office, the norms of party unity and shared party principles will operate to ensure that attempts to downplay the role of party, that might result from the introduction of elected mayors, are neutralised.

Elected mayors separate out notions of representation from ideas of governing a council area and as such go some way to resolving the tension between these two, often competing, concepts. The mayor receives a direct mandate to govern from the electorate across the whole of the council area, as a result councillors and parties no longer need to assume a governing mandate from votes aggregated and seats won across a number of wards. The mandate theory, so beloved of councillors and their parties, is given new life and meaning, but it appears not to be one to which many councillors want to subscribe to.

Elected mayors can lead to a form of politics that political parties have long sought to avoid, that is a politics driven by the qualities, strengths and weaknesses of the individual seeker of office, rather than the platforms and policies of political parties. Party people become suspicious of individuals that become too prominent, too well known and, such is the extent of the party persons experiences with a publicly unpopular pass time – party politics – even candidates that are too popular. When directly electing a mayor, to serve as the political and executive head of the council, the electorate will wish to be convinced of rather more than the candidate's willingness to stick to the party line. They will need to be convinced of the personal qualities of the rivals for office and their *ability* to deliver what they promise, rather than *just* what they promise. Rather than making a voting decision based on the political affiliation of the candidate alone, electors may want a candidate that can navigate the complex and diverse world of local and national politics and provide clear political leadership – it could happen!

As a result of the enormous potential for the mayoral office to change the dynamics of local politics and the way in which local politicians view local politics, the experiment so far has been somewhat disappointing. The mayors elected to date have so far failed individually and collectively to find a national voice and to redress the balance of territorial politics between the political centre at Westminster and

Whitehall and the localities. That is as much a failure related to the traditional practices and focus of party politics within the localities, as it is with the new mayoral offices.

Yet, elected mayors must look beyond the confines of the geographical territory of their council, to what they can contribute to the national local government scene and to the national political debate. Political parties as local and national organisations have not encouraged such a shift of emphasis, and with so few elected mayors at the moment they are unlikely to do so in the near future. Moreover, political parties act as agents that unify local and national politics and subordinate distinctive local concerns beneath displays of national party unity. Parties may campaign for more resources for their council or region, but such local campaigning is conducted within a clear understanding of the supremacy of the centre over the local and the role of parties as national rather than local constructs, an approach which Labour and Conservative parties have collaborated in maintaining,[17] and an approach which they will no doubt continue to pursue to ensure elected mayors are not able to level out the local and the national political dynamic and power balance.

Elected mayors represent an as yet unfulfilled potential to change the dynamics of party politics, and, more widely, the conduct and inclusivity of local politics and democracy. Yet, parties will not simply cede their dominance of the local political scene and council control to elected mayors without a fight. The resilience of party at the local level and the depth to which it has penetrated the processes of local democracy and the degree to which party politics drives the local political and council culture requires more than institutional change to overcome party dominance. Whilst mayors may encourage greater involvement from non-party sources in both electoral politics and wider political decision-making, a more powerful challenge is required; there is currently little alternative available to the dominance of political parties at the local level. Local democracy needs to alter its base from one solely related to the needs and activities of party politics to one based on broader shifting coalitions of interest and alliances around issues and events of local importance and concern. The advent of elected mayors is a small first step in that direction.

Notes

1 G. Stoker, P. John, F. Gains, N. Rao and A. Harding, *Report of the ELG Survey Findings for ODPM Advisory Group*, Department of Government, Manchester: Manchester University Press, 2002.

2 DTLR, *Public Attitudes To Directly Elected Mayors*, 2001.

3 M. Hodge, S. Leach and G. Stoker, *More than the Flower Show: Elected Mayors and Democracy*, London: Fabian Publications, 1997.

4 *Municipal Journal*, London, Hemming, 15 May 2003, p. 18.

5 C. Copus, 'Local Government and the Media: The Impact on Citizen Interest and Participation', *Local Government Management Board*, January 1999.

6 R. Hambleton, 'Directly Elected Mayors: Reinvigorating the Debate', LGA discussion paper, 1999.

7 J. Leitch, 'Securing a Yes Vote in a Mayoral Referendum', *Local Governance*, 28 (2), 2002, pp. 125–129.

8 G. Stoker and H. Wolman, 'Drawing Lessons from US Experience: An Elected Mayor for British Local Government', *Public Administration*, 70, (2), 1992, pp. 241–267.

9 S. Bullock, 'The Road to the Lewisham Mayoralty', *Local Governance*, 28 (2), summer 2002, pp. 131–138, particularly 137.

10 DETR, *Modern Local Government: In Touch with the People*, 1998, paras 3.19–3.22.

11 C. Copus, 'Consulting the Public on New Political Management Arrangements: A Review and Observations', *Local Governance*, 26 (3), autumn 2000, pp. 177–186.

12 Game, C., Elected Mayors: More Distraction than Attraction? Conference paper to Eleventh One-Day Conference of the Political Studies Association Urban Politics Specialist group, November 2002, p. 10.

13 D. Widdicombe, Committee of Inquiry into the Conduct of Local Authority Business, *Research Vol. III, The Local Government Elector*, Cmnd 9788, London: HMSO.

14 Mayor Frank Branston, *Municipal Journal*, 15 May 2003, p. 18

15 Mayor Mike Woolfe, *Municipal Journal*, 15 May 2003, p. 19.

16 R. Giuliani, *Leadership*, London: Little Brown, 2002, p. 152.

17 J. Bulpitt, *Territory and Power in the United Kingdom: An Interpretation*, Manchester: Manchester University Press, 1983.

10

Political parties: dominating local politics

The book started out by posing the questions: 'what is it that political parties do to the processes of local politics and local representative democracy?' and 'whom or what is it, that benefits from local democracy and representation?'. The existence of political parties organised to play a particular role within local politics and the politics of the council has a profound affect on the way political decisions are made, on those decisions themselves and on the relationship between the councillor and the citizens and communities he or she represents. Moreover, political parties generate a very particular type of political dynamic when it comes to the relationships within and between parties and between parties and the broader local political environment. It is crystal clear that the conduct of politics locally, the issues on which it focuses, the players involved and the decisions made, are different because parties exist, organise and conduct politics, than if they were not present. Whether political parties lead to the creation of a healthy local democracy or not is far less clear.

Assuming control of the local polity

Representative democracy calls forth the need for political, economic and social interests to organise resources, effort and bias, and to mobilise support for the purpose of capturing control of representative institutions at any and all levels. That organisational need manifests itself in the political party, which is a cohesive coalition, structured and co-ordinated so as to contest elections, and if public support is sufficient, to act as a governing or opposing *bloc* in the representative institution that is the council. As political parties do not differentiate between this electoral role and purpose nationally and locally, they are able to fundamentally distort the nature and conduct of local politics and representation into a geographically smaller version of the national party political conflagration.

The exploration of political parties in relation to local government and local politics conducted within this book has not been with the aim of removing parties from council chambers or more broadly from local politics, that would be undemocratic, unnecessary and largely a fools errand. The purpose of the exploration has been to carve out a notion of local politics as distinct from national politics; the distinction is often blurred, particularly in the view of the party person, but it is a distinction nonetheless. Moreover, our exploration of political party in the locality has sought to question and challenge the assumptions about politics, democracy and representation held by party people and which manifest themselves in the way political parties organise for, and conduct, local politics and the politics of the council.

The assumptions which underpin party political activity at the local level are: first, that parties represent the only legitimate source of political authority, an authority assumed from the local election; secondly, elections provide parties with a right to govern locally because they signal the acceptance by voters of a manifesto or policy platform or because they simply give a particular party a majority. If no majority is secured, as in the case of a hung council, then the election is seen more simply as the legitimisation of party interaction on the council. Indeed, for parties, elections are the sole and only source of legitimisation required when conducting local politics. As a corollary of these assumptions a further set of assumptions arise to underpin the activities of political parties: that parties are the only way in which local representation can be organised and representatives held to account; that any other source of political activity outside of a party has a suspect legitimacy, or is simply not politics and therefore lacks any legitimacy. Moreover, parties are what link the interests of sections of the community to the interests of the general good or general well being, which in turn is firmly secured to the interests of the party in question. Yet, there is little in these assumptions that speak specifically of the local realm, being as applicable to national as to local politics. Some refinement is therefore required.

When turning to the relationship between political parties and a specifically local dimension to political activity, including that of the council chamber, a further set of assumptions emerge. These assumptions underpin further the dominance of the party over local politics and are used to justify, to the satisfaction of the party and its membership, its position as the local political *elite*. The first assumption is that parties have an equalising affect on local political participation in a pluralistic context, which is dominated by a particular type of citizen. The typologies of the non-party politically active citizen seeking to influence political decisions are designed to suit the political bias and prejudices of the party concerned and rest largely on social stereotypes, for example: the educated and professional, white male, middle aged and middle class; the working class, trade unionist council tenant agitator; or those working for equal opportunities and causes associated with women, ethnic minorities or gays and lesbians. Political parties serve to represent or to confront, in very broad terms, sets of politically defined, sectional interests, but can and do achieve this in a specifically local context. Thus, every political issue locally can be party politicised and the protagonists assumed to be either political friends and allies, or they become opponents by the simple process of adopting a different view on an issue from the party and party group on the council.

The second assumption related to the local dimension of politics, which enables parties to claim the locality as its own realm, is simply that the election of representatives and a representative-based system is the only way to organise a local democracy. Parties do not distinguish between different types of democracy being appropriate to different territorial purposes. Thus, whilst locally parties can accommodate a degree of citizen consultation or participation in local affairs, parties and elected representatives must make the final decisions, because that is what democracy means. Thirdly, local politics is a far messier and less distinct process than national politics, focusing, as it often can, or very small communities of place or interest and generating conflicts within and across those communities. The political party serves to bring to bear on such issues a cohesive coalition of generalised purposes and intentions that can take a broader view of the specific local issue and come to a conclusion on a suitable solution, thus arbitrating between competing local sectional interests. The argument runs that no other organisation or individual is practically or legitimately placed to act as an alternative to the party voice in these circumstances, coming, as others do, with a set of specific interests to articulate and pursue. Whilst political parties come to local politics from exactly the same perspective of course, that is with a specific notion of interests to pursue and articulate and some sectional concerns to promote, party people believe they do quite the opposite and promote a sectionally unbiased approach to governing a locality.

Finally, the party person assumes that local citizens are distinctly apathetic about local politics and local government, an apathy that extends beyond disconnection with national politics and party political activity. The citizen exists in a natural state of apathy, which even the occasion of the local election can rarely overcome. Such electoral apathy often results in councillors and parties feeling 'let down' by the electorate. As one councillor who had narrowly held his previously safe seat, on a greatly reduced turnout commented: 'They let us down, the people on that [named] estate just let us down by staying at home.' Here we see how parties often view their electorate and that it is possible for parties and party people to feel deeply betrayed if the electorate they perceive they own, refuse or fail to turn out and vote. That the party may have failed to stimulate the electorate to turn out because of a perfunctory or non-existent election campaign or simply by being invisible and irrelevant between elections is not the issue: the electorate has a duty to vote for the party, whether it deserves them to or not. A similar view was expressed by a Labour councillor commenting on the application to join his party by an individual who had previously been a member of the Liberal Democrats and had unsuccessfully stood on that platform against the Labour councillor: 'Why should we let him join; he took our votes, our votes, and we could of lost the seat.'

Party people assume that not only are the electorate apathetic about voting, but that they are also generally disinterested in local affairs, unless an issue specifically and particularly affects the individual or a particular community. Being motivated by self-interest, either individual or collective/community self-interest, for the party is not an appropriate or acceptable basis on which to conduct local politics. Moreover, such self-interest has a specifically local dimension, which manifests itself differently from notions of national voting intention and is concerned with the preservation or promotion of more immediate and selfish concerns. Simply put, parties must govern locally and dominate the local political realm because they do so from far more pure and honourable motivates than ordinary citizens or any sectional interest group.

As a consequence of the hierarchy of assumptions held about local politics by party people the party becomes easily elevated above all other contributors to the politics of the territory concerned. What is more, despite the political, economic, social and cultural traditions and historical development of the territorial areas conveniently lumped together to form a council, the assumptions explored here manifest themselves in all parties, wherever they are located. Moreover, the general assumptions underpinning the role of party locally held by party people mean that, rather than being vehicles for the display and promotion of local differences, parties serve to iron out territorial differences in political culture, interest and processes within and across our territorially convenient councils.

At the same time as voicing concern about local issues, priorities and autonomy, parties act as homogenising agents, submerging notions of locality and local diversity beneath a national concern for the advancement of the party at all local costs. Parties generate a self-fulfilling and self-serving prophecy of what local politics means and how it should be conducted. Moreover, political parties display all the characteristics of those political actors outside the party that they seek to de-legitimise; political parties are powerful sectional interests with a particular objective to pursue and become intensely active and interested when its own well-being is involved.

It is these assumptions about the role of party that make it necessary, in any critical questioning and analysis of political party at the local level, to distinguish between the local party outside the council chamber and the manifestation of party within it – the party group. Whilst local party and party group are separate but intertwined organisational facets of party, they interact with the politics of the local territory in different ways, but to similar affect, as their interactions are supported by the same set of assumptions about the world of local politics. Moreover, whilst distinct organisationally, the party group and local party are focussed on the same set of objectives: control of the council (or opposition to a controlling administration); winning extra seats or holding the ones already captured; party unity and cohesion in public; the avoidance of politically embarrassing events whilst maximising and exploiting the embarrassment of political opponents; excluding what parties consider to be politically illegitimate interests and concerns from the political arena; and the smooth internal running of the party organisation.

Political parties are organised, hierarchical structures designed to focus on the machinery of representative democracy, which in turn provides a cloak of legitimacy for party dominance.[1] That dominance encompasses not only the council but also the activities of any individuals or organisations that stray from civil society into party territory. Moreover, it means that local politics is not only dominated by the activities of political parties but also by the representative institution that is the council. One consequence of this is that political representation becomes conflated with managerial and administrative processes linked to the provision of public services. The main political parties and councillors will judge themselves less by the quality of political representation, accountability, transparency, openness of political process and responsiveness to citizen opinion, and more by the quality of services provided by the council. Councillors are less likely to say 'I have articulated and fought for the views of my electorate', rather 'my council provides an excellent road maintenance service'. Yet again we are led to the conclusion that at the local level, parties distort the meaning and actuality of political representation to fit an interpretation that suits not only the domination of politics by the party, but also a focus on the management of local services. Politics and representation are in fact, doubly distorted and the space for public involvement and public political discourse is reduced as a consequence.

We see then, that despite being the vehicles for political participation, parties serve to create an exclusive political environment, which welcomes only those prepared to share the interpretation of democracy and politics held by party people. Moreover, whilst parties reject other interpretations of the way in which local politics should be configured and conducted, they seek to draw those wishing to participate in local politics into sharing the assumptions on which parties operate. They do this by making questionable claims to be the only vehicles through which electoral politics can be conducted and through which representation can be fairly and appropriately secured. Representation becomes government and government requires a broad set of policy interests and concerns, congruent with the services provided by councils. Moreover, to govern locally parties must act as publicly unified, disciplined and cohesive expressions of the will and interests of those they claim to represent and govern. Thus, a barrier is formed between the party, its elected representative and the citizen and the elected representative cannot cross that barrier without being seen as disloyal to the party.[2]

In the setting of local politics, the barrier created by the party between its elected representatives and local citizens and communities ensures the representative serves the interests of the party above other interests and articulated views. Those joining a party to pursue some very specific community object, rather than a party political one, are immediately made aware of the distance the party places between community objectives and party-based government.[3] Whilst the councillor will make special pleas for the needs of his or her ward or division and will rest those pleas on how connected he or she is to the ward and the communication networks he or she has been able to develop, the party will ensure that ultimately a broader governing responsibility is adopted by the councillor. Ultimately, the councillor's political party is the single most important factor when it comes to his or her acting as a representative and in governing an area. Councillors are more willing to be guided by their parties view of the needs of the communities governed, than mandated by those communities. Thus, the councillor acts from a Burkean belief in the freedom of the representative from the represented and the consequence of this transference of representative relationship from voter to party is that political parties are able to dominate all facets of local council politics. At best all that the electorate can hope to secure is the councillor's wiliness to accommodate some general guidance from the electorate when carrying out in his or her political activities.[4]

By acting as a consistent and permanent pull on the activities of the councillor, the political party and the council party group are placed at the centre of the councillor's assumptive world. It is the party the councillor ultimately comes to 'represent', because in that way the general well-being of the citizenry is served, not the sectional interests clamouring for attention and resources. Placing the party at the centre of his or her assumptive world, ensures that the party is not seen for what it is, just another sectional interest clamouring for attention and resources, but as the only viable vehicle though which representation and government of a locality can be secured. Whilst degrees of public cohesion and unity amongst party groups may vary across place and party, and whilst Liberal Democrats maintain an at best ambivalent relationship to notions of a group whip, party unity does become an end in itself. It is the solidification of bias around the party that secures its elevation above any other players in the field of local politics. Thus, government at the local level and indeed the entire spectrum of activity that is local politics is, for the party person, rightfully the domain of the party.

The dominance of the political party is not threatened by those that see community politics as an alternative to an unresponsive local representative democracy; community politics does not amount to the replacement of the representative system with a participative variant. Community politics is also, not exclusively the property of the Liberal Democrats; exponents of a more community focus to the activities of the party exist across the political spectrum, but this approach to politics remains focused on the party as the mechanism through which community views can be articulated and community interests pursued. Yet again, it is possible for the party person to equate the interests of the party with the pursuit of community concerns. Indeed, political parties in some areas have sought to 'out community' each other in the desire to display their credentials as the only true vehicles through which community concerns can be addressed.

Parties are able to dominate local politics because they focus their activities on obtaining representation on, or control of, a council. The very presence of a party on a council enables it to claim legitimacy for its actions, which extends beyond anything obtainable by non-electoral means. Whilst local politics is not just what councillors, councils and parties do, the legitimacy parties accrue as a consequence of the public vote enables them to squeeze out from the public political space other voices or those conducting politics through non-party means. Those involved in fighting elections and acting within a representative institution that is the council, hold public unity and loyalty above all else. They do this because of the belief that public disagreement within parties is fatal in electoral terms, and because acting as a unified coherent unit, either in the council or the wider community, is essential to achieving a set of political ideals or pursuing a set of policy preferences.

Parties exhibit a form of tribalism when it comes to the conduct of politics, in that the sworn enemies it has in the shape of other parties and community activists must, on each and every issue, be fought and defeated. Above all, right or wrong the party must win. Indeed, the question of right or wrong is not one that is addressed, as by their very nature parties will act with a perceived monopoly of wisdom on each and every issue. Moreover, any politically orientated organisation, or organisation indulging a political activity outside of party politics, if it cannot be colonised and controlled, must be marginalised or defeated in the same way as any party political opponent. Parties, as institutions, are insular and introspective mechanisms designed to focus on a very narrow range of external activities and on the internal working of the party itself. Yet, it is these bodies that systematically control the conduct and focus of politics both inside and outside the council, serving to direct local political attention and activity towards the council and consequently towards that distinct element of the party that is the council party group.

Party groups: a systematic approach to the politics of the council

The way political parties approach council politics and the impact they have on the conduct of political decision-making, have led many to consider the existence of party systems of one sort or another.[5] These systemic analyses are useful for classifying types of party organisation and activity and the partisan interactions between party groups, but they do not explain the style of politics adopted or the intensity of the relationships between the party groups. It is one thing to categorise party systems based on the political composition of a council and the numbers of party to non-party councillors, or on notions that councillors have different views of what constitutes an appropriate display of partisan politics to those of the voter; it is another thing to recognise the impact on local politics, both inside and outside the council as a result of the intensity and nature of the interactions between and within the parties. It is not so much that there are different types of party systems that matter, but that parties exist and conduct business in a broadly similar and highly systematic way. Simply, if we are to understand the impact of party on council politics and beyond, the only system that we need to consider in any depth is the group system.

We considered earlier four models of party group dynamics: *the partner, arbitrator, filter and leviathan*. These models explored the different degrees of cohesion existing amongst party groups as facets of the group system rather than being presented as systems themselves. The models provide a mechanism by which the intensity of party dynamics can be understood and the rigidity of the boundaries parties draw around themselves illuminated. What these models also highlighted was that the nature of the party group system, whether groups act in a fluid and deliberative fashion or in a highly disciplined and authoritarian way, culminates in a broadly similar approach to the business of council politics across council and party.

What the political party group provides is a regularity of process and a systematic approach to the business before councillors, an approach that is shared by the three main political parties in the conduct of council and group business. It is a regularised approach based on a system of councillor conformity, avoidance of public dissent and adherence to policy and decisions made by private group meetings. The system is held together partly by rules and regulations, but also by shared values and beliefs which in turn are underpinned by the rhetoric of party politics, not by public political deliberation and discourse. The rhetoric of party politics, the way in which public political debate is conducted through the loudspeaker that is the party, exemplifies the nature of the relationships between the parties and highlights the tone in which political discourse takes place.

A Conservative councillor from a metropolitan authority commented:

> The ruling Labour group are a very difficult bunch, basically insecure I think. They cannot debate with us, or accept any questioning or challenge without resorting to political name-calling. Even the most innocuous of enquiries in scrutiny will set them off and then you get a barrage of party mud slinging. Always this business about the 'manifesto' or 'you Tories did such and such', as if anyone reads their manifesto.

A Labour councillor commented in a similar vein about the Liberal Democrat controlling group on his council:

> A very, very touchy lot; they've never had control before so they're nervous about making mistakes. It's very easy to wind them up and you can do it without meaning to. It makes things very difficult because whenever we ask a question all we get is 'when you were in charge' or 'after years of Labour misrule, blah blah', that sort of thing. They're going to have to toughen up and also realise the council is a place for political battles, otherwise is going to be a very unpleasant few years.

The tone of debate between the parties is a product not only of party differences but also of the group system's tendency towards intensifying the rigidity of party boundaries. That rigidity comes from notions that the party group is a collective entity responsible for providing an administration or government, or a coherent, cohesive opposition *bloc* to any administration.[6] Collective responsibility can only be assured if the group acts in a systematic and organised fashion when conducting the affairs of the council and its own internal business. As a Liberal Democrat council leader interestingly put it: 'We are in charge here, no one else, just us, and we must act accordingly: as a united force.'

The group system generates a particularly mechanistic and authoritarian style of politics at the local level, and, whilst it has elements of the ethos and culture of party politics at Westminster, it also displays an intensity that is decidedly local in nature and context.[7] The party group system is more authoritarian and disciplined than the party system in Parliament; it is more extensive in that the reach of group discipline extends beyond the council chamber into every facet of the councillors activity and the entire range of *theatres* within which he or she can act. It is less tolerant of dissent and more willing to act in a formal and informal sense against councillors that find themselves publicly at odds with their colleagues. It is far less sophisticated when dealing with recalcitrant members than its Parliamentary counterpart and is far more willing to put the needs of government and for that matter effective opposition against the articulation of public views and public deliberation.

The party group and the party group system do not distinguish between the executive activities of a council cabinet and the council chamber as a deliberative forum, as Westminster parties are more inclined to do. Indeed, the group has far more control over the council executive than parliamentary parties have over the central executive. Finally, the group has a close and deep relationship with the local party, having a series of institutionalised links with it and often seeing itself as an extension of the local party, or at least clearly connected and responsible to it. On top of which is overlaid a series of informal personal, social and political networks that are the glue holding the party locally together.

Any consideration of the group system must be tempered with a cautionary note concerning differences in the way in which groups conduct political affairs that result from the political tradition of the authority concerned, the state of relationships between the parties and personalities within them and, above all, party affiliation. It is always possible to claim that a generalised approach does not account for the subtleties that are required when exploring the intricacies of politics on individual councils and within particular local areas. It will be remembered that this book started with the assertion that local politics is not only interesting but also exciting. That excitement comes form the fact that the parties, personalities, issues and events across local government are varied and that no two councils are identical in the political environment they inhabit locally. Neither is any political party faced with an exact replica of issues, personalities, problems and processes to that of a group of party colleagues in a neighbouring authority. Add to this, party affiliation and political beliefs tempered and shaped by geographical, social, economic and cultural factors and it is a wonder we can claim that any categorisation of local politics is possible at all.

Yet, the political party has such a resonance with councillors, provides such a robust systematic approach to council politics and is able to provide shape, form and coherence to a complex environment, that the party group system transcends any specifically local set of circumstances. Indeed, whatever the nature of politics within any council, elements of the group system will be present and it will be clear that councillors are cohering in *blocs* around some label or another. Despite local circumstances, local politics and the politics of the council are drawn into a broadly similar pattern of interactions and events, which display themselves within and between the workings of party groups. Indeed, the party group system is maintained by patterns of political interaction and behaviour that have been barely touched on in all the talk about the political modernisation of local government.

Political modernisation: an incomplete project

Party politics in local government, until quite recently, displayed itself through the distribution of leadership positions, committee chairs and

other patronage positions, such as the mayoralty and appointing councillors to represent the council on outside bodies. In addition, council
and committee could be used by councillors for displays of party political grandstanding and theatrical displays of inter-party strife (real or
imagined). Yet, the political representation of the electorate found little
outlet in the politics of local government, with the councillor's attention heavily focussed on the running of local services through the committee system.

The old anti-party adage that there 'is no socialist or Conservative
way of digging a ditch' attempts to indicate that party politics has no
role to play in service administration and provision. There may indeed
be no specific party approach to the actual digging of a ditch, but there
certainly is a socialist and Conservative view about how many ditches to
have, who should dig them, were they should be and who should pay
for them. Thus, when working on the details of service provision in
committee it could appear to councillors and the casual observer that an
intensely party political process was in operation and the interests of the
electorate were being served by their party political representatives.

Yet, little 're' presenting of the views of the electorate, save for in
very general circumstances, was evident from the business of most
council committees. Moreover, immersion in huge quantities of information presented via officers' reports to councillors in committee, produced an illusion to the public and councillors themselves, that
councillors were in 'control' or using political power on behalf of the
citizenry. In addition, committee agenda and reports setting out in
great detail what the council was doing or proposing to do in regard to
some area of service provision, gave councillors the impression that they
had swaths of information and as a consequence knew what was going
on in the council. Political parties locally collaborated in the deception
and self-delusion that local politics and representation was what councillors did in committee when running vital public services. By so doing,
they defended themselves from the need to respond to public pressure
aimed at altering some council decision, or from articulating some set
of opinions or deliberating some complex political issue.

The committee system reduced much of what should be a political
process to a set of dry administrative procedures; political modernisation
needs to be about putting the politics back into local government but, at
the same time, recognising that politics exists outside of political parties.
Political modernisation so far enacted under the Local Government Act
2000 concentrates on changes at the level of institutional structures and
procedures, but tied to a broader aim of reinvigorating and renewing

local democracy and local government. By focusing on structural change, rather than a thorough re-assessment of local democracy and politics, political parties have been able to ensure that they continue to dominate the new executive political decision-making processes. Indeed, as far as political parties are concerned, the real disturbance generated by the arrival of executives – leader or elected mayor and their cabinets – is in the dynamics of political interaction within and between the parties. The role and power of political party groups in council and wider local politics have been left undisturbed and the representative framework of local government untouched.

The favoured executive option of parties and councillors – the indirectly elected leader and cabinet – has been adopted by all but 11 of those authorities to which executive arrangements were compulsory. Thus, when it comes to the type of executive preferred by councillors, political affiliation makes no difference at all. Rather, political affiliation displays itself more in levels of power given to council leaders, rather than in the choice of which executive option to adopt. Stoker *et al.* point out that Labour gives less formal power to its leaders than Conservative groups and Liberal Democrat cabinets are less dominated by one party.[8] In addition, the Stoker survey indicates clear lines of party influence over the new scrutiny committees existing. Indeed, with pre-meetings before overview and scrutiny meetings a fairly regular occurrence, it appears political parties are taking few chances that these new bodies may lead to independent, public political deliberation taking place that has not been previously considered by the party group in private.[9]

Party groups have shown themselves to be a force for inertia and the status quo when it comes to the question of reforming and revitalising the way in which the politics of the council are structured and conducted. The three parties prefer that the electoral constituency for the leadership of the council is councillors themselves, rather than the electorate and that re-structuring of council political decision-making processes reflects, as far as is possible within the new arrangements, the old style committee structure. Indeed, when reforming council political decision-making many of the new arrangements have been configured so as to reinvent the committee system, rather than display a new approach to the politics of the council.[10] Whilst many councillors still bemoan the passing of the 'good old days' of the committee system, others have quickly adapted the new processes to suit existing patterns of political behaviour when it comes to the interactions between and within the parties.

What has changed under the leader and cabinet model is that party groups can come to feel as though they are fractured, with some of its

membership drawn off into a closer relationship with the council than
that existing for members outside the executive. Such an impressionis-
tic reaction to the new structure by councillors, ignores the fact that the
situation was much the same for committee chairs. The dynamics of
party groups have been altered, however, to accommodate for this new
impression and as a consequence some groups have attempted to 'whip'
the executive, whilst others have concentrated on preserving party unity
in overview and scrutiny committees. For the opposition groups little
has changed, save that there is a greater tendency for majority groups to
countenance the opposition holding some overview and scrutiny chairs.
Sharing out chairs with the opposition is something that would not have
occurred with the old committees and is perhaps an indication that
majority groups do not feel threatened by overview and scrutiny. It is
possible over time that overview and scrutiny councillors and executive
members will come to see themselves as primarily focussed on these specific functions and processes, rather than as representatives of their political parties. As a consequence an unclogging of political interaction and
involvement from unnecessary party practices could occur, councillors
then will see themselves as overview and scrutiny or executive first and
Labour, Liberal Democrat and Conservative second. There is little evidence, however, to suggest that such a sea change in attitudes is about
to occur.

So, if the latest attempt at modernising the political decision-
making structures of local government has fallen far short of modernising and renewing the nature and conduct of party politics – which is
hardly surprising as that was not the target any way – we need to look
elsewhere in seeking change. The focus of this book has unashamedly
been that political parties and party groups need to change the way they
interpret, understand and conduct local politics and the politics of the
council chamber. It is only an end to the dominance of local politics by
the political party that will bring about citizen re-engagement and interest in local affairs and lead ultimately to a renewal of local civic pride and
with it new forms of civic leadership. Moreover, the future political
independence of local government from central control rests as much
on developing a new political role as it does on the quality of service
provision; a new political role for local government can only come about
when parties are just one of many contributors to local politics and to
the politics of the council and where councillors are required to use their
political skills and acumen to seek out single issue alliances with a range
of individuals and organisations outside of the council. The notion that
councillors will be able to conduct political affairs in council, without

relying on the consistent and regular support of a publicly united *bloc* of councillors cohering around a party label, fundamentally undermines the party group system and political parties more generally. Moreover, approaching council politics through a series of negotiated single-issue coalitions or alliances, forged between a wide range of organisations and individuals, not just parties, requires parties that are much more fluid and flexibly formed particularly at council level, than is currently the case. It is not the culture of British politics, nationally or locally, that such a situation or the circumstances leading to it could arise.

Political parties in Britain are monolithic organisations. Whilst it would be wrong to suggest that the parties nationally and locally do not talk to each other about a range of political and organisational issues, and equally wrong to suggest that parties locally do not engage in negations and arrangements, electorally or to form a council administration, such communication as does occur is driven by events and circumstances. It is not the product of a culture of exchange and positive interaction between the parties. Moreover, the winner takes all approach to political power and patronage that is the dominant political culture, locally and nationally, does not encourage positive political exchange and deliberation between parties. Such cultural change as would lead to a more fluid political organisation and exchange and a less rigid and hierarchical approach to local politics requires radical surgery at the local level.

Cultural change within British local politics is more likely to result from a radical rethinking of local government and politics, rather than come from structural tinkering alone. But, any such radical change must emerge from a long process of examination of the place of local government and politics in relation to a new national political settlement between the localities and the centre. Assuming that settlement will be based on the principles of representative democracy (it need not of course), but tempered with a much more participative edge and with widespread public participation at its centre, then a responsive and politically representative local democracy can emerge.[11]

A simple, if not simplistic, and immediate solution to the problem of realigning the position of political parties in council politics, alongside the introduction of new players into the game, is a change to the way in which we elect councillors. The use of the blunt instrument of first-past-the-post for local elections is designed to do locally what it does nationally, provide a government. Except at the local level we are not electing governments that are masters in their own house, but administrations that are prone to central interference. In that case, it becomes even more important that political parties do not conduct their business, and the business of the council, from the dull conformity of the confines of the party, as though they were on a governing crusade, but more from the perspective of community representation, responsiveness to citizen input and a recognition of the rich and diverse nature of local politics.

A move to the use of the single transferable vote (STV) at the local level would encourage organisations and individuals, other than party candidates, to contest elections, as seats would no longer be the property of political parties. At a stroke politics would change, as it in unlikely that STV would deliver clear and stable majorities. As party councillors would be faced with councillors from a non-party background, compromise, negotiation and coalition building would be required to move forward on any single political issue. Moreover, the many and varied voices with which local communities speak would not be drowned out by the noise of the parties, but find articulation within the council chamber. Councils would still be politically representative institutions; indeed, they could be vastly more representative institutions than they currently are. A move to STV would help bring together the local political and civil societies within the framework of representative democracy. As councils become open to more than just political parties, a more participative environment could spring forth as those non-party groups forged a different and more acutely responsive relationship with the electorate, or at least sections of it, than political parties are willing and structurally able to create. STV does bring local government and politics closer to the realisation of Ostrogorski's exhortation of *down with the party and up with the league* and brings forth the notion that political organisations may not always seek a permanent life. Active and influential in local politics, alongside those that seek a continued but general interest and involvement through political parties, will be those interested in a very specific involvement for the life span of a particular issue or event.

Yet, in seeking to realign political and civil society as a vital part of modernising local government and politics, a longer-term and much more difficult and complex solution is required than a simple change of the voting system. The need to revive civil society and to focus it on a clearer understanding of its position and role in more acutely political terms must first be recognised by those involved in local party politics, as well as those involved in wider non-party political concerns and interests. Party people, particularly those experiencing representative office and political power, are less concerned to stimulate interest in local politics beyond voting at a local election or joining a political party. Indeed, party people interpret politics and representative democracy as requiring party membership to gain admission to political processes and practices. Moreover, councillors, in particular, are often sceptical as to the motives of citizens who wish to intermittently contribute to politics and of any participants in local politics that are from outside the world of the political party.[12] Unless of course, they share the aims and beliefs of the party concerned, but even then they are not truly part of the 'political system', merely an adjunct to it. Politics as it displays its self locally is the property of the party.

Politics, democracy and representation: the realm of the party

The political party is the *Leviathan* that straddles the separate but interlinked concepts of local politics, democracy and representation. In addition, parties dominate all facets of local government political decision-making. They can do this because they are organisations best placed to cope with the ambiguities that are political life and dynamics.[13] Yet, parties in coping with uncertainty and chaos by seeking order and stability in local political action serve to produce conformity and regularity to local political processes, particularly in the council chamber.

Parties fail to reflect or address the range of views on local issues that exist within and across communities of interest and place. Moreover, parties exist in a local environment comprising for the most part fluctuating levels of interest and involvement by the citizen. The party person finds such fluctuations both frustrating and suspicious, leading them to conclude that the motives for involvement by the citizen are self-centred if not selfish. As a consequence, dominance of the local political scene by the party, whichever one or more it may be, ensures local government and politics are conducted for the general well being rather than any notion of community or communities, or what the party would see as sectional interests. Political parties, of course, may argue that they govern in the interests of the whole, but as organisations and sets of political processes parties are no more than sectional interests themselves. Indeed, local representation becomes representation of the party above all other interests and concerns.

Whilst Mill argued that a healthy political life depends on the existence of parties of order and stability or parties of progress and reform, at the local level the existence and activities of either sort of party, result in a rather unhealthy if not anaemic political condition.[14] Mill, of course, saw local government as representative government thus:

> The proper constitution of local representative bodies does not present much difficulty. The principles which apply to it do not differ in any respect from those applicable to the national representation. The same obligation exists, as in the case of the more important function, for making the bodies elective; and the same reasons operate as in that case, but with still greater force, for giving them a widely democratic basis: the dangers being less, and the advantages, in point of popular education and cultivation, in some respects even greater.[15]

Mill here clearly sees no need to distinguish between national and local politics when it comes to the type of democratic systems appropriate: it should be representative. As a consequence, parties emerge locally to control those representative institutions and to govern much along the lines of national government: through the mechanisms of the party. Yet, the diverse and complex set of interests that exist locally are not adequately represented, nor have their views articulated sufficiently through local political parties, acting either in the council or outside of it. Indeed, it is the failure of parties locally to approach local democracy and representation from a local perspective that often leads the electorate to look elsewhere for representation, or for a more participative input to political decision-making over and above the choice of councillor at election time. As one Conservative councillor succinctly put it: 'The role of the electorate is to choose the party that runs the council; the role of the council is to govern locally. The electorate can choose to re-elect us, or elect someone else. That's what representation and democracy is about.' This is a view which has its echoes amongst Labour and Liberal Democrat councillors. Indeed, for the councillor of a party background, politics, democracy and representation cannot, and should not be separated, and each exists within the representative mould, enabling the party to dominate all three aspects of political life. Moreover, councillors and other party people, conflate politics, democracy and representation, employing them casually to mean the same thing: politics is about party activity, democracy is how the electorate choose the party to govern them, or can be how parties govern themselves, thus being the embodiment of democracy, and representation is what parties do for and on behalf of all the electorate. Anything that sits outside this very constrained definition of the ideals of politics, democracy and representation, and so sits outside the party, does not conform, for the party person, to any legitimate interpretation of political activity.

Parties and party people, then, define the concepts of politics, democracy and representation and local variants of them, and in so doing create these definitions in such a way as to ensure party has a dominant position locally when it comes to the practical, day-to-day workings of political life. This political life is based on notions of representation that Pitkin described as: 'very general, abstract, almost metaphorical idea – that the people of a nation [and a locality] are present in the actions of its government',[16] to which of course, can be added its local government. It is these very broad, general, yet shared interpretations by all party political actors, irrespective of their political affiliations, and of the nature of political life that are responsible for local representatives coming to represent the party above all else. Whilst councillors may be willing to act as a trustee or politico in relation to the electorate, it is only in relation to their party that they are willing to act as a delegate, bound by instruction and by a deeper loyalty than that felt in regard to the citizen or community. Moreover, it is only the views and beliefs that coincide with the political beliefs of political parties that are able to find an effective expression and outlet within the local arena. Political voices and involvement are not only constrained by the beliefs of any one party, but also by how the members of it and its elected representatives interpret notions of politics, democracy and representation and how they act upon those interpretations.

Whilst parties serve locally to exclude and constrain political activity and the expression of political opinion, and particularly to constrain opinions on non-party political issues, the reality is that parties remain, and will remain, the prime mechanism by which the electorate can find an outlet for a range of views. That is so because, despite considerable experiments with public participation in local government, its representative and electoral basis has never been seriously questioned. The continued representative nature of local government is not in doubt, forcing those concerned to be involved in local democracy to configure their organisations and activities in certain ways and to aim those activities at certain targets, namely: councils, elections and political parties. As a Labour council leader commented: 'we actively consult with a wide range of groups on a range of issues; we encourage people to become involved. It is the council that makes the final decision, we have a duty to listen and then a duty to act as we think fit.' 'We' being by implication the council, but by intention the party and party group.

Whilst diverse non-party political organisations do exist, take part in local politics and make an enormous contribution to political dynamics and in smoothing off the rough edges of a representative democracy, they do so in a political world dominated by party and party concerns. That domination by party reduces to a minimum the input and impact that non-party groupings can have on local politics generally and particularly reduces their contribution to council politics to negligible proportions. Yet, the electorate in a few cases return to council chambers a small but significant number of Independent councillors (all of whom have their own party political views and party preferences), and in some cases return councillors from very local, non-party, but inherently and overtly *political* organisations.

Political organisations from a non-party pedigree contest local elections and in some cases have been successful, even to the extent of taking control of a council. A Residents Association currently controls Elmbridge District Council; then there is the celebrated case of 'Health Concern' which not only over a period of time became the largest and then the controlling group at Wyre Forest, but also succeeded in returning under its banner the only independent MP at the 2001 general election. In addition, various non-party independent organisations have had some electoral success; as we saw in chapter 9, directly elected mayors have opened up the political field to independents and candidates from a non-party background.

The existence of councillors from a non-party organisation or from a body calling itself a party but stemming from a local, rather than a national base, such as the 'Better Bedford Party', indicates one clear and striking feature of our political processes: that political representation, political policy-making and decision-making about the provision of local services need not be undertaken by party politicians to be effective. Those outside the walls of the party are quite capable of representing and even governing locally. Moreover, councillors from such organisations and with a non-party background can just as easily be held to account by the electorate at the local election. Thus, political accountability is not a feature that only political parties can effectively contribute to local democracy.

When minor, locally based parties, or non-party organisations secure a degree of local electoral success it indicates that the party *Leviathan* has some limitations. The limitations of party as a vehicle for democracy are most evident when it comes to the expressions of views, which conflict with its political philosophy. That is of course understandable to a degree, but parties also restrict the articulation of views which are simply at variance with a decision taken by the party, or at the local level, more likely by the council party group. Parties construct their activities for the convenience of government or opposition at the local level, rather than for a broader democratic purpose. Whilst parties may not be the 'evil inherent in free governments' that Tocqueville envisaged, they do serve to reduce the public space for democratic debate and deliberation and reduce the number of actors involved in the political processes. Those with a political interest, but not wishing to sign up to the rigours of party discipline or to a complete box-set of political principles, find no home in a party and thus no direct and influential access to the levers of political power at the local level. Moreover, those with an interest in a specific local issue will find that parties will attempt to insulate themselves from such single, but important issues, rather than engage with them; or, where they do engage it is within the confines of a very narrow, party politically drawn definition of what constitutes legitimate political activity. Issues are the property of sectional interests and concerns, broad policy objectives and the provision of public services are the territory and concern of the party. At least that is the reasoning of the party *Leviathan*, a reasoning which does not match the reality of local politics as it confronts the citizen or community, rather one that matches the practice of local politics by the party. Moreover, for the party, single local issues do not really exist outside a broader policy perspective; the stand-alone issue that cannot be related to some party policy or another is a rarity.

Local government does not escape the view that modern politics is 'party politics' and 'political parties are the main actors in the systems that connect the citizenry and the governmental process'.[17] Yet, this view does not bear out the reality of party politics in the localities, where politics is certainly party politics, but where parties serve to disconnect the citizenry from the local governmental process and act as a barrier to wide-spread public engagement in the political processes. Parties conduct local politics despite the locality within which they are based, rather than because of it. Political campaigning, electioneering and the wielding of local political power through the council is seen as Westminster government in miniature, a tendency that will increase as a result of the new executive arrangements based on an indirectly elected leader and cabinet.

As a consequence of party dominance the politics of the locality are continually squeezed out of the limited political space available for its expression, and are replaced by a focus on party as the only legitimate vehicle for expressions of political concern and political decision-making. In the view of political parties, representative democracy and politics are the only way of configuring political processes and dynamics, a view and approach which bears responsibility for a growing disenchantment with local politics and an increasingly cynical attitude taken by the electorate towards parties in local government. By the interpretations of the role of party and the nature of democracy that parties hold and display, and as a result of the way in which they conduct local politics, parties distort local representative democracy, transforming it into rule for, by and on behalf of the party. Moreover, parties undermine public confidence that important local issues are dealt with in a way that reflects local needs and not the interests of political parties, or in a way designed to maintain party domination of the local political realm.

Political parties make grandiose claims about democracy, representation and accountability when it comes to the conduct of local politics and their role within it. Parties also make great claims to be 'representing' or speaking on behalf of the citizens that placed them into office and so legitimised their political role by the public vote. The reality described here is the reality of the party person; the political reality for citizens and communities is somewhat different. Political parties in the conduct and control of local politics and council chamber politics have only the most tenuous link to the citizens and communities they claim to represent and govern. Links between political parties and civil society are all but non-existent in any meaningful sense; parties are hermetically sealed from the troublesome outside world and seek mainly to engage in defensive sorties outside when circumstances demand. Party people, by and large, are unable to look beyond the consequences of any political situation further than to the party itself. That is why those taking up a position at variance with the party's are often unjustly party-politicised and become a legitimate political enemy to be defeated, rather than a politically complementary element to be embraced. Such inability to look beyond the party interpretation of local issues and citizen motivation constrains and distorts the search for political solutions and is displayed in the frightening levels of political myopia parties display in local government. It is only that parties face little or no competition for dominance of the local political realm that enables them to maintain their grip on the institutions that are local councils.

Conclusions

Partisan divisions run deep within council chambers and within the broader politics of the locality, yet political affiliation accounts for little when considering the impact of political parties on the governance of the localities in Britain. Parties have a generic impact on the conduct of politics that is the same for Conservative and Labour parties and the Liberal Democrats. Councillors and other party people, share a broad interpretation of what party means, what it expects, how it conducts local politics and the politics of the council and how it interacts with other parties and the non-party contributors to local democracy. Moreover, a shared view exists of what representation and democracy means and how the democratic and representative processes should be conducted. Whilst the broad sweep of party philosophy, value systems, policy differences and political loyalties result in varying degrees of intensity of inter- and intra-party conflict, the role of party and the basic tenants of representation are uncontested between and by the parties.

Despite claims by party people, that their own party has the monopoly of wisdom when it comes to solving political problems, and representing the electorate, each party conducts council affairs and local politics from the same mould. Differences in political beliefs between parties only affect political activity at the margins and recourse to party loyalty and discipline leads to an over simplification of complex political concerns and reduces the space for genuine consideration of different ways of conducting local politics. Political parties in the various territorial units of local government have had a homogenising affect on the spatial dimensions of political life and concerns. Moreover, party loyalty and discipline has reduced the public space for genuine political deliberation and has had the devastating effect of reducing local politics to a team sport and a spectator one at that. Loyalty to the team that is the party transcends all other considerations for the party person and results not only in the stifling of local political life, but also confines political activity to certain practices acceptable to party politicians. Politics must be processed through the political party and it is party as an institutionalised set of practices and procedures, rather than party as an articulation of diverse political opinions, where we see the real and powerful impact of party in the local setting. Party as an institution and set of procedures fundamentally distorts local representation and democracy and profoundly affects interpretations of politics held by party people. Parties simply have a different meaning of what it is to be involved in politics and how to do local politics than the wider citizenry they seek to represent and govern.

Political modernisation should not be confined to the council chamber, new political executives and overview and scrutiny committees in themselves, will fail to reinvigorate local politics and enhance citizen engagement if parties do not radically alter the way they approach council and wider local politics. Modernisation, or at least willingness to rethink political activity, is a requisite for all parties, yet this challenge represents a dangerous journey for parties. It means recognising that politics is not the domain of the party alone, but a territory shared with a wide range of players that will come and go as issues demand. Whilst parties do add stability to an otherwise chaotic political system in a constant state of flux, that stability can also lead to stasis and worse, an atrophying of political life. Parties must accept that they hold responsibility for much of the cynicism with which those not concerned or involved with party politics view them and political activity.

Two possible scenarios for the long-term development of local politics present themselves for consideration. The worst case scenario is as follows: In a council with a political culture of secrecy and intense group loyalty, the adoption of a political executive makes no difference to the way in which political decision-making is conducted. The power of the party group would be retained through discipline and expectations of loyalty, but secrecy would be increased through executive decision-making, which would remain effectively unscrutinised, at least in public. Only symbolic public scrutiny would occur by majority party backbenchers that had previously discussed and decided upon issues in private group meetings. Moreover, existing one-party states would remain intact with the problems of democratic accountability intensified.

In the worst case scenario executive councillors could attempt to whip their party scrutiny colleagues and impose discipline on them to support the executive in public. Or, scrutiny members may use the group to attempt to control or at least direct the executive in its activities. As members of the same group, it would be convenient for executive and overview and scrutiny councillors to use any party majority, or where no majority exits, to ensure identifiable and coherent party groupings, to continue to avoid public criticism and to co-ordinate party political attacks against the opposition. Or, the non-executive members in the majority within the overall group would be able to impose a whip on the executive to support, in public, group decisions. Public scrutiny of a political executive would fail if councillors were bound by some form of whip or group discipline to act in a predetermined way in public, and, as a consequence, would remain conducted in private group meetings. As a result, local councils with new powerful political executives would be further distanced from the communities they represent and the health of local democracy damaged – perhaps terminally.

In this worse case setting, political parties conduct their activities with scant regard for notions of public involvement or engagement in the political processes. Indeed, parties conduct activities despite the existence of local citizens, communities and political interests outside the party that are motivated by issues and events of local importance. Parties continue to act in a form of splendid isolation from events and pressures outside its walls or the walls of the council. Politics is very narrowly defined and overly focused on the council and the interest of parties seeking power and seats on it. Representation means acting as a delegate of the party, not as a conduit for a wide range of voices and views existing outside the party and within the community. Local communities and citizens become increasingly disenchanted with the political processes and more and more disengaged from the parties that seek their votes and from local political concerns. A deepening spiral of disillusionment and disconnection develops amongst local communities, which suits the parties fine, as they can get on with the business of politics with no interference from the outside world.

Alternatively, the best case scenario sees political parties embrace a new political culture and new approach to conducting council affairs. On adopting a new form of political executive back-benchers are freed by the group to play a genuine scrutiny and representative role, even in councils were one party has dominated the council for some time. Public and open deliberation of local issues returns to the council chamber, which also regains its importance as a real decision-making body where councillors consider issues, speak and vote according to their beliefs, opinions and the views of those they represent. Council chambers become the place where local democracy is expressed by councillors unfettered by current patterns of group discipline and political behaviour.

In these new circumstances party groups will still meet to decide broad policy responses to the major issues impacting on the council and the area it governs. Councillors will then support the outcomes of group meetings, not as a result of disciplinary processes, but because they reflect choices based on a shared political outlook amongst party colleagues. Those that remain unconvinced will be free to express their doubts and to vote accordingly. Local democracy becomes more fluid and the outcome of council meetings more difficult to predict; the council becomes a politically exciting, challenging and meaningful body that sees its role as a platform for the exchange of views and public deliberation resulting, in a more legitimate form of representation and local governance. Ultimately councillors and councils achieve a fully developed community leadership role, based on intense connection between citizens and representative, rather than spurious claims to a governing mandate through a manifesto. Such circumstances only come about because at least one party has radically rethought its role and how it conducts politics and because other parties have willingly or unwilling, followed suit. Parties start to reach out beyond their own very narrow confines, to a wider range of organisations and communities of interest and place when conducting political activity. Common ground is sort and where possible public deliberation leads to a refining and shifting of views by parties and those with which they interact. Parties approach the business of politics as one of many players in a pluralistic framework; they seek common cause where it can be found, form coalitions around specific issues or problems and operate on the basis of shifting alliances rather than solid party *blocs* of regularised support.

Parties begin to interact with communities, single-issue or interest leagues and other parties. They do not cease to be political parties with political objectives, designed to pursue power in a coherent fashion, but they recognise the multifaceted nature of politics, political players and degrees of political activity, and accommodate them accordingly. Politics just gets more exciting. Ultimately the health of local democracy is enhanced and the community comes to view the council as a genuine representative body, reflecting its concerns and priorities, not the dictates or interests of preserving the dominance of the political party group and the wider local party.

The evidence suggests however, that it is the former scenario, not the latter that is emerging from experimentation with political modernisation – parties have yet to recognise fully their own need to reform and rethink both the organisation and process of local politics. Indeed, parties must explore locally the very culture of politics they have created and the way in which they approach local representation and democracy. Whilst this book could be criticised for taking too critical and cynical a view of party involvement in local politics, it has not been fatalistic. Parties have so many defenders in the academic and political worlds, willing to trumpet loudly and clearly the positive affect of parties, which is why this book has taken a deliberately alternative view to the impact of political parties on local politics. The book has, however, raised the prospect that parties can begin, and in some places are beginning, to consider what they do to local politics and as a result change. There is the glimmer of hope that parties may start a journey which brings them to realise that, whilst they are the major players in the world of local politics, they are not the only players. Moreover, they have a responsibility to constantly challenge political orthodoxy. If they do not, others will do that for them and as parties currently represent political orthodoxy they could find themselves becoming increasingly irrelevant to the demands from local politics made by diverse and dynamic communities and the citizens that comprise them.

As a party member of 26 years standing the author's cynicism and the faint traces of bitterness that any reader may detect as underpinning much of this work, can I hope be forgiven. Whilst anti-party in terms of local government and local politics, I am paradoxically still a party member and activist. But, one that has long recognised how vital it is to our understanding and conduct of local political dynamics to critically explore the impact of party politics on the conduct of council affairs and more widely on local politics and democracy. It is not the existence of party politics within our council chambers and within the local polity that is objectionable, rather it is the rigidity of the boundaries parties place around themselves, council politics and political decisions about important local issues and events that is the objectionable and sinister feature of party domination of the locality. It is the way in which local politics are partyfied and the resultant partyocracy (rule of the party, by the party and for the party) that develops, where all issues are the domain of the party and must be addressed with reference to party concerns and advancement, that serves to create an exclusive, rather than inclusive local democracy.

Political parties locally take good people, committed and dedicated to the local area and its interests, concerned for its well being and seeking a way to contribute to a vibrant and healthy democracy and transform them into party people. Party people can not see beyond the party, they party politicise every facet and element of the political processes, they perceive the council or the local political arena as their domain and come to despise those that wish to conduct politics through different means. Parties can take good, committed and virtuous people and can turn them into office hungry despots that think little of conducting the dark arts of politics to their own ends, or that see the party and its advancement as an end in itself. Yet, parties are also full of good people to which such a transformation has not occurred and much of this book will resonant with them; those that have not succumbed to such a metamorphosis are vital to local democracy.

A local democracy, in which only party people and well placed ones at that can genuinely contribute to politics, is a restricted and disconnected entity. If parties continually fail to display the vitality, relevance and excitement of local politics to the communities they conduct their activities around, the bond between the political and civil worlds is loosened and the worlds drift further apart. It need not be that way, however, parties can reflect the dynamism of political exchange, by recognising that politics is far more than what parties decide it is and how they decide to play it. Parties as vehicles of representative democracy, can also be the vehicles for profound and far-reaching change, not just in policy but in the very nature of the local political system and the conduct of local politics

Local politics and local democracy are too valuable to be left to parties alone, but party domination locally will not change without parties being prepared to share political space, influence and power with those outside the world of party and with those that view politics from different perspectives and interpretations. If political parties are unwilling to face up to the challenges of re-engaging a cynical and disenchanted citizenry in the local political processes, the health of local democracy and the fabric of politics will continue to deteriorate. A new local accommodation is needed between parties and those they seek to represent and govern; parties need to re-interpret and reinvent their entire approach towards representation and accept that political activity outside the party is equally legitimate and also politically representative. As a councillor speaking in an overview and scrutiny committee said of voluntary representation on the committee 'We need to be very careful that these people are representative and don't just come along and act as a lobbyist for their organisation.' But that is just how political parties portray themselves to the public: as *lobbyists* for party advancement and the promotion of party interests.

Finally, of the greatest difficulty to all those involved in party politics is the need to redefine what it is to be a party and a party member and to reconsider notions of rigid party discipline and unity. It is necessary to move beyond seeing parties as the bodies responsible for conducting politics and government in private and to see them as organisations responsible for generating open, vibrant and fluid public deliberative space where political issues can be considered. The reward for party people in rising to this challenge is to see those organisations to which they give so much of their time and energy become meaningful and relevant and even popular with their fellow citizens. The problem to overcome is that their are just too many people involved in party politics that enjoy things just the way they are.

Notes

1 T. Wright, *Citizens and Subjects: An Essay on British Politics*, London: Routledge, 1994, p. 6.

2 M. Ostrogroski, *Democracy and the Organisation of Political Parties*, Vol. II, New York: Macmillan, 1902, p. 635.

3 N. Dennis, 'Community Action and Quasi-Community Action and Anti-Community Action', in P. Leonard (ed.), *Sociological Review*, 1975, pp. 143–163.

4 J. Kuklinski, 'Representativeness and Elections: A Policy Analysis', *American Political Science Review*, 1978, pp. 165–177.

5 J. Bulpitt, *Party Politics in English Local Government*, London: Longmans, 1967. G. W. Jones, 'Varieties of Local Politics', *Local Government Studies*, 1 (2), 1975, pp. 17–32, D. Wilson and C. Game, *Local Government in the United Kingdom*, Basingstoke: Macmillan, 2002.

6 D. Green, *Power and Party in an English City: An Account of Single-Party Rule*, London: George Allen & Unwin, 1981, pp. 66–69.

7 S. Weir and D. Beetham, *Political Power and Democratic Control in Britain*, London: Routledge, 1999, pp. 410 and 481.

8 G. Stoker, P. John, F. Gains, N. Rao and A. Harding, 'Report of the Evaluating Local Governance Survey for the ODPM Advisory Group', November 2002, p. 42.

9 Ibid., pp. 48–49.

10 S. Snape, S. Leach and C. Copus, *The Development of Overview and Scrutiny in Local Government*, ODPM, 2002.

11 C. Pateman, *Participation and Democratic Theory*, Cambridge: Cambridge University Press, 1970, p. 111.

12 C. Copus, Re-engaging Citizens and Councils: The Importance of the Councillor to Enhanced Citizen Involvement, *Local Government Studies*, 29 (2), summer 2003, pp. 32–51.

13 D. Held, *Models of Democracy*, Oxford: Polity Press, 1987, p. 46.

14 J. S. Mill, *On Liberty*, Cambridge: Cambridge University Press, 1992.

15 J. S. Mill, *Considerations on Representative Government*, in McCallum (ed.), Oxford: Basil Blackwell, 1948, p. 280.

16 H. Pitkin, *The Concept of Representation*, Berkley and Los Angeles: University of California Press, 1967, p. 235.

17 H. D. Klingemann, R. Hofferbert and I. Budge, *Parties, Policies and Democracy*, Boulder, Co: Westview Press, 1994.

Bibliography

Adonis, A., *Parliament Today*, Manchester: Manchester University Press, 1993.

Almond, G. A. and S. Verba, *The Civic Culture: Political Attitudes and Democracy in Five Nations*, Princeton, NJ: Princeton University Press, 1963.

Association of Liberal Democrat Councillors (ALDC), *Model Standing Orders For Liberal Democrat Council Groups*, Hebden Bridge, 2000.

Ballard, J., *Running A Successful Council Group*, 2nd edition, Association of Liberal Democrat Councillors, Hebden Bridge, 2000.

Barker, B., 'The Operation of Bristol Labour Party: A View from the Edge', School of Advanced Urban Studies, Working Paper 27, Bristol University, 1983.

Barron, J., G. Crawley and T. Wood, *Councillors in Crisis: The Public and Private Worlds of Local Councillors*, Basingstoke: Macmillan, 1991.

Batley, R., 'An Explanation of Non-Participation in Planning', *Policy and Politics*, 1 (2), 1972, pp. 95–114.

Bealey, F., J. Blondel and W. P. McCann, *Constituency Politics: A Study of Newcastle-under-Lyme*, London: Faber & Faber, 1965.

Beloff, M. (ed.), *The Federalist or the New Constitution*, Oxford: Basil Blackwell, 1948.

Birch, A. H., *The Concepts and Theories of Modern Democracy*, London: Routledge, 1993.

Birch, A. H., *Representation*, Basingstoke: Macmillan, 1971.

Bloch, A. and P. John, *Attitudes to Local Government: A Survey of Electors*, York: Joseph Rowntree Foundation, 1991.

Blunkett, D. and K. Jackson, *Democracy in Crisis: The Town Halls Respond*, London: The Hogarth Press, 1987.

Boaden, N., M. Goldsmith, W. Hampton and P. Stringer, *Public Participation in Local Services*, Harlow: Longman, 1982.

Brand, J., 'Party Organisation and the Recruitment of Councillors', *British Journal of Political Science*, 3 (4), 1973, pp. 473–486.

Brier, A. P., 'The Decision Process in Local Government: A Case Study of Fluoridation in Hull', *Public Administration*, 48 (2), summer 1970, pp. 153–168.

Budge, I., J. A. Brand, M. Margolis and A. Smith, *Political Stratification and Democracy*, Basingstoke: Macmillan, 1972.

Bullock, S., 'The Road to the Lewisham Mayoralty', *Local Governance*, 28 (2), summer 2002, pp. 131–138.

Bulpitt, J., *Territory and Power in the United Kingdom*, Manchester: Manchester University Press, 1983.

Bulpitt, J., 'Participation and Local Politics', Manchester in Parry, G. (ed.), *Participation in Politics*, Manchester University Press, 1972, pp. 281–302.

Bulpitt, J., *Party Politics in English Local Government*, London: Longmans, 1967.

Butterworth, R., 'Islington Borough Council: Some Characteristics of Single Party Rule', *Politics*, 1, May 1966, pp. 21–31.

Chamberlayne, P., 'The Politics of Participation: An Enquiry into Four London Boroughs 1968–74', *London Journal*, 4 (1), 1978, pp. 49–68.

Clements, R. V., *Local Notables and the City Council*, Basinsgstoke: Macmillan, 1969.

Cochrane, A.,'Community Politics and Democracy', in D. Held and C. Pollit (eds), *New Forms of Democracy*, London: Sage, 1986, pp. 51–77.

Cockburn, C., *The Local State: Management of Cities and People*, London: Pluto Press, 1980.

Colenutt, B., 'Community Action over Local Planning Issues', in G. Craig, M. Mayo and N. Sharman (eds), *Jobs and Community Action*, London: Routledge & Kegan Paul, 1979, pp. 243–252.

Commission for Local Democracy, Final Report, *Taking Charge: The Rebirth of Local Democracy*, Municipal Journal Books, 1995.

Committee on the Management of Local Government, *Vol. I, Report of the Committee*, London: HMSO, 1967.

Committee on the Management of Local Government, *Research Vol. II, The Local Government Councillor*, London: HMSO, 1967.

Committee on the Management of Local Government, *Research Vol. III, The Local Government Elector*, London: HMSO, 1967.

Committee on the Management of Local Government, *Vol. V, Local Government Administration in England and Wales*, London: HMSO, 1967.

Conservative Party, *Conservative Council Groups: Draft Model Rules*, London, 1998, revised 2001.

Copus, C., 'Re-Engaging Citizens and Councils: The Importance of the Councillor to Enhanced Citizen Involvement', *Local Government Studies*, 29 (2), summer 2003, pp. 32–51.

Copus, C., *It's My Party: The Role of the Group in Executive Arrangements*, Local Government Association, Designing Governance, Issues in Modernisation Series, April 2001.

Copus, C., 'Citizen Participation in Local Government: The Influence of the Political Party Group', *Local Governance*, 27 (3), autumn 2001, pp. 151–163.

Copus, C., 'Community, Party and the Crisis of Representation', in N. Rao (ed.), *Representation and Community in Western Democracies*, Basingstoke: Macmillan, 2000, pp. 93–113.

Copus, C., 'Consulting the Public on New Political Management Arrangements: A Review and Observations', *Local Governance*, 26 (3), autumn 2000, pp. 177–186.

Copus, C., 'The Attitudes of Councillors since Widdicombe: A Focus on Democratic Engagement', *Public Policy and Administration*, 14 (4), 1999, pp. 87–100.

Copus, C., 'The Councillor and Party Group Loyalty', *Policy and Politics*, 27 (3), July 1999, pp. 309–324.

Copus, C., 'The Party Group: A Barrier to Democratic Renewal', *Local Government Studies* (special edition), 25 (4), winter 1999, pp. 77–98.

Copus, C., 'The Party Group: Model Standing Orders and a Disciplined Approach to Representation', *Local Government Studies*, 25 (1), spring 1999, pp. 17–34.

Copus, C., 'Local Government and the Media: The Impact on Citizen Interest and Participation', *Local Government Management Board*, January 1999.

Copus, C., 'The Councillor: Representing a Locality and the Party Group', *Local Governance*, 24 (3), autumn 1998, pp. 215–224.

Corina, L., 'Elected Representatives in a Party System', *Policy and Politics*, 3 (1), September 1974, pp. 69–87.

Crick, B., *In Defence of Politics*, Harmondsworth: Penguin Books, 1982.

Cutler, H., *The Cutler Files*, London: Weidenfeld & Nicolson, 1982.

Dahl, R. A., *Who Governs?*, New Haven: Yale University Press, 1961.

Davis, J., 'The Progressive Council, 1889–1907', in A. Saint (ed.), *Politics and the People of London: The London County Council 1889–1965*, London: Hambledon Press, 1989.

Dearlove, J., *The Politics of Policy in Local Government: The Making and Maintenance of Public Policy in the Royal Borough of Kensington and Chelsea*, London: Cambridge University Press, 1973.

Dennis, N., 'Community Action and Quasi-Community Action and Anti-community Action', in P. Leonard (ed.), *Sociological Review*, 1975, pp. 143–163.

DETR, The Local Government Act 2000, *New Council Constitutions: Guidance Pack*, 2001.

DETR, *Local Leadership: Local Choice*, 1999.

DETR, *Modern Local Government: In Touch with the People*, 1998.

DETR, *Modernising Local Government: Local Democracy and Community Leadership*, 1998.

Drewry, G., 'Select Committees and Back-Bench Power', in J. Jowell and D. Oliver (eds), *The Changing Constitution*, Oxford: Clarendon Press, 1985.

DTLR, *Public Attitudes To Directly Elected Mayors*, 2001.

DTLR, *Strong Local Leadership: Quality Public Services*, 2001.

Eulau, H. and J. Whalke, *The Politics of Representation*, California; Sage, 1978.

Eulau, H., J. Whalke, W. Buchanan and L. Ferguson, 'The Role of the Representative: Some Empirical Observations on the Theory of Edmund Burke', *American Political Science Review*, 53 (3), September 1959, pp. 742–756.

Fishkin, J. S., *The Voice of the People: Public Opinion and Democracy*, New Haven: Yale University Press, 1995.

Fraser, D., *Power and Authority in the Victorian City*, Oxford: Basil Blackwell, 1979.

Game, C., 'Elected Mayors: More Distraction than Attraction?', Conference paper to Eleventh One-Day Conference of the Political Studies Association Urban Politics Specialist group, November 2002.

Game, C. and S. Leach, 'The Role of Political Parties in Local Democracy', Commission for Local Democracy, Research Report No. 11, London: Municipal Journal Books, 1995.

Garner, R. and R. Kelly, *British Political Parties Today*, Manchester: Manchester University Press, 1993.

Gillespie, J., 'Municipalism, Monopoly and Management: The Demise of Socialism in one County, 1918–1933', in A. Saint (ed.), *Politics and the People of London: The London County Council 1889–1965*, London: Hambledon Press, 1989, pp. 103–125.

Giuliani, R., *Leadership*, London: Little Brown, 2002.

Glassberg, A., *Representation and Urban Community*, Basingstoke: Macmillan, 1981.

Goldsmith, M., 'Representing Communities: Who and What?', in N.Rao (ed.), *Representation and Community in Western Democracies*, Basingstoke: Macmillan, 2000, pp. 10–23.

Grant, W. P., 'Non-partisanship in British Local Politics', *Policy and Politics*, 1 (3), 1973, pp. 241–254.

Grant, W. P., 'Local Parties in British Local Politics: A Framework for Empirical Analysis', *Political Studies*, 19 (2), 1971, pp. 201–212.

Gray, C., *Government Beyond the Centre: Sub-National Politics in Britain*, Basingstoke: Macmillan, 1994.

Green, D., *Power and Party in an English City: An Account of Single-Party Rule*, London: George Allen & Unwin, 1981.

Green, G., 'National, City and Ward Components of Local Voting', *Policy and Politics*, 1 (1), September 1972, pp. 45–54.

Green, P., 'A Review Essay of Robert Dahl, Democracy and its Critics', *Social Theory and Practice*, 16 (2), 1990, pp. 217–243.

Gregory, R., 'Local Elections and the Rule of Anticipated Reactions', *Political Studies*, 17 (1), 1969, pp. 31–47.

Guardian, Thursday 23 May, Thursday 30 May, Friday 2 August 1996.

Gyford, J., 'The Politicisation of Local Government', in M. Loughlin, M. Gelfand and K. Young (eds), *Half a Century of Municipal Decline*, London: George Allen & Unwin, 1985, pp. 75–97.

Gyford, J., *The Politics of Local Socialism*, London: George Allen & Unwin, 1985.

Gyford, J., *Local Politics in Britain*, London: Croom Helm, 1978.

Gyford, J. and M. James, *National Parties and Local Politics*, London: George Allen & Unwin, 1983.

Gyford, J., S. Leach and C. Game, *The Changing Politics of Local Government*, London: George Allen & Unwin, 1989.

Hain, P., *Radical Liberalism and Youth Politics*, London: Liberal Party Publications, 1974.

Hambleton, R., 'Directly Elected Mayors: Reinvigorating the Debate', LGA discussion paper, 1999.

Hampton, W., *Democracy and Community: A Study of Politics in Sheffield*, London: Oxford University Press, 1970.

Harrison, M. and A. Norton, 'Some Effects of the Presence or Absence of Party Politics on the Operation of Local Authorities', Committee on the Management of Local Government, *Vol. V, Local Government Administration in England and Wales*, London: HMSO, 1967, chapter 5.

Haynes, P., *An Islington Councillor: 1971–1992*, London: Haynes, 1994.

Heath A. and R. Topf, 'Political Culture', in R. Jowell, S. Witherspoon and L. Brook (eds), *British Social Attitudes: The 1987 Report*, Aldershot: Gower, 1987, pp. 51–69.

Heclo, H., 'The Councillor's Job', *Public Administration*, 47 (2), 1969, pp. 185–202.

Held, D., *Models of Democracy*, Oxford: Polity Press, 1987.

Hennock, E. P., *Fit and Proper Persons: Ideal and Reality in Nineteenth-Century Urban Government*, London: Edward Arnold, 1973.

Hill, D. M., *Democratic Theory and Local Government*, London: George Allen & Unwin, 1974.

HMSO, *Community Leadership and Representation: Unlocking the Potential*, The Report of the Woking Party on the Internal Management of Local Authorities, July 1993.

Hodge, M., S. Leach and G. Stoker, *More than the Flower Show: Elected Mayors and Democracy*, London: Fabian Publications, 1997.

Jackson, W. E., *Achievement: A Short History of the LCC*, London: Longmans, 1965.

Jennings, W. I., *The British Constitution*, Cambridge: Cambridge University Press, 1947.

Jones, G. W., 'Varieties of Local Politics', *Local Government Studies*, 1 (2), 1975, pp. 17–32.

Jones, G. W., 'The Functions and Organisation of Councillors', *Public Administration*, 51 (2), summer 1973, pp. 135–146.

Jones, G. W., *Borough Politics: A Study of Wolverhampton Borough Council 1888–1964*, Basingstoke: Macmillan, 1969.

Jones, G. W. and J. Stewart, 'Party Discipline through the Magnifying Glass', *Local Government Chronicle*, 30 October 1992.

Jones, G. W. and J. Stewart, *The Case for Local Government*, London: George Allen & Unwin, 1983.

Judge, D., *Representation: Theory and Practice in Britain*, London: Routledge, 1999.

Judge, D., *The Parliamentary State*, London: Sage, 1993.

Kavanagh, D., 'Political Culture in Great Britain: The Decline of the Civic Culture', in G. A. Almond and S. Verba (eds), *The Civic Culture Revisited*, London: Sage, 1989.

Keith-Lucas, B., *The English Local Government Franchise*, Oxford: Basil Blackwell, 1952.

Kingdom, J., *Local Government and Politics in Britain*, Hemel Hempstead: Phillip Allan, 1991.

Klingemann, H. D., R. Hofferbert and I. Budge, *Parties, Policies and Democracy*, Boulder, CO: Westview Press, 1994.

Kuklinski, J., 'Representativeness and Elections: A Policy Analysis', *American Political Science Review*, 1978, pp. 165–177.

Labour Party, *Labour Group Model Standing Orders*, London: Labour Party, 2001, updated 2002.

Labour Party, *The Labour Party Rules*, London: Labour Party, 2000.

Labour Party, *The Labour Councillors Handbook*, London: Labour Party, 1999.

Lambert, J., C. Paris and B. Blackaby, *Housing Policy and the State: Allocation, Access and Control*, Basingstoke: Macmillan, 1978.

Lansley, S., S. Goss and C. Wolmar, *The Rise and Fall of the Municipal Left*, Basingstoke: Macmillan, 1989.

Leach, R. and J. Percy-Smith, *Local Governance in Britain*, London: Palgrave, 2001.

Leach, S., *Starting to Modernise: Reviewing Leader and Cabinet Models, a Practical Guide*, London: NLGN, 2001.

Leach, S., *Making Overview and Scrutiny Work*, Local Government Association, 2001.

Leach, S. and G. Ben-Tovim, *It's our Party: Democratic Problems in Local Government*, London: Local Government Management Board, 1998.

Leach, S. and C. Copus, 'Scrutiny and the Political Party Group in Local Government: New Models of Behaviour', *Public Administration*, forthcoming.

Leach, S. and C. Game, *Political Parties and Local Democracy*, in L. Pratchett and D. Wilson (eds), *Local Democracy and Local Government*, Basingstoke: Macmillan, 1996, pp. 127–149.

Leach, S. and J. Stewart, *The Politics of Hung Authorities*, Basingstoke: Macmillan, 1992.

Leach, S. and D. Wilson, *Local Political Leadership*, Bristol: The Policy Press, 2000.

Lee, J. M., *Social Leaders and Public Persons: A Study of County Government in Cheshire Since 1888*, Oxford: Clarendon Press, 1963.

Leitch, J., 'Securing a Yes Vote in a Mayoral Referendum', *Local Governance*, 28 (2), 2002, pp. 125–129.

Liberal Democrats, *The Constitution of the Liberal Democrats*, London: Liberal Democrats, 2002.

Liberal Democrats, 'Political Speech and Race Relations in Liberal Democracy', 'Report of an Inquiry into the Conduct of the Tower Hamlets Liberal Democrats in Publishing Allegedly racist Election Literature between 1990 and 1993', London, December 1993.

Livingstone, K., *If Voting Changed Anything, They'd Abolish It*, London: Fontana, 1987.

Lowndes, V., G. Stoker and L. Pratchett, 'Trends in Public Participation: Part 2 – Citizens' Perspectives, *Public Administration*, 79 (2), 2001, pp. 445–455.

Lowndes, V., G. Stoker, L. Pratchett, D. Wilson, S. Leach and M. Wingfield, *Guidance on Enhancing Public Participation*, DETR, 1998.

Manin, B., *The Principles of Representative Government*, Cambridge: Cambridge University Press, 1997.

Maor, M., *Political Parties and Party Systems: Comparative Approaches and the British Experience*, London: Routledge, 1997.

Marsh, A., *Protest and Political Consciousness*, London: Sage, 1977.

Meadowcroft, J., 'Community Politics: Ideals, Myths and Realities', in N. Rao (ed.), *Representation and Community in Western Democracies*, Basingstoke: Macmillan, 2000, pp. 114–137.

Michels. R., *Political Parties*, Glencoe, IL: The Free Press, 1949.

Mill, J. S., *On Liberty*, Cambridge: Cambridge University Press, 1992.

Mill, J. S., *Considerations on Representative Government*, in McCallum (ed.), Oxford: Basil Blackwell, 1948.

Morris-Jones, W. H., 'In Defence of Apathy: Some Doubts on the Duty to Vote', *Political Studies*, 2 (1), 1954, pp. 25–37.

Muchnick, D., *Urban Renewal in Liverpool*, Occasional Papers on Social Administration, the Social Administration Research Trust, London: Bell & Sons, 1970.

Municipal Journal, London: Hemming, 15 May 2003.

National Union of Conservative and Unionist Associations, *Model Rules For Constituency, Branch and European Constituency Councils*, 1993.

Newton, K., *Second City Politics: Democratic Processes and Decision-Making in Birmingham*, Oxford: Clarendon Press, 1976.

Norton, P., 'The Changing Face of Parliament', in P. Norton (ed.), *New Directions in British Politics? Essays on the Evolving Constitution*, Aldershot: Edward Elgar, 1991.

Ostrogorski, M., *Democracy and the Organisation of Political Parties*, Vols I and II, New York: Macmillan, 1902.

Owen, D., *The Government of Victorian London, 1855–1889: The Metropolitan Board of Works, the Vestries and the City Corporation*, Cambridge, MA: Harvard University Press, 1982.

Parkinson, M., 'Central–Local Relations in British Parties: A Local View', *Political Studies*, 19 (4), 1971, pp. 440–446.

Parkinson, M., *Liverpool on the Brink*, Policy Journals, 1985.

Parry, G., *Political Elites*, London: George Allen & Unwin, 1971.

Parry, G., G. Moyser and N. Day, *Political Participation and Democracy in Britain*, Cambridge: Cambridge University Press, 1992.

Pateman, C., *Participation and Democratic Theory*, Cambridge, Cambridge University Press, 1970.

Phillips, A., *Local Democracy: The Terms of the Debate*, Commission for Local Democracy Research Report No. 2, London: Municipal Journal Books, 1994.

Pinkney, R., 'Nationalizing Local Politics and Localizing a National Party: The Liberal Role in Local Government', *Government and Opposition*, 18, 1983, pp. 347–358.

Pinkney, R., 'Nationalizing Local Politics and Localizing a National Party, from I. Hopton, *Directory of Liberal Party Resolutions*, London: Liberal Publication Department, 1978.

Pitkin, H., *The Concept of Representation*, Berkley and Los Angeles: University of California Press, 1967.

Prior, D., J. Stewart and K. Walsh, *Citizenship: Rights, Community and Participation*, London: Pitman, 1995.

Quagliariello, G., *Politics without Parties*, Aldershot: Avebury, 1996.

Rallings, C. and M. Thrasher, *Local Elections in Britain*, London: Routledge, 1997.

Rallings, C., M. Temple and M. Thrasher, *Community Identity and Participation in Local Democracy*, Commission for Local Democracy, Research Report No 1, London: Municipal Journal Books, 1994.

Rallings, C., M. Thrasher and J. Downe, *One Vote, One Value: Electoral Re-Districting in English Local Government*, Aldershot: Ashgate, 2002.

Rao, N., *Reviving Local Democracy: New Labour, New Politics?* Bristol: Policy Press, 2000.

Rao, N., Representation in Local Politics: A Reconsideration and Some New Evidence, *Political Studies*, 46 (1), 1998, pp. 19–35.

Rao, N., *The Making and Unmaking of Local Self-Government*, Aldershot: Dartmouth, 1994.

Rao, N., *Managing Change: Councillors and the New Local Government*, York: Joseph Rowntree Foundation, 1993.

Rees, A. and T. Smith, *Town Councillors: A Study of Barking*, London: The Acton Society Trust, 1964.

Riddell, P., *Parliament Under Pressure*, London: Victor Gollancz, 1997.

Rose, R., *Politics in England: Change and Persistence*, Basingstoke: Macmillan, 1989.

Saint, A. (ed.), *Politics and the People of London: The London County Council 1889–1965*, London: Hambledon Press, 1989.

Sartori, G., *Democratic Theory*, Detroit: Wayne State University Press, 1962.

Saunders, P., *Urban Politics: A Sociological Interpretation*, London: Hutchinson, 1979.

Schumpeter, J. A., *Capitalism, Socialism and Democracy*, London: George Allen & Unwin, 1974.

Scottish National Party, *Model Standing Orders*, Scottish National Party, Edinburgh, 1998, up-dated, 2002.

Sharpe, L. J., 'The Politics of Local Government in Greater London', *Public Administration*, 38 (2), summer 1960, pp. 157–172.

Sharpe, L. J. and K. Newton, *Does Politics Matter? The Determinants of Public Policy*, Oxford: Clarendon Press, 1984.

Snape, S. and S. Leach, *New Forms of Political Management Arrangements*, IDeA/DETR, 2000.

Snape, S., S. Leach and C. Copus, *The Development of Overview and Scrutiny in Local Government*, ODPM, 2002.

Soldon, N., '*Laissez-faire* as Dogma: The Liberty and Property Defence League 1882–1914', in K. Brown (ed.), *Essays in Anti-Labour History: Responses to the Rise of Labour in Britain*, London: Macmillan, 1974.

Stanyer, J., *Understanding Local Government*, London: Fontana, 1976.

Stanyer, J., 'Social and Rational Models of Man: Alternative Approaches to the Study of Local Elections', *Advancement of Science*, 26, 1970, pp. 399–407.

Steed, M., 'Participation through Western Democratic Institutions', in Parry (ed.), *Participation in Politics*, Manchester: Manchester University Press, 1972, pp. 80–101.

Stewart, J., *The Nature of British Local Government*, Basingstoke: Macmillan, 2000.

Stewart, J., *From Innovation in Democratic Practice Towards a Deliberative*

Democracy, The Institute of Local Government Studies Occasional Paper No. 27, April 1999.

Stewart, J., *More Innovation in Democratic Practice*, The Institute of Local Government Studies Occasional Paper No. 9, May, 1997.

Stewart, J., *Further Innovation in Democratic Practice*, The Institute of Local Government Studies Occasional Paper No. 3, May, 1996.

Stewart, J., M. Clarke, D. Hall, F. Taylor, R. Hambleton and G. Stoker, 'Practical Implications: New Forms of Political Executive', Local Government Management Board, London, 1998.

Stoker, G., *The New Politics of British Local Government*, Basingstoke: Macmillan, 2000.

Stoker, G., 'Local Political Leadership: Preparing for the 21st Century', Mimeo, Strathclyde University, 1998.

Stoker, G., *The Politics of Local Government*, Basingstoke: Macmillan, 1991.

Stoker, G. and V. Lowndes, *Tower Hamlets and Decentralisation: The Experience of Globe Town Neighbourhood*, Luton: Local Government Management Board, 1991.

Stoker, G. and H. Wolman, 'Drawing Lessons from US Experience: An Elected Mayor for British Local Government', *Public Administration*, 70 (2), 1992, pp. 241–267.

Stoker, G., P. John, F. Gains, N. Rao and A. Harding, *Report of the ELG Survey Findings for ODPM Advisory Group*, Department of Government, Manchester: Manchester University Press, 2002.

To Whom Much is Given: New Ways of Working for Councillors following Political Restructuring, Audit Commission, 2001.

Tocqueville, A. (J. P. Mayer (ed.), *Democracy in America*, London: Fontana, 1994.

Wainwright, H., *Labour: A Tale of Two Parties*, London: The Hogarth Press, 1987.

Weir, S. and D. Beetham, *Political Power and Democratic Control in Britain*, London: Routledge, 1999.

Widdicombe, D., Committee of Inquiry into the Conduct of Local Authority Business, *Report of the Committee*, Cmnd 9797, London: HMSO, 1986.

Widdicombe, D., Committee of Inquiry into the Conduct of Local Authority Business, *Research Vol. I, The Political Organisation of Local Authorities*, Cmnd 9798, London: HMSO, 1986.

Widdicombe, D., Committee of Inquiry into the Conduct of Local Authority Business, *Research Vol II, The Local Government Councillor*, Cmnd 9799, London: HMSO, 1986.

Widdicombe, D., Committee of Inquiry into the Conduct of Local Authority Business, *Research Vol. III, The Local Government Elector*, Cmnd 9799, London: HMSO, 1986.

Widdicombe, D., Committee of Inquiry into the Conduct of Local Authority Business, *Research Vol. IV, Aspects of Local Democracy*, Cmnd 9801, London: HMSO, 1986.

Wilson, D. and C. Game, *Local Government in the United Kingdom*, Basingstoke: Macmillan, 2002.

Wiseman, H. V., 'The Working of Local Government in Leeds: Part I, Party

Control of Council and Committees', *Public Administration*, 41 (1), spring 1963, pp. 51–69.

Wiseman, H. V., 'The Working of Local Government in Leeds: Part II, More Party Conventions and Practices', *Public Administration*, 41 (2), summer 1963, pp. 137–155.

Wolman, H. and M. Goldsmith, *Urban Politics and Policy: A Comparative Approach*, Oxford: Blackwell, 1992.

Wright, T., *Citizens and Subjects: An Essay on British Politics*, London: Routledge, 1994.

Young, K., 'From Character to Culture: Authority, Deference and the Political Imagination since 1945', in S. James (ed.), *Political Change in Britain since 1945*, Basingstoke: Macmillan, 1997.

Young, K., 'Bright Hopes and Dark Fears: The Origins and Expectations of the County Councils', in K. Young (ed.), *New Directions For County Government*, London: Association of County Councils, 1989.

Young, K., 'Local Government and the Environment', *British Social Attitudes: The 1985 Report*, in R. Jowell and S. Witherspoon (eds), Aldershot: Gower, 1985, pp. 149–175.

Young, K., 'Political Attitudes', in R. Jowell and C. Airey (eds), *British Social Attitudes: The 1984 Report*, Aldershot: Gower, 1984, pp. 11–45.

Young, K., *Local Politics and the Rise of Party: The London Municipal Society and the Conservative Intervention in Local Elections, 1894–1963*, Leicester: Leicester University Press, 1975.

Young, K., 'The Politics of London Government 1880–1899', *Public Administration*, 51 (1), spring 1973, pp. 91–108.

Young, K., 'Political Party Organisation', in G. Rhodes (ed.), *The New Government of London: The First Five Years*, London: Weidenfeld & Nicolson, 1972, pp. 16–49.

Young K. and M. Davies, *The Politics of Local Government since Widdicombe*, York: Joseph Rowntree Foundation, 1990.

Young, K. and P. Garside, *Metropolitan London: Politics and Urban Change 1837–1981*, London: Edward Arnold, 1982.

Young, K. and N. Rao, 'Faith in Local Democracy', in J. Curtice, R. Jowell, L. Brook and A. Park (eds), *British Social Attitudes: The Twelfth Report*, Aldershot: Dartmouth, 1995, pp. 91–117.

Young, K. and N. Rao, *Coming to Terms with Change? The Local Government Councillor in 1993*, York: Joseph Rowntree Foundation, 1994.

Websites

www.conservativeparty.org.uk
www.labour.org.uk
www.libdems.org.uk

Index